Library of
Davidson College

LANGUAGE and POWER

LANGUAGE and POWER

Edited by
**Cheris Kramarae
Muriel Schulz
William M. O'Barr**

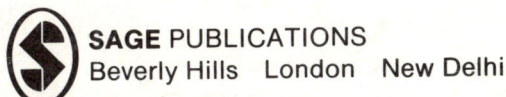
SAGE PUBLICATIONS
Beverly Hills   London   New Delhi

Copyright © 1984 by Sage Publications, Inc.

All rights reserved. No part of this book may be reproduced or utilized in any form or by any means, electronic or mechanical, including photocopying, recording, or by any information storage and retrieval system, without permission in writing from the publisher.

For information address:

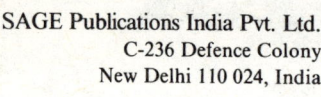

SAGE Publications, Inc.
275 South Beverly Drive
Beverly Hills, California 90212

SAGE Publications India Pvt. Ltd.
C-236 Defence Colony
New Delhi 110 024, India

SAGE Publications Ltd
28 Banner Street
London EC1Y 8QE, England

Printed in the United States of America.

Library of Congress Cataloging in Publication Data
Main entry under title:

Language and power.

    Includes bibliographical references and index.
    1. Sociolinguistics—Addresses, essays, lectures.
2. Power (Social sciences)—Addresses, essays, lectures.
I. Kramarae, Cheris. II. Schulz, Muriel. III. O'Barr, William.
P40.L287 1984   401'.9   84-3412
ISBN 0-8039-2255-8

FIRST PRINTING

CONTENTS

Acknowledgments   7

Introduction: Toward an Understanding of Language and Power
    CHERIS KRAMARAE, MURIEL SCHULZ,
    and WILLIAM M. O'BARR   9

1. Networks and Hierarchies: Language and Social Stratification
    PATRICIA C. NICHOLS   23

2. Education, Ideology, and Class/Sex Identity
    NOËLLE BISSERET MOREAU   43

3. Problems and *Prob*lems: Power Relationships
in a Medical Encounter
    PAULA A. TREICHLER, RICHARD M. FRANKEL,
    CHERIS KRAMARAE, KATHLEEN ZOPPI, and
    HOWARD B. BECKMAN   62

4. Determination of Guilt: Discourse in the Courtroom
    RUTH WODAK-ENGEL   89

5. Black Language as Power
    GENEVA SMITHERMAN   101

6. Language and Power in the Family
    SUSAN ERVIN-TRIPP,
    MARY CATHERINE O'CONNOR,
    and JARRETT ROSENBERG   116

7. Effecting Social Change Through Group Action:
Feminine Occupational Titles in Transition
    MARLIS HELLINGER   136

8. Planning for Language Change in the United States:
The Case of Monolingual Spanish Speakers
    JOAN RUBIN   154

9. The Alchemy of English: Social and Functional
Power of Non-Native Varieties
    BRAJ B. KACHRU   176

10. Defining Reality: A Powerful Tool
    DALE SPENDER   194

11. Minority Writers: The Struggle for
    Authenticity and Authority
        MURIEL SCHULZ   206

12. Studying Power in Literary Texts
        JEAN F. O'BARR   218

13. Francophonie: Language Planning and
    National Interests
        BRIAN WEINSTEIN   227

14. Discourse, Consciousness, and Literacy in a
    Puerto Rican Neighborhood
        ADRIAN T. BENNETT and PEDRO PEDRAZA, Jr.   243

15. Asking the Right Questions about
    Language and Power
        WILLIAM M. O'BARR   260

References   281
Index   305
About the Contributors   315

Acknowledgments

WE HAVE WORKED TOGETHER, across countries and seas, to compose a collection of linked but varied discussions of the relationship of language and power. Collaborative work is always challenging. In this case, we have deliberately employed multidisciplinary and multinational approaches, which has necessitated a great deal of interaction and correspondence from many people, including some whose work is not explicitly represented in the essays that follow.

The collection has its origin in an international Language and Power conference organized by Muriel Schulz, Cheris Kramarae, and Dale Spender and sponsored by the Rockefeller Foundation at its Study and Conference Center in 1980 in Bellagio, Italy. Based upon the discussions at the conference, the papers given there, and our own continuing reading and thinking, we have selected some of the issues that seem important to theoretical, informational and methodological analyses of the relationships between language and power. Some of the papers were begun at the conference and revised after collaborative discussions. Others we solicited from other researchers who are working on the ways language is used to acquire, transmit, or block the flow of social, economic, and political power.

We have been appreciative, throughout the planning and editing processes, of the cooperation from all the conference participants, the authors whose work appears in this volume, and those readers who have provided critiques as we have worked together. The process has been more lively than that for many other scholarly volumes, because in this case most of the authors are actively and explicitly involved with the people and the issues they discuss. We have not tried to mute these voices or to deny that these writers, as others, have an interest in whether social conditions change or remain much the same. Their differing training, assumptions, and social concerns have, of course, an impact on the ways each author documents and analyzes language and power relationships, and bring valuable diversity to the collection.

We give special thanks to the following people who have helped with this project: Pierre Achard, Sherida Altehenger-Smith, Hans Arndt, Johanna DeStefano, Murray Edelman, Martin Hoyles, William Mackey, Trevor Pateman, Tove Pedersen, Helen Roberts, Gill Seidell, and Albert Verdoodt. We also record our appreciation of the firm support provided by the staff of the Rockefeller Foundation; Michel Blanc; John Attinasi; Judy Page; the anonymous readers of our manuscript; the Scholars Travel Fund at the University of Illinois, Urbana-Champaign; the secretarial staff at Duke University; Robert Dilligan of the University of Southern California; and Roberto Celli of the Rockefeller Foundation Study and Conference Center.

INTRODUCTION
Toward an Understanding of Language and Power

Cheris Kramarae, Muriel Schulz, and William M. O'Barr

IN DESCRIBING THE WAY language functions, scholars have variously described it as rule governed, a container, a transmitter, a symbolic system, and a social leveler. Some have focused on the universals, while others have focused on variation among and within languages. A growing number of researchers concern themselves with the relation of language to its spatial, temporal, and social contexts. Although considerations of language in context can be traced back at least as far as Greek and Roman scholars, it is only within the latter part of the twentieth century that the study of language implies for most scholars simultaneous concern with society. Language is, after all, spoken by people in social contexts as they communicate about human concerns. This volume is intended as a contribution to the study of language and society by focusing on the relation of language to one of the most basic social concerns: power.

In inviting researchers to contribute chapters, we have provided no limits for this exploration. Rather, we have encouraged each author to consider how language and power are intertwined in the issues they study. This freedom to explore so broadly the relationship between language and power has yielded some exciting analyses and has shown the utility of joining topics and approaches seldom linked in common effort. It has also made it difficult to describe fully encompassing boundaries for the scope of our concerns or to provide comprehensive definitions for the key concepts of *language* and *power*. We believe, however, that this effort—which indicates rather than exhausts the possibilities that emerge from the consideration of language and power—more than outweighs the disadvantages. Such limited definitions, although they appear to fit each succeeding case as if all were researched by a single scholar, would be too general to be of any real use.

At least two major reasons lie behind our decision to encourage expansion rather than to set restrictions on these analyses. First, the contributors to this volume did not begin their research efforts with a common set of concepts and concerns. Each focused on a particular topic or setting (for example, language policy; a literary tradition; or an institution like schools, hospitals, or courts) and researched it from the vantage of one or more disciplines (including such widely differing ones as political science, psychology, speech communication, literature, and sociolinguistics). It would be an error on our part to attempt to shove and push, to remold and fit these distinctive contributions into a single framework. Instead, it is more appropriate to recognize and appreciate what each one can teach.

Second, many of these papers were presented in earlier versions at an exploratory, interdisciplinary conference, where the guidelines given to contributors encouraged thoughtful consideration of just how language and power are related in their own research. These analyses have been joined by several other papers that have, in our opinion, helped round out some of the issues and approaches that received less than adequate attention initially. Thus, the chapters of this book are a collection, in its finer sense, reflecting how 22 scholars conceive of the relationship between language and power. We will not attempt to gerrymander topics, approaches, or conclusions or to provide post hoc definitions that might, with the clearer vision of hindsight, be claimed to have been in use throughout. Everywhere we have looked—from the simplest dyadic relationship to the most encompassing global interactions—we have learned something important about the relationship between language and power, leading us to the firm conclusion that consideration of either ultimately entails the other.

Although we offer guidance and suggestions in the following pages for those just beginning to consider how language and power are related, we encourage both those who are just beginning and those who have been developing their own ideas and views not to mistake our efforts in this introduction as an attempt to circumscribe a field nor to be limited in their own thinking about language and power.

THE CONCEPT OF POWER

In common usage and in scholarly writings, the concepts of *power* and *politics* are so closely linked that they may even be used sometimes as synonyms. Yet, there is an important difference we seek to underscore by electing to define our subject as language and power, not language and politics. "Politics" often implies power, persuasion, and influence; but it may also connote its earlier, more restricted etymological association with the state or government (being derived from the Greek, *polis*). We choose "power" over "politics" in this volume because not all expressions of influence and control are governmental. In making this choice, we do not wish in any way to minimize the mammoth significance of government and language. Rather, we seek to show how essentially similar processes operate in both governmental and nongovernmental situations. For example, some contributors to this volume (notably, Rubin, Weinstein, Wodak-Engel, Kachru, and Smitherman) deal with governmentally based associations of language and power; whereas others (for example, Schulz, J. O'Barr, Hellinger, Bisseret Moreau, Ervin-Tripp et al., Treichler et al., and Spender) focus on language and power relations that are much less directly related to the formal, public authority structure of the societies they study.

In a highly useful review of theories about power, Wrong (1979) offers this basic definition: "Power is the capacity of some persons to produce intended and foreseen effects on others." He moves on to differentiate intentional from unintentional influence. Intentional influence may be achieved through authority (a contractual acceptance of another as competent to wield power), manipulation (concealed power), persuasion (argumentation), and force (physical or psychic). And we note that it is possible to realize most of these effects—except for physical force—through language.

If power is defined quite differently, as for example both Miller (1976) and Rich (1976) have done, language also is intricately tied to how power is actually manifest. For Miller and Rich, power is conceived as autonomous action based on one's own beliefs and abilities not necessarily entailing domination of others. Others offer another critique of the winner/loser studies of power. They suggest that instead of assuming that there is present in any interaction a finite amount of power—so that if someone or some group loses it—acts of nurturance in interdependent relationships can be understood as acts of strength and power (Lips, 1981; Gilligan, 1982). Power has been conceptualized in a number of useful ways (depending on basic assumptions about relationships and on the stress laid upon various features of the aspects to be described); but, regardless of its definition, the resources available to exert or resist influence are recurrent, similar, and—in societies at peace—chiefly *verbal*.

Most classical dictionary definitions of power treat it as static rather than processual. Although one unit of any relationship is likely at any one time to be stronger than another, seldom is one so strong that the other has no bargaining ability whatsoever (Janeway, 1980a,

1980b). Interest in presenting power as interactive and all discourse as hierarchical has lead Foucault, among others, to set forth an anlysis of power as internal to all relationships, not "held" or exercised by individuals but, rather, developed through interaction in a multiplicity of relationships. Power, in his analysis, is not a limitation of freedom, not a possession, not a control that can be stored or a system of domination exercised by an individual or group over another individual or group. Rather, power comes from below as well as above, in a shifting relationship of force and resistance. It is not merely negative or repressive, but also positive and implicit in the constitution of discourse and knowledge. Foucault encourages us to study the specifics of power relationships within a particular institution at a particular time, to study overall structure and discourse within an institution and to study these relationships to other practices and institutions (Foucault, 1972, 1973, 1980; Lemert and Gillan, 1982; Sheridan, 1980).

Some critics have noted a critical limitation of Foucault's approach; it seems to be more useful in studying well-defined institutions (such as medicine and psychoanalysis) but not as useful in suggesting how most discourse is bounded or how institutions related. Most human communication and interaction seem not to be contained within a single, specific institution, but to encompass many situations and contexts, including, for example, religion, education, and family. Foucault's analysis focuses on the regularity of structures and relationships during struggle (such as Marlis Hellinger, for exmple, describes in Chapter 7). Foucault uses *discourse* to mean both language practiced and social practices, without providing clear indications of where discourse ends and the rest of social life begins (Weedon et al., 1980: 194-216; Lemert and Gillan, 1982).

Still, his emphasis on the relational nature of power and on the importance of studying interaction within institutions and within a complex of relationships is similar to that encouraged by others who believe that, in understanding the working of inequality, we must also study the entwining and changing of relationships. This does not deny the existence within a society of relatively dominant and subordinate groups with greater or fewer resources to employ toward their respective goals. But an approach to power as relational does begin differently, highlighting different issues, asking new questions, and prompting alternative explanations. It is with such a focus that most of the contributors to this volume have proceeded in their considerations of language and power. Hence, the topics discussed here as well as the approaches and the conclusions emerging from these studies are different from those that have come from more narrowly conceived studies of language and politics and from more rigid views of power as structured rather than flexible in its social distribution.

RELATING LANGUAGE AND POWER

The degree to which language *and* power have been considered differs greatly by discipline. For example, sociolinguists—by considering language and society—at least implicitly deal with power. In a few instances, studies have focused directly on language and power. Political scientists who consider language at all represent a small fraction of the discipline, and most of them deal almost exclusively with language and its entanglement with governmental expressions of control. Some literary critics have discovered the importance of the social and political contexts within which authors write, but traditionally any concern with power has been more incidental than intentional. Language teachers, whether in instructing students in the usages of mother tongues or foreign languages, have typically given no concern to the association of power with concepts like *dialect, standard language*, and so on. Through the contributions to this volume, we seek to adjust the study of language—from whatever discipline or academic background—to attend to the problematic aspects as well as to the utility of language.

Adequate understanding of the relations between language and power may be several sociolinguistic years away. Patricia Nichols argues in Chapter 1 that current definitions of social stratification, even though they include several types of social measures (e.g., class and gender), ignore many types of speakers, making it impossible to include them with any degree of accuracy or reliability. Nevertheless, research emphasis is changing, and research efforts are yielding evidence that speech functions in different ways for different cultures as well as for different individuals and groups within a culture, and that language behaviors differ depending upon such variables as geographic location, social groups, sex, and age. Yet, little is said about the linguistic asymmetries of everyday life, about unequal distribution of influence and the resulting social and economic impact, or about causation.

The "descriptions" of relatively static relationships between people and their language use (sometimes called objective, noncontroversial, scientific, and unbiased analysis) do help us understand the social, political, and administrative relations and institutions in our society. But they are partial; they often imply, through omission, that the relationships between linguistic means and social meaning are interesting, statistical regularities rather than problematic arrangements involving unequal distribution of resources. Missing is an explicit discussion of asymmetrical influences and of the resulting strains and emotions resulting from the ways linguistic markers are used by some individuals or groups to keep others in "their places" and of the responses to or efforts to change the situations of conflict. The essays in this volume deal with such topics, and in doing so work to unmask implicit authority relationships among speakers.

Not all previous considerations of language and society have assumed egalitarian, benign relationships among speakers. Several writers have provided questions and theoretical models that aid in systematic exploration of the language-power relationship. For example, Fishman (1972) encourages consideration of who speaks (or writes) what language (or language variety) to whom, why, and to what end. He suggests that researchers ask questions like the following: What are the patterns and causes of change in the social organization of language use? What are the norms for speaking in particular social networks and communities?

Similarly, Ross (1979) suggests that researchers conduct simultaneous and complementary studies of (1) institutional structures, power hierarchies, and kinship networks; and (2) studies of the language used by individuals in particular settings. And Hymes (1974: 72) reminds us that a language is conceived of as "what those who have it can do with it—what they have made of it, and do make of it; and ... in consequence, notable differences in facility and adequacy may be encountered that are not accidental, but integral to the language. The linguistic system, he argues, is a part of the larger social context; thus, the study of language should *begin* with an analysis of that social context. Since speech abilities and opportunities for speaking are unequally distributed, we must study these along with the values, beliefs, reference groups, norms, practices, and knowledge of speakers in order to have a better understanding of language in society.

Pride's (1979: 29) list of factors involved in determining the place of language in speakers' lives is "what people do (i.e., linguistically), think they do, say they do, think/say others do/think/say, hear themselves/others doing, consider best to do/say, think/say others consider best to do/say, and so forth." In order to explore fully the role of language in social life, we might add to his list the following considerations: Which people and what institutions have the most influence in determining the structure of the factors he has enumerated? What are the consequences of the structures and its supporting ideologies?

Many of the contributors to this collection argue against the conception of individuals as vessels of power or subordination and reject the notion that power is simply prohibition and repression. Power, they demonstrate, results from human activities and interactions. It is a system of relationships running through the whole of society, producing incongruent and often conflicting definitions of reality (see Foucault, 1980, for an extended discussion). The authors of the chapters that follow study relationships by focusing on how power is constituted within them.

In addition to the difficulties we face in attempting to provide a uniform definition of power, we note several problems encountered as well in the conceptualization of language. First, since researchers do not always agree on what language is and how its functions vary, we cannot assume a unified perspective on what is meant by the term "language." Depending upon their definitions, the advocates of the various approaches set themselves different puzzles to solve, in order to understand cognitive and social processes or to offer advice for immediate language planning policies. For example, Geneva Smitherman in Chapter 5 discusses her efforts to persuade the courts that Black[1] English is a separate language, not a dialect of English. In doing this she drew upon the work of theoretical linguists, who study language as abstract grammatical systems, as well as upon that of sociolinguists, who focus upon language as that which occurs in social interaction.

Second, sociolinguistic studies usually focus upon language as a resource of the speakers, not as a problem for them. Thus, most discourse analysis attempts to illuminate how it is that language does what it does, almost as though speaking had no real-world consequences for the participants (other than communication). Conversation analysts usually work with relatively discrete episodes of behavior, often with little concern for the context of the interaction (including past interactions and the social, political, economic, and administrative practices that may have an impact on the interaction). In Chapter 4, Ruth Wodak-Engel joins some other analysts of conversation (e.g., Watson, 1983) in arguing that the pragmatic meaning of utterances depends upon who says them in what setting. Wodak-Engel finds that the meaning and value set upon speakers' words and class-based differences in speech style have serious consequences for defendants in courts of law.

Third, many contemporary considerations of language focus upon speech, rather than upon writing. Little attention has been paid by linguists in recent years to problems related to written language. Even the studies in this book deal primarily with asymmetry in verbal interactions. Two authors, however, address this question. Jean O'Barr's analysis (Chapter 12) of the novels of Kenyan women writers shows the value of using sources other than spoken language and public documents in the analysis of social processes. She argues that fiction presents opportunities to understand political phenomena that may be virtually inaccessible otherwise. Muriel Schulz (Chapter 11) discusses ways in which access to publication is frequently denied to minority writers and analyzes the consequences of this fact for their attempts to "speak themselves."

Fourth, although many speakers think of language as a conduit through which information flows from sender to receiver (Reddy, 1979), some scholars emphasize the important observation that language contains, comunicates, and perpetuates the ideologies of those in power (for example, see Edelman, 1964). Noelle Bisseret Moreau, in Chapter 2, traces the ideology embedded in French language and culture. She shows that absence of an ideology can be just as problematic. Dale Spender's chapter considers the difficulties women have articulating their experiences in a language structured to overlook and ignore them. Marlis Hellinger (Chapter 7) addresses a question frequently raised in discussions of language and gender: Does a change in language result in a change of attitudes? Hellinger's answer, based upon a longitudinal study of semantic responses to oc-- cupational titles in Germany, is affirmative.

LANGUAGE AS A HUMAN PROBLEM

> It is striking that we have no general perspective on language as a human problem, not even an integrated body of works in search of one. Salient problems, such as translation, multilingualism, literacy, and language development, have long attracted attention, but mostly as practical matters constituting "applications" of linguistics, rather than as proper, theoretically pertinent parts of it ... for about a generation thought in the United States has seen in the role of language in human life only something to praise, not something to question and study [Hymes, 1980: 20-21].

The editors of a recent atlas of the "state of the world" include a map with each country colored according to the relationship between the language of rule, that is the language "which is used by the governing classes and which helps to secure their dominance" (Kidron and Segal, 1981) and the vernacular of the citizens. The color scheme illustrates the following distinctions:

(1) Tan—The language of rule is widely spoken throughout the country or in the appropriate region.
(2) Lavender—The language of rule is spoken by most people in a creole form.

(3) Mauve—The language of rule is spoken by the majority but not by many of the poor.
(4) Purple—The language of rule is not the language of the majority.
(5) An exploding star—A "significant linguistic conflict" exists.

India is purple, with a star. Most countries of Africa are purple (but without stars). Ireland is patchy purple and tan. (In fact, the map is primarily purple and tan.) The United States, France, and the United Kingdom are all calm tan, with an exploding star only in nearby Wales.

This dramatic pictorial device gives a visual introduction to language and power issues at a national level. But the map is small and static, and the problems are large, complex, and dynamic. Even in areas in which most people speak the same language (as is the case in the United States), multilingualism and dialect differences create problems for speakers paralleling those in areas with radical differences.

Since our interest in this volume focuses upon language interaction, the concept of what it is that empowers a prestige language variety is central to our investigations. The fervent language loyalty of purists would suggest that the standard form of a language rises to the surface quite naturally—like cream—because of inherent attributes, and that any infiltration from below will inevitably lead to a dilution of the richness of the prestige variety.

Ferguson (1959) presents quite a different theory of the origin of standard languages. He identifies two kinds of languages: high languages, which are used in performing the major public activities of a culture (those dealing with education, religion, literature, law, business, and government); and low languages, which are everyday vernaculars, usually restricted to conversational use. Because of their different uses, low and high languages differ in form as well as function.

High languages develop word stocks necessary to the contexts in which they are used but are relatively impoverished in words relating to affective relationships and to the basic values of the people, subjects generally discussed in the vernacular. Syntactic differences develop as well. Ritual use, for example, contributes to the survival of syntactic formulas that may have no life in the spoken version of the language, and writing is likely to be rich in syntactic constructions seldom used in speech. Even phonological differences develop between high and low varieties.

Because they are often used by speakers who are relative strangers, there is pressure on high varieties to be explicit and clear, pressure that inhibits elipsis and favors careful articulation. Ironically, speakers of high languages take this clarity to be evidence of a natural superiority, rather than simply a response to specific contextual demands. Such linguistic chauvinism is supported, in part, by the literary tradition that exists for most high languages. When a language has encoded most of what is considered the literary canon of a culture, and when the ideas expressed in that canon are not found encoded elsewhere in quite the elegant form of the familiar models, it is easy to believe that the language is the source of that thought. Thus it is that the high varieties of language are often venerated and defended against dilution and corruption from below. To this end, grammars, dictionaries, and handbooks help codify and perpetuate the high language in an unchanging form.

Low varieties are not without status, however. Especially in western European countries, great loyalty to local vernaculars exists. Because they are used primarily in conversation, these may develop a range of affective devices that render them capable at once of registering and embodying feeling. While such devices may find their way into the "high" literature, they have no place in the documents and deliberations most frequently couched in the high language.

If low varieties are the vernacular of the people, where do high varieties come from? Ordinarily, there are two conditions, either or both of which may contribute to the establishment of a high language. One is literary. If an enormous body of literature exists in a language—especially but not necessarily religious literature—that language may be preserved as the vernacular diverges from it in everyday life. Latin's long persistence as a high language in western Europe results from just such a situation, for instance. The second, and more frequent, source of high languages, however, is through the imposition of one language variety upon another by a ruling group, one either conquering from without or rising to power from within. Part of the colonialization process is generally the imposition of the colonizer's language as the "high" language of the dominated culture, as is illustrated by the presence of European languages in Africa and Asia.

Although in the past high languages emerged gradually over a period of time, decolonization often occurs abruptly and rapidly in the twentieth century, as the colonizing power withdraws from the scene. Emerging nations often need to settle upon a high language quickly if they are to maintain a world position (as was the case in India) or to create a unified sense of nationhood (a problem throughout the Third World). When the choice must be made deliberately, two possibilities present themselves (Joseph, 1983). The colonial language may be retained, a solution that has several advantages. It is often already a world language, one that can be used internationally as well as intranationally. It has already functioned as a high language in the culture at hand. No adaptations are necessary to fit it to the functional requirements of the high variety. And further, existing documents need not be translated into a new high variety. The disadvantage of such a solution is, of course, the association of the colonial language with the imposed rule—with its culture, its values, and its abuses.

The second choice is to elevate a local language or dialect, gradually adapting it to the functions fulfilled by a high language. While this avoids the disadvantages associated with the colonial language, the selection of a local language creates other problems. The local variety may not readily adapt to the requirements of a high language (Hymes, 1980: 51). Furthermore, in superimposing one local variety above others, one is thereby elevating one portion of the populace, since its native speakers automatically form a new elite, having greater access to the power structure than do speakers of other varieties. But even more serious, the local variety generally cannot serve as the vehicle for international discussion, for which a world language must be available.

Thus, while it is theoretically possible for local varieties to become the high languages in the Third World—and it has occurred—nevertheless, English has remained dominant throughout Africa and Asia, often yielding a diglossia so widespread that Mazrui (1975) asks how we should define "first language." Is it the language first learned or the one most often used? When, for speakers of different languages, English becomes both the language in which they conduct their public lives and a lingua franca in their private lives, it becomes the first language in both senses for the subsequent generation. Thus, Mazrui calls growing numbers of African blacks speaking English as their native language—a populace resulting from just this situation—"Afro-Saxons," predicting that by the year 2000 there will be more blacks who speak English as their native tongue than there will be British. In fact, there may already be more for whom it is the "first" language in a functional sense.

The selection of an official language, traditionally determined through natural processes over a long period of time, can now be achieved more or less instantaneously by language planners. Two authors consider the consequences for local speakers when the official language is other than the native tongue. Braj Kachru looks at the place of English in the fortunes of India and of Indians. Brian Weinstein takes a similar perspective on the place of French in former colonies and protectorates of France.

The high language in the United States is English, and we are accustomed to the situation in which goods and services are provided through the medium of that language. However, since English is not the official language of the nation (Heath, 1981a), it has been argued successfully that public services must be provided for monolingual speakers of other languages when a sufficient number is present in a community. Joan Rubin (in Chapter 8) examines some of the federal, state, and private activities designed to overcome language barriers in providing services in several domains: public health, law, employment media, citizenship participation and representation, social welfare, and education. She focuses her attention on Spanish speakers, but her remarks apply, as well, to the growing number of Asians in the United States who are not learning English well enough to become bilingual (and to the people throughout the world who do not happen to speak the high language of the nation in which they live).

Geneva Smitherman discusses the problems of such speakers in her account of the circumstances surrounding the King case in Ann Arbor, Michigan, in which legal action was required to assure equal educational opportunity to a group of Black students. Although there is a legal precedent in the United States for charging educational bias because of language differences, there is none for charging bias because of dialect differences (a technicality that has led to unresolved problems in areas where, for example, Appalachian children form a significant minority of the school population). Smitherman's essay shows how the linguist may play an important role in power struggles involving language.

People often talk about language as if it were a lever, aiding anyone who learns to "speak well" to open doors and pole vault to new social heights. Much education policy is based on the belief that different language varieties are rivals, and that the comparative values of languages can be determined by the social status of the speakers of each. Kachru (in Chapter 9) disagrees. Although he acknolwedges that the political and social vitality of English results from its history as a high language in India and its usefulness as a world language, still he implies that English possesses a power (one that might come to reside in any high language), such that acquisition of it works a transformation upon the speaker and writer. In a somewhat different vein, Weinstein (Chapter 13) chronicles the efforts of French-speaking nations to deal with the declining use of their language in world communication. He analyzes the consequences this change has had for them.

Many linguists hold an alternate view; that is, they assume that speakers are internally unaffected by the language variety they happen to speak. Whatever differences they experience as a result of their language are generally attributed to outside responses to their speech. Thus, Bolinger (1980) argues that "attitudes toward a form of speech are hardly other than attitudes toward the speakers," so that "inferior" people are believed to speak in inferior ways, "naturally." The social groups whose speech is looked down upon are told, by those who enjoy prestige, that their language is one of their problems; learning to speak "correctly," they are told by educators and sometimes by parents, is a way to move up through the strata of society. Although this approach to language does recognize divisions between hierarchical rankings of speakers, it focuses on individual change and ignores the inequities and discrimination that keep the majority of the stigmatized social groups socially and economically at the bottom of the hierarchy.

Even though it is something other than the language variety they speak that keeps such groups in the lower strata of society, their speech serves as an invidious marker of that stratification. Many studies have demonstrated that control of the standard language variety is a positive asset, that speakers of the standard language (whatever their social classification) are evaluated more favorably than speakers of low-status language varieties, whether these are different dialects or different languages (see, for example, Lambert et al., 1960; Giles, 1970; Lambert et al., 1975; Giles and Powesland, 1975). We know less, however, about the consequences suffered by nonstandard speakers as a result of unfavorable social evaluations.

Foucault (1980) suggests an approach that may reveal such difficulties when he suggests that we study the specifics of power in a specific situation and a particular time. We might look at any situation in which the high language is the spoken norm and assess how successful speakers of the low language are in procuring their rights and privileges. It is a critical question, in fact, since a significant proportion of the world population speaks a language variety that denies them direct access to the economic and political institutions of the country in which they live. As a consequence, they must depend upon speakers of the high language to represent them in securing their entitlements. When representation is not possible—when they must speak for themselves—we can observe the consequences, and several papers in this collection do just that.

The classroom provides a useful setting for studying the consequences of such language variation. In this volume, Noelle Bisseret Moreau discusses some long-range consequences of unequal educational opportunities in France, and Geneva Smitherman's paper documents the difficulties encountered by nonstandard speakers in the classroom. The courtroom is very much like the schoolroom, in that roles are clearly defined and most of the activity involves spoken communication (O'Barr, 1982). Wodak-Engel demonstrates that the tension created by their inability to control the standard speaking style results in incompetent testimony by working class defendants. The doctor-patient medical encounter presents a special set of problems because the power asymmetry is highly institutionalized in such a setting, and because failure to transmit vital information may have serious implications in the prescribing of medical treatment. In their chapter, Treichler et al. discuss a doctor-patient interview in which such a problem occurs. The analysis of the interview developed from a program in which techniques are being studied for restructuring the doctor-patient encounter so that power asymmetry does not result in failure to obtain the needed information.

The family, too, provides a situation in which roles are often highly structured and much activity is carried on verbally. An added advantage to studying the family, discussed in the chapter by Susan Ervin-Tripp et al., is that we can observe the process whereby social norms are internalized by children. Because age differences translate into power differences within a family setting, we can observe the strategies used by younger children to try to overcome such power differences.

The essays that follow consider these topics, inquiring into the process of language and the society that uses it. These are not presented as "standard notions" about language and power, but as searches that can be pursued either independently, or collectively as part of theory-building. The authors encourage consideration of power not only in terms of legislation and prohibition, but as a network of processes that produces, among other things, discourse. The perspectives and topics are deliberately varied; all, however, are concerned with power asymmetry in interaction—its sources and its consequences.

NOTE

1. Fluctuation between *Black* and *black* in this volume reflects the different points of view of the authors using each spelling. Those who prefer to capitalize do so to reflect their view of *Black* as the designation for race (replacing *Negro*); they argue that *white* does not designate race in the same way, since most whites label themselves Italian, Polish, British, or some other nationality. Those who do not capitalize consider that doing so would reflect a patronizing attitude toward one minority category unless the same capitalization procedure were applied to all such categories. In this chapter we capitalize the term, reflecting the preference of the majority of contributors to this volume.

1

NETWORKS AND HIERARCHIES
Language and Social Stratification

Patricia C. Nichols

EVERY SOCIETY and every living language is stratified in many different ways. People divide themselves and each other into groups along lines of class, status, and power. In the study of language stratification, analysts find such things as "high" and "low" varieties (Ferguson, 1959), standard and nonstandard dialects (Wolfram and Fasold, 1974), spoken and written codes—all having different functions and different evaluations within their social groups. Why do we as human beings rank each other and submit to ranking by others? Why do we use language as one of the primary vehicles for this ranking? Language, as Wittgenstein (1969) puts it, is a "form of life" and, as such, is one of the forms through which our social relationships are manifest. Language is one of the primary vehicles through which our relative social status is shown, often in ways that remain below the conscious level of participants in the speech act.

Studies of language use in recent years have given us both access to this not-always-conscious ranking of each other and also the means of exercising conscious control over language use as well as language evaluation. These studies provide potential guides for the redistribution of social power at all levels of the social body. As William Labov has shown us, the nonstandard speech of Black adolescents in urban U.S. ghettos may express a greater degree of logical reasoning than the standard speech of their middle-class counterparts (Labov, 1972b). His sustained crusade to force the public schools to examine the prevailing judgments about the correlation of intellect and dialect culminated in the testimony he and other linguists gave during the 1979 Black English court case in Ann Arbor, Michigan (Labov, 1982; Smitherman, this volume).

Penelope Brown's analysis of politeness and deference in women's speech has shown the relationship between a social position of inferiority and the use of negative politeness (Brown, 1980). The study of a kind of language use characteristic of subordinate groups across cultures (Brown and Levinson, 1978) gives us the possibility of exercising conscious control over these aspects of linguistic behavior and of furthering social changes underway in a given society. As Cheris Kramarae (1981) observes, however, careful use of such studies is needed, so as to distinguish between actual language use of such groups and stereotypes held about it. In discussing the use of such studies of women's speech in the currently popular assertiveness training courses in the United States, Kramarae (1981: 151) notes that careful attention must be given to the range of language use and evaluation across social classes within a given society, if changes in language use are to effect changes in the social structure. For all subordinate groups, both study and social change is probably most effective when the groups themselves are actively engaged in the inquiry. As William Labov notes for the Black English trial in Ann Arbor, the entrance of Black linguists into the study of this language variety was in large part responsible for outcome of the court case: "The only permanent advance in the condition of life in any field occurs when people take their own affairs into their own hands" (Labov 1982: 195-196). For subordinate linguistic groups to make their own analyses of their language use would almost certainly result in more comprehensive studies, as well as provide the foundation for changes in the social structure.

The use of language is part of a social interaction that requires essential agreements about meaning between the participants in the interaction and reflects the consensus among participants about their relative social "worth" as speakers and hearers. Language, almost beyond any other form of life, can give us insight into the consensual relationships that obtain between participants in the speech events as to their relative positions on the social scale at any particular time and place. With awareness can come the potential of withholding consensus on the part of the weak, as Elizabeth Janeway has suggested in her *Powers of the Weak* (1980b). And on the part of the powerful who are also rational and see beyond themselves, a willingness to participate on terms of greater equality can come with recongnition of the arbitrariness of all power relationships.

LANGUAGE STANDARDS

Studies of linguistic attitudes in recent years indicate that languages are stratified according to varieties associated with a specific social class, race, ethnic group, or gender. Little work has been done on attitudes associated with age-grading, but the fact that young children characteristically speak differently from adults in their speech communities—and that these differences are predictable across languages—has been documented the world over (Ferguson and Slobin, 1973). Provocative research by Zimmerman and West (1975) has shown that language use by children and adults parallels that by women and men: Children talking with adults and women talking with men are consistently and frequently interrupted by their speaking partners, as well as ignored or unsupported when they attempted to choose the topic of conservation. We must assume that evaluations of the speaking rights of children are similar to evaluations of the rights of women in conversation with men.

For all languages, there seems to be general agreement among speakers and hearers that there is a standard variety and that this variety is in some important sense "better" than other varieties of the language. This judgment holds true whether or not a listener customarily uses the standard (Labov, 1972a). (See Bisseret Moreau, this volume, for an interesting perspective on how and why the standard evolves to serve the needs of the dominant population.) In the United States, which has no language academy and no officially designated standard, speakers across a variety of social and ethnic backgrounds agree in ranking a dialect typical of "network newscasters" highest of six regional and ethnic varieties, though the variety ranked lowest changes with the personal dialect background of the listener (Tucker and Lambert, 1969).

In countries that have more than one competing language, one of the languages is consistently ranked as better than the other. In Canada, before the advent of French nationalism, both English and French speakers rated English speakers higher than French speakers (Lambert et al., 1960); in Peru, bilingual teachers rate Spanish speakers of higher status than Quechua speakers (Wölck, 1972).

Which language or dialect receives the highest ranking in a particular social context depends on power relationships that obtain at the time. These power relationships may shift within the lifetime of speakers, as the editor of *American Speech* has noted recently for the United States, where dialect patterns of the Sun Belt states of the south and west are rising to prominence in the popular music and speech of the young concurrent with economic prosperity in these regions (Butters, 1983). Or the power relationships may shift over centuries, as with the status of French as a prestige language in medieval England (when the Norman French held political power) but that of a nonprestige language in colonial Canada (after English speakers had reclaimed political dominance in England and attained it in much of North America). In both contemporary England and Canada, the prestige of English has been associated with the political power of its speakers. As a general rule, a society selects for its "standard" that language variety associated with its most powerful ethnic groups and social classes. The "registers" within this standard that are most highly esteemed are those associated with the most powerful gender (men) and with the most powerful age group (adults). (See Hughes and Trudgill [1979] for a recent discussion of how a standard dialect is determined, and Ellis and Ure [1969] for a discussion of the relationship between language variety and register.)

LANGUAGE STANDARDIZATION IN TWO COMMUNITIES: AN EXEMPLUM

Although we have abundant evidence that all human societies recognize a standard language variety, we have only recently begun to examine the processes by which subgroups within a given society select or reject the standard for their own language use. Since the pioneering work of Labov (1966) in New York City and the recogniton of its usefulness as model for the study of change in progress (Weinreich et al., 1968), sociolinguists have found it possible to obtain an overview of an entire community's relationship to the standard of the wider society. Over the past decade I have undertaken such a study in two rural communities in the American South and have examined the social and linguistic processes through which both communities are adopting the regional standard language as a replacement for their older nonstandard varieties.

Coastal South Carolina, as one of the oldest of the new-world settlements that brought together European, African, and native American peoples, provides a contemporary setting for the study of the interaction of language and social stratification. From the six European, forty African, and thirty indigenous groups of people already settled there, two major ethnic groups have emerged: white and nonwhite, which I will call "Black." The Black group has been marked throughout its history in South Carolina as having fewer rights than the privileged white group, from denial of baptismal rights in Christian churches in the early colony and the literacy rights that accompained membership in them, to denial of voting rights and access to public accommodations like restaurants, hotels, libraries, and schools well into this century.

I have chosen to call these *ethnic* rather than *racial* divisions for several reasons. While there has been considerable mixing between individuals of European, African, and Amerindian ancestry, sharp social and legal boundaries have been maintained between groups. An individual of mixed ancestry usually assumes the ethnic membership of his or her nurturing family, acquiring its traditions, customs, and status within the wider community. In the plantation belt of the American South, however, this practice was often supplemented by legal designations of persons as "Negro" even though they had less than twenty percent African ancestry. Because of the power relationships that obtained between Amerindian, European, and African in the early colony, African and Indian women frequently bore children by European men; thus children who were racially of partly European stock were often raised with non-European ethnic traditions. In terms of language use, the ethnic traditions of the nurturing speech community have been far more influential than the racial history of individuals. Furthermore, the Black/white distinction has been more important than the old-world religious and racial distinctions between Jew and Gentile. Unlike much of the Western world, South Carolina has historically granted significant political power to its Jewish population (originally Sephardic from Spain and Portugal)—electing an upstate man to the Second Provincial Congress from South Carolina, merchants to civic offices of prominence in the early port of Georgetown, a jurist to Supreme Court Justice after the Civil War, and a legislator from Barnwell County to the powerful position of speaker of the House of Representatives in this century (Elzas, 1905; Joyner, 1983; Dinnerstein and Palsson, 1973; Bass, 1972). On several counts, then, an ethnicity based only partially on racial differences emerges as the salient feature of the social hierarchy that characterizes South Carolina.

This major ethnic division stems from the early enslavement of African and Indian peoples by the European colonists and from the fear that arose from the increasing numbers of Blacks after 1720, as Africans began to constitute the majority of the colony's population. "White" emerged as the cover term for those colonists who could claim land and accumulate property; old-world distinctions between Welsh, Scots, English, Germans, French, and Sephardic Jews, which might have been important in another time and place, were virtually forgotten in the economic sphere. New-world distinctions between the

Siouan, Iroquoian, and Muskogean nations disappeared also, as native Americans died of disease and war or moved to frontier areas—the few remaining becoming assimilated into either the Black or white ethnic group. Only a small band of Catawba remain in the upstate county of York and a few marginal triracial groups scattered around the state, known by names like "Turks," "Brass Ankles," and "Red Legs." Gone also are the distinctions between African cultural groups from Senegambia, Nigeria, and Angola, even though these groups formed the majority of the colony's population for much of its early history.

Within two generations, the English language became a unifying factor among all these diverse people. Some Europeans acquired it as a second language, using it in commerce and education, often intermarrying with different European ethnic groups and requiring such a unifying language for the home. The Africans, excluded from intermarriage with the Europeans by the prevailing Protestant and English attitudes toward this practice (unlike the Catholic and Spanish attitudes that prevailed in South American colonies) and excluded from certain kinds of social interaction because of their slave status, usually acquired the English-based creole Gullah as their common language.[1] A few house slaves who had regular conversational interaction with native English speakers would have learned English as a second language, but the great majority of the Africans did not have such access to English-speaking models. The few surviving Amerindians spoke the English of the major ethnic group with which they assimilated. Language thus became one of the distinguishing marks of the two new ethnic groups, with the white group speaking English and most of the Black group speaking the English-based creole, Gullah.

Today the living and marriage patterns of these two ethnic groups display rigid segregation, though the work patterns are now becoming more integrated. It is still possible to find small rural communities that are exclusively Black or white, with members from each meeting in a nearby urban center to work at common jobs. I studied two such rural communities for the insight their language patterns give into the interaction of such social factors as class, ethnicity, gender, and age and their influence on language use. I was initially interested in the relationship between Gullah and Black English Vernacular and in the changes now under way in the creole as its speakers have become increasingly integrated into the mainstream during the past two decades. While varieties of Black English had been studied extensively in northern settings, little systematic work had been done on the language use of Black speakers in communities where they have lived longest.

As a white South Carolinian, I had learned a variety of Black English as a child from a Black woman who cared for me daily at the time that I was also acquiring the language of my ethnic group. I was personally curious about the relationship between these language varieties and subsequently expanded the work to include a comparison of a white community that was similar in size and socioeconomic background to the Black one. A linguistic analysis of this three-way relationship between Gullah and Black English Verncacular and White Southern English is under way (Nichols, forthcoming). The social factors underlying the movement of both the Black and white communities toward the regional standard have been of particular interest for the light they shed on the questions of language and social stratification. The two communities have existed in a relatively isolated part of coastal South Carolina for almost two centuries; although they lie less than twenty miles apart along the same river, the communities have maintained two different nonstandard language varieties over this long period. Recently, however, their isolation has been broken and they are sharing more of the same educational and occupational opportunities. With these changes, some members of each community have begun to use the regional standard language. In examining the factors underlying the contemporary movement toward the standard variety, I have found that certain kinds of social interaction available within and without the groups have crucially influenced the language choices made by segments of each community.

Demographics

The all-Black community in which I worked for five months and studied over a period of five years would be classified as working class by the criteria commonly used in social stratification theory. (See Nichols [1976, 1983] for a discussion of this community research.) It has existed on a river island of the Waccamaw Neck since the early 1700s and constitutes a single social class, as most of the male heads of household work at construction jobs on the mainland to which they commute daily by motor boat and automobile, and most women work in the seasonal tourist industry of the Grand Strand as servants or retail clerks.

All adults except one can read and write, most adults having finished elementary school and the younger generation now obtaining a high school education. A few island women in past years have gone to college; women with college educations usually do not return to the island to live. In recent years several young women and men have joined the armed services for careers and have left the island at least temporarily.

The income level per household is not much above the poverty level, even though all adults except the very old work during some part of the year; most own their houses and the small plots of land on which they rest, sharing family land as young adults set up their own households. Families are large, some caring for foster children as well as their own. All families own a small motorboat by which they get to the mainland, and most keep a car parked at the landing on the mainland. Fuel and upkeep for these vehicles are a continual drain on family resources. Two or three families also keep a truck or similar vehicle on the island itself, where all roads are deep sand or mud. The county maintains a large schoolboat for transporting the children to school daily. The children, on the basis of family income, usually qualify for free lunches at school. In terms of the occupation, education, and income of the head of household, island families would be classified as working class.

The all-white community I have studied over the past four years is located on the mainland bordering the Waccamaw River approximately twenty miles north of the river island. During the past century, when the river was the major transportation artery, the two communities were served by the steamships that made regular trips between the port of Georgetown to the south and the neighboring county seat of Conway to the northeast. Today the distance between them seems greater because travelers must now use narrow country roads and the broad highway connecting the cities of the Grand Strand.

The community is connected to the resort center of Myrtle Beach by well-maintained paved roads, and the children are bused daily to school. Most adults and children have attended elementary and high school within their own community, having long had one of the oldest and most respected high schools in the county.

The men of the white community hold service jobs associated with the tourist industry of the Grand Strand. Men of the older generation farmed tobacco and cotton, but farming as the major family livelihood has almost stopped in the last two decades. Women are either full-time housekeepers or hold service jobs in addition to their home responsibilities. A few hold professional jobs as nurses or teachers, continuing to live in the community of their birth.

A link with farming as a livelihood is maintained by renting out the family tobacco allotments (government permission to plant a certain number of acres in tobacco) to large corporations which own expensive farm machinery and can dispense with scarce hand labor. Some families obtain additional income from the old farmland by renting out small parcels to workers in the resort communities or on the nearby military base; some of these rentals are organized into trailer parks. By the criteria of income, education, and occupation of heads of household, this community would be classified as lower middle class, using conventional social stratification methods.

Language Differences

Language differences in the two communities can best be illustrated by stories told by two young boys about dogs, a favorite topic of discussion throughout this region. While the standard orthography does not illustrate important differences in phonology, the grammatical differences in the verbal and nominal systems are evident:

> I have this dog and we have a bunch of chickens back at my uncle's and at my house. And this dog, he went after the chickens the other day and he killed, he killed two roosters and four hens and went after some more. And when he did, my uncle shot him in the leg and made him go on. And he came back yesterday and almost got some more. We ran him off again. We had to go take him to town and put him to sleep 'cause he was real badly hurt. So we had him pretty well fixed up, so we could bury him. [White male, age 11 years]
>
> One day, yesterday, me and Darryl, we were going in the yard. Me and Darryl hear a car say, "Bump, bump." And then Teria dog . . . and he say, Darryl said, "Teria dog done get hit." Then me and Darryl run up there and the dog bleed all over. Then Bubba bring um in the yard. Then Bubba gone get ee gun and shoot um. [Questions from audience]. Yeah, he been dead. [Black male, age 11 years]

Although the white boy's language is characteristic of that of the white community, this child was actually a student in the same classroom as the Black boy. They were both from working class families, both poor students in school, and both orphans being raised by grandparents. They were exposed to the older generation's language, because of these circumstances, as well as to the language usage of their peers in school situations. The white child uses, at least in this story, standard grammatical patterns for verb tenses and nominal plurals and possessives; the Black child, by contrast, uses the creole aspect marker *done* to indicate completed action, zero tense marking to indicate action clearly in the past (though this varies with standard past tense marking and with the creole marker *been*), zero possessive marking for *Teria dog,* and the creole pronoun *ee* to indicate third person possession. The children in this classroom seemed to understand each other, although the white teacher often did not understand the Black children. They, on the other hand, understood her problem well enough to switch from creole to standard forms when asked for clarification from her.

Some of the younger adults in both the white and Black communities are changing their language patterns in the direction of the regional standard, abandoning nonstandard patterns long used in each community and still used by the older generation. Those Black and white speakers who are changing are beginning to sound more like each other than like the older members of their own communities. Older Blacks speak a creole-influenced variety of English, often lacking gender marking for the personal pronouns and tense marking for action verbs; the creole infinitive-marker *fuh* and the habitual aspect marker *duh* can sometimes be heard in their speech. Older whites speak a dialect of English that originated in the northern counties of England and in the Lowlands of Scotland (Nichols, forthcoming). The neuter pronoun *hit,* which has been in continuous use in these dialects since 400 A.D.,is heard in their speech; they often use past tense verb forms no longer heard in the regional standard language variety.

Brief excerpts from tape-recorded speech of two adults from the separate communities—one a Black woman of 88 years and the other white man of 99 years—illustrate the older speech patterns characteristic of the two speech groups:

> I been know June, yeah Lord. I been know June so long till ee ain't funny. June been a baby in ee ma hand when I been know June. 'Cause ee mother-them been living—just how they got this road gone right straight through where they living, where they house, where she house there over there—ee mother-them house was right there. And ee father. And, but now she duh work now to Brookgreen. 'Cause ee brother die—I hadn't seen her since ee bury ee brother. I just hear about ee brother died. And how I hear about ee brother die: I put this radio in the morning-time, and anything like that come on that battery on that radio. And that how I heard about him. But I ain't see she—bout his brother—but I ain't see she fuh tell um nothing, but I pass he house all the time when I ride. [Black woman, 88]
>
> And I come here, and me Daddy had an option on this place. I stayed all day over yonder to Burroughs and Collins looking to his places. And there's nice little places, but they were too high. And I come on down here. There weren't no house on it—there weren't no house on it, but I

knowed the land was all right. I tended—watched that, looked out for that—and I examined it and I found the soil was all right. And I turned in and I bought this. And then there's a high school there. And that's the way I got by—I, I wanted my children to have an education. Twelve head of um. And then for me—I didn't want ne'er one to be as sappy as I was. I wanted my children to get an education if they could be got. And hit was—looked like hit was free if I could get close enough to it. [White man, age 90]

For a sociolinguistic study of each community, I tape recorded male and female adult speakers between ages fifteen and ninety and analyzed their speech for the presence or absence of selected morphosyntactic variables characteristic of the speech of their communities (Nichols, 1980, 1983, forthcoming). I made these recordings in the homes of speakers with their consent and often in the presence of other family members. Older speakers talked about community history and changes they had witnessed; younger speakers talked about their perceptions of the community and their plans to stay or leave.

In the Black community I worked as a volunteer aide in the elementary school which the children attended. I also taught a college-preparatory composition class on a voluntary basis in the community itself one night a week; this class was attended by some twenty pupils ranging from junior high to college age. In the white community I was officially sponsored by the county historical society and did interviews that complemented its recent study of the early families and churches of the community.

Older members contributed additional facts about community history, and younger people talked about their decisions to remain in the community or their plans to leave. My kinship ties with some members of this community and my personal knowledge of its history proved valuable in formulating relevant interview questions. In the Black community my daily contact with its elementary school children and my obvious concern for and help with their studies proved valuable in making interview contacts. In both communities my observations outside the formal interview situation enrich and confirm the findings of the quantitative study of speech variation.

My most difficult interview occurred in the white community with a relative; the speaker was anxious to convey his position about an old family feud over his land holdings, and I knew far less about the issue than he supposed. I fared much better with speakers I knew little about personally, in both Black and white communities. Only one speaker, an older woman in the Black community, refused to be tape recorded; her position was that she was not really a native of the community since she had come there as a bride some fifty years before.

In the recorded interviews, both young and middle-aged woman of the Black community used exclusively standard forms for two of the variables, while one young and one middle-aged woman used some nonstandard forms for a third variable. Young men in this community used more nonstandard and creole variables than middle-aged men. By contrast, young women in the white community used exclusively standard variables, while middle-aged and older women used some nonstandard forms. Middle-aged and older men, as well as younger men, used nonstandard forms variably with standard ones; younger men used fewer than their elders, however.

The language patterns associated with occupation, as well as the role models within their communities, are the factors associated with changing speech for selected portions of these communities. Young and middle-aged women in the Black community and most young women in the white community are now in service jobs that entail interaction with a wide spectrum of speakers who visit the resort area each year and who sometimes retire to live in areas adjacent to the white community. While some young men of the white community are now in service jobs also, most young and middle-aged men of the Black community are working in jobs associated with the construction industry—jobs that do not entail extensive interaction with speakers outside their social group.

Unlike middle-aged women of the Black community, women of this age in the white community frequently work at home, caring for their own homes and children daily and, thus, not having extensive interaction outside the immediate community. This last point is interesting because of the slight difference in social class between the white and Black communities; having higher social status than women of the Black community, one might expect the women of the white community to use language forms that have greater social prestige. Just the opposite is the case. Internal patterns of language interaction, rather than external social variables, account for this community pattern and lead us to examine the importance of social networks in determining linguistic behavior.

THREE VIEWS OF LANGUAGE IN SOCIETY

Those who study language use in social groups work, however loosely, within some model of social organization. At least three major models can be indentified: structuralist or functionalist, conflict, and symbolic interactionist.

The model that has dominated American sociology and American linguistics until recently is the *structuralist* or *functionalist* model. In this view of social organization, a number of social structures of institutions are seen as functioning in some kind of balance with each other. The social classes are discrete and static structures, defined by attitudes toward outside indicators of social class; occupation is the foremost of these indicators. While movement of individuals between social classes is possible and even expected in a relatively open society like the United States, the classes themselves remain fixed in relation to each other.

Labov (1966) worked within such a framework for his landmark study of language use in New York City. He used a social survey of the Lower East Side that had been conducted along the structural view of social stratification, treating the family as the basic social unit and male head-of-household as the source of the family's social status. An entire family was assigned to a given social class based primarily on occupation of the male head-of-household. An implicit assumption in this language study was that social position correlates with language use. When subgroups within a social class were found to deviate consistently with the language use generally characteristic of that class, explanations were sought from within the language users rather than from within the system of social classification itself. Women in Labov's study were assigned to the social class of their husbands or fathers; when they exhibited language use more prestigious than that of men of their class in formal situations and less prestigious in informal ones, they were labeled "linguistically insecure" (Labov, 1972b).

To his credit, Labov did recognize that social variables like gender and ethnicity influence language use significantly. He found it necessary to include descriptions of sex and ethnic differences in this study, whereas previous dialect studies in the United States had focused on the correlation between language variety, social class, and age. He also documented convincingly the wide range of language use available to a single speaker in different social situations. After his New York study, no longer would the study of language in society be one that correlated only language variety and social class. Building on his work, my South Carolina study suggests that it is often individual and subgroup participation in occupational networks that influences language use at least as much as participation in the family unit; the occupational networks of individual family members often differ in ways important for language use.

The *conflict* model of social organization has been much more influential in Europe, particularly in France, than in the United States. It emphasizes the economic basis of class divisions and sees them as organized in relation to the mode of production; it stresses exploitation, oppression, and social conflict as important factors in social organization. In this view, "class" refers to positions defined by the social relations of ownership and authority, rather than to positions defined by such factors as status, style of life, and income (Dahrendorf, 1959; Kallenberg and Griffin, 1980).

The authors of a recent study of language use in Canada are indebted to this view of social organization, rejecting any attempt to correlate language use and social class overtly: "directly correlating linguistically variable behavior with social class membership, whether defined stratificationally or dialectically, is not a well-motivated procedure" (Sankoff and Laberge, 1978). In a study of Montreal French, Sankoff and Laberge attempt to correlate language use with economic activity, applying the notion of *linguistic market* developed by Bourdieau and Boltanski (1975) in an examination of the educational system in France. For this study Sankoff and Laberge developed a profile of each speaker's socioeconomic life history and asked a panel of judges familiar with language use in the city to rank each speaker on the basis of the relative importance of the "legitimatized" or standard language variety in his or her personal history. This study relies, to some measure, upon a speaker's relationship to the economic system, as determined by an outside evaluator, and directly examines the place of language in those interactions that center on economic concerns.

Applying this concept to the South Carolina study, we observe that the difference between the economic activities of young women in both the Black and white communities and those of young men in the Black community is a difference between service jobs and blue-collar jobs. Language plays a central role in this difference in economic activity; the regional standard language is an important part of every transaction in the service jobs but not in the construction jobs. Although the jobs held by young white men are different from those of women in both communities, they also entail face-to-face interaction with people of diverse language backgrounds. Using the conflict model of social organization, therefore, we obtain some measure of explanation for the divergent language use among subgroups in the two communities. Although it is more comprehensive than the functionalist reliance upon occupational status as the primary indication of social position, the conflict model does not address the issue of speaker choice or intention, nor is it clear how it would treat speakers outside the economic system. If we, for example, ask why the housewives in the white community of South Carolina use more nonstandard variables than the women who work in service jobs within the Black community, the conflict model cannot offer an adequate explanation. As Bisseret (1979) has observed, the focus on *linguistic capital* leads to an emphasis on the language of the dominant without a consideration of the important relationship between the language of the dominant and that of the dominated. This model does not address the possibility that the language of the dominated may be chosen as the preferred language within the community when there are no outside economic pressures to speak the language of the dominant.

In addition, the definition of "power" in the conflict model is unnecessarily limited. Randall Collins, in an influential discussion of conflict sociology, acknowledges that the kinds of contacts each individual has are major influences on behavior and mental constructs. He goes on to place major importance on very limited kinds of contacts, however: "Power relations, situations of giving and taking orders, seem to be the most important behavior-shaping experiences in the world of work" (Collins, 1975: 54). In his view, *occupation* is of major importance as a human activity, since it is the way people keep themselves alive and is the reason for their fundamental importance. Occupations, in his view, shape the differences among people and are essentially "power classes within the realm of work" (p. 62). He maintains that the most powerful effect on a person's behavior is the sheer volume of occupational deference given and received; the greater cosmopolitanism of the higher occupational levels is one key to their outlooks, since the volume and diversity of personal contacts is often greater at these levels.

The defect in Collins's analysis can be seen in the different linguistic behavior of men and women in the Black community of South Carolina. Although women in service jobs such as waitress and retail clerk are giving no more orders than men in such positions or in blue collar construction jobs, they exhibit language behavior that would suggest that they do, in Collins's analysis. These women do indeed have a greater diversity and volume of personal contacts in their occupational activities than do men, but the occupational deference is not different in kind or degree. The income of these women in white collar service jobs is far less than that of men in blue collar laboring jobs, another important indicator of occupational deference. According to Collins, members of the working class are characterized by having steady jobs, but giving no orders to anyone in the name of an organization. Given that both men and women of the Black community belong to the "working class" in this framework, why would they exhibit such different language behavior even when they belong to the same family units? Since neither women nor men give orders in their jobs, some other explanation must be offered for their difference in linguistic behavior.

The *symbolic interactionist* model of social organization shows promise of overcoming major defects of the other two models, in that it considers both individual choices or intentions and also relationships between subgroups within a given society. It provides a more holistic consideration of the way in which people organize themselves into social groups, and it is dominated by the notion of process rather than structure; it makes room for the dynamic interaction that changes the participants in the process of the social act. The American philosopher George Herbert Mead is perhaps the first proponent of this orientation in sociology and one of the first sociologists to recognize the importance of language in the social process:

> If your recognize that language is . . . just a part of a co-operative process, that part which does lead to an adjustment to the response of the other so that the whole activity can go on, then language has only a limited range of arbitrariness. . . . There is . . . a range in our use of language; but whatever phase of this range is used is a part of a social process, and it is always that part by means of which we affect ourselves as we affect others and mediate the social situation through this understanding of what we are saying [Mead, 1934: 75-75].

This view of social organization places relations between people at the center and recognizes that human interaction is a shaping process in its own right (Blumer, 1966), without limiting this interaction to order-giving and receiving situations. In an insight relevant for language use, Herbert Blumer (1969: 19) observes, "It is the social process in group life that creates and upholds rules, not the rules that create and uphold group life." Both Mead and Blumer deny that institutions have life and vitality of their own, but focus rather on the meanings attributed to situations by individuals and the actions they take as a consequence of their definitions.

The elements of internal choice for group members is a central notion within this analysis of social organization, and the concept of *social networks* has evolved as a primary concern. Within both anthropology and sociology, an analysis of social networks has focused on those internal social groups within small villages or larger cities around which individuals center their interaction. (See Barnes [1954] for an early analysis of class within a Norwegian island parish, and Bott [1956] for analysis of conjugal role and social network in the city of London.) In such a framework, social groups are described from within, using the perspective of interactional links between people, rather than from without through the use of external indicators of socioeconomic class.

Social networks, or those long-term and voluntary associations into which people enter, has been a particularly useful construct for those who would study naturally occurring social groups; not all symbolic interactionists have used it. Susan Gal, in a recent study of language choice in a bilingual Austrian village did use this framework to ascertain which factors seemed most to influence the choice between German and Hungarian as a speaker's primary language. By counting an individual speaker's contacts with peasants in the village over a set period of time, Gal determined that the percentage of peasant contacts was correlated with the speaker's primary language identification (Gal, 1979). The greater involvement with others who were peasants, the more likely the speaker would prefer Hungarian as the primary language; the greater the involvement with industrial jobs outside the village, the more likely the preference for German.

This framework has been further developed for linguistic analysis in the more recent work of Leslie Milroy in a study of language use in Belfast, Ireland. Defining social network as "the informal relationships contracted by the individual," Milroy finds it a more useful construct than that of social class, because "the Network concept, unlike that of socioeconomic class, is not limited by intercultural differences in economic or status systems" (Milroy, 1980: 174). All human beings, whatever their nationality, race, or ethnic heritage, enter into such informal relationships. The more dense (that is, the more contacts between various members of an individual's network) and the more multiplex the social network (the more individuals interact with each other in a variety of capacities such as kinship, occupation, neighborhood, and friendship), the more linguistic norms are apt to be affected. Milroy assigns a network score to each individual speaker based on five factors of network interaction, finding that "even when variables of age, sex, and social class are held constant, the closer an individual's network ties are with his local community, the closer his language approximates to localized vernacular norms" (Milroy, 1980: 175). The degree of participation of individuals in such social networks accounts for, Milroy maintains, the frequent observation that speakers of very similar social backgrounds (even from the same family unit) show very different patterns of language use. It is the network participation that is the salient factor in language use, according to Milroy, rather than external social variables usually measured in structural sociology.

If we apply Milroy's concepts of the density and muitiplexity of social network to the South Carolina communities, we find more adequate explanations for the different linguistic behavior in the two Black and white groups and in the different gender and age subgroups within each. Occupation remains a salient feature of sociolinguistic interaction, but now we focus on the place of occupational interaction in the entire spectrum of interaction. Young women in the white community have worked outside the community in jobs that entail interaction with non-community members for a large proportion of their waking hours, while middle-aged women in this community work daily as housewives within their own homes. Thus middle-aged and older women have a denser social network within the community than do younger ones, retaining their older nonstandard dialect speech patterns for these frequent community contacts. The younger women, moreover, have a less multiplex network than do older ones, in that their occupational co-workers frequently do not know other members of their community, and friendships made outside the community often do not overlap friendships within it.

Young men of the white community work outside in jobs that the community itself refers to as "public work" to distinguish it from farming, and some middle-aged men have begun to work in such jobs in midcareer as they have abandoned farming as a major occupation. The greater use of the regional standard dialect by younger men than by middle-aged ones is similar to that for women in their community—for much the same reason.

In the Black community, both young and middle-aged women work outside the community with non-community members, usually in jobs where no other community member has ever worked. Young and middle-aged men, on the other hand, frequently work with each other on construction jobs, which entail little or no interaction with non-community members. Thus the greater use of nonstandard and creole features in the speech of young and middle-aged Black men than in the speech of Black women of the same age is not a gender difference per se, but a feature of their denser and more multiplex social network within the community. People tend to speak most like those they speak with most frequently and interact with in a variety of different social roles (as kin, as neighbor, as friend, and as co-worker).

CONCLUSION

All three of the major models of social organization find that occupation plays a central role in the way we stratify ourselves and others into social groups. An examination of how language as a "form of life" enters into the social dynamic, however, sheds some crucial light on the adequacy of these models themselves. The structural model of social class does not adequately account for the linguistic behavior of either gender differences or ethnic differences. The conflict model of society attempts to explain our linguistic behavior in terms of how some external linguistic market rewards our production; it focuses on our economic activity without considering the strength of factors like kinship, friendship, and neighborhood in influencing our speech patterns. The interactionist model manages to incorporate the constructs of social class and individual economic activity, without assuming that either is the overriding factor influencing language use. By examining the nature and frequency of social contacts, the social network approach within this larger model takes into account contacts that occur as a result of social class and of economic activity, while letting us also consider how some contacts may have greater influence on language use than others.

The social network framework's major defect is that it sheds virtually no light on how individual choices of network interaction are made. Some individuals abandon dense multiplex social networks in favor of social mobility, leaving community and family-of-origin for "life in the big city." Along with such geographic and social choices go language choices. To be sure, external constraints condition some of these choices, and the insights of the conflict model of sociology may help us understand some of these. Some speakers have very little choice about their marginal position relative to localized social networks. Where there is some degree of individual choice, however, the question of how these choices are made must be addressed if we are to have a fully adequate understanding of language and social stratification.

Recent work has been done in social psychology on the question of how individual participants in social interaction arrive at a mutual definition of the situation. Howard Giles and his associates at Bristol have examined perceptions, stereotypes, and attitudes that affect language use, constructing inference models to account for how various information is combined. These factors, they believe, underlie both individual interactional and individual language choices (Giles et al., 1980). These social psychologists have developed an "accommodation theory" to refer to the process of style-shifting by speakers in order to encourage further interaction (Giles and Smith, 1979) and have also addressed issues like the persistence of low-prestige language varieties and the relationship between speech and ethnic identity (Ryan, 1979). While this approach is not yet fully developed, it points the way to a method of describing both individual choices that seem anarchic and also the relationship of such choices to what we perceive as the structured patterns of a larger social group. With such a perspective, language can be seen as a symbol of both personal identity and group membership.

Using this modified social interactionist model of language and social stratification, we make it more possible to see that power flows among and between those who have chosen to speak and listen to each other—not merely from top to bottom from those who have more external attributes of social status to those who have less. From this emerging perspective we are able to see language as encompassing the power to transform, as well as transmit, forms of social life.

NOTE

1. A creole is a language variety that arises when a pidgin becomes the primary language of a speech community. It is more complex in structure, vocabulary, and function than a pidgin. A pidgin is a contact language used between speakers who share no common language.

2

EDUCATION, IDEOLOGY, AND CLASS/SEX IDENTITY

Noëlle Bisseret Moreau

POWER RELATIONSHIPS exist between groups when one, the dominated group, is submitted to a system of real economic, political, juridical, and ideological constraints by the other, the dominant group. Dominated and dominant groups do not exist as realities per se; the identity of each group is actually constituted through the relationship itself. So it is necessary to use the expression *power relationships* instead of *power*, a term that emphasizes only one side of the relationship (that of the dominant group), as if it could be defined per se, as if it were an entity.

Groups are often perceived as static sets condemned to a "natural" destiny, not currently defined by the power relationships that historically constituted them as classes with antagonistic interests. A difference in "essence" among human beings supposedly predetermines the place of the individual in a social order considered immutable. This essentialist ideology, which originated along with the establishment of those structures constituting class societies (Guillaumin, 1972; Bisseret, 1979: 6-32; Capitan Peter, 1981), bases all social hierarchy on the transcendental principle of a "natural," "biological" order.

This ideology arose at the end of the eighteenth century and acquired a scientific language in the nineteenth. As soon as the new bourgeoisie in France found it necessary to protect its own political order from the people, who were demanding de facto equality, it began to build an ideology justifying the concrete relations it had established between possessors and dispossessed. So that the bourgeoisie would not appear to have usurped power, it had to substitute another principle for the nobility's declining principle of

---

*This chapter is a revised (1981) version of Chapter 2 of *Education, Class Language and Ideology* (London: Routledge & Kegan Paul, 1979). Reprinted by permission.

legitimacy. As it could no longer claim that its power derived from divine right, the bourgeoisie sanctified the elements in whose name it had seized power from the nobility: knowledge, merit, ability, and the like. In order to legitimize its domination, it transformed these qualities into intrinsic indivividual qualities that defined its own members alone.

But changes in language that are significant of group relationships had begun to occur well before the Revolution. When the feudal society of France was transformed into a trading society, when economic power came into the hands of the bourgeoisie, the social referent changed: there was a transference of power from one social group—the nobility ideologically defined as a *collectivity* whose practices incarnated the will of a transcendent object, God—to another social group—the bourgeoisie, defined as a sum of *individual* wills acting on their own behalf over the world and over men. At the same time as this bourgeoisie acted, it saw its practices as issuing from a free and creative subject, and it invented a new way of speaking the world. The stress was displaced from the action to the doer of the action; the uttering subject, the "I," became the center around which, with the help of possessives and demonstratives things and human beings were hierarchically ordered (Bisseret, 1979: 67-89). Linguistic forms changed to correspond to the new hidden referent of dominant discourse: a new definition of the *human being* founded on material possessions.

In the nineteenth century, when scientific knowledge became increasingly an instrument of economic power, its possession became, at the same time, an important means of legitimizing power in *all* its forms. The social agents involved in a class system interpret the possession or lack of knowledge according to the irrational logic that the dominant ideology imposes on each individual, whatever her or his position in the system of power relationships. Far from being perceived as the result of sociohistoric forces, current social inequalities are attributed to a dynamic principle existing prior to and independently of them, to a so-called natural force: aptitude. Success or failure at school would be a manifestation of constitutional and hereditary intellectual aptitudes, according to a system of interpretation that has been generally imposed by the bourgeoisie. Its underlying, and often unconscious, postulate is that certain physical characteristics which are socially marked as constituting a "lack" (e.g., of white skin, of a penis, of corporal or verbal facility) necessarily entail a "lack" of mental and psychological characteristics that would qualify those who "possess" them to be the ruling "elite."

This ideology denies the impact of *material* power relationships on the constitution of mental and psychological structures.

Statistical regularities (evidenced by a study of the success or failure of students at the university [Bisseret, 1974: 74-149]) have demonstrated that school and occupational choices are socially imposed on each group and each individual according to her or his class/sex position. The income hierarchy in society is a result of all the orientations that have operated in the life of the individual since the first day of school as a constant factor of differentiation: Dominant class boys can expect the highest incomes and dominated class women, the lowest. At all levels men come out ahead, followed by women. Differences within each sex group occur according to social class origins. The majority of women occupy situations of economic exploitation inside the institution of marriage (domestic work and child care) and, hence, of physical and monetary dependence.

In fact, the appropriation of knowledge and power in all its other forms is basic to the maintenance of dominated and dominant classes. The school system expresses and strengthens power relationships between *social* classes (in the classical sense of the word, "position in the system of production based on a monetary economy") and between *sex* classes—social classes in which one would include (and this is yet to be further analyzed) the production relations based on the material appropriation of women (Guillaumin, 1981: 3-28) and on work without pay (Benston, 1969; Delphy, 1980).

Ideology is the global system of meaning rooted in material relationships. The process is dialectic: The scheme organizing the material action of human beings which transforms the world and social reality is reorganized in return by the material result of that action (Goldmann, 1966; Lukacs, 1971; Piaget, 1977a). Ideology, the global system by which power relationships are interpreted, is *social discourse* about the world and about the human beings. This is perpetually created by social agents through their practices, through unconscious—perceptual, motor, and verbal—behavior as well as through systematized mental constructs (thought and values of the hierarchy). Although ideology often takes the form of a conscious and rational discourse on reality, it draws its dynamic strength from its unconscious dimension, its unstated assumptions.

The essentialist ideology imposes on every social agent his or her class/sex identity, as can be seen by the analysis of the discourses of dominated and dominant groups. The concept of identity is a sociological one: In a class society each social class takes on and shapes its identity and gives meaning to its practices only by referring to a dominant definition of "being." In our culture, a definition of "Man," based on possession, is the hidden referent of social discourse. This hidden referent has two dimensions: a concrete one, which is based, in fact, on material possessions (including—for men—possession of their own body) but embodied in human beings, and a symbolic and imaginary dimension, drawing its identity as a subject of power from the identity of the dominated as object. One way this can be studied is through an analysis of the contents of the speech of males and females from different social classes, through an analysis of the way in which they express their views on the history of their school and on their occupational choices, several years after their entry into the university. The young adults quoted here are all students of the humanities (literature, languages, history, and so forth).

INCOMPLETENESS AND WHOLENESS

In social discourse, the dominated are defined (collectively) as incomplete, while the dominant are singularized and defined as the incarnation of achieved human nature. Dominant speech certainly assigns each one her or his place, but only the dominant individuals have the place of singular beings, and apart from the collection of unique individuals to which they belong, only masses of undifferentiated elements are distinguished: "the people" or "Blacks" or "women." Indeed, in the world "order" created and articulated by the dominant, the dominated have no individuality or singularity, and particularities attributed to their group suffice to define them completely.

Students define themselves differently according to whether they come from the dominated or the dominant class, and whether they are men or women. Children of the dominated class always announce in some way, right from the start, a social origin that seems to them to make sense of their history and of the speech that restores it:

My parents were workers.

I'm from a very working class background.

My family is very, very simple.

There are very few of us from the working class at the university.

On the other hand, in their discourse, members of the dominant class seek only to individualize themselves, not to define themselves in terms of social origins or class membership. They may eventually allude, in passing, to their class background, but only so as to explain a detail of their history:

> My father, whose work is advertising books, has a lot of contacts in literary circles, with editors, authors.
>
> My father wanted me to go in for a mathematical discipline because he's in one himself.
>
> I did *classique* because my father, being a Latin teacher, thought he could give me all possible initial advantages.

Unlike men, women, whatever their class of origin, define themselves as part of a category:

> I think I shall have a less good job than my father (my mother doesn't work). Less good because, being a woman...
>
> A difficult exam for a woman...
>
> It's not really a job for a woman...
>
> Good pay for a woman...

On the other hand, men do not refer to their masculine status. They never qualify utterances by adding "for a man." Since the social characteristics of the dominant never suffice to define their identity, they are not uttered. Only the dominated groups are named, specified. But "woman," "the worker," "the Jew," "Blacks"—these are banal labels which are significant only in relation to what is never mentioned: a referent who is male, bourgeois, Christian, white, and so on. The hidden referent has all the characteristics of the perfect dominant.

SPATIALIZATION

If the dominated (unlike the dominant) announce the category to which they belong, it is because they are marginalized in social discourse. They are thrown into a closed, limited world—as it is expressed by a collection of spatial metaphors. Topologically the representatives of the dominated-class are "under":

> I don't want to sink back.
>
> I wanted to rise in the world.
>
> Pulling oneself up by one's bootstraps...

Those who, thanks to relatively favorable conditions, were able to have at least a secondary education consider that they have escaped, that they are now distanced from their class origins, that they have clambered out or jumped over the barriers. If there is a closed area, this can only be by reference to an open space—which is the place of the dominant.

The universe of the dominated category of women is an equally closed, limited, circumscribed world. Women's and men's discourse assigns women a defined space—namely home, family, or domestic interests—where they "go round," "stay within the four walls," "become bogged down," lead a "secluded" life, become "limited," "dull," and even "cut off" and "isolated" from the rest of the world. This symbolism of enclosure applies equally to domestic activities and to occupational activities, where the woman's dependent status is especially marked. Secretaries, for example, speak of themselves as being closed in, blocked, and confined. The same general opening function filled for dominated-class children by education is filled for women by paid employment. By working away from home or "outside," it is possible to "get out of the house" and to "broaden one's horizons," to have "an opening into the outside world" and be "integrated into collective life," to "develop fully."

The idea of women obtaining fulfillment through work is held especially by those who have what they call free, independent or lucrative jobs. This idea is sometimes accompanied by the idea that women should work only if they have a job they like. Would this be the view of a class that defines work only as a free and creative activity? Yet some women, for whom work is all the more constraining because they are also in charge of family tasks, talk both of overwork and fulfillment. Despite the psychological connotations of its formulation, the idea of fulfillment or freedom, which goes along with that of constraints, is the sign of a sociological contradiction: Work, which is a source of alienation for the working class in general, can paradoxically become a first condition of release from alienation for women, whose bodies and labor have been appropriated by men.

The notions of enclosure, and their corollaries—getting out and opening up—illustrate the weight of ideology. Accordingly, a worker or woman is secluded, far from the mythical center where the bourgeois man is situated. But the place of the dominant is never designated. One never says of a man, for example, that he works "outside." In the dominant discourse topological classifications serve the ideological function of disguising the existence of material power relationships by transmuting them into relations of a formal, geometrical character—i.e., by spatializing them. But this space itself, which is the sign of a reification of social reality, of the dynamics of power relationships, is not neutral; the dominant is always there as the implicit referent.

Dominated Sex

Dominant discourse assigns women a supposedly natural social status (Mathieu, 1978). But how can we explain the undeniable fact that the majority of women are to be found in literary and nonscientific areas, in devalued sections of activity, in positions where their status is low in the hierarchy?

In general, the dominant discourse accounts for women's choices by attributing to them a deepseated incapacity. If they direct themselves toward the humanities it is because they have specific aptitudes and because they can succeed educationally only in ways adapted to a supposedly minor form of intellegence—one more intuitive, more nurturing, and less necessary.

Their "natural" biologically based destiny is motherhood. They are thought to be able truly to "fulfill" themselves only by having and raising their own children. A reified "mother" occurs as a leitmotiv in the accounts analyzed. The mother's *presence* (it is not said *work*) is essential, necessary, and irreplaceable. This is a recent form of the dominant ideology's masking of domestic exploitation and giving women an illusion of power, since the "power" exerted over the children—the most sociologically dependent category—has been delegated by men.

A child needs its mother.

The mother is the only one really capable of raising her children...

The first years are the determining ones.

If the women do not have children, it is generally considered to be desirable if not necessary that they be employed. It is important for a woman to "avoid idleness" and a "trivial life" by "giving herself something to do," a job which will "give her something to think about," since "idleness is the mother of all vices." These suspicions are shared by both sexes. The dominant discourse denies members of the dominated sex the status of a moral person. (Psychoanalytic theory, according to which women are supposed to have a weak "superego," is a particular form of this dominant discourse.)

Dominated Class

And what of children from so-called "deprived" backgrounds? Why do they experience educational difficulties from the start of their schooling? If we enumerate the qualities necessary for success, we can already supply the elements of the implicit reply to this question. A child's educational success presupposes "something" within his or her genetic inheritance. There is a rich terminology applied to this metaphysical principle: intelligence, aptitude, capacity, disposition, facility, intelligence quotient, mental structure, taste, interest, open-mindedness, critical judgment, or intellectual curiosity, for instance.

> You need personal abilities, you cannot make up for a lack of these [dominated-class son]
>
> Unfortunately, on the intellectual plane, my brother doesn't really have the disposition or the taste. [dominated-class daughter]

Intelligence (defined as a substantive characteristic) is necessary but not sufficient. Other psychic and moral qualities are needed—such as personality, character, courage, will, a strong disposition, enthusiasm, application, and seriousness. Finally, you need a "good family background," which encourages, supports, induces, stimulates, frames, supervises, and which shows its availability, will, firmness, strictness, and the like. If some are convinced that "only the least able stay as laborers" (dominated-class male student) or that "the children of workers and peasants have often inherited less aptitude for study" (dominated-class male student), it is very rarely that anyone refers equally explicitly to the ideology of aptitudes. People don't say straight out that dominated-class children have fewer aptitudes—quite the opposite:

> I'm absolutely certain the opposite is the case.
>
> Heavens, no.
>
> No, no, no, not at all.

The denials and the repetitions seem to be symptoms: One must repress what one cannot consciously avow.

Sociology has taken over from psychology, substituting a new scientific prop for the theory of aptitudes. Social background factors and "cultural" inequalities provide a rationale used more and more in the universal discourse as the new principles explaining differences in educational achievement. That this represents a simple shift in the essentialist view of social reality is shown by the remarks noted. Far from being defined in relation to the system of economic, political, and social interactions—which alone give it an identity—the "background" (often reduced to the family background) is considered to be an entity. The cultural differences involved are in the end differences *sui generis*.

What do those who fail lack *culturally?* "A way of expressing themselves," "a critical mind," "openness of mind," "a taste for nonutilitarian culture," "a theoretical mind," "a conceptual mind," "certain values." They have "concrete minds," 'they value material things too much," "peasants are more practical—they have a relationship with nature—and don't feel the need to intellectualize problems." All such elements are considered as absolute characteristics, as transcendent and independent of the relations of dominance on which they are based.

If the background is not "open," "curious," "stimulating," "provident," "aware of the need for qualifications," nor concerned for the "individuality of the subject," it is because it is deemed to be the carrier of biological and moral defects. This belief, which is sometimes expressed explicitly ("the defect of hereditary alcoholism," for example), may generally be interpreted like the reverse of the accounts given of "good" families, those whose children succeed: "a balanced and nondisturbing background," "a reliable family," "stable," "quiet," "harmonious," where there is a "good atmosphere," "serene and caring," a "regulated life," where "the family situation is clear," a "healthy climate." If we compare these sorts of comments with those on the dangers of idleness for childless women we can infer from both of them a belief in the amoral nature of the dominated.

As we have already seen in relation to the use of spatial metaphors, the dominated are defined in universal discourse only in a negative fashion with regard to the dominant. They are enclosed somewhere else, they are irreversibly lacking in something. In the end, if the dominated, unlike the dominant, always indicate in one way or another what category they belong to, it is because the social groups to which they belong, and only these, are socially designated as a species apart.

THE DIVIDING UP OR UNIFYING OF IDENTITY

The self of the dominated, defined in terms of incompleteness, is divided or split, whereas that of the dominant is unified. The minority of individuals who, because of their class and sex, belong to the group that has economic, political, or ideological power at its command, never doubt their capacities. It seems that male students from the dominant class have never questioned their "aptitude" for higher education. Their aptitudes are revealed early and are altogether singular and exceptional, distinguishing them from other people as a unique subject.

> I've always wanted to be a writer, even when I was quite young. I started to make up poems when I was 6. ...I still write today.
>
> I chose Indian studies mainly out of interest, and a bit out of a whim.
>
> At ten years old I already had a passion for politics.

Failure does not make the dominants question the high ideas they have of themselves. When they consent to use the common reasons of laziness and dilettantism, it is so as to remove blame from themselves. The poor organization of the educational system and the "uninteresting subjects" are in the end the true culprits, according to the dominants. When asked if some particular circumstances influenced the unfolding of their life, they never make any reference to sociological explanations (unlike the children of both sexes of the dominated class, and girls from the dominant class, as we shall see).

For the dominants, their social situation is the fruit of their quite singular subjectivity. What was determinative for them?

> The fact that I was raised in absolute fear of the devil and that I then had the courage to resist it...
>
> The face of my grandmother, a certain sunset...

Denying that concrete power relations have an influence on the formation of identity, the dominant class has formulated the idea of "personality," or personal identity, to define itself, to express the vision it has of itself as a collection of "I's", of free and responsible individuals. This is a disincarnated, asociological conception of social relations whereby, through its use of material power and of language, this class creates a mass of undifferentiated beings that it relegates to the sphere of impersonal things, of "objects."

Dominated Class

Through their class origin, the children of both sexes in the dominated class have a dissociated identity. Children of the dominated class are aware of having been designated as different, as marked with the sign of incompleteness:

> The people around me more or less knew that I was from a working-class family and hence I had a few hitches in that respect.
>
> Some teachers used some very unkind words, saying that one was not society's rubbish, but almost.
>
> I remember that the drawing teacher used to say...[he] worked from the principle that workers' children couldn't understand art.
>
> In hearing remarks to those with scholarships that they should make a greater effort than the others, because they were scholarship girls, I felt a bit vexed.

The constraints are imposed on dominated-class children far too long and in too imperious a fashion for them to think of their educational orientations in terms of pure freedom:

> It was my teacher who put me in for the entrance examinations in the *sixième*.
>
> I was advised to go to the *lycee*.
>
> It was the French teacher who found out that I was good at literature.
>
> My teacher encouraged me by saying that I shouldn't stop there. He came home and persuaded my parents.
>
> I took this channel because I lacked information and ambition. [the son of a laborer]

Opposite the active, personal form used by the dominants—"I chose," "I decided"—is frequently set the impersonal form of the dominated (in English, usually the passive)—"it was decided," 'I was allowed," "I was permitted," or "they decided." Also the "I" of the dominated does not always have the same meaning as that of the dominant: The personal referent is object rather than subject.

It, thus, seems that the dominated have a certain degree of insight into the social determinations that have weighed on their orientations; but this does not imply that they have a reflexive awareness of the relation between their class membership and their history. They cannot escape the system of rationalizations that is culturally imposed. If they have been distinguished, it is because they are particular. In addition, despite everything, they reinterpret their educational and occupational orientation by the dominant logic of taste and interest.

> I was interested in geography, in geography and history, as one may be in the *sixième* and *cinquième* and then later, given my educational background, there was nothing else I could do. ... it was fortunate since it interested me.

The same student further on:

> One thing I regret is not having done medicine. But I could never have been a doctor. It wasn't possible.

What they are socially they consider to be due to personal and family qualities that distinguish them from their class:

> I'm going to boast, perhaps I was more successful.
>
> My parents really took their responsibilities seriously; they are true parents.

The implicit discourse is the following: We are workers but we are worthy, and we want to be recognized in the name of this worth. If there is an attempt to value themselves in the name of this merit, this dominant value, it is because they believe unconsciously (the unconscious draws its content from the dominant discourse) that to be a worker is to be dirty, immoral, and shameful, it is to be "less than nothing":

> I'm not ashamed of having parents like mine.
>
> In my home there was a decent family life.
>
> My parents managed to make a family life which was agreeable and everything. ... After all, many people remain less than nothing.
>
> You understand, I can say that I was never ashamed of my parents. Indeed I admire them very much.

All these efforts and those of their parents are directed to the sole aim of proving that one is not of less value than others:

> I wanted to be the best because I'd been put down again.
>
> I wanted to prove to myself that I was capable of higher education.

But to want to prove to oneself and others that one is "better than that" is to deny part of oneself, and this denial engenders a split identity. Dominant in imagination (who am I?), dominated in reality (what am I?), the ego lacks cohesion, hence the contradiction and incoherence of the social practices. Dominated-class children think in terms of aptitudes, tastes, and interests because at each step in their education their success has progressively convinced them that they are not less than nothing intellectually; but at the same time they profoundly doubt themselves.

The comparison with others cannot be centered around a devalued and denied "me," so it is polarized by the "I" of the dominant, which for the dominated is incarnate in the person they would like to be, in the first instance—a primary school teacher (not a single dominant-class child said they had dreamed of being a primary school teacher) —and then, the person they imagine being (using dominant-class success limits)—a secondary school teacher, an engineer, doctor, film director, or higher civil servant. As has already been seen, the content of choices (teaching) often signifies the socially assigned limits of their desire to get out. Even the most ambitious choices are marked by the experience of economic insecurity (a fundamental element of the class position of the dominated class) since stability of employment is taken into account. The ideal for one teacher was "to be a higher civil servant of the École Nationale d'Administration type—high for prestige and income; a civil servant for a secure job." However, for men the gap between what they actually are and what they imagine themselves to be is smaller than for women.

Dominated Sex

The definition of their identity is not obvious for women, whatever their class origin. Taking the dominant discourse into account, they think of themselves both collectively and singularly. Certainly, just as their masculine counterparts stay in the dominant class, women who are dominated within this same class think they have chosen their direction quite freely. However, after certain decisions, experienced as free choices, they question little-by-little their idea of an autonomous self: They are overwhelmed by the situation that they have "chosen." Marriage and maternity above all introduce a break in the unfolding of an education or occupational history hitherto lineal and without jolts. Whether they see marriage and motherhood as losses or gains, for women it is always an event that introduces a discontinuity in their future:

> If I wasn't married I would have accepted a job needing a lot of moving about.
>
> My husband was very keen for me to act as his collaborator.
>
> My marriage and the birth of the first child...afterwards things went very swiftly.
>
> After the birth of the first child I couldn't work anymore and I had to follow my courses alone at home, which is why they were so seriously delayed.
>
> I married very young, which made me become a primary school teacher after the *bac*. Then my children and my trip to the United States with my husband made me interrupt my work, then my divorce obliged me to work again before having finished my course.

In alluding systematically to what they have experienced as individual circumstances, they are only expressing a condition that imposes channels on all those in their sex and class. These channels are also imposed on women from the dominated class. As compared with women of the dominant class, their marriage has much less often been the occasion for interrupting a course or their occupational activities. Their class origin is for them the explanation of what happens to them, but this does not imply that they do not make reference elsewhere to their marital status. They do not overlook the fact that marriage and the birth of children has introduced (or is in danger of introducing) changes in their present lives. Men, in contrast, whatever their class, rarely allude to that which objectively has not introduced any discontinuity to what happens to them. Their marriage and family are absent from their field of discourse.

That women refer themselves to a system of social constraints does not mean that they are necessarily aware of the relations of power between the sexes. They may wish to convince themselves of their freedom by speaking of their singular aptitudes in the way that the sons of the dominant do, but they cannot at the same time avoid expressing by their words the restriction of this freedom:

> When I was young, I was good at English because it interested me.

> One of the things which made me successful was that I liked what I was doing. Well I liked it. I loved English. I love it as a language and as a culture.

The repetition doubtless fulfills a reassuring function for the author of this account because she could not ignore the fact that the majority of women who are at the university are devoted to the humanities and particularly to languages.

> You see, I was tempted to be an archaeologist because I adored ancient history, but for that you must go to the École des Chartes and in the end, I really don't remember the train of events, but in addition you need a certain personal fortune to get there, and it's not really a woman's job. ... So then I wanted to be a librarian...up to the time when I went in for teaching; but even so, basically it was teaching since I was a child.

The same informant further on:

> I've always wanted to be a secondary school teacher; when it's deeply fixed in you I don't think one can want anything else.

In these two cases, the speaker sought and reintroduced coherence later on: "deeply fixed in you," "vocation." The dominant discourse provides them with the elements of singularization of the "me" and with this they try to wrest themselves away from specification—the group specification to which these women are doubly subject (as women and as dominated-class children). In affirming that "I was gifted at English and not at math," "teaching was always my vocation," "I love children," in exalting sensitivity, affection, the realization of oneself in motherhood, they all want to convince themselves of their singularity. But this attempt to give value to their "me," whose limits are those assigned to their "species," openly leads to enclosing them within these same limits.

Of course, the replies are a little different according to the nature of the handicap the women encounter owing to their social origins. Women from the dominated class whose projects for individual promotion were blocked said that they would have liked to be teachers. But it is in their replies that the dissociation sometimes appears in the form of statements: "pilot, surgeon...or air hostess," "doctor or hairdresser."

It was only because of their sex category that women from the dominant class could not realize some of their projects. One would have liked to have been a doctor, another a designer, but their parents opposed these orientations. Others followed specialized studies but without getting the desired occupation:

- A married woman without a job who had actually followed a course in publishing and bookselling would have liked to run a bookshop.
- A single woman with a degree from the École du Louvre (art school), who wanted to be an archaeologist, ended up as a filing clerk.
- A married woman without a job, who failed at the Institut des Sciences Politiques, had wanted to be a minister

Some of them stressed that it is because they were women that they encountered particular social prohibitions. One wanted to go to a hotel and catering college but she knew there were no openings for women. Another wanted to be an agricultural engineer but gave up because of her sex. What they could not and cannot be in reality, they live in their imaginary world. Certain slips are symptomatic of the division between their social self and their unconscious I. For example, in reply to the question, Sex: M or F?, several women had marked the first possibility (male), but no man made the opposite mistake. Although women may not consciously seek to share the economic legal and political power with men, they are unconsciously aware of the possibility—through that power—of asserting one's self as social subject, as incarnation of humanity and not as a subspecies of humans.

Women, even when they speak against the myth of the housewife, cannot define themselves only by their occupational status or their housewife status. They are always divided between an "inside" and an "outside," whatever their concrete situation may be. Single women do not escape this: Their personal status, whether it is experienced as a free choice or as the result of chance, sought or accepted, has meaning only in relation to the situation of the majority of women. They are socially defined as lacking children and, as such, as incomplete women. Some seek out this status saying that "work is more intelligent than baby-minding" and refusing to become "cabbages," but reference to a hypothetical or missing "inside" is often implicit or explicit in the accounts of single women:

> It seems to me preferable that the mother should bring the children up herself, but personally I need an outside activity. [Unmarried teacher]
> Being unmarried and without problems, I can devote myself completely to my work. If I was married, this position would be too demanding. [Buyer]
> I like what I do, I hope only to progress. ... I was obliged to leave my family and my country to achieve this. ... I might get married. That would change a lot, especially if I had children. [French teacher in Canada]

The contradictions experienced and expressed by the women and the incoherences in their practices reinforce the incoherence of their "me." What are they? This devalued, closed me or this free and powerful I, which can only assert itself in relation to that of the dominant, as its negative? In their own words ("I love the humanities," "I've always dreamed of devoting myself to children") they are only reinforcing the splitting of their identity. This split cannot be removed as long as the relations of power are maintained, as long as the dominated can only interpret their social condition by the logic of the natural order of things.

CONCLUSION

The hypothesis underlying my analysis of power relationships at work in language is as follows: Dissimilarities between language practices are meaningful only in the light of the social organization. Language is the medium through which the dominant and the dominated consciously and unconsciously perceive and interpret the appropriation by a small social group of the means of subsistence and of other human beings. Each class speaks itself, in other words, takes on and shapes its historical identity *according to the same hidden referent*. This social referent is the dominant group, whose identity is based on what it possesses (including knowledge and norms of language practice). It is the group which legitimizes its material power by defining itself as a collection of individuals incarnating the perfection of "humanity," a collection of "subjects," of "I's." Because the social referent is the same for all classes, class language practices are not homogeneous, and this nonhomogeneity is necessary for domination.

We have seen that the group in possession of the means of subsistence articulates the coherence of the universe, of its universe. The dominated articulate the split in that universe. It is the order of the world as created and articulated by the dominant which forces the dominated to express themselves by means of signifiers that unconsciously have the same historical significance for all: It is "bad" to be powerless (woman, worker, Jew, black, and so on), to be "other," "different," or a "species apart." One should certainly analyze the language practices of the categories whose age, sex, or color of skin assign them a collective, dominated place. For example, their speech almost inevitably announces the specified category to which they belong. The concrete and verbal practices of the dominant seem to impose an identity on the dominated that induces them to adopt specific language practices, but not arbitrarily. Certain practices of all dominated show that they both reject and submit to power: The working classes' "coarse" language, women's "frivolous" language, school children's slang, are ways of taking refuge and attempting to assert self, ways that at the same time lock one into the definition imposed by the dominant. Dominant ideology acts as the principle ordering differential linguistic "choices," not only the content of speech, its semantic aspects studied here, but also its morpho-syntactic aspects (Bisseret, 1979: 67-89).

Socially rejected "elsewhere," in order to avoid the annihilation of their "me," the dominated have no other option but to identify *individually* with the hidden referent of the social discourse. This shows the effectiveness of dominant ideology: While it is a unifying principle for the identity of the dominant (his actual me—the set of his practices—and his imaginary I being two homogeneous realities), it is a dissociating principle for the dominated (her or his imaginary I and her or his social me being two heterogeneous realities). The me and the I can be homogeneous (ego) only for the dominant.

Dominant and dominated languages are the scene of a power struggle. The dominated's search for a unified ego gives rise to a passionate interest in the facts of language. Silence is often the language of the powerless, the only possible solution when the contradictions are insurmountable. Pejorative words of popular origin that designate the act of talking allow one to suppose that words are suspected by the dominated. They unconsciously know that the dominant impose their own definition of their world order through the totality of their practices, including verbal practices, and thereby justify their power (Fanon, 1952, 1970). A minority attempts to "deconstruct" language. But that attempt presupposes the possibility of a relative material liberation also. Those who deconstruct language to express the split in their identity are conscious that they cannot become an individual subject by identifying with the dominant. They say the split can be removed only if historical conditions entail a collective consciousness of the domination and the possibility of a movement toward liberation (Wittig, 1980, 1981).

Historical changes (for example, the French Revolution of 1789) have proved that concrete violence is an effective language used by the dominated to signify their refusal of material and ideological domination. It operates by itself the deconstruction of the apparent coherence of social discourse about the world, by which the dominant try to ward off the idea of the potential instability and illegitimacy of their social order.

3

PROBLEMS AND *PROBLEMS*
Power Relationships in a Medical Encounter*

*Paula A. Treichler, Richard M. Frankel,
Cheris Kramarae, Kathleen Zoppi,
and Howard B. Beckman*

Physician: What are you feelin' down a*bout*?
Patient: Stomach problems, back problems, *side* problems
Physician: *Prob*lems problems
Patient: Problems and *prob*lems

This chapter reports a collaborative effort by the authors to analyze a videotape of a routine clinic visit between a patients and a medical resident. Our overall purpose is to illuminate dimensions of power in this particular encounter and in medical settings generally. At one level, we define our scholarly task as learning more about the real-time organization of power as manifested in observable interactions on the videotape. At another level, we are interested in better understanding some of the formal and informal practices that accompany our individual and collective efforts as researchers. Finally, as citizens and consumers concerned with the distribution of health care resources, we are interested in connecting the results of our research to more broadly based questions about power in medical encounters. This chapter, then, is an analysis of a medical encounter that we present as a model of collaborative, interdisciplinary research on power in medical settings.

*We would especially like to thank the individuals who agreed to let us videotape, analyze, and publish the results of this investigation. Partial funding for this research was provided by a grant from the National Council of Teachers of English to Paula A. Treichler, a grant from the Ruth Mott Foundation to Howard B. Beckman and Richard M. Frankel, and a Program Development Grant for Residency Training in Primary Care Internal Medicine, NIH PE 15226-02.

POWER IN MEDICAL INTERACTIONS

There are many reasons to examine power in medical interactions. As patients we sometimes feel excluded from knowledge and decision making that affect our health and well-being. As consumers we may feel ineffectual or neglected in our attempts to affect the organization and delivery of health care services. As health care professionals, we sometimes feel frustrated by patients' seeming unwillingness to adhere to our therapeutic programs, and by the difficulties of delivering high-quality care under stringent time constraints. As researchers we observe that practitioners routinely take the lead in regulating the conversational exchanges through which patient problems and needs are identified; in consequence, patients' concerns are sometimes assessed on the basis of incomplete or narrowly defined knowledge. All these difficulties may be said to involve issues of power.

Though power is often taken for granted as a component of medical encounters, its conceptualization and discussion remain problematic and elusive (see Foucault, 1975; Heath, 1979; Giles, Scherer, and Taylor, 1979; Starr, 1983). This is true in part because there is no clear-cut consensus among researchers on what power means, how it functions in clinical practice, nor what individual, community, and societal consequences flow from its exercise. Further, there is no independent, uncompromised stance from which studies of power can be viewed and interpreted.

But the major difficulty arises from the prevailing view that power in medical settings is a social fact, established a priori by the differential position of individuals or groups within the social structure (e.g., patients and physicians). Much like actors who have memorized and rehearsed their lines before a performance, participants are seen as bringing power with them to the health care encounter: differences in rights, duties, and obligations are known in advance. Any change in the script—for example, a physician's attempt to be primarily a listener or a patient's attempt to ask many questions—is viewed as exceptional and deviant. Thus, power is seen as a static property emanating from one individual (usually from the practitioner) or as a force applied by one individual to another.

We examine power in a different way: we view power relations as negotiated within the context of face-to-face interaction. Though we acknowledge that such "preconditions" as status, gender, and race influence participants' attitudes and expectations, we suggest that it is also important to examine the *interactive behavior* of the participant. Power as a dynamic concept emerges within patterns of communication over time and space, and cannot be located as a property of the individual. Rather, power becomes the negotiated product of a mutually constituted and mutually administered interaction system. From this standpoint, any assessment of power must take the details of interaction—for example, sequential and other complex relationships among utterances—into account.

If we think of power as a process, as bound to a relationship, then patient-physician interaction becomes not just evidence that opportunities and resources are differentially distributed, but the site where they are established and negotiated. An ongoing locus for such relations, for example, is in the exchange of information in the medical encounter. Patients generally know little of their physicians' training, career expectations, or personal life; they generally know little of what the physician remembers about them nor what is contained in their medical records. Yet they bring to the medical interaction considerable knowledge about their own physical symptoms, medical histories, and potential causes of illness; based on their lifetime experience as patients, they also bring knowledge about the nature of medical encounters. Physicians, bringing specialized knowledge and training to the encounter, nonetheless are dependent upon patients for information that will yield accurate diagnosis and treatment. The medical encounter involves a sequence of complex interactional structures in and through which knowledge and expertise are actualized.

Our view of power, then, focuses on mutual, but asymmetrical influence, and recognizes the control physician and patient exert on each other's actions. In the analysis that follows, we attempt to identify and explore the creation of power relations among the participants in a medical encounter—a physician, a patient, and a medical student. We also attempt to position ourselves as researchers in relationship to the analytic process.

METHOD OF STUDY

The encounter we report is a routine follow-up visit between Dr. David Toffer, a white second-year medical resident in a Primary Care Internal Medicine Training Program, and Mr. Joseph Stittler, a 38-year-old Black man. A third participant in the encounter is Allan, a white second-year medical student who joins the resident as part of his medical school's Introduction to Clinical Medicine curriculum and talks with the patient at the conclusion of the resident's formal interview. (All participants' names have been changed to protect their privacy.)

The data were gathered through a research and training program developed at Wayne State University School of Medicine by two of the authors—Richard Frankel, a conversational analyst trained in sociology, and Howard Beckman, an internist. Medical interviews in their program are routinely videotaped; some are transcribed and analyzed in detail for research and teaching purposes. In some cases (including this one), the physician and patient are invited independently to review and comment upon the videotaped interview; their comments, audiorecorded and then superimposed upon the original tape at relevant points, make the tape an important source of information about participants' points of view (Frankel and Beckman, 1982). A further analytic procedure was used in the current study: three researchers in addition to Frankel and Beckman, trained in different fields (linguistics, sociolinguistics, and health education), analyzed the videotape from the perspectives of their respective disciplines. This approach to communicational analysis (Pittinger, Hockett, and Danehy, 1960) yields a layered, multidisciplinary exploration of medical interaction.

THE PATIENT AND THE PHYSICIAN

This is the fifth visit between Dr. Toffer and Mr. Stittler. Prior to a follow-up visit of this kind, the physician reviews the patient's record and develops an agenda for the visit based on previously identified problems and treatment plans. Mr. Stittler's previously identified problems include hypertension, nausea and vomiting, chronic fatigue, liver enlargement, low white blood count, bronchitis, and ulcer disease. The medical record from the immediately preceding visit noted abdominal pain associated with vomiting and cough. The patient is being treated with antibiotics and antacids. The physician thus confronts a patient with multiple problems; he must determine their current status as well as assess the results of two treatment regimens. From his point of view, this is not a visit designed to uncover new problems but rather to review old problems and continue testing to refine the diagnosis. The patient, since his last visit, has stopped receiving social security disability payments.

The Encounter

The patient, the resident, and the medical student enter the examining room. The resident opens the interaction; addressing the patient as "Mr. Stittler," he shows him where he can put his jacket and where to sit, and explains the presence of the medical student ("Allan"). The patient talks briefly with the student, and then the resident begins the interview. (A guide to the system of transcription used to present the verbal data appears in the Appendix.)

    Physician: Great. So how you doing today Joseph.

    Patient: Not too good doct//or

    Physician: Not too good. I see you kinda hangin' your head low there.

    Patient: Yeah.

    Physician: Must be somethin' up (˚) or down I should say. Are you feelin' down?

    Patient: Yeah

    Physician: What are you feelin' down a*bout* (0.7)

    Patient: Stomach problems, back problems, *side* problems.

    Physician: *Prob*lems problems

    Patient: Problems and *prob*lems

    Physician: Hum. What's:: we- whats goin' on with your stomach. Are you still uh- havin' pains in your stomach?

The patient initially makes eye contact with the physician and student. But as the physician gets to the official agenda—"So how you doing today"—the patient drops his head. For most of the interview he sits slumped in the chair, head down. He seldom introduces topics, usually agrees with the resident or expands his comments slightly, and speaks at an unusually slow pace. Information is gathered by the resident without comment, although at one point the resident suggests that a problem of holding down food cannot be too severe since the records show the patient hasn't lost much weight over recent months. The physician offers the following summaries of the patient's information, and the patient confirms them: He is still throwing up food; the nausea has been worse since December; it is bad most of the time; he is having fever; he feels he's getting a cold; he feels nauseated during the day; there is pain in his lower back; he has only an occasional beer and nothing stronger. He contributes little other information except short statements of his problems. The resident moves from general questions to more specific questions about the patient's physical problems, a commonly used "funnel" approach. The topics and the preferred range of answers introduced by the questions are supplied primarily by the physician (see the sequence marked B in the Appendix). Eight minutes into the interview, the resident shifts his approach:

> Physician: (O:kay) (3.2) What do you think is uh — is goin' on here. Wadda you — what do you think has been happenin' with ya. Any ideas?
>
> Patient: Lots of worriation
>
> Physician: Lots a what?
>
> Patient: Worriation
> (0.2)
>
> Physician: Worriation? Lotta worryin' y' mean? =
>
> Patient: = Yes
>
> Physician: What've you been worried about.
>
> Patient: Well I don't have no income anymore.

In response to the resident's direct query, the patient offers his explanation of the problem. In the dialogue that follows (see the sequence marked C on the transcript in the Appendix), the patient explains that his social security checks have been discontinued; as he talks, he initiates sustained eye contact with the physician for the first time since the beginning of the interview. As the doctor asks questions and provides encouraging feedback ("um hum"), the patient's answers become longer than in the preceding "funneling" section of the interview. He explains that his continuing problems began with a blow to his head 13 years earlier.

The physician then asks, "just out of curiosity," how this blow to the head occurred. (This initiates the sequence marked D on the transcript.) The patient tells the story of how he was paralyzed on his left side "for life" when he was hit from behind with a tire iron. Based on this injury and the diagnosis of a lifetime disability the patient stopped work and began to receive social security compensation. He knows this story well and, once encouraged to speak by the physician's questions and comments, tells it with animation. Although the physical problems including pain and paralysis are still present, the social security checks supporting him for years have recently stopped coming, and he has suddenly been told that he must find work. He believes he is unable to work. The doctor listens to this recitation, asks several clarifying questions; and then shifts the topic of the discussion back to the present set of problems:

> Physician: O:kay well (more) to your cu:rrent problem right now. What you (·) you know are descri:bin sounds like a *flu*-like kind of syndrome.

The resident returns the interview to his domain of expertise—analysis and treatment of the patient's biomedical problems. He does so by sharing his evaluation of the information as a summary statement about flu. He does not comment on or assess the problem identified by the patient (loss of income), nor does he at this point or at any other point in the discussion offer a remedy. The question thus raised is one of the negotiation and status of patient problems and the selective attention paid by the provider to the biomedical dimensions of care. An additional question is the patient's unwillingness or inability to pursue his concern over the loss of income from what he understood was a long-term disability.

For the remainder of the interview the resident concentrates on the analysis and treatment of the patient's biomedical problems. He carries out a physical examination. He spends time describing the nature of vitamin B-12 deficiency and the test the patient will undergo to rule this out as a cause of the patient's medical problems. In closing the interview, he acknowledges that the patient is "down," and expresses the hope that the test results will provide a basis for timely and efficient treatment.

Use of Questions

Several specific features of the interview are noteworthy. One is the use of questions. A general sequential property of questions is that they limit the domain of what will count as a conversationally appropriate next action (Sacks, 1966). Frankel (forthcoming) and West (1983) found that physicians routinely (99% and 91%, respectively) ask questions, and patients routinely provide responses. In a speech exchange system in which one party chronically occupies the initiating position and the other party occupies the responding position, it follows that the initiating speaker exerts a form of organizational control over the respondent.

In the particular interaction we have been describing the physician may feel it necessary to ask so many questions (and suggest responses) because the patient is slow in offering information that can be used to construct the record of care and to make a diagnosis. For example, in one section of the transcript (see sequence marked A in the Appendix), six utterances are initiated by the physician; four of these contain questions. (One of those four contains two questions, which may raise a problem for the patient; see Shuy [1976].)

In contrast, all six of the patient's utterances are responses. Interestingly, one response—"Nervous tensions (˙) can't sleep"—contains information that was not specifically solicited by the physician's previous question. More will be said about this utterance momentarily, but it is worth noting that the physician's response to the information is minimal. He acknowledges with the token, "I see." It is notable that with the exception of *"Prob*lems problems," the physician gives only minimal responses; mostly, he produces token acknowledgements: "Hum," "Hmh," and "I see." The significance of this pattern lies in the contrast between clinical problem-solving talk, in which the professional assembles a data base and tests hypotheses in an attempt to "solve" the client's problem, and casual conversation, in which a trouble or complaint is responded to much more immediately with assessments like "That's too bad" or "I'm sorry to hear that" before a solution is offered or searched for. The lack of such responses is a general characteristic of physician-patient discourse and is often attributed to the desire or goal to remain clinically detached or neutral during the data-gathering phase of an encounter (Frankel, forthcoming). Discourse strategies that yield neutral responses to highly emotional or charged information offered by a client have not been examined in the context of patient satisfaction or outcome; the physician's lack of effective response may be, in this context, an important dimension of power and control.

The Written Record

The physician's written record of care that accompanies each encounter is an important feature of the medical encounter. Like many other institutional files, the clinic's written records on patients are a "bureaucratic collection of details" (Heath, 1982) that routinely function as "factual" accounts of the patients' consultation with doctors. Since we are interested in various dimensions of influence on the communication situation itself, those record-keeping practices that occur as the encounter is ongoing provide another significant dimension in which control may be examined. At a very gross level, we can say that the decision to take notes during the encounter itself represents an influence on the physician-patient relationship. From the point of view of interaction structure, the act of writing while discourse is ongoing creates multiple sites of attention. It is well known (for example, see Kendon, 1967) that coparticipants routinely look at one another from time-to-time during face-to-face interactions. Since note-taking almost invariably draws the physician's gaze away from the patient and to the record, interpersonal attention to the patient has effectively been "cut-off." Another way of stating this proposition is to say that the act of writing affects the very interaction for which the text stands as a representative.

Using the transcript in conjunction with the videotape of the encounter Frankel has recently developed a technique for mapping the location of each episode of writing to its location relative to the discussion of the patient and physician. In this way the relationship of talk to the written record can be studied. The segment of transcript already examined (the sequence marked A in the Appendix) contains two writing episodes and is presented below. The numbers and brackets above the utterances indicate the onset and offset point for each episode in terms of elapsed time in seconds since the beginning of the visit. The left-hand margin of the transcript shows the entries made by the physician during each of the writing episodes. Quotation marks enclose each text entry.

                    Physician: What are you feelin' down a*bout* (0.7)

                    Patient: Stomach problems, back problems, *side* problems.

                                            [086

                    Physician: *Prob*lems problems

"2/9/82"   Patient: Problems and *prob*lems

                                           090]

                    Physician: Hum. Wha'ts::we- whats goin' on with your stomach. Are you still uh- havin' pains in your stomach?

                    Patient: Yeah it's- can't hold no *food* water

                    Physician: How 'bout uh- ::are you- y' still throwin up?

                    Patient: Oh yes.

                    Physician: Hmh

                              (2.0)

                              [105

	Patient:	Nervous tensions (˙) can't sleep.
		111]
"Still	Patient:	hhh
N&V"	Physician:	I see. An::d so this has be::en since December you've been havin' this (0.2) nausea =
	Patient:	= Oh. yeah =

It is clear even from this small sample of discourse that what is said and what is recorded do not necessarily stand in a one-to-one relationship. For example, at an elapsed time of 86 seconds into the encounter, the resident begins to write. At this point he records not the list of ailments mentioned by the patient, but the date. Parenthetically, this is also the point at which he has just completed the possibly ironic "*Prob*lems problems." The resident's "cut-off" almost immediately after this remark suggests its potentially hostile nature. The physician's writing continues across the patient's reply "Problems and *prob*lems," and into the beginning of the physician's next utterance. Given the timing of the writing episode that coincides with the patient's response to a request for a presenting complaint, the patient might conclude that the content of the physician's record is somehow tied to the information he has been giving. This possibility has particular relevance since the patient does not have visual access to the content of the entry, knowing only that writing occurs as he completes his statement of concerns.

In fact, the physician's entry has no tie whatsoever with the ongoing discourse; it is simply the recording of the date of the visit. There is, then, an ambiguity that exists between writing and its relationship to the ongoing discourse—an ambiguity whose structural features amount to a form of control regardless of content.

The second writing episode, like the first, begins after an affirmative resonse by the patient to a question by the physician. After minimally acknowledging the response with "Hmh," the physician pauses for two seconds and then begins to write. The content of this entry is directly tied to the previous sequence; "Are you— y' still throwin' up?" followed by, "Oh yes," produces the entry "Still N & V" (nausea and vomiting). Thus we see the physician exercising options about how and when to record pertinent information and how such options may limit the patient's participation or representation in the clinical picture that the record documents.

"Worriation" and the loss of income, the topic that was the patient's basic concern and took the most time to complete, was never entered into the record: it thus becomes a topic with no "official" status even though it may be pursued informally from visit to visit. It is also worth noting the fate of the patients' unsolicited offer of the complaint "Nervous tensions (·) can't sleep," since this concern also occurs while the physician was making an entry into the record. While the physician does provide the token acknowledgement "I see" at the conclusion of the writing episode, the information voiced by the patient is otherwise ignored for the duration of the visit. The fact that this concern was not recorded or addressed suggests that it may have been lost during the resident's record-keeping activities. This is perhaps another way in which the decision to take notes during the encounter influences the clinical picture.

PROBLEMS AND PROBLEMS

We have spent some time on the sequence in which the phrase "problems and problems" occurs (the sequence marked A in the Appendix). The resident here acknowledges, in his question, that the patient is depressed—"feelin' down." At this early point in the interview, the patient responds by listing general *medical* complaints, yet his litany seems to point the way to a problem not contained within the list; in other words, the list may signal the patient's sense of being overwhelmed with problems, yet without moving explicitly into the more troubling realm of "feelin' down." The intontation of the patient's utterance mirrors that of the physician's, with the major stress falling at its conclusion. At this point the physician *might* have pursued his opening question about "feelin' down," taking the patient's response *as* a response. Instead, however, he focuses on the first item in the patient's list, "stomach problems," and indicates that it is a known continuing condition that is being followed since he offers "are you— y' still throwing up?" This transition signals a shift out of the identification of current problems and concerns, including his own observation of the patient's depressed condition, and into an assessment of previously identified problems. Thus, at a point in the visit reserved for new problem identification and negotiation of an agenda for the day's visit, the resident has opted to concentrate on a previously established problem.

In playing back the tape, the resident commented about the patient's medical and psychosocial problems. Yet in the interaction itself, his "*Prob*lems problems" comes off as an ironic commentary on the patient's list. His emphasis on the first syllable suggests that any noun can fill the slot—that the patient's problems are multiple and ongoing and, in some sense, not interesting at all. The irony, then, is in the acknowledgement that the patient's list is "more of the same old thing" and is not a real response to why he is depressed. Yet it is also a dismissive comment, for it now makes the patient's entrance into the realm of depression even more difficult.

The patient's counterresponse captures the ironic dismissal: "Problems and *prob*lems," with the stress at the end of the utterance, highlights the physician's actual language, virtually parodying it. Literally the patient's phrase suggests that there are, indeed, two categories of problems; yet he is acquiescent when the physician, in the next utterance, singles out his stomach problems as the complaint to be taken up.

It is commonplace for sociomedical researchers to assert the dominance of the biomedical model in medicine and its preeminence over other forms of inquiry (see, for example, Engel, 1977; Kleinman, 1983; Todd, 1983). In this sequence we can perhaps see some of the complexities of this model in practice, and some of the consequences it can have for actual care. It is worth remembering that this physician is in a training program for residents, which attempts to integrate psychosocial information within a biomedical framework. In this particular interview, however, he finds this difficult to do.

Indeed, this seems to be an interview with "problems and problems." There is a sense in which what did not get said is more striking than what did. In the next section we see a medical student addressing these problems somewhat differently.

THE MEDICAL STUDENT

Following the physical examination and concluding phase of the interaction, the resident closes the chart to signal the close of the official interview; he then asks the patient to participate in a more informal interview with the medical student who has been sitting in on the session:

> Physician: Well, I'm gonna go order some tests for you here and if you don't mind Allan would like to maybe talk with you for a couple of minutes before you split, okay, so we'll maybe try to get all your paperwork all done so you don't have to wait too long.

In several ways the resident marks the different status of the medical student's interview: "if you don't mind" suggests (at least rhetorically) that the patient can refuse to be interviewed; similarly, "Allan would like" makes this a personal and rather minor favor to Allan rather than a clinical or institutional goal or requirement. The use of the student's first name as well as the qualifiers "maybe" and "a couple of minutes" further downplay significance, as does the departure from technical language in "before you split" and the suggestion that the patient has to wait anyhow for the paperwork to be done.

The medical student takes the resident's seat at the desk and opens his interview with low-key diffidence, in keeping with its unofficial status:

> Medical student: I'm just kinda curious um about the pain you're having now. Has it been um progressively getting worse?

The language is simple and clear; the mildly technical term "progressively" is deflated by "um." But the key word in this opening sequence is "curious." For this is a curious word in a medical interview. The request to be educated expresses a rather open-ended interest in the patient in a way we do not routinely expect to hear from physicians. Curiosity, in other words, is not what drives the typical medical interview. Indeed, the resident qualified a question about the patient's head injury with the phrase "just out of curiosity" and bracketed the lengthy response it elicited as irrelevant to the "current problem" (sequence marked D in the Appendix). For the medical student, in contrast, an expression of curiosity and what it elicits are central to his concerns at this stage in his training. Perhaps as important, the medical student's curiosity is linked to a critical interpersonal behavior: the ability to remain silent.

Into these silences the patient begins to tell his story. Unlike the resident, the student allows pauses to occur and shows a willingness to wait while the patient finds his own words. We have noted how the resident's "*Prob*lems problems" seemed rhetorically to trivialize the patient's concerns. The medical student refers to problems quite differently:

> Medical student: You said you had lots of sad problems. Is the [loss of social security payments] the major one? Is there anything else?

He waits three seconds. When the patient then mentions confusion, he says, "Tell me a little more about your confusion." He waits seven seconds. The patient mentions anger. The medical student says "Yeah," encouraging him. The following exchange then occurs:

Patient: I have killed before and I could do it again—easy.
Student: Uh huh.
Patient: And I know that the court won't hold this against me cause I got a mental case—brain damage [moving hands; slumps].
Student: I see. So that was since you—since 1968?
Patient: Yes.
Students: Um hmmm. I see.

The medical student handles this new and rather startling information with considerable *sangfrois* (see Part II of the transcript in the Appendix). For the rest of the interview, the medical student continues to encourage the patient to talk, eliciting new and sometimes surprising information he cannot have anticipated from the resident's interview. He learns that the patient sees a psychiatrist regularly, he has gone through an alcoholic detoxification and rehabilitation program, and he regularly takes Thorazine, a powerful antipsychotic medication that the patient feels may have a direct bearing on his stomach problems.

These are significant pieces of information, medically as well as psycho-socially. Particularly the information about Thorazine is of immediate relevance to the medical diagnosis and treatment of the patient's chief complaint. Yet none of these items appeared on the patient's official record, nor was there any provision for the medical student's interview to be incorporated into the ongoing care being provided. It appears that the medical student's role in this encounter was to practice his skills with a real patient; it was not assumed that the information obtained might have clinical relevance.

The medical student, then, though encompassed by the profession, does not yet fully embody it; his actions are minimized in terms of his impact on the actual delivery of care. Perhaps precisely because medical students often have little apparent "real" impact, most studies of medical professionalization focus on residents or mature physicians; certainly as far as the scholarly literature on language goes, we know more about such subcultures as pickpockets than we do about medical students (though the nonscholarly literature, notably fictionalized and autobiographical accounts of medical training, is rich in linguistic detail).

Yet it is as medical students that physicians first acquire the basic grammar and vocabulary of the profession, learn the techniques for eliciting and evaluating information, are required to begin integrating technical and nontechnical language, and encounter the central and unique intellectual project of the art and science of medicine: that of translating a language of flesh into a language of words, of building an intricate multidisciplinary verbal model of the human body. Along with these linguistic changes during medical school come changes in students' relationships to power and authority and in the way the human body is perceived, interpreted, described, and controlled.[1]

THE RESEARCH PROCESS

In describing and interpreting this medical encounter, we have treated power and control as the negotiated product of face-to-face interaction, derivable through formal analysis. Our findings in this way speak on behalf of the participants, implicity subsuming their views and their voices as though they were homologous with each other and with the outcomes of our analytic strategies. Such an assumption may not be warranted.

We can supplement and refine our analysis by asking the participants themselves to comment on the encounter, drawing upon their own knowledge and expertise and comparing their responses with our own conclusions. In this case, the resident and the patient independently viewed the videotape of their interaction, stopping the tape to identify and comment upon problems and concerns. Dr. Toffer, the resident, stopped the tape ten times. Twice he commented on the patient's depressed affect; the rest of his comments dealt exclusively with his hypotheses about the patient's biomedical problems (e.g., possible B-12 deficiency, upper gastric tenderness, neurologic problems secondary to trauma to the head). It is interesting that his first comment about depression occurred at a point we have discussed at length (the asterisk marks the point where the tape was stopped):

Physician: What are you feelin' down a*bout*
Patient: Stomach prob[*]lems, back problems, *side* problems
Physician: *Prob*lems problems
Patient: Problems and *prob*lems

The physician:

> It's obvious when he came in, he just looked like a dishrag—just limp lying there. It's obvious he had fairly depressed affect. I don't think I've seen anybody that dramatic come into the office like that.

Thus, at least insofar as the professionals were concerned, there was agreement that a problem existed at the beginning of the encounter.

Mr. Stittler, the patient, stopped the tape four times, focusing on the stresses caused by his loss of income after 13 years of disability payments; he talked about his family problems, the test to determine disability he has been required to undergo, and his seeking psychiatric care. He was asked whether he was satisfied everything bothering him at the time of the interview had been addressed. "Not exactly everything," he responded. "I was depressed and my nerves was shot." By incorporating the patient's point-of-view, important information that could only be speculated at or proposed on the patient's behalf appeared in the same process of review. The result is a naturally controlled environment for studying the responses of the participants in their own words and under the same viewing conditions. In this way some of the problems in traditional analyses of power and control are minimized.

Frankel and Beckman (1982) report initial results from this playback technique that suggest that physicians and patients often (more than 60% of the time) independently stop the tape at identical points and comment on the same problems. Though their interpretations may vary, this high degree of concordance seems to indicate a shared orientation to the problems and concerns that unfold in the course of medical interactions. In the visit we report, in contrast, none of the commentaries occurred at the same points nor, with the exception of the physician's two comments about depression, did their topics converge. This structural evidence, tallying with the results of formal analysis, points away from a shared orientation between the patient and physician. It is perhaps significant that the patient did not return for the follow-up visit scheduled after the visit we have described.

A final perspective is provided by the medical student. In keeping with the status of his interview as informal, that portion of the videotape was not routinely transcribed for research and was in fact discovered only in the process of reviewing the "real" interview between the patient and the resident. Contacted some months later, the medical student nevertheless remembered the encounter clearly and in particular remembered that he had not discussed his findings with Dr. Toffer. Like the other participants in the encounter, he evidently also judged his interaction with the patient as unofficial and placed a different, perhaps lesser, value on the information he elicited.

The other participants involved in the study of this encounter are the researchers, who, collectively, make up the "we" of this published account. Our participation involves goals different from those of the original participants; likewise, we bring different perspectives and resources to the tasks of analysis and interpretation. While our interests, training, and analytic strategies as researchers overlap, we nevertheless acknowledge differences. A major challenge of collaborating on this project has been to achieve language and logic that all five of us, trained in different fields, find appropriate and illuminating. (The title of this chapter should only in part, however, be read as a commentary on the collaborative research process.)

CONCLUSION

In summary, both formal analysis and participants' commentaries suggest that the physician and patient in this encounter had very different concerns, only some of which were addressed during the visit. In particular, the physician's emphasis on biomedical aspects of the case, together with his style of interviewing and method of recording data, hindered a full expression of the patient's concerns and the development of a mutually agreed-upon agenda for the visit. Paradoxically, concerns expressed more readily to the medical student remained, in the absence of a mechanism that would incorporate them into the medical record, officially unspoken.

We believe that this method of analysis, which layers formal elements with the perspectives of individual participants and of researchers, enables us to look at some of the dynamic aspects of power in the medical encounter. We believe, further, that this process of acknowledging and codifying different perspectives holds promise for developing programs of intervention that are useful to all participants in medical encounters. It is important, as well, to examine our own relationship, as researchers, to our training, to our colleagues, to our audience, and to the "subjects" we are analyzing: If we want our work to have genuine impact, we need to be self-consciously reflective about our own power as researchers—power that is also not a static property but constructed in the course of our relationship with others.

APPENDIX: TRANSCRIPTS

Transcribing Conventions

The transcription method we used was developed by Gail Jefferson, at the University of California, Irvine, in the course of collaborative research with Harvey Sacks. The transcription system is intended to act as a guide to speech production activities as they occur on a micromomentary scale. The mapping of text entries from the medical record onto the discourse was developed by Richard M. Frankel.

Physician:	[Right	The onset of simultaneous speech is indicated with either a double or single left-hand bracket depending on where it occurs. Double brackets are used to indicate simultaneous turn beginnings; single brackets indicate interruption or overlap of ongoing speech. Single right-hand brackets indicate resolution points for simultaneous speech.
Patient:	And] if there's anything	
Patient:	[[No (0.3) an' nothing since] Not at all]	
Patient:	Something I wanna//do]	An alternate method of indicating overlap is the use of double oblique lines as the point of overlap or interruption.
Physician:	That's the whole-]	
(1.3)		Numbers in parentheses indicate pauses or breaks in speech production and are indicated in tenths of seconds. Pauses are marked both within and between speaking turns.
. ? , ?		Punctuation marks are used to indicate intonation and not grammar. A period indicates a sharply falling intonation; the question mark a sharply rising intonation. Commas and question com-

Patient:	hh U:hm the: uh: (0.5) the back	mas (?) indicate intontation blends. , = slightly rising or slightly falling intonation. ? = moderately rising intonation. Stressed syllables are italicized. Colons indicate a sound stretch or prolongation of an immediately prior syllable. Each colon represents one-tenth of a second.
Physician:	That's the whole-	A hyphen indicates that the immediately prior syllable has been cut off.
Physician:	Y' put half a' pound on this time. =	Equals signs are used to indicate that no discernible time has elapsed between the completion of one speaker's utterance and the beginning of another.
Patient:	= I don't know what tuh	
hh hh		Breathing patterns are signified using hh's. A period followed by "hh's" marks an inhalation; "hh's" alone stand for exhalation.
"Feels warm last week"	Dr: Don't have one. You just feel warm? [259 Pt: Ye:s (3.0). Nose bleeds. Dr: I see 265] Pt: Y'r nose bleeds?	Brackets to the left of speaker designations indicate points in the interaction during which writing occurred. A single left-hand bracket and number indicating elapsed time in tenths of seconds shows the onset of writing; a single right-hand bracket and number shows its completion. Quoted text in the left margin shows what was entered into the medical record during the writing episode.

I.

Dr. Toffer [Dr] and Mr. Stittler [Pt]; Allan is the medical student [MS].

Dr: Have a seat there Mister Stittler (Right) over here you can put (·) jacket right behind there. (Right) over here there you go:. (0.5) An =' have a se:at (0.7) (Hum) (0.7) Uh toda::y we're having medical students sit in with us if you don't mind this is Allan // (Mister) Stittler
Pt: (Hi how you doin')
MS: = Fine thank you
Pt: I have seen you *some*where before
MS: Oh really?
Pt: Yeah (   )
MS: ((laughs))
Dr: Maybe he:s been wandering around the medical center here//(
Pt: ((laughs)) (oh yeah everywhere)
MS: ((laughs))
Dr.: Great. So *how* you doing today Joseph
Pt: Not too good doct//or
Dr: Not too good. I see you kinda hangin' your head low there.
Pt: Yeah.
Dr: Must be somethin' up (·) or down I should say. Are you feelin' down?
Pt: Yeah

"2/9/82"

A {

Dr: What are you feelin' down *about* (0.7)
Pt: Stomach problems, back problems, *side* problems.
[086
Dr: *Prob*lems problems
Pt: Problems and *prob*lems
090]
Dr: Hum. What's:: we- whats goin' on with your stomach. Are you still uh- havin' pains in your stomach?
Pt: Yeah it's- can't hold no *food* water
Dr: How 'bout uh-:: are you- y' still throwin' up?
Pt: Oh yes.
Dr: Hmh
(2.0)
[105
Pt: Nervous tensions (·) can't sleep.
111]

"Still N & V" Pt: ·hhh
Dr: I see. An::d so this has be::en since December you've been havin' this (0.2) this nausea=
Pt: =Oh. yeah=
Dr: =and stuff. (1.3) Has it gotten any *bet*ter, worse or-
Pt: Worse
Dr: Worse? Have you been able to *hold* down any *food*?
Pt: Well certain things
Dr: Certain kinds of food. Since Let's see well sinc:e (·) Oc*to*ber ((shuffling paper)) Let me see where your weigh- oh here=
Dr: =We are we start over (again) one eighty-six (1.0) probably if you're one seventy-eight now so you maybe have lost about (·) five pounds since - since October twenty-seventh which isn't a whole lot (·) which suggests that you must be holdin' down at least a little bit.
Pt: Yeah just a little
Dr: what kind of things do you seem to be able to hold *down*.
Pt: We:ll (like) fruits
Dr: Fruits?
[170
Pt: like lemons
"No Prob w/ Fruits" Dr: Mmh hmh
Pt: Grapes, oranges, apples
180]
Dr: Uh huh (·) what kind a'things aren't y-seem t' be able tuh holding down. (0.3) What things come up pretty *ea*sily=
Pt: =Well (0.8) (like) heavy food like (0.5)
Dr: Heavy food?
Pt: Yeah
Dr: What would you call heavy food, *maple* syrup or mashed potatoes or
Pt: Yes. *beans pea:s*
(0.7)
[200
Dr: *Veg*etables kinda in general?
"Vegetables bother stomach" Pt: Oh ye:s
(1.2)
206]

	Dr: How bout uh::- (0.5) *meat*. Have you been able to eat any kinda meat 'at all? (1.0) chicken or hamburgers or (1.0) fish or anything? fish or anything like tha- has that been able to stay down?
	Pt: No::
	Dr: That's been comin' up, *All* the time er j'st some time.
	Pt: In general *most* of the time.
	Dr: Most of the time. (1.3) I see. (0.7) Uh::m(·)hmh: Have you been havin' any fever or chills at all?
	Pt: Ye:s fever.
	[237 242]
"Fever"	Dr: Been havin' a fever? How long have you- have you been havin' fevers.
	Pt: Oh (4.7) (for-) (2.1) over a *week* now.
	Dr: About a week?
	Dr:⌈Have you taken your
	Pt:⌊ Ye:s
	Dr: temperature with a thermometer?
	Pt: I don't have none.
	Dr: Don't have one. You just feel warm?
	[259
"Feels warm last week"	Pt: Ye:s (3.0) Nose blee:ds
	Dr: ⌊I see:
	265]
B	Dr: Y'r nose bleeds?
	Pt: Yes
	(1.2)
	Dr: That's just somethin' recently? (1.0) Just recently *start*ed
	Pt: Yeah.
	Dr: Does it start by itself or is it like after you blow your nose or pick your nose or somethin like that =
	Pt: =A *cough* or (·) *sneeze* somethin' like *that*
	Dr: Mmh hmh how many t:imes does this actually happen to you that your nose starts bleeding
	[256
Seq: "Nosebleed 2-X a day"	Pt: Two sometimes three times a day.
	Dr: Two uh three times a day
	Pt: Yeah.
	297]

Dr: An:' when did you first *start* noticin' that you were gettin nose bleeds.

[A portion of the transcript is omitted here.]

"Claims no ETOH"

C {

[380   389]

Dr: (O:kay) (3.2) What do you think is uh - is goin' on here. Wadda you - wha'do you think has been happenin' with ya. Any ideas?
(4.0)
Pt: Lots a' worri*a*tion
Dr: Lots a what?
Pt: Worriation
(0.2)
Dr: Worriation? Lotta worryin' y mean? =
Pt: = Yes

Dr: What've you been worried about.

Pt: Well I don' have no income anymore.
Dr: You don't (1.0) Because you're not workin'
Pt: No de:y (0.7) stopped my checks last month.
(0.3)
Dr: What your::-uh
Pt: Social Security =
Dr: = Social Security isn't payin' any more?
Pt: No

Dr: Hmh (1.0) How come- why did they do that (1.0) Any idea? =
Pt: Back in No*vem*ber I took a: (5.0) a de*ter*mination us *tes*//They-
Dr: Um hum
Pt: = said I was able to *work*.
Dr: Mmh hmh
Pt: My *law*yer say (·) y' got a good *case* cuz uh- he has no more complaints from the Jefferson clinic. (·)//((loudspeaker in background)) =
Dr: Um hum
Pt: That's all they did
Dr: All they did was ask you ques//stions
Pt: Told me to raise my hand (and) walk backwards ask me a a few questions.
Dr: Um hum
Pt: I'm able to work.

Dr: Oh that was your evaluation for social//security.
Pt: Yes yes
Dr: I: see. Do you think you're able to work?
Pt: No.
Dr: Wadda you feel would be keepin' you from workin' right now.
Pt: Uh- I *can't* use my left side.
Dr: You *whole* left side?
Pt: Yes - my a:rm my le:g
Dr: It feel- it feels weak on that side
Pt: Yes I can't hardly (walks and move)
    (0.3)
Dr: You had mentioned that a*while* before um: (0.3) how *long* (0.5) has this been botherin' you this weakness on your (0.3) left side.

"L side weakness"
Pt: Well (4.2) (first sta:rt to) on social security (0.8) back in November of sixty-nine.
Dr: Um hum
Pt: The doctors told me say - this'll your (life//(·)) ((loudspeaker in background)) (·) be paralyzed for left-=
Dr: (Right right)
Pt: =for life on your left side=
Dr: =did they tell you why: you were paralyzed for life d//n you left side?
Pt: (Somethin' wrong with the limbs)
                                                          [539
Dr: Did they say what the problem was at the time?

"(Since 1969)"
                                          543]
(3.0) Did they//say what ca:used the weakness.
Pt: Yes
Pt: Yes it was a blow to the *head*
Dr: A *blow* to the head.

"2° blow to head"
Pt: Yes.
                    550]
Dr: So you've had this problem ever since (·) that blow to your head.
                                        [555
Pt: Yeah that happened back in April the *twel*fth nineteen sixty-eight.
    (0.8)

"1968"
Dr: Um hum
Pt: Philadelphia Pennsylvania.
    (0.3)
                   560]

86 LANGUAGE AND POWER

Dr: How di- how did you get hit in the head just out of curiosity.
(0.5)
Pt: I was workin' at Temple University Hospital
Dr: Um hum
Pt: And this was on a Wednesday
Dr: Um hum
Pt: Pay day // used to be paid every two weeks.
Dr: Um hum
Dr: Um hum.
Pt: I (had) *caught* the *sub*way home - I was stayin' in *North* Philadelphia
Dr: Um hum
Pt: I got off uh- was goin' home I passed a Lo:dge
Dr: Um hum
Pt: About six or seven people out there (bunch) of prostitutes asked me if I wanna turn a trick you know.
Dr: Heh
(0.3)
Pt: Said I got enough problems at *home*
Dr: Yeah
Pt: One of these jokers jumped out on me and I - I start puttin' it on 'm I was doin pretty *good* too
Dr: Um hum
Pt: Somebody was behind (I heard this *trunk*) (·) car trunk slam?
Dr: Um hum
Pt: He has a ti:re iron

D {

Dr: Um
Pt: Cut me across the head.//I =
Dr: Hum
Pt: = wind up in the sa:me hospital I was workin' in
Dr: O:h no::
Pt: Stayed in a coma three r' four days.
[629

"Was in Coma 3-4 days"

Dr: In a *coma* three or four days?
Pt: They was looking- wasn't lookin' for me to live.
Dr: *Hum* well you certainly did.
636]   [638
Pt: I was in a wheel:l chair for (0.6) three t' four months.
(0.7)

"Was in Wheelchair"

Dr: Hmh:
Pt: =couldn't *walk*.
(1.0)

"w/paralyzed
L side?"

Dr: What was it that kept you from walkin:
Pt: Paralyzation.
   (1.0)
Dr: What- was it just on your left side or//both sides
Pt: Yes
   (1.0)
Dr: Did you have a skull fracture or anything like that at // the time =
Pt: Yes. They had t' put a *plate* in my head.
   663]
Dr: I: see. So this has really been (·) since the a:ccident. =
Pt: = Oh yes.
Dr: You've had this weakness. O:kay well (more) to your cu:rrent problem right now. What you (·) you know are descri:bin' sounds like a *flu*-like kind of syndrome. Although u::h you do have some other problems that we're workin on u:m: one thing was we had talked about you had this B-12 deficiency.
Pt: Oh yeah.

[The transcript of the rest of the interview is omitted.]

II.

Allan [medical student: MS] and Mr. Stittler (patient: Pt]. Brackets enclose nonvocal behaviors and pauses. (U) = unintelligble vocalization.

MS: I'm just kinda curious um about the pain [looks at pt] you're having now. Um has it been um progressively getting worse?
Pt: Oh yes [looks up, slumps, plays with left shirt cuff]
MS: Uh huh. I see. Does it seem to be worse in the morning? Or at night?
   [2 sec]
Pt: Yes — morning
MS: Usually in the morning?
Pt: Umm [yawns]
MS: Uh. Does your left leg and arm bother you a lot?
Pt: Oh yes — there's pain.

MS: Does it tingle a lot sometimes like little needle pricks, or-
Pt: -(U) [points to upper left arm] Right here in the muscle. [slumps]
MS: Um Hmm. That's been since 1968 or so, right?
Pt: Yes
MS: Um hmm. And so you've been getting social security until just a month ago then?
Pt: Yes
MS: Um hmm. That really is a disturbing thing then when that went away. [Pt. picks at left shirt cuff] [pause] Is there anything else that's troubling you that way? You said you had lots of sad problems. Is that the major one? Is there anyting else?
[3 sec]
Pt: Umm. Get confused easy.
MS: Uh huh. Confusion. [looks at pt] Tell me a little more about your confusion.
[7 sec]
Pt: Get angry. (U) [vocalizes, moves right hand] (U) violent intentions. (?)
MS: Yeah
Pt: [looks at MS] I have killed before and I could do it again — easy.
MS: Uh huh.
Pt: And I know that the court won't hold this against me cause I got a mental case — brain damage [moving hands — slumps]
MS: I see. So that was since you — since 1968?
Pt: Yes
MS: Um hmm. I see.

NOTES

1. General discussions of medical professionalization include Becker et al. (1961), Bosk (1979), Bucher and Stelling (1977), Freidson (1970), and Larson (1977). For a discussion of medical students and linguistic change that touches on the changing relationship of the physician-in-training to power and authority, see Treichler and Zoppi (1983). Increasingly, postgraduate programs such as Frankel and Beckman's are emphasizing communication as an element of primary care practice; such instruction occurs relatively late in the trainee's educational career, however, and seems different from the initial acquisition of a medical repertoire.

4

DETERMINATION OF GUILT
Discourse in the Courtroom

Ruth Wodak-Engel

Judge: I know he's guilty, he is sweating.
Interviewer: But it's hot!
Judge: No, I know these people.

In this chapter I discuss justice in the courtroom, specifically whether the social class of the defendant makes a difference in what happens there. I first examine existing sociolinguistic theories about socialization and class-specific behavior, and then go on to develop an approach of my own, including hypotheses about courtroom interaction.

In support of those hypotheses, I give some details from an empirical study of behavior in the courtroom. The goal of the pilot study reported here is to arrive at an explicit analysis of courtroom interaction in terms of sociolinguistics and textlinguistics (discourse analysis), and to discover the significance of socially derived linguistic barriers (especially their contribution to communicative difficulties) in an interaction that has serious consequences for some of the participants.[1]

The questions I pose here are these:

- Is there evidence that the social class of the defendant determines the degree of impartiality of the judgments that may be expected from the court?
- To what extent does the defendant's linguistic behavior contribute to the outcome of a court hearing?
- What factors in the courtroom situation affect the linguistic behavior of the defendants?

The combination of sociolinguistics and textlinguistics used in this chapter has enjoyed increased interest among linguists in recent years. The microanalysis of courtroom interaction (specifically, that between judge and defendant) at the textlinguistic and phonological level helps us to arrive at general conclusions about the significance of interaction at court and helps verify (or contradict) theoretical sociolinguistic hypotheses about the consequences of class-specific socialization and about the resulting strategies selected by participants for interacting in institutional settings. Analyses of these strategies have serious implications for such practitioners as judges or therapists (Wodak-Leodolter, 1980). Thus, the choice of a specific institutional setting for sociolinguistic analysis is legitimized not only by practical considerations (norms and rules being explicitly stated and known, deviant behavior being recognizable, and conversational rules being easily derived), and by theoretical concerns (the results providing insights into the validity of sociolinguistic and linguistic theory), but by the fact that such studies can have sociopolitical justification: They can enable practitioners to understand and perhaps to *change* the processes and dynamics of a social interaction that might otherwise go unnoticed.[2]

SOCIOLINGUISTIC BACKGROUND

Some sociolinguistic controversy has arisen out of two (superficially) contrasting theories: those of Bernstein (1962a, 1970a, 1970b) and of Labov (1966, 1972a). Bernstein analyzes sociolinguistic (speech) behavior using a theory that middle-class children master elaborated codes and working-class children, restricted codes. Working-class parents, he hypothesizes, enunciate decisions that are often neither discussed nor explained. Consequently, their children fail to internalize the flexible rule system available to middle-class children, a system that prepares them to communicate on an abstract and a metatheoretical level. Labov shows that black children are able to communicate very well in their own group and do not behave at all in a restricted way, except when they have to interact with white authorities. Therefore, Labov argues, both working-class and middle-class language varieties are equivalent.

Unfortunately, Labov does not address the *social* consequences that arise due to the differential power and prestige of speech varieties that are linked to social class. It is precisely in middle-class social situations that working-class speakers experience difficulty—in school, for instance, where the standard language rules are the norm. In a situation perceived as hostile and unfamiliar (the school or, as I show, the courtroom) such speakers have difficulty drawing upon their own elaborated codes, and these fail to match the elaborated codes positively sanctioned in the courtroom, anyway. Every speech situation is restricted by norms and rules of varying degrees of definition, depending upon whether the situation is open or closed, formal or informal, institutionalized or not. So we cannot speak about abstract *modes* of discourse as being "restricted" or "elaborated." More likely we have to do with interaction rituals positively sanctioned (if they conform to local norms) or negatively sanctioned (if they do not). Whether they are considered "better" or "worse" depends not upon the rituals themselves but upon social values placed on them by the members of the society.

That is why I propose a different sociolinguistic theory of socialization and verbalization. The internalization of institutional norms succeeds most ideally if the dialogues through which children develop their linguistic repertoires replicate the dialogues that they will encounter in social situations. Such a hypothesis fits well with the theories and findings of psycholinguistic research (Habermas, 1970; Wodak-Leodolter, 1980).

Interactional role theory presents us with categories useful in describing such an ideal of communication. Role distance, empathy, and role ambiguity are fundamental strategies used in displaying a speech identity. Those typically internalized in middle-class families prepare children well for the roles required of them when they must perform in middle-class institutional settings.

INTERACTION AT COURT: AN OUTLINE OF THE STUDY

The empirical portion of this study was carried out in Vienna in a special courtroom for hearing cases dealing with serious automobile accidents. During a period of several months, fifteen trials were tape-recorded and analyzed qualitatively and quantitatively. The central sociolinguistic question was to discover if the verbal interaction in the courtroom could be correlated with the social class of the defendants. Sociolinguistic, sociological, and psychological frameworks and categories had to be used, and the statistical analyses were of a text-linguistic and phonological nature. The entire material for this study is published in Leodolter (1975a), where it is subjected to a different analysis.

The general hypotheses based on the outlined sociolinguistic socialization theory underlying the empirical study can be formulated in the following ways. First, individuals with different status and positional role combinations differ basically in their modes of interaction. Second, their behavior in the courtroom will vary accordingly. Third, situational factors of the courtroom procedure induce varied behavior among the participants in the interaction at court. Fourth, a microanalysis of the very specific speech situation in a courtroom setting can provide evidence to support (or refute) theories about the processes and consequences of different kinds of socialization.

I chose the courtroom situation for study, initially, because it provides an institutionalized speech setting where many norms are explicitly stated and deviant behavior is easy to identify. The courtroom also provides a setting where verbal interaction is of great importance, having significant consequences for the participants and for society. Finally, it is possible to control for consistency in the courtroom setting by using the same room, the same judges, and the same researcher throughout the study.

I chose to analyze hearings dealing with automobile accidents, since such offenses are less class-specific than theft, murder, or corruption. In all of these cases, one or more deaths had occurred, and the purpose of the trial was to determine the degree to which the defendant was responsible. Consequently, the proceedings were extremely serious, and sentences ranged from minor fines to extended prison terms, depending upon the judge's evaluation of the defendant's responsibility for the accident. Since these hearings are usually short, four or five being held on a single day, it was not difficult to get a fair sampling of hearings in a relatively short time. The empirical investigation took ten months (February to September 1973), during which I attended ten days of hearings, observing the first four days and taperecording the procedure the following six days.

Fifteen court cases were taped, in all. The defendants knew they were being recorded (it was necessary to secure their permission in advance), but, given the formality and seriousness of the situation, they concentrated so intently upon the interaction that they seemed to forget the existence of the microphone rather quickly. Observation helped us to understand the participating individuals and to discover implicit norms in the interaction. The textlinguistic analysis demonstrated that speakers used different strategies of image-making in telling their stories, strategies related to social class.

Hypotheses

The court situation is an institutionalized speech setting. Individuals are able to maneuver successfully only if they know the explicit and implicit values and norms of the courtroom and are able to verbalize their knowledge in spontaneous interaction. As a consequence of this necessity, we hypothesized that defendants would behave differently in court as follows:

(1) Working-class (WC) defendants will perform poorly, since they have not internalized the norms and values of the courtroom, or the modes of interaction that are positively sanctioned in such public situations.
(2) Lower middle-class (LMC) speakers will be insecure, but they will differ in their behavior at a purely linguistic level.
(3) Middle-class (MC) defendants, who have internalized the strategies that enable them to cope with the questioning to which they are subjected, will perform well in the courtroom.
(4) Previously convicted (PC) defendants, even if they belong to the WC, have acquired a good knowledge of the norms of courtroom interaction —obtained in previous courtroom experience—and they will benefit from this knowledge by performing more capably.

My observation of the courtroom interaction procedures demonstrates that Luhmann (1969) was incorrect in arguing that courtroom proceedings operate independently of the everyday roles of the participants. In fact, judges arrive at their decisions following quite different criteria in different cases, and defendants' roles outside the courtroom quite naturally become involved in the decisions made there. Decisions sometimes depend upon the impressions the judge has formed based upon the speech of the defendant, and on such details of nonverbal behavior as clothing, bearing, and so forth. Luhmann classifies such factors as "exceptions," but I believe that such factors comprise explicit and implicit norms in the procedures of the courtroom. In chats with the researcher before the hearings began, the judge occasionally revealed a very definite bias ("This is a woman; they cannot drive anyway" or "This is a previously convicted defendant; we know what to expect here," and so forth).

The Sample

The sample consists of 15 defendants (13 men and 2 women). Of these, 4 were MC, 3 were LMC, and 8 were WC. The WC defendants consisted of 5 first-time offenders and 3 PC (previously convicted, who had been in jail 13 times cumulatively). The classification as MC, LMC, and WC is based upon Oevermann's scale (1973), using income, education, and profession of the defendant as indicators for social class.[3] There are (as Patricia Nichols points out elsewhere in this volume) difficulties in assigning social class on the basis of such static items as education and income, especially for women in the study, but those problems are perhaps less severe in a society like Vienna's, where there is relatively little social mobility.

Image-Making

Recent textlinguistic studies of speech behavior indicate that image-making has a lot to do with language behavior. Speech styles can be correlated with the ability to construct a socially acceptable image (Holly, 1977; Wodak-Leodolter, 1980). In order to get a fair hearing, it is important for the defendants in court not only to behave in an adequate way and to answer all of the questions posed by the judge, but also to create "good" images. Especially important are the strategies used in the initial story-telling: the manner in which defendants handle the directive, "Now tell me what happened." Does the story fit with the facts? Is it obviously memorized? Or does the defendant succeed in convincing the court that he or she is spontaneously telling the turth? Does the defendant use a technical vocabulary? Is the story consistent and coherent? How does the defendant evaluate the situation? We will see that the answers depend somewhat on the socioeconomic class of the defendant.

By using categories provided by an interactionist theory of role relationships, I first observed how the defendants built up their images. Second, I compared the implicit rules of the court (gained by observation of the hearings) with the explicity stated rules voiced by the judge in making his decisions. At the beginning of the hearings, all the status and positional roles of the defendant were known: previous convictions, work, schooling, marital status, and so forth. Information necessary to assign social class to the defendants was gathered quite early in the dialogue between the judge and defendant. In these exchanges it became obvious that occupation plays an important role in evaluation of the person: People with prestigious occupations, like "university assistant" or "student," were treated in a completely different manner from nonacademic defendants.

In addition, some MC defendants were able to succceed in showing their own identities favorably, by using the strategies of maintaining "role distance," "role ambiguity," and so forth. For example, the defendant who said "Although I certainly was wrong, I was very shocked....I tried to change [lanes]....It never happened before"—by performing both the role of a guilty person and, simultaneously, the role of a sufficiently contrite person—succeeds in presenting himself as contrite, capable, and socially acceptable. For some reason, most WC defendants pleaded not guilty, although everyone knew they were guilty. For whatever reason—through confusion or lack of confidence in the courtroom procedure—these defendants did not appear to understand that the question of guilt was less important to the court than showing oneself to be responsible, honest, remorseful, and sincere, though guilty. Failure to plead guilty or to apologize suggests both a lack of comprehension of the seriousness of the accident and a lack of contrition.

Yet another factor was the empathy of the defendant in role-taking. If the defendant demonstrated a flexible verbal behavior, able to adapt quickly to all of the questions and expectations of the judge, he or she was likely to fare much better than the defendant who had memorized a version of what happened. WC defendants often presented the first version of their story in a standard but, for them, unfamiliar dialect. When the judge questioned them, they found themselves in the position of having to reply and to rephrase their stories in their own, less acceptable dialects. As a consequence, the memorized version appeared to differ significantly from the spontaneous version.

Textlinguistic Analysis

The strategies used in Account 1 and Account 2 to answer the question "What happened?" are different in important ways, constituting almost two different text types (see Appendix).[4] In the first account the defendant tells a consistent story, embedded in a metacommunicative framework. He expresses his shock, fear, and guilt, while delivering a complete evaluation to the judge. The technical vocabulary is so well-applied that no questions need be asked to fill in details. Very precisely woven into the story are all the details that might be important in judging responsibility for an accident. ("Did he look in the mirror?" "How far into the street was the pedestrian?" "Which lights were on?") By presenting a valid explanation for the accident, he makes work easier for the judge. Although the story from the MC defendant is obviously prepared beforehand, it does not occur in a completely different sociophonological speech style from his usual one. There is no style shifting in the testimony of the MC defendant. He switches style very little in spontaneous interaction and seems perfectly secure. Linguistically the text is characterized by personal perspective, by the completeness of the story structure (Labov and Waletzky, 1967), by the explicitness of evaluative speech acts, and by very coherent phrasing (almost like written discourse).

The second story, from the WC defendant, is almost no story at all. A scene is described, but neither metacommunicative frame, nor orientation, nor evaluation, nor explanation is supplied. The event itself is described—the minute of the crash and the panic felt—but no other parts of the story are told. Because the initial version of the accident is incomplete, the judge must ask her questions about it. To answer these she finds it necessary to switch into dialect, a variety she clearly considers to be inappropriate for courtroom proceedings. The switch into dialect from a formal speech style during the initial narrative is obvious, indicating that the defendant has learned her version by heart. Under the situational stress, she finds it impossible to rephrase statements. ("I couldn't brake" is repeated twenty times during the trial.) She is blocked, and the judge makes it worse with his cynical questioning. This may be a consequence of her doubly negative status role: She is a woman and she is from the working class. He uses her momentary uncertainty about the verb "swerve" as a basis for lecturing her on the purposes of the steering wheel. The combination of her situational discomfort and the judge's overt hostility evidently disorient her, and she is unable to draw on her verbal resources to defend herself.

The previously convicted defendants, although members of the working class, behaved competently and comfortably in the courtroom as a consequence of their knowledge of the norms and rules of behavior. They knew that the courtroom interaction was of less consequence to the judge's decision than was their previous conviction, and they knew (from past observation) something of the norms and expectations of the courtroom. As a result, the interaction was for the PC something of a game. They succeeded in manipulating the courtroom procedures in a positively sanctioned way. As a consequence, they were comfortable in the courtroom and were able to joke and to express camaraderie with the officers of the court. Their verbal ease provides a stark contrast to that of the other working-class defendants: The PC engage in no style-shifting in the courtroom. They speak entirely in the vernacular in which they are at ease.

The outcome of these trials is not surprising. The first defendant had to pay a nominal fine, although he was guilty of manslaughter. The second defendant received a three-month jail sentence, although she was less responsible for the accident in which she was involved than was the first. Although the sample is small, the WC and LMC observed here received more severe sentences (especially prison terms) than did the MC. For the defendants in my sample, difficulty with image-management in an institutional setting had clear and serious consequences.

For the previously convicted, a prison sentence is less disastrous, in that it is something with which they have already come to terms. The judge wants a quick trial. If the defendant pleads guilty, does not argue, has reasonable explanations, tells a believable story, can answer everything, looks honest on paper (no previous convictions), speaks nicely, and is well dressed, such trials take only half an hour. Only MC defendants were able (or were permitted) to act in the prescribed way, thus correlating well with the prejudices of the judges.

Results

The results when using text linguistic indicators to analyze the text from all defendants to see how they went about image-making suggests the following conclusions:

(1) MC individuals are able to build up an image valued by the court; they know the strategies and values dominating courtroom interaction. They plead guilty. Their stories are consistent and the facts are plausible: The accident happened because of some "objective misfortune" (the technique of neutralization).
(2) LMC defendants *can* speak in a manner that is positively valued by the judge. However, they fail to succeed in building up a positive image, and they violate the court custom of pleading guilty.
(3) WC defendants don't succeed in the courtroom. They don't know what to expect, and their behavior reinforces a variety of prejudices and stereotypes held by the judge.
(4) PC defendants speak in a way that illustrates their knowledge of courtroom procedure to their advantage.

SUMMARY

It is possible from this pilot study to see that justice relates to class and that language is evidently a significant factor in establishing or verifying class-related prejudices. The implicit speech norms in the courtroom are acquired by MC children during their socialization, but not necessarily by WC children. Consequently, defendants not socialized in these norms of language use are discriminated against, and only MC defendants succeed, as a rule, in good image management before the judge.

That these results are of great practical importance seems evident. Judges should be trained to consider language behavior differently, as manifestation of the socialization of the defendant (see also Smitherman, in this volume). They should be acquainted with the results of sociolinguistic studies on variation and should alter their behavior according to these findings. Judges should be aware of factors affecting their decisions in the courtroom situation (including social class, familiarity with the rules, and language) and should strive to render the decision-making process more explicit and transparent, so that it is clearly understandable to the defendants.

Perhaps the study of sociolinguistics should be part of the education of lawyers. (How do I lead an interrogation? What are the stereotypes evoked by varied speech styles? How can the attitudes arising as a consequence of these stereotypes be combatted?) But the judges and lawyers should not be the only courtroom participants who discuss the meaning and values associated with varied speech styles. Perhaps the growing literature on language in the courtroom can be used in teacher-training programs, so that teachers and their students—the defendants-to-be—discuss and challenge the speech evaluations that shape, in part, their possibilities and restrictions in the classroom, courtroom, and other institutions.

APPENDIX: TRANSCRIPTS

Middle-Class Male Speaker

J: = Judge; D: = Defendant.

J: G.F.?
D: Yes. Good morning.
J: You are a Ph.D.?
D: Yes.
J: In what field?
D: Philosophy.
J: Philosophy? How does that relate to your athletic activities?
D: I have been a member of the Austrian Alpine Club for several years. I have led expeditions and have undertaken difficult climbs...
J: You are single? You live at...
D: Yes.
J: Average income?
D: 6000 shillings.
J: 6000 shillings? No capital? No maintenance obligations?
D: No.

J: No previous convictions. Do you plead guilty or not guilty.
D: Yes, I plead guilty to not having seen the woman, even though I was paying full attention...
J: [Naming the place of the accident.] Flotzersteig, near the Wilhelminenspital. Now, what happened?
D: Yes, I was in the second lane because there were cars parked on the right-hand side, and about at the place where the accident occurred, the row of parked cars ended. I wanted to change lanes because the right lane was clear ahead, and so I looked in the mirror, and then suddenly I saw in front of me, or rather, to the left of me, a figure, and my first thought was that it's completely impossible, and I was really quite shocked that something could appear in front of me to my left at all, and before I could start braking, the collision happened and somehow I also realized that the vehicle behind me had skidded. Together with this, I realized that the woman had been thrown toward the curb, and this was my first thought: no further accident if, behind me, cars crash into me, and—therefore—eh, I set—I had subjectively the impression that the car went to the left. After this, after thinking it over, this had to be explained; it was due to the deformation of the wings on the right side; I braked. I wanted to steer the car to the right in order to stop it at the curb, so I had the impression that the car went to the left. Then I would be able to orient myself and brake the car and stop at the curb...

[After sentence has been passed]

D: I wish to thank you for the conduct of the trial and, especially, for the mild sentence; and I accept the sentence.
J: I hope it will go all right in June. Then you will become a professor?
D: This can be applied for, after a certain time, the professorship, after the habilitation, after three years it can be applied for.... It is difficult.
J: Will you earn more then?
D: Professorship: Yes, one can live on that quite well.
J: More than now?
D: I think the starting salary is about 10,000 shillings, the starting salary.
J: Okay. Thank you.

Working-Class Speaker

J: Religion?
D: Catholic.
J: Married?
D: Yes.
J: And you live...?
D: In the 22nd [district].
J: Vienna 22.... So, and now we need the education.

D: Primary and secondary school.
J: Each four years.
D: Yes...
J: Yes, and what else?
D: Yes, I was near the crossing, suddenly the car came from the right. I saw it, but I couldn't manage to brake, so...
J: You couldn't brake? Couldn't you try to swerve somehow?
D: No.
J: Do you know what that is?
D: No.
J: You can't answer that question either?
D: Yes, to steer somewhere else did you mean? Or...?
J: Yes. Every vehicle has a steering wheel. If one turns it around, the direction changes, doesn't it? If it's not broken. If one turns this thing, it is called "swerving," to put it briefly. Understood? Yes?

NOTES

1. Details of the linguistic analysis of the data, as well as facts related to the framework of sociology of the law (in the narrow sense), are available in Leodolter (1975a, 1975b) and, for reasons of space, are dealt with only briefly in this paper.
2. Follow-up studies of the research reported here done in Germany (especially Hoffman, 1979) have led lawyers to a new awareness of the consequences of different verbal styles in the courtroom.
3. The empirical part of the study, a Ph.D. thesis, was done in Vienna in the traffic court where trials were held concerning automobile accidents resulting in fatalities. During a period of several months, 15 trials were tape-recorded and analyzed qualitatively and quantitatively. The central sociolinguistic question was to discover whether verbal interaction in the courtroom could be correlated with the social class of the defendants. Sociolinguistic, sociological, and psychological frameworks and categories were used; the indicators for the statistical analysis were of a textlinguistic and phonological nature. The entire study is published in Leodolter (1975a).
4. The two transcripts are brief examples, chosen from the entire data set for illustrative purposes. In the study, it was possible to verify the hypotheses with the help of textlinguistic indicators.

5

BLACK LANGUAGE AS POWER

Geneva Smitherman

THE CONTEMPORARY MERGER of linguistics and the law can be a mechanism of social change for Black Americans. In the courtroom, sociolinguistic information can arouse public consciousness about the relationship between language and oppression, thereby creating arenas for debate and yielding possible solutions to some of the glaring contradictions in American society. Further, the combination of such scholarly and legal strategies can be used as the basis for arousing and unifying the Black community to change educational and other social institutions that often impede the development of future Black leaders. Problematic in this endeavor, however, are the popular confusions about Black English as a language and as a dialect, and about the relationship between class and race.

The linguistic confusion results from differing conceptualizations about language. After all, the distinction between a language and a dialect ultimately depends on how we define "language" in the first place. The language-dialect issue is a contradiction because language is an abstraction; we know it only as it manifests itself concretely in dialect. The concepts "language" and "dialect" are dual aspects of the same reality, the human communication system; one can call one "heads," and the other "tails," but it is the same coin. The class-race confusion results from analyses and perceptions of the cause of oppression in American society. Is Black oppression the result of conflict between two racial groups, Blacks and whites? Or is it the result of conflict between a dominant socioeconomic class (which, depending on how and where one draws the line, might include some Blacks as well as whites) and the oppressed socioeconomic class (which, again, might include both Blacks and whites)?

To understand these popular confusions and conceptual contradictions, our analysis of the courtroom as a mechanism for social change for Blacks must take into account the scholarship in theoretical Chomskyan linguistics (hereafter Cartesian linguistics), languages-in-contact research, and the Black American intellectual tradition. Although I shall not discuss each of these areas of inquiry and research separately in detail, it should become apparent that each is necessary to advance our understanding of the power of language to aid speakers in changing social conditions.

THE AFRICAN PAST AND AMERICAN ENSLAVEMENT

A rich empirical data base indicates that the sub-Saharan African/European language contact situation produced similar sociolinguistic phenomena wherever Africans and Europeans interacted as a result of the African slave trade (Schneider, 1966; Alleyne, 1980; Dillard, 1972; Valdman, 1977; Herskovits, 1941; Turner, 1949; Harrison, 1884; Bokamba, 1982; Hall, 1966). This contact led to the creation of various pidgins and creoles, formed by grafting European words onto basic African language patterns, producing a variety of Africanized forms of European speech. In this historical process over time, there was borrowing between the two language communities, and both the European and African languages were transformed. Although much of this research has focused on language structure to the unfortunate subordination of language function and use, still it has been important for documenting the existence of Africanized language varieties and establishing an empirical data base to validate a linguistic continuum from Africa to the new world.

This history is critical to our analysis because it highlights a fundamental failure in the American democratic experiment. Given the goals and objectives of the American ideal (the economic free enterprise system; "life, liberty, pursuit of happiness"), the logical consequence of the North American-African language contact situation should have been linguistic assimilation of America's Blacks. The fact that this has not occurred can be accounted for by examining America's educational, social, economic, and political systems, which have maintained both Black linguistic difference and Black oppression.

To be sure, among North American Blacks, as compared to Blacks elsewhere around the globe, this language variety, known as Black English, has undergone the greatest degree of de-creolization, that is, de-Africanization of Black English in the direction of Euro-American "standard" English (hereafter White English). However, due to the continued existence of two separate societies in America, the de-creolization process remains incomplete. Thus, today Black English still reflects fundamental linguistic differences from White English, in both the Cartesian "deep structural" and sociolinguistic senses. For example, Black American English has retained the African language semantics of an aspectual verb system, albeit superimposed upon an English lexical structure. Consider the sentence "He be hollin at us and stuff" (Smitherman, 1981) spoken by a Black child in reference to one of the Ann Arbor teachers in the internationally publicized King ("Black English") federal court case of 1979 (of which, more later). This use of the White English verb "to be" conveys the speaker's meaning with reference to the qualitative character and distribution of an action over time. The White English verb system of past, present, and future tense cannot accommodate this type of construction, whereas the Black English verb usage has actually captured all three tenses simultaneously. The closest White English equivalent would be (1) He is always hollering at us; (2) he frequently (or often) hollers at us; or (3) he sometimes (or occasionally) hollers at us.

Such deep structure differences operate not only in the realm of language structure. There are important *sociolinguistic* deep structural differences between Black and White English, so intensive that one may question whether it is accurate to label Black English a "dialect" of White English, rather than a language in its own right. Further, such differences raise the question of methodological adequacy in differentiating languages and dialects by a linguistic analysis that separates structure from use. The sociolinguistic phenomenon of Black English vividly illustrates the limitation of Cartesian linguistics as well as the inadequacy of empiricism, though both paradigms dominate American academic intellectual thought.

For example, Muhammad Ali, hero and rapper par excellence to virtually the entire Black English-speaking community, nearly caused an international diplomatic disaster by using the rules of "talkin Black" when he said,

> There are two bad white men in the world. The Russian white man and the American white man. They are the two baddest men in the history of the world.

Although the Tanzanians, to whom he was speaking at the time, apparently understood his meaning perfectly well, the standard White English-speaking world did not. He was castigated for using a term interpreted in the Websterian tradition as evil, wicked, negative, or not good. In the semantics of inversion used by the descendants of African slaves, however, "bad" can mean powerful, omnipotent, spiritually or physically tough, outstanding, wonderful, and, with emphasis, very good. In this historical linguistic tradition, in which something can be so good that it's "terrible," such poetic license is not merely the exclusive property of the artist, but every speaker's rightful domain.[1]

The example of Muhammad Ali and the contrasting Black and White American interpretations of his verbal showmanship place the language/dialect controversy in bold relief. Although Ali's language appears to be White English, the correct interpretation of his meaning requires the listener to have access to sociocultural data outside the realm of White English.

Ali represents the bad man of words in the Black oral tradition. Through boastful talk, pungent rhymes, verbal repartee, and clever "signifyin" (indirect language used to tease, admonish, or disparage), the rapper establishes himself or herself as a cultural hero solely on the basis of oral performance. Preachers, politicians, and other Black leaders reflect this tradition. A clever rapper can talk himself out of a jam, and in sessions of ritual insult such as "playing the dozens" (talking about somebody's momma and/or other kinfolk) tension is relieved and fights often avoided. Those who are verbally adept at the art of "selling woof (wolf) tickets" (boasting) often do not have to prove anything by action. It is believed that the African concept of Nommo, "word power," can indeed "psych your opponent out." Thus, when Ali engages in the art of Black braggadocio, the louder and badder he talks, the more Blacks applaud him, and the more whites, lacking cultural experience in this tradition, censure him. Ali symbolizes a cultural value manifested in Black language behavior, suggesting that we are dealing with a language, not a "dialect."

Combining the African past with African American enslavement, Black America forged a new language. It became a primary force in which the cultural consciousness—"Race memory"—of a people in bondage adapted to and created a new reality. This language variety became a source of power and attraction because the Africanized style of speaking was fully understood only by those born under the threat of the lash. Forced by sociolinguistic necessity—as a result of the slavers' deliberate mixing of African slaves from different ethnic-language groups into a single slave community—to talk *in* the oppressor's language, the oppressed were not *of* it. They used the slave master's words, but not his meanings. This African-derived style of speaking in indirect and even ambiguous ways led to the creation of, for example, the Negro spirituals. These are songs based primarily on the biblical Old Testament and sung by long-ago darkies on slave plantations, where "steal away to Jesus" and "this train is bound for glory" referred not so much to the Christian journey as to the journey from slavery in America to freedom in Canada. But all this is as it should be. After all, in the deep structure, the lexicon of the captor cannot possibly serve the semantics of the captive. Perhaps writer James Baldwin put it best in a piece written for the *New York Times* (July 29, 1979) two weeks after the King trial:

> [I]t is late in the day to attempt to penalize black people for having created a language that permits the nation its only glimpse of reality, a language without which the nation would be even more whipped than it is. ... This was not merely, as in the European example, the adoption of a foreign tongue, but an alchemy that transformed ancient elements into a new language. ... Now, if this passion, this skill, this (to quote Toni Morrison) "sheer intelligence," this incredible music, the mighty achievement of having brought a people utterly unknown to, or despised by "history"—to have brought this people to their present, troubled, troubling, and unassailable and unanswerable place—if this absolutely unprecedented journey does not indicate that black English is a language, I am curious to know what definition of language is to be trusted.

The Black English language-dialect controversy reflects a fundamental contradiction within linguistics itself as to how language is to be defined, conceptualized, and studied. The classic dichotomy between *langue* and *parole* (speech/language) is evident in the differences between Cartesian linguistics and "socially constituted" linguistics. The Cartesian school (Chomsky, 1966, 1972) abstracts language from social context and focuses on its structure—sound patterns, grammatical structure, and vocabulary. The socially constituted school (Hymes, 1974) more broadly conceptualizes language within the framework of culture and society, and focuses on the use and users of language: their history, culture, values, world views, and social structure are considered basic to understanding a given language. Expressing this in terms of the languages-in-contact tradition (for example, Weinreich, 1963), there are both structural and nonstructural interference phenomena between Black and White English (that is, mismatches in phonology, lexicosemantics, and morphosyntax as well as differing attitudes, uses of speech and conflicting values about the two speech systems and the individuals who use them).

Our analysis of Muhammad Ali's speaking style illustrates interference in both realms and points to a fundamental theoretical inadequacy in the Cartesian language model. The relationship between structural and nonstructural phenomena—between language structure and language use, between speech and language—is a dialectical and interactive relationship. The separation of this reality into distinct, dichotomous entities creates an analytically convenient *but artificial* schema that merely lends itself to empiricism.

Elsewhere (Smitherman, 1977, 1979) I detail the relationship of this general controversy in linguistics to study and research on Black English. The point is that the semantics within which one formulates a general theory of language can determine whether one views the issue as involving Black language or Black dialect. If one considers only words, grammar, and sounds as the essence of language, then Black speech data might tend to look more like a dialect of White English. If one also considers the history and social rules that govern the use, production, and interpretation of the words, grammar, and sounds, then Black speech data more nearly resemble a different language.

Research and scholarship on language use (as opposed to structure) in the Black American community has been sparse (see discussions in Mitchell-Kernan, 1969; Smith, 1969; Smitherman, 1977). Such an analysis demands that we concentrate on the language users and their history, culture, values, world view, and social structure, which govern the production and use of language from their perspective. No racially chauvinistic claim is being made for only Black linguists to study the Black community, but I am issuing a sad statement of explanation and a heavy note of caution. The explanation: Some outstanding research, which should have once and for all put the lie to the linguistic impoverishment myth about Blacks, was soundly rejected by the Black community and by members of the white community, because the data were inappropriately gathered, analyzed, and disseminated without regard for demographic variables influencing Black language behavior, rules, and norms of interaction for appropriate speech behavior within the Black community, implications for public policy decisions, and most of all because the data were set forth in a seemingly apolitical (if such is possible) framework. Thus, in the American media, Black verbal ability was caricatured (and ultimately dismissed) as so much "dem, dat, dose jive talk about muthafuckas and pussy-copping."

This brings us to the caution: Future research on Black English must be grounded in a thorough understanding and conceptualization of the Black American experience, which is certainly possible, albeit difficult, for outsiders. Consider that it took the Black linguist Lorenzo Turner 15 years of living among, working with, and researching Gullah Black folk before he was able to publish his *Africanisms in the Gullah Dialect*. This is not to indict the work of white American scholars, whose research, after all, has proved important groundwork for those of us keen enough to separate the wheat from the tare. (See Smitherman and McGinnis [1977] for references to such work.)

DOUBLE CONSCIOUSNESS AND AMERICAN "FREEDOM"

From the seventeenth century until the end of the Civil War, the race-language connection in America was sharp and fairly discrete. That is, Black English was spoken by and objectively prevalent throughout the African slave communities. This is not to assert that the slave community was monolingual; on the contrary, African language forms were richly present, as well as several varieties of more or less Africanized English. However, as long as slavery existed and all Blacks could be categorized as slaves (whether they were slave or free), such sociolinguistic complexity did not have widespread objective consequences in the larger social system. Black English began to assume a significant class dimension as Blacks, both by choice and force, began to be Americanized. This assimilation became greatly dominant and pronounced with the transition from slavery to citizenship, and the postemancipation years saw large numbers of Blacks enter the economic, cultural, and linguistic mainstreams.

Yet, high phenotypical visibility prevented complete Black assimilation; thus, segregation of the races, whether through de jure or de facto means, was routinely and easily maintained. This set of factors meant that regardless of a Black person's socioeconomic status, she or he was forced to reside, socialize, and be educated in the Black community. Thus, middle-class Blacks, though they became fluent in White English, had to retain their ability to "talk dat Talk" (Black English) or at least to understand it, because it continued to be the *lingua franca* of Black workers and the Black underclass (the so-called masses). The question of Black English thus raises the fundamental contradiction between class and race in the American national character.

On the other hand, Black language commands little respect in the white world since it is the language of a racial minority who have been depersonalized and dehumanized and are considered the dregs of

American society. Yet, features of this same language are adopted by white American heroes—athletes; entertainers; the "beautiful people"; those in feminist, hippie, and other contemporary American social movements; and even U.S. presidents. Thus, whether whites acknowledge it or not, and whether they even consciously realize it or not, much of their popular speech has been borrowed (stolen?) from Black America. The language has enriched mainstream American language and culture to such an extent that Ralph Ellison (1953) argues that all of authentic American culture has been borrowed from Black people. However, because Black language has become a double-edged sword, Blacks tend to be ambivalent about it—hence double-consciousness and what I have described as "linguistic push-pull" (Smitherman, 1977).

Double-consciousness was first used by W.E.B. DuBois (1903), who defined it thus:

> After the Egyptian and Indian, the Greek and Roman, the Teuton and Mongolian, the Negro is a sort of seventh son, born with a veil, and gifted with second-sight in this American world—a world which yields him no true self-consciousness, but only lets him see himself through the revelation of the other world. It is a peculiar sensation, this double-consciousness, this sense of always looking at one's self through the eyes of others.... One ever feels his twoness—an American, a Negro: two souls, two unreconciled strivings; two warring ideals in one dark body. ... The history of the American Negro is the history of this strife—this longing to attain self-conscious manhood, to merge his double self into a better and truer self. In this merging, he wishes neither of the older selves to be lost [1903:16-17].

The manifestation of double-consciousness in Black speech is reflected in the push toward Americanization (i.e., de-creolization) of Black English counterbalanced by the pull of its Africanization. Both linguistic forms have been demanded for Black survival in White America—Black language for use in the Black community where "talkin proper" is negatively equated with "talkin white," white language for use in attempts to get admitted to the White American mainstream.

In analyzing the psychological schism created by this linguistic push-pull, psychiatrist Frantz Fanon (1967) spoke on it thus:

> The Negro of the Antilles will be proportionately whiter ... in direct ratio to his mastery of the French language.... Every colonized people—in other words, every people in whose soul an inferiority complex has been

created by the death and burial of its local cultural originality—finds itsself face to face with the language of the civilizing nation...because he wants to emphasize the rupture that has now occurred.... In every country of the world there are climbers, the ones who forget who they are and, in contrast to them, the ones who remember where they came from. The Antilles Negro who goes home from France expresses himself in the dialect if he wants to make it plain that nothing has changed [1967: 18-37].

Although Fanon here speaks specifically of the Afro-French situation, it directly applies to the Afro-English situation in America and, in fact, through the Diaspora. As noted earlier, linguistic phenomena have developed in a similar fashion wherever the slave trade brought Africans and Europeans into contact. Such languages-in-contact situations reflect similar sociolinguistic realities "whether the contact is between Chinese and French or between two subvarieties of English used by neighboring families" (Weinreich, 1963).

With the coming of "freedom" in the nineteenth century, double-consciousness became a serious and pervasive threat to the Black community and the coherent development of Black personality. Concomitantly, linguistic push-pull became pronounced and created fundamental questions about Black language and culture. As long as a slave was still a *slave*; as long as a Black person, whether slave or free, had, like Dred Scott, no rights, legal or otherwise, which a "white man was bound to respect" (Dred Scott court case, 1856); and finally, as long as White English was primarily spoken by and thus generally associated only with the oppressor, circumstance and psychology ensured the existence of large numbers of Black English speakers and kept linguistic double-consciousness at a minimal level.

The Emancipation Proclamation of 1862 and the American Civil War—fought, as many of the slaves believed, on their behalf—opened up new vistas and possibilities as a people released from bondage dreamed of being absorbed into and accepted by the country built on the blood, agony, and unpaid-for sweat of their ancestors. Leading up to these events, Frederick Douglass and other Black leaders of the nineteenth century had soundly rejected the goals of the American colonization movement to solve the problem of slavery by resettling the slaves in parts of West Africa. History notes that even Abraham Lincoln—who is revered for having "freed" the slaves—staunchly supported this movement as a way to avert the impending Civil War between the Northern and Southern capitalist classes vying for power over the American political economy. History also notes that those

American Blacks who bought the trick bag of nineteenth-century back-to-Africa resettlement established the colony of Liberia, which, with the 1980 coup by indigenous Liberians, has now freed itself from the capitalist dominance of the expatriated, formerly-enslaved Black Americans (the so-called Americo-Liberians).

The reconstruction years and the creation of the Freedmen's Bureau to assist ex-slaves (suddenly "displaced" by freedom) saw the election of ex-slaves to political office throughout the American South and saw the legalization and institutionalization of Black education on a mass level. However, with the abrupt end of Reconstruction, Blacks had to face the two great betrayals of American freedom—one educationally related, the other economically based.

The first betrayal was the failure to receive land or any other material compensation for the nearly 300 years of free African labor on American soil. With no resources, the freed men and women were ruthlessly thrown into the labor market; but education came to the rescue. Although reneging on its promise of forty acres and a mule, America was willing to offer literacy because the demands of an emerging technological society, on the brink of becoming a world superpower, required literate workers—though not small landowners who would threaten the developing alignment of the southern master class with northern capitalists (Bond, 1966).

The literacy programs came in the form of private and publicly supported *Black* "separate but equal" educational institutions, which rapidly began to rival indigenous Black community institutions (e.g., the family, the church) in the socialization of Black youth. As Carter Woodson (1969 [1936]) tells us, the education was always away from—not toward—Black culture, language, and community. In surveying nearly fifty years of Black education, Woodson (1933) noted that

> In the study of language in school pupils were made to scoff at the Negro dialect as some peculiar possession of the Negro which they should despise rather than directed to study the background of this language as a broken down African tongue—in short to understand their own linguistic history, which is certainly more important for them than the study of French Phonetics, or Historical Spanish Grammar.

This continues to be the dominant linguistic value paradigm in American education, which creates intensive sociolinguistic conflict in the schools (McGinnis and Smitherman, 1978) and persists despite sustained support for and use of Black language among Black artists, musicians, writers, preachers, politicians, doctors, lawyers, Ph.D.s, domestic workers, factory laborers, students and plain everyday people functioning in the Black community (Taylor, 1975; Smith, 1972; Wolfram, 1969; Mitchell, 1970, 1975; Kochman, 1972; Smitherman, 1973a, 1973b; Fasold and Shuy, 1970; McWorter, 1969).

THE DOUGLASS-DuBOIS-WOODSON LEGACY

In the tradition of Frederick Douglass, W.E.B. DuBois and Carter G. Woodson, Black linguists, social scientists, educators, and others inspired by the Black intellectual tradition have used the tools of their training to aid Black people in our liberation struggles. Of course, this has not been characteristic of *all* members of DuBois' "talented tenth" (the upper 10% best educated, best trained of the Blacks), many of whom have gone the way of the colonized petit bourgeoisie elsewhere, aiding and abetting the oppression of their people. Nonetheless, there has been a historically persistent thread of resistance and rejection of the values of capitalist culture by America's Black intelligentsia. One of the fronts on which this struggle has been consistently waged has been American courts.

My own work and research in this area has combined the scholarship of linguistics and the law. My experience began in 1969 with the case of a revolutionary Black attorney, and climaxed in the victorious federal ruling in the King case a decade later. In between, there were several less highly publicized court cases in which I conducted sociolinguistic research to construct legal arguments on behalf of Black plaintiffs. Each case involved an attempt to use principles of language and law to effect social change. I shall here discuss only the King case.

The King case called attention to the failure of American education to bring Blacks "up from slavery." Indeed, literacy efforts of American schools are succeeding, as Margaret Mead put it (referring to a different but highly similar social situation) only in making the "preliterate illiterate."

The case of *Martin Luther King Junior Elementary School children v. Ann Arbor School District Board* was, on one level, a language case. On a more fundamental level, *King* and the ruling legitimizing Black English and affirming the legal obligation of school districts to educate Black children was about the literacy and, thus, the survival of Black people in the most technologically advanced capitalist state in the modern world. As the white judge, Charles W. Joiner (1979) himself said,

> It is a straight-forward effort to require the court to intervene on the children's behalf to require the defendant School District Board to take appropriate action to teach them to read in the standard English of the school, the commercial world, the arts, sciences and professions. This action is a cry for judicial help in opening the doors to the establishment. ... It is an action to keep another generation from becoming functionally illiterate.

To be functionally illiterate in twenty-first-century America is, in fact, to be doomed.

Briefly, the background facts of *King* are as follows. On July 28, 1977, attorneys Gabe Kaimowitz and Kenneth Lewis of Michigan Legal Services filed suit in Eastern District Court, located in Detroit, on behalf of fifteen Black, economically deprived children residing in low-income housing on Green Road in Ann Arbor. By the time the case came to trial in the summer of 1979, one family with four children had moved out of the school district, leaving eleven plaintiff children to litigate the case. I served as the chief consultant and expert witness for the children during the two years of litigation and the four weeks of trial. The case, which aroused national and international attention, was featured in more than three dozen national and local television and radio shows and occasioned more than 300 articles in the national, international, and local press.

Ironically, the so-called Black English case did not begin as a language case. Although the possibility of a language barrier was alluded to as a part of the legislative provision used to frame the issues, the original complaint did not emphasize the language matter as an issue of litigation. And this was certainly not the concern of the mothers, most of whom headed single-parent families receiving public assistance. Their complaint was that their children, over several years, had not learned to read. Further, the children continued to experience academic and behavioral problems at Martin Luther King School, where Black children formed thirteen percent of the school population, which consisted predominantly of white, upper-class children.

School officials had persuaded the parents that their children should be placed in learning disability classes and other types of special classes for slow learners and retarded children. Owing to their use of Black English, some of the children were assigned to speech pathology classes. Yet, neither the language pathology instruction nor any of the special education instruction provided the solution. In fact, some of the children performed even more poorly academically than they had when they were in regular classes. The mothers knew that their children were normal, intelligent kids who could learn if taught properly.

Initially, our legal argument in *King* was based on the failure of the school system to recognize and make adjustments for the fact that the cultural, economic, and social backgrounds of the Black children differed critically from the white, middle-class orientation of American education. These claims were dismissed by Judge Joiner; there are constitutional guarantees around the question of race, but not class. In Joiner's reasoning, then, it was necessary to focus the issues in *King* on a legal, if decidedly narrow, set of arguments. Dismissing all of the plaintiff's claims except one, he forced the lawsuit to be tried solely on 1703(f) of the Equal Educational Opportunity Act, which reads in part,

> No state shall deny equal educational opportunity to an individual on account of his race, color, sex, or national origin, by...the failure to overcome language barriers that impede equal participation by its students in its instructional programs.

Restricting the case to the issue of language barriers, Joiner instructed us to specify the nature of the barriers, the lack of appropriate action to overcome them, and the resulting denial of educational opportunity based on race.

Yet, the concerns of these children could be addressed solely on the basis of race; their use of Black English set them apart from their Black middle-class peers at King School who were fluent in both Black and White English, such bilingualism being both a racial and class marker. While Judge Joiner ruled against our introducing issues of culture, economics, and class into the case, asserting that such issues were "irrelevant under the language barrier statute," it is in fact virtually impossible to discuss the linguistic, educational, and literacy—hence survival—crises of Black English speakers without discussion of culture, class, and race. Thus, it was inevitable that such commentary was reintroduced in expert witness testimony, in portions of the *Complaint*, and in the discourse of national debate on the Black English case.

The critical issues of whether Black English is a language or dialect and whether the problems are tied to class or race were at the heart of the Ann Arbor case. To the popular mind, languages have high social status, dialects do not; languages identify nations; dialects do not. Calling a variety of language a "language," rather than a "dialect," brings that variety more respect. Were there available a body of literature and research on Black English from socially constituted and dialectical paradigms, there would be no way, legally or socially, to separate the issue of Black English from cultural, social, and economic issues; and it would be viewed as a language.

It is not a question of Cartesian *or* socially constituted linguistics, but of *both*. Cartesian linguistics should become an integral dimension of a holistic conception of language, and deep structure should thus be redefined as the sociolinguistic construction of reality. Or, as I put it in my Latinate Black English, *Dico, ergo, I bees*. To resolve the Black English language-dialect controversy—and, hence, to further our understanding of class and race dynamics in American life—requires that we shift from what has deteriorated into a narrow paradigm of knowledge and science to an epistemology and cosmology that sees all of life, reality and knowledge as a system interacting and moving in dialectical progression. When Black English speakers be talkin and testifyin, we jes say, "Everything is everything," and that takes care of it.

Further, with a dialectical language model, we would be able to neutralize the negative reaction from the Black middle class and enlist their aid in devising legal, linguistic, and educational policies to effect social change (Smitherman and McGinnis, 1977). The Black middle class, you see, is plagued by the research answers given to the late poet Sarah Webster Fabio's question: "Who speaks Negro?" As defined by the narrow empiricism of most descriptions of Black English, the answer to Fabio's question becomes, only nonliterate, poor Blacks caricatured by "who dat say who dat when I bees sayin who dat?" (Smitherman and Daniel, 1979). Yet, "speaking Negro" is more than eight or ten features of morphosyntax or cuss words. It is the expression of the sum total of the African experience and struggle on the North American continent. It is a sociolinguistic construction of reality manifested by virtually the entire Black American community—this includes poets and professors; preachers and pimps; reverends and revolutionaries.

As a federal ruling, then, the *King* decision could have implications across school districts throughout America. Yet, although it established a precedent, subsequent litigation will be needed to push the language-dialect and class-race issues forward (Smitherman, 1981).

The contention here is that the merger of linguistics and the law is a potential instrument of social change. However, no claim is being made that the nature of the judicial process in itself is revolutionary. Rather, court cases such as *King* are social catalysts that raise up the glaring contradictions in American society and create arenas for debate on critical issues of political economy.

Of course, on one level, the initial victory in *King* is that the research and scholarship tradition on Black English has been written into U.S. law and is now a matter of federal court record. But the broader social victory is the arousal of national consciousness and concern, especially in the Black community, about the educational welfare of Black America's children and, hence, the development of future Black leaders. Thousands of Black children and youth throughout America have been failed by the same educational system, which after the Civil War so quickly took up the cause of Black literacy in order to supply a technological capitalist economy with the necessary literate labor pool. Now a hundred years later, U.S. monopolistic imperialist capitalism is faced with a changing world economic order—dwindling markets abroad and a surplus labor force at home. Thus, there is no real effort by the American state to stem the tide of Black functional illiterates being produced by the nation's schools. From the perspective of the state, this is as it should be. After all, if the niggers become literate, they just might read the handwriting on the wall.

NOTE

1. For this feature of language use in Black English, Dalby (1969, 1972) cites linguistic parallels in Mandingo and several other African languages. His work remains the most rigorous treatment of the lexicosemantic system of Black Language from a diachronic perspective. See also Dillard (1977) and Major (1970).

6

LANGUAGE AND POWER IN THE FAMILY*

Susan Ervin-Tripp, Mary Catherine O'Connor, and Jarrett Rosenberg

IN FAMILY LIFE, as in other face-to-face situations, the actions of other people sometimes aid and sometimes collide with ours. For this reason, we are inevitably led to perform acts of control: offers, requests, orders, prohibitions, and other verbal moves that solicit goods or attempt to effect changes in the activities of others.

Any analysis of control and manipulation through language must deal with the fact that virtually all "control acts" have a dual nature, both social and utilitarian. The specific content of a control utterance may principally be an assertion of power over another (Mitchell-Kernan and Kernan, 1977). "Can you change the channel?" may really mean "Comply with my wishes." "I'm cold" may mean "Show concern for me." Other acts may have companionship as their goal, as does, at bedtime, "Mommy, get me a cracker." Such requests generally require that the other person be in a better position than the speaker to fulfill the act requested, but their primary goal is social. Utterances such as these could be called *person-centered control acts*.

At other times we have specific ends in which the services of others are means to goals we cannot easily accomplish ourselves ("Forceps please" and "Hand me that dishcloth"). These could be called *task-centered control acts*. Since even such utilitarian acts are intrusive on hearers, they too have social consequences; Brown and Levinson (1978) have claimed that all control acts are face-threatening—potentially destructive to the autonomy or the self-esteem of the listener.

Although the distinction between task-centered and person-centered is an important one, it is a difficult distinction to make.

---

*Work on this project has been funded by Grants MH 26063 and NSF BNS #7826539. The data collection and analysis owe a great deal to David Paul Gordon, Georgette Stratos, Ruth Bennett, Julie Gerhardt, Miriam Petruck, and Iskender Savasir.

Task-related purposes are easier to identify, since their goals are usually conscious and explicit, but almost all control acts have social meaning as well. In this chapter we will not be delving into questions of the internal nature of control acts or the intent of speakers in using them. We will be focusing primarily on the development of power relations in the family as expressed indirectly, through the use of control acts, by children eight years of age or under, within the context of family interactions. As such, we will be talking about the externally observable aspects of linguistic control acts: the form they take, who uses them, to whom they are addressed, and what results they reap.

One might ask how the use of linguistic control acts is reflective of power. In some sense, all kinds of power have in common one factor: the ability of the powerful person to control the goals and behavior of others. Thus, although a parent appears to have absolute power compared to a three-year-old child, we can easily find examples of that child controlling the parent, exerting power in the form of demanding the attention and goods to which a helpless dependent is entitled. All members of a family exert power over other members in some way; we have tried to examine how their relative power is expressed through language use.

CONCEPTUAL BASES

Effective Power

In this analysis, we shall distinguish between *effective power* and esteem. Effective power in face-to-face interaction is the ability to get compliance from an addressee. A powerful person gets what she says she wants. Does the possession of power in the economical and political system guarantee more effective power in verbal interaction? Face-to-face power, or the ability to gain compliance in conversational interaction, may be enhanced by the capacity to give rewards or by rights and obligations of the social system involved. On the other hand, addressee compliance can be affected by factors involving personal relationships; for example, the possibility of compliance may be increased if the control act occurs within a network in which past experience has present consequences, such as reciprocity or personal feelings of fear, love, or esteem. To complicate matters further, there are individual differences in the effectiveness of various strategies. Additionally, we can find instances of local power, when an individual who is low in real-world power nevertheless holds a position within a smaller system and is able to base requests and control acts on her status within the system. For example, children may expect a high level of compliance from care-givers when requesting goods and services due them.

A prerequisite to compliance is *attention*. Part of our measure of effective power is how much attention is paid to a speaker. Speakers low in effective power are less likely to be noticed and, because their moves are ignored, have to make special efforts to get the floor.

Esteem and Verbal Deference

Effective power can be investigated separately from what we will call "esteem" (which constitutes another kind of power). Esteem can be measured by analyzing the type and degree of compliance achieved, as we do in this study. A speaker who is high in esteem has the right to receive verbal deference from others and can make control moves boldly, without offering deference to those who are lower in esteem. There are three kinds of deference expressions by which we propose to measure the power revealed through the commanding of esteem in face-to-face interaction: overt marking, justifying, and allusion or hinting. In Labov and Fanshel's (1977) discussion of speech acts in a therapeutic context, these three types of deference are called "mitigations" because they seem to qualify the control act and soften its threat.

First is expressed deference, which indicates that the addressee is held in high esteem and is marked by the use of *overt marking* by conventional forms. These are often taught to children explicitly. It has been shown experimentally that when children are asked to be more polite, they add "please," and then move to conventional control frameworks like "Could you" or "Can I" (Bates, 1976; James, 1978).

The second type of expressed deference is *justifying*. The requester explains why the control act is necessary or is based on common norms (and is not just a power-grab): "Dad I'm gonna take your car because I might get mugged on the subway." Such justifications are also used by addressees in refusing control acts. If the addressee feels that the speaker is someone who must be held in high esteem, then an excuse or justification is called for: "I can't work late tonight. It's my husband's birthday and his mother is coming over, and ..."

The third type of expressed deference is *allusion* or *hinting*, in which the goal of the control act is not made explicit. "It's really chilly in here" can be a polite, covert way of asking someone to shut the window while still expressing esteem for them by giving them the choice of ignoring the implicit request. According to Ervin-Tripp (1976), hints are very common in some American solidary groups that share assumptions.

Both the ability to gain compliance with one's expressed wishes and the ability to elicit deferential behavior (or expressions of esteem) are evidence that a speaker has power of some sort. Of these two reflexes of power, should we consider the ability to command esteem the less important? It is a secondary consequence of real-world and effective power? We have all observed the kind of deference offered to those who wield a lot of social and/or economic power.

On the other hand, we have also probably observed the use of forms of deference to distract from economic inequity—a woman who has doors held open for her by male peers who earn fifty percent more than she does may become suspicious and resentful of the symbolic power that is being imputed to her. Such social behaviors as duels and other fanatic defenses of honor or face remind us that in some cases, mere symbols of prestige, honor, and group membership can command deep allegiance. What we do not know is whether the internal dynamic of real and effective power is regularly affected by symbolic relations such as expressions of esteem.

In this chapter we will examine how the development of effective power is related to the manipulation of expressions of esteem. By exploring early development in the family, we can see some of the background assumptions regarding status, sex, and deference that are learned very early.

Compliance and Resistance

In order to use compliance as a measure of effective power, we need to determine what factors will feed into a speaker's decision to comply with or refuse another speaker's control act. We can expect that compliance will not just be a result of the verbal control act or "asking nicely." Other factors may determine the outcome of an attempt at control to a greater extent than politeness will. These include the activity context, the nature of the request, and the relationship of the speakers.

The activity context within which the control act is performed will often determine how successful a speaker is in achieving compliance. When children are engaged in types of activities that require cooperation, as do cookie-making or role-playing, for instance, then compliance will be common. In other activities, such as choosing objects, roles, and territories for play, where they are competing for scarce resources and expressing dominace, the frequency of refusal will rise. When the speaker and the addressee have not been engaged in joint activity, or when the addressee is otherwise occupied, we can also expect the frequent refusal or ignoring of control moves. So we can expect that cooperative joint activity will facilitate compliance, and competitive joint activity or separate engagement will reduce compliance.

We have organized these and other factors that are likely to lead to resistance or noncompliance into a notional category called "cost." The four components of cost are *joint involvement* of speaker with addressee in activity or talk; *trajectory* of addressee's current activity (Is the request of speaker going to fit with the plans of the addressee?); *possession* of objects in question (Does the request refer to an object that is the addressee's?); and *authority* (Is the control act aimed at someone who has authority over the speaker in the current activity?).

Control acts are more likely to be resisted or have a "high cost" in the following circumstances:

(a) The control act interrupts the addressee's conversation.
(b) Compliance would undo the addressee's present or planned activity.
(c) The proposed good is expensive or the activity is difficult.
(d) The possessions at issue are owned by or in use by the addressee.
(e) A subordinate is trying to control someone in authority, beyond normal rights.

We expect that compliance will also be related to social factors such as solidarity and rank. In our study, age difference is the chief determinant of rank. We expect younger children to comply with older children more than the reverse, and we expect older children to have more power to capture attention. Since males have more power in the larger society, we expect that fathers may refuse more than mothers. In addition, mothers have the traditional family role of servants to their husbands and children. If this family role affects cooperativeness, we can expect mothers to respond more than female researchers to children's requests. Predictions from solidarity would also favor maternal cooperation, especially with girls. If mothers are expected to be helpful, will girls perceive females as agreeable, or docile, and therefore be more compliant than boys? Female roles would also lead to the prediction that in order to avoid explicit refusal, girls—and possibly mothers—would hedge, favoring passive aggression or the ignoring of requests.

The Development of Deference

In adult use of language, higher-cost requests often display more politeness in the form of deference, flattery, or allusions to solidarity between speaker and hearer (Brown and Levinson, 1978; Ervin-Tripp, 1976); in short, the petitioner pays for the higher cost in terms of symbolic power. Just as low-status persons in society must have more experience or education to get the same pay, so in face-to-face interaction, the petitioner's status can require that higher symbolic payments be made in order to get compliance. We can ask several questions about the expression of deference on the part of children in the family. First, we can ask how children eventually acquire the system: What factors are important in provoking the use of deference or the expression of esteem? We can expect developmental differences in the types of forms learned and in the social features to which the children are sensitive.

We expect that of the three forms of symbolic payment, formal marking will be learned first, both because it is explicitly taught and because it is conventionally correlated with social features. Justifying and explaining, which involve analysis of the addressee's motives, will be learned second. Finally, indirection or avoidance of mentioning the goal of the control act will become deliberate in the older children.

In being more polite in making high-cost demands, we expect that younger children will be more sensitive to the cost factors of relative authority and possession rather than to trajectory and involvement, since the latter two call for more awareness of the perspective of the conversational partner. In terms of social features, we anticipate that the obvious features of relative age and familiarity will be important. As adults, researchers and parents will be high in esteem, and deference to them will be greatest; older children will receive more deference than younger ones. On the grounds of distance versus familiarity, we expect fathers and researchers to receive more deference than mothers.

Further, we can ask why children learn to be more deferent to their seniors and to be more deferent in framing higher-cost requests. They could learn to express deference and esteem through positive or negative reinforcement. If the child learns by reinforcement, then it is likely either that the child succeeds more often by being deferent for higher-cost requests or that the child is praised or rebuked for the form used. Family instruction is usually limited to "please" in English-speaking families, and occasionally to "May I" and other idioms that we consider to constitute formal marking. Thus, the other forms of deference—justifications and implicit suggestions—are not explicitly taught. These must be learned either by positive reinforcement (by being more effective) or by modeling (the child identifying with and imitating the others). In the theory of modeling and identification, learning occurs because of secondary reinforcement or the pleasure of sounding and acting like loved, admired, or powerful models. We can test the hypothesis of greater effectiveness by examining our data. If we find that learning cannot be explained by greater compliance with or attention to deferential forms, then we are left with implicit modeling as an explanation, for which we cannot—from these data—provide further tests.

Research on Deference

Two recent studies of children's role-playing illustrate that children are aware of symbolic power and manipulate the forms associated with high- or low-status roles in order to establish dominant and submissive relationships between the "characters" in their role-play. Mitchell-Kernan (1969) asked Black American children, aged 7 to 12 years, to role-play scenes using puppets. The only constraints were provided by the puppets available. In the role-playing, the symbolic contrast between superordinates and subordinates was clearly marked linguistically, both in the frequency of orders given to subordinate characters by their superiors and in the form selected for these orders. Addressees who were lower in rank than the speaker received over five times as many directives as those who were higher in rank.[1] Within this set of control acts, the children directed imperatives to Subordinates eight times as often as to Superordinates. Subordinates did use imperatives to Superordinates, but only in circumstances of pleading, high emotion, or tension.

A more structured role-play study by Elaine Andersen (1977) asked white, middle-class children, aged 4 to 7, to enact family scenes using puppets. The roles of Father, Mother, and Baby gave us role-play analogues of our family scenes. As in the Kernan's study, one indication of relative power was the frequency of directives. As the age of the participant children increased, and presumably their sensitivity to the power relations in the family increased, they had the puppet Mothers produce fewer directives when addressing the Fathers. In the play of the oldest group of children, the Husband gave more than twice as many directives to the Wife as the reverse.

Besides reflecting status through different frequency of speech-act types, Andersen found that the children were sensitive to and used formal variations, as well. There were more imperative commands from puppet Parents to Children than from Children to Parents. The Children's directives to Parents took the form of statements of desire ("I want a cookie") and used explicit mitigating markers such as question forms ("Could you get me a cookie?") and *Let's* forms ("Let's play" versus "Play with me"). Interestingly, the Mother and the Father—though both high-status adults—were treated differently, and this difference was reflected even in the role-play of the earliest age group. The Child puppet addressed six times as many imperatives to Mothers as to Fathers, and eight times as many "Let's" (solidarity-evoking, mitigating) forms to the Fathers as to the Mothers.

This difference ties in several of the parameters we've discussed so far. One explanation for the high number of nonpolite imperatives to the Mother is that the Mother's real-life role is typically one of providing for all the daily needs of the Child. As a result, requests for her will be lower in cost, at least with respect to the trajectory of her action. Since her role is one of care-giving at all times, requests for care cannot be considered a major intrusion or unusual demand, as they might be toward the Father. In addition, in Andersen's data, the puppet Husbands were less polite and ordered the Wives around more than the reverse, so children using parents as models evidently see the mother as being held in lower esteem (Andersen, 1977: 99).

Other studies, summarized in Ervin-Tripp (1977) and Becker (1982) have shown that by the age of 2½ years, children are sensitive to variation in social features governing the use of polite forms. But none of the researchers has controlled cost by closely analyzing age, sex, and familiarity as factors affecting compliance and deference in naturalistic settings.

DATA BASE AND METHOD

We chose four cooperative middle-class families with 2 or 3 children between the ages of 2 and 8 for videotaping naturalistic interaction over a period of more than a year. Table 6.1 shows the age and sex distribution of the children in the families. Since the families were not selected for distribution of sexes among peers, there is an imbalance in the sample, which limits the number of utterances that can be compared with respect to differences balanced for age *and* sex. In addition to interaction with siblings and parents, we included child visitors and researchers. The transcripts coded for this chapter were chosen for the diversity of the interactants' ages. From 10,000 utterances transcribed in this sample, 891 control acts by children were coded. These were unambiguous attempts to alter the behavior of one or more addressees. For purpose of the cost analysis, we had to remove some ambiguous cases; in analyses of compliance we also removed unclear-results cases (for example, when the response was

TABLE 6.1 Ages of Children During Study Span

Family A	Family B	Family C	Family D
Female 7;3–7;8	Female 6;3–6;9	Female 3;11–5;0	Male 4;2–4;10
Female 5;7–6;0	Male 4;6–5;0	Male 2;9–3;10	Female 2;4–3;0
Female 3;9–4;2	Female 2;2–2;8	Female 1;3–2;4	Female Infant

off-camera or ambiguous). As a result, the numbers vary on different tables.

RESULTS

Getting Attention

The first problem to be solved in a successful control maneuver is to get attention. We found that younger children were more often ignored when they attempted to get the attention of someone who was already engaged in talk with another person. When children over 4½ interrupted for reasons considered to be irrelevant by the addressee, they were ignored 79 percent of the time; when younger children did the same thing, they were ignored 94 percent of the time. Even when they interrupted for reasons considered to be relevant, the younger children were ignored 83 percent of the time (Ervin-Tripp, 1979).

The tendency of older speech partners to ignore children is exacerbated by the children's failure to seek the floor before speaking. As children get older, their strategies for breaking into a conversation change. They use a wider range of verbal attention forms ("Hey Sandy"; "Lookit"), and they use more of them. Of 2-year-olds' control moves to already busy addressees, 89 percent were made without getting the attention of the addressee first. This ineffective behavior decrease with age: 78 percent of the children at age 3 and 31 percent at ages 5 to 8 failed to use an attention form to seek the floor when the addressee was not attending to them.

Getting Compliance

The major factors in gaining compliance, which are shown in Table 6.2, are the cost of the request and the status of the addressee. These factors interact. The parents—chiefly the mother—cooperated regardless of cost; even for high-cost requests they complied over half the time. Researchers and the children themselves were highly sensitive

TABLE 6.2 Compliance by Cost and Addressee Type (percentages)

Addressee:	Child			Parent			Researcher		
Cost Level:	Low	Med	High	Low	Med	High	Low	Med	High
Response:									
Comply	50	47	23	48	55	55	54	35	25
Refuse	26	30	58	42	24	24	29	54	71
Ignore	24	23	19	10	21	21	11	11	4
N	92	64	73	31	85	41	35	37	24

to the cost, to the nature of the act requested, and to its fit with ongoing activity.

The most important determinant of compliance besides cost was relative age. Older children were significantly more likely to refuse or ignore the control acts of younger children than the reverse ($p < .01$, $N = 528$). Overall, younger children complied with 47 percent of the control moves of children of different ages, while the older children complied with only 27 percent of such moves. We can see this difference in effective power even more clearly if we look at elliptical control acts: those consisting of only a noun or an adverb. In these cases the speaker is clearly not trying to be carefully persuasive, but the younger children complied with 60 percent of these moves, compared with 27 percent compliance by the older children in response to younger ones.

In examining effects of sex on compliance, we restricted the set of utterances used to those performed by children aged 3 and 4. This was the age group with a relatively balanced sex ratio, so that age was not a confounding factor in our results (although, of course, the sample is smaller). First, we found that in their tendencies to comply with control moves, mothers were biased by the sex of the speaker. Although they ignored requests from both boys and girls at roughly the same rate—about 15 percent of the time—mothers complied with the control acts of girls 55 percent of the time, while boys got compliance for only 10 percent of their utterances. They boys were refused 73 percent of their requests. (See Table 6.3.)

It was also the case that male and female children used different strategies in response to control moves by other children. Although their noncompliance rates were similar, boys almost always chose either to comply or to refuse—refusing to comply with the control acts of others 53 percent of the time and ignoring only 16 percent of the re-

TABLE 6.3 Sex Differences in Response Strategies at Ages 3 and 4 (percentages)

Response Strategy	Female Addressee	Male Addressee
Ignore	33	16
Refuse	35	54
Comply	31	32
N	83	51

quests. Girls refused only 35 percent of the requests directed to them, ignoring 33 percent (compared with the boy's use of this strategy, which amounted only to 16 percent).

Age Changes in Forms of Deference

Deference is expressed in different ways by children of different ages. We predicted that there would be a change in the use of different forms with increasing age; first explicit markers would be learned, then mitigating explanations, and last, hints.

(1) The earliest common deferent forms were "please," permission questions, and polite requests, such as "Can I" or "Could you" followed by a specification of the goods and services wanted. Permission questions accounted for about the same percentage of control utterances at all ages, but polite requests and the use of "please" decrease with age. In all, these politeness markers, which adults explicitly teach their children, dropped from 78 percent of mitigated forms at ages 2 and 3, to 39 percent at 4, and 43 percent from 5 to 8.

(2) Children aged 2 and 3 provided explanations or justifications for only six percent of their control utterances, whereas older children added them to about 14 percent of theirs. Only 22 percent of the deferential control moves of the children aged 2 to 3 included explanations, whereas 52 percent of the older children's deferential utterances did. Functionally, explanations seem partially to replace formal politeness markers for the children aged 4 and over.

(3) Although hints may convey the same information as justifications, they omit the explicit request or order. Overall in our sample, the children's speech was highly explicit. Unlike adults, they rarely used hints or inexplicit control acts as a major part of their control methods; in only 7 percent of their acts was the purpose hidden. In the

age range we sampled, the percentage of hints among all deferential forms did not change, remaining at around 14-17 percent.

Deference, Status of Addressee, and Cost

To whom were the children deferent? At ages 2 and 3, they deferred mainly to the researchers, who received polite forms 60 percent of the time. For parents, the ratio dropped to 10 percent, while for other children it varied from 14 percent to 24 percent. The children aged 5 to 8 displayed a conventional pattern of differentiation; adults received more polite forms than children, and other children more than younger ones. As a group, the 4-year-olds displayed no consistent pattern of contrast, although some individual ones followed the older children's patterns. When we grouped together all moves toward parents, we found that children used significantly more imperatives to mothers than to fathers. In addition, more mitigating explanations were added to requests addressed to fathers ($p < .01$, $N = 109$).

But were they sensitive to the cost? We had argued that some aspects of cost, such as the consideration of whose property was at stake, would be reflected in deferent forms. Even 2-and 3-year-olds made such a distinction. If they wanted a child addressee's goods, they chose polite forms 44 percent of the time, but these forms were chosen only 9 percent of the time when neutral goods were involved. They were rarely polite to parents, with requests involving the parents' possessions being the only incidents occasioning deferent usage. They were much less sensitive to the cost of a request in terms of the hearer's proposed activities and present actions, and they seemed oblivious to whether or not the hearer was already engaged in conversation.

By ages 5 to 8, these children were aware of the listener's activities to a greater extent: They were polite only 12 percent of the time in the context of activities in which the listener was already cooperating, but 54 percent of the time when the request would interrupt the listener. Higher cost led to more deference, to a reduction from 60 percent to 27 percent of the use of impolite imperatives, but also to an increase in statements of desire or need, which the children may consider explanatory or persuasive justification.

Deference and Compliance

Finally, we examined the question of the interaction between the use of deference and addressee compliance (Table 6.4). We considered

TABLE 6.4 Adults' Responses to Polite and Nonpolite Control Forms (percentages)

	Ignore	Refuse	Comply
Polite form	.04*	.50	.46
Nonpolite form	.20*	.43	.36

*Difference p < .001.
Polite: Polite questions, permission forms, explanations or justifications, implicit questions or statements of consequences (N = 80).
Nonpolite: Imperatives, cries, gestures, ellipsis, "I want, I need" (N = 168).

the following forms to be polite or deferent: any request that was accompanied by an explanation or justification; explicit question prefixes such as "May I" or "Can you"; and implicit questions and statements, whose indirect, hinting character renders them deferential.

When factors such as relative age and cost were held constant, *we found no increase in compliance in response to deference.* For example, in the group aged 5 to 8, who appeared most socialized to the issue of cost and to the conventional patterns of deference, *all* the polite requests from peers were ignored or refused, regardless of costs. The more polite requests used by 4-year-olds to researchers (including those that were explicitly polite and those that contained justifications or explanations) were refused more often than they were successful.

Although we found no significant increase in compliance with the use of polite forms, we did find a behavioral result that we consider extremely important. In virtually all cases, adults *did not ignore* requests that were polite in form.

DISCUSSION: COMPLIANCE

Getting Attention

The first problem of a successful control maneuver is to get attention. Younger children were ignored more often than older ones when they attempted to get the attention of someone who was already engaged in talk with another person. Some of the problem can be attributed to the younger children's inability to follow conversations. Although we found that young children can appropriately alternate turns when talking with peers, they do not recognize the appropriate points at which to interrupt older speakers because these conversations are not adapted to their level. Thus they miss the gaps and topic changes in the conversation where they could successfully break in, and their interruptions are often delayed replies to what went earlier.

Even when young children's interruptions were relevant, they were ignored at a rate greater than that for older children. At least part of this effect is due to their lack of control over attention-getting devices. However, no matter how pertinent or well-timed a younger's point may be, the odds are greater that the young will be seen and not heard. In terms of power to gain attention, the effects of age are very strong.

Other researchers' findings can augment our conclusion about the correlation between power difference and age. Wood and Gardner (1980) have found that in addition to power based on age, power based on social dominance is a consistent determinant of compliance in the interactions of children. They asked nursery school teachers to make judgments about the relative social power of the children in their classes. Using these judgments, they established dyads and observed the ensuing interaction. They found that fewer than one-third of the responses by dominant members of a dyad were compliant. The compliance rate between equals was 50 percent, but the most interesting finding, for our purposes, was that the subordinate members of the dyads complied at a much greater rate than the dominant members, when age was held constant. In older pairs, subordinates complied with 74 percent of the dominants' control moves, while in younger pairs, subordinates complied with 91 percent.

Cost and Status

The major factors in compliance, as shown in Table 6.2, are cost of request and social distance of addressee. These factors interact. For example, parents in these observations are very compliant, regardless of our estimate of the cost of the demand. Mothers, who constitute the bulk of the parent audiences, may have been sensitive to the demands of their care-giver role. They were expected by the children to collaborate in the child-organized role-play scenes, and they were perhaps more cooperative because they were before the camera. However, our finding of high compliance in the mother's case seems to be more than an observational artifact. The children recognize and use the fact that mothers in their culture are supposed to be responsive to their wants and discomfort, since they routinely use their assertions of helplessness or of their wants as means of getting mothers to comply, even under conditions of high cost. This assumption—that mothers are there to provide for one's needs—may explain the following attempt by a seven-year-old to gain his mother's compliance with a request: "If you don't give some now, I won't want any later." This strange utterance would function as a threat only in a social situation where the mother is assumed to derive benefit from fulfilling the care giver role. In some sense, this makes our dimensions of cost irrelevant in some cases of mother-child interaction. A request that would be high-cost if addressed to a researcher may be part of a mother's normal trajectory of activity. (The researchers complied less than the parents. Since they were often confronted with requests to use their camera equipment, they refused at a high rate.)

Our analysis of cost—our expectations of how it would contribute to the rate of compliance—was borne out to some extent by these data. Both adults and children gave behavioral responses that seemed sensitive to whether or not the control move they were responding to involved their possessions or disrupted their ongoing activity. The children's own views of cost became apparent in their justifications and excuses. Possessions, as we expected, were an important element. Children's inclusion of minimizers such as "just a little" in their requests suggests an awareness of cost in terms of difficulty. Our evidence suggests that the notion of intrusion, which involves awareness of what the other is doing or planning, is acquired later than sensitivity to possessions.

Compliance and Sex Differences

We found a sex difference in parent responsiveness: mothers were more cooperative with the demands of girls than of boys. We are dealing with a small group—four mothers only. But if this difference is confirmed in larger studies, we may be seeing evidence of sexual alliance formation in families.

What can we make of the sex differences in children's behavioral responses to others? At first glance, the finding that boys refuse more requests than girls do might lead us to expect that the girls were being more compliant in general. However, the real importance of the finding lies not in the fact that boys refuse more than girls, but that girls ignore others as much as they refuse or comply, thereby using a wider range of response strategies than boys, while not complying any more frequently than did the boys. Again, our sample is small, but if it is confirmed, we may see early evidence of the contrast Sutton-Smith (1979) and others have noted in play groups. He comments that boys' groups involve more struggles for dominance and explicit arguments (corresponding to our refusals), whereas girls are more concerned with inclusion/exclusion (in our sample, attention versus ignoring).

DISCUSSION: ESTEEM AND DEFERENCE

Age Changes in the Form of Deference

Our predictions as to the order of acquisition of different polite forms were partly borne out. Explicit permission questions and polite forms were used by even the youngest children. The use of justification as a mitigating device increased markedly in children after the age of four. Hints, or inexplicit control acts, are used infrequently and may just reflect children's lack of focus on problems or goals rather than on explicit means.

Use of Deference
Determined by Addressee

We confirm that children are, from a very early age, sensitive to social features of their relationships with their addressees. Two findings in particular support this hypothesis. First, children address significantly different forms to mothers and fathers. Children use the less polite imperative to their mothers, while using more mitigating explanations to fathers. Interestingly, this finding parallels Andersen's 1977 role-play results, in which children had the Child puppet use more polite forms to the Father puppets than to the Mothers. At the time of Andersen's study it was not clear whether this pattern was a reflection of the child's conception of role stereotypes or of a pattern of use found in real family interaction. However, the results of our study show that the mother and father may, indeed, elicit different types of control-act behavior from children.

The second finding that bears on the question of children's awareness of the social features of their addressees concerns their use of justifications. All the children used justifications, although their use definitely increased with age. Although the form of the justification was the same in all cases (a supporting statement issued right before or after the control act), we noted an interesting difference in the content of the explanations, depending on the relationship to the speaker. When addressing an adult, either a parent or the researcher, the child would use supporting information that evoked the care-giver role in the adult. Beth, 5 years, to mother:

> Mommy, I want you to open all of them—the paint, so I won't have to have trouble.

Lisa, 4 years, to researcher:

> OK, we can't know all these pages, so you read 'em.

By referring to their own inadequacies, the children were clearly appealing to the superior abilities of their caretaker, and they clearly considered the statement of the contrast in abilities enough of a justification to mitigate the request.

Explanations or justifications used to younger speakers, on the other hand, centered on a reason for the addressee's compliance that did not refer to the addressee's role vis-à-vis the speaker. Instead, reference was made to a behavioral norm that must be satisfied, a goal the child may expect if she complied, or a fact about the world that should guide her decision. As such, these justifications serve an informing, socializing function. Ellen, 8 years, to Beth, 5 years:

> Beth? Don't do that. That water is too fast to water those plants. And don't pee on the grass.

Ann, 8 years, to Caren, 4 years:

> We have only a little more, OK? So don't use one on every Valentine.

Ellen, 8 years, to Beth, 5 years:

> Catch that fly so we can squish it up.

Lisa, 4 years, to Saul, 2 years:

> Get out of my space. This is *my* space.

Thus, by the age that justifications are used, children have internalized nuances of social structure that go beyond simple status categories to norms and expectations for their occupants.

The Use of Deference and the Cost of a Control Act

The following exchange is between Saul (S), 3 years, and an adult female researcher, Patty (P), during a morning taping session. It illustrates how forms and strategies can be influenced by cost, relative status, and perceived role.

S: Hey, I'm hungry.
P: Didn't you eat your breakfast?
S: No, I didn't. I just go to bed, and I want to eat. I'm hungry.
P: You're hungry.
S: Could you get me something to eat?
P: No I can't. You have to ask your mom.
S: Well, Momma won't give me something.
P: (Laughing) Well, why not?
S: Because he ... he ... won't fix me anything.
P: Doesn't she usually?
S: No. Do you have a lot of cake at your house?

Saul starts out the exchange as though Patty were a regular care giver and, thus, should be expected to fulfill his needs. He simply states his need: "I'm hungry." To make sure that she attends to his request, he prefaces the need statement with the attention bid of "Hey." When Patty does not immediately provide him with food, he responds with a justification for the implicit request, centering mainly on his needs: He wants to eat, he is hungry. If she is to respond to this sort of request, she will be responding as a care giver who is attuned to his needs. She evades the issue. Saul responds with a direct, but more polite request ("Could you ..?"). It is obvious that this request is higher in cost than he thought, or else Patty is not a member of the same class of care givers as is his mother. She refused his direct request and redirects him to the real care giver, who is obviously in charge of food. Saul answers this by claiming that his mother will not fulfill his needs in this area. Patty laughs at this attempt to cast aspersions on his mother's ability or willingness to fulfill the care-giving role, and in the next few utterances probes Saul on the issue to get him to spell out his improbable argument. Finally, Saul retreats to an indirect hinting form. Although this is a matter of interpretation, the formulaic utterance "Do you have any (cake, cookie, M&M's)?" often brings a positive response from adults who are primary care givers, whereas it is not likely to work with Mom.

Deference and Compliance

What can we conclude about the acquisition of politeness from these data? Surprisingly, the polite requests were the *least* successful at each cost level. This suggests, at least, that politeness cannot be learned from immediate reinforcement of the type that we might expect—that is, from a higher rate of compliance with one's requests.

One of the ironies of politeness is that it can be heard as an admission of speaker's evaluation of the request. Seen from this angle, we might expect that an assertive stance would succeed more frequently and would, therefore, predict a functional decoupling of deference and compliance. However, children do continue to produce more polite forms (as well as more types of polite forms) with age; Bates (1976) shows that children from an early age believe polite forms should be more effective.

One explanation is suggested by our finding that polite control acts are virtually never ignored by adults. They thus differ significantly from other utterances in terms of the attention paid to them by adults. This must explain at least part of the motivation for using polite forms, and it may represent the principal force toward the acquisition of politeness.

It is possible that peers' greater compliance with polite requests (Wood and Gardner, 1980) outweighs inefficacy in the family. Another alternative is to propose that deference is learned, at least partially, because it sounds appropriate, despite its lack of efficacy in getting one's way. There are long-term and subtle payoffs to sounding like a member of one's group, at whatever level. Adults may not be more likely to grant a high-cost request, even if the child "asks nicely," but in the long run their estimate of the child's social knowledge and level of maturity will be affected, with consequences that may not appear in specific day-to-day interactions such as these.

The proposal that sounding like a competent speaker is highly motivating is not new; it has been the most favored explanation for the mastery of nuances of correctness in first and second language learning. In this domain, as in the area of politeness, differential effect alone does not seem to account for learning (Brown et al., 1969).

CONCLUSIONS

We have examined power and deference displays in the natural interaction of family members by isolating children's attempts to control others—researchers, parents, siblings, and friends. Effective power and esteem were related to age in this sample. Children aged 2 and 3 had learned formal politeness markers and were selectively deferential in addressing requests to unfamiliar or older people and for borrowing possessions. The older children (who received more deference and compliance from younger children) began to take into account the preoccupations of addressees, gaining attention before proceeding, scaling up deference to those who were busy or would be disturbed by cooperating, tuning justification to the hearer's beliefs and knowledge.

What brings about these changes? Though the adults, especially the mothers, were more attentive to polite control moves, neither they nor other children were any more compliant with them. We propose that the learning of deference in families such as those in our sample may be based on identification with models and social attention rather than on efficacy.

The mothers in our sample were an important exception to the pattern of power and esteem correlating with age. In their role as care givers, they received nondeferent orders, suggesting that the children expected compliance and believed their desires to be justification enough. They were right; the mothers cooperated, even when the tasks were difficult or intrusive.

One might expect that because of this pattern, girls (in copying their mother's behaviors) would be more cooperative than boys. In our sample, this was not the case. Instead, girls used the strategy of refusing less openly, ignoring rather than refusing outright to comply with requests. Interestingly, the mothers cooperated more with their daughters than with their sons. Though based on a small sample, these findings suggest many areas of family interaction that provide the training ground for later patterns of social behavior. In many respects, the structure of power and deference in adult life is prefigured in the families.

NOTE

1. We have capitalized the referents to puppet characters (Mother, Father, Subordinate) to differentiate them from real-world referents throughout this chapter.

7

EFFECTING SOCIAL CHANGE THROUGH GROUP ACTION
Feminine Occupational Titles in Transition

Marlis Hellinger

The liberation of language is rooted in the liberation of ourselves [Daly, 1973:8].

Contrary to the assumption that language merely reflects social patterns such as sex-role stereotypes, research in linguistics and social psychology has shown that these are in fact facilitated and reinforced by language (Blaubergs, 1978; Bate, 1978; Martyna, 1978, 1980; Kramer et al., 1978; MacKay and Fulkerson, 1979; MacKay and Konishi, 1980). Thus, the exclusion, subordination, and degradation of women in educational materials serve to perpetuate the image of women as a muted group (Spender, 1980: 76-77). Women in many Western countries have, therefore, insisted on planned language changes with the goal of eliminating sexism from language use, at least in official communication. One visible outcome of these efforts is the creation of numerous guidelines that identify sexist usage and offer neutral alternatives (Miller and Swift, 1976; Nilsen et al., 1977: 181-182; Tromel-Plotz et al., 1981). Women have begun to reclaim the right to name themselves and the world.

It is appropriate, then, to place this chapter in the wider context of language planning. Language planning has been defined as the conscious and systematic interference with the dynamic processes of a language,

> channeling such processes into a specific direction, artificially accelerating or retarding them, encouraging some of their facets at the expense of others, or even introducing into the language features that lie outside their rules and setup [Wurn, 1977: 336].

On the other hand, language planning may be concerned with the existing social and functional status of a given language, "broadening and/or elevating its role and standing, or narrowing it to the point of suppression" (Wurm, 1977: 336). Typical examples for the latter, external, type of language planning are found in multilingual (and often, but not necessarily, developing) countries, where decisions must be made on such matters as the future of coexisting languages (perhaps including a former colonial language), the choice of an official language, or the social and functional role of minority languages (including immigrant and refugee languages). The former, internal, type of language planning has traditionally worked on the standardization of a language at various linguistic levels—from the construction of an orthographic system to the elaboration of the lexicon and the creation of special registers.

Language planning presupposes the identification and analysis of a current communication problem. Conflicts may arise from the existence of competing languages or language varieties, from the absence of a standard or prestige model, from either structural or lexical deficiencies that become evident when a language assumes new social functions, or from substantial interference from a foreign language (Wurm, 1977: 345). In restricting the discussion to "communicative problems," however, one obscures the real nature of their origin and trivializes proposals for solutions. There are usually important underlying social, political, and/or cultural conflicts that are typically rooted in asymmetries in a society's power structure. Language planning strategies cannot be understood (nor successfully implemented) unless this covert nonlinguistic level has been analyzed.

The question—who initiates a language planning measure on an individual, a group, or a national level—is a salient one, since the successful implementation of any such measure depends on access to and perhaps control of the "authorities" such as the media, the press, the educational institutions, and the legislative or executive bodies. When initiated or supported by the dominant group (perhaps as a result of pressure from a subordinate group), the goal of language planning is often explained in terms of the emancipation of the subordinate group, or the improvement of the communicative capacities of the language. But on a deeper level, language planning measures imposed "from above" will frequently serve to maintain and stabilize existing power hierarchies. On the other hand, a subordinate group may define its own language planning strategies as part of a wider political framework, typically in the sense of ethnic and/or cultural identification.

Language planning strategies will most likely develop from intricate motivational patterns and fulfill a variety of functions. Take, for example, the case of an English-based creole speech community, where the creole language may be "granted" the status of a primary-level educational medium (thus contributing to the emancipation of the subordinate group), while at the same time the use of English is reinforced on the level of higher education as well as in other prestigious interactions. Thus the white middle-class speech norm is maintained (Hellinger, in prep.).

IDENTIFYING THE CONFLICT

In this chapter I am concerned with internal language planning on a micro level, focusing on strategies used by women in an attempt to achieve equal treatment of the sexes in the area of professional terminology. For women, a serious communicative and even identificational conflict derives from their linguistic status as a relatively invisible and unnamed group.

In naming the most important areas of human reality, men as the dominant group have followed a semantic rule that Schulz (1975) has described as "male as norm." This rule implies that professional terms such as *politician, engineer,* and *poet* are not neutral, although they are morphologically unmarked. Their true masculine nature is revealed by their primary association with male referents (see Stanley, 1977). While men may always be included in the reference of *pilots* and *taxi drivers,* women are generally faced with ambiguous reference. In English, as in many other languages, regardless of their typological structure, most occupational terms are understood to refer to males and will only occasionally include females, simply because the concept of genericness is not generally available as a psycholinguistic reality. Very few titles are inherently feminine, and these usually denote occupations with low social status, as in the case of *maid, nurse, housewife,* or *prostitute.* In social areas where the presence of women is exceptional or regarded as inappropriate, speakers may feel the need to use feminine markers to identify female referents. Thus we get *woman pilot, female lawyer,* and *lady doctor.* Also, derivational morphemes are used to yield pairs such as *author/authoress, major/majorette,* and *governor/governess,* where the suffix often has a weakening, trivializing or even sexualizing effect on an occupational activity which for a man may connote power and prestige.

> Calling a woman a poetess may not only serve to define her as not belonging to the general order of poets, but may also suggest that her

contribution is not equal to a man's—that she is only a pale and lesser imitation [Eakins and Eakins, 1978: 116].

The following quotation from *Time* (February 16, 1981: 33) illustrates the semantic assymmetry between feminine and masculine terms:

> so solid was [Ella Grasso's] reputation as a politician that when she ran for Governor in 1974, sex was not an issue, aside from a few snide remarks about a "Governess."

In English, the use of masculine terms perpetuates the morphological and psychological invisibility of women, whereas morphological marking of female referents often implies semantic derogation. As in other social areas, women are here confronted with a double bind.

Below I will discuss two strategies that women have devised to resolve this conflict: *the generic strategy* and *the visibility strategy*. I will briefly describe the situation in the United States, Great Britain, the Netherlands, Sweden, and Norway as evidence of the first strategy; and that in Italy, France, and West Germany as evidence of the second. In an attempt to broaden the sociolinguistic approach by a psychological perspective, I will also consider factors of association and attitude connected with selected occupational titles. Finally, I will speculate on the future of the proposed changes in light of early reactions from the dominant group.

THE GENERIC STRATEGY

Women advocating the generic strategy insist on the systematic use of morphologically unmarked occupational terms for female referents. The underlying hypothesis is that through consistent reference to both sexes, these terms will become truly generic in the future. They believe that words can be "recycled," that the old word may "become new in a semantic context that arises from qualitatively new experience" (Daly, 1973: 8; see also Spender, 1980: 188-189). Where the morphological structure of a term makes such a semantic change unlikely, as in the case of English *cameraman, businessman,* or *insurance man,* the creation of new terms is suggested: *camera operator, business executive,* or *insurance agent.* I will call a strategy that emphasizes changes in the nouns, the "weak form" of the generic strategy.

Languages that have neither grammatical gender, nor natural gender—as is the case for English according to Stanley (1977)—fail to provide speakers with gender-linked rules for developing or maintaining elaborate morphological devices for gender marking. Here, feminine suffixes are used sporadically and for special purposes, frequently with the subconscious intention of demeaning women. If semantic derogation is felt by women to be inherent in the process of morphological marking, then the generic strategy appears to be a logical solution to the double-bind situation described above. This is, however, a solution that is not easily accepted by many members of the speech community, particularly since its success depends upon the modification of a deep-rooted semantic and psychological rule ("male as norm").

Where, as in English, the linguistic visibility of women can no longer be achieved by syntactic devices such as determiners or adjectival concord, a heavy functional load falls on pronominalization. In other words, in English the generic strategy may not achieve substantial gains for women unless the prescriptive rules for the so-called generic *he* are changed simultaneously, by encouraging the use of alternative constructions such as *he or she,* generic *she*, or singular *they*.[1] This reinforcement of semantic changes in the nouns by modified pronominal usage I will call the "strong form" of the generic strategy.

Steps Toward the Implementation of the Generic Strategy

Women have been able to win considerable administrative support for the implementation of the generic strategy in some countries. In 1975 the United States Department of Labor revised the official list of occupational titles, substituting neutral terms for discriminatory ones—for example, *business executive* for *businessman* (Guentherodt, 1979). In Great Britain the Equal Opportunities Commission issued guidelines for employment advertising practice, based on the Sex Discrimination Act of 1975. The general introduction says that

> use of a job description with a sexual connotation (such as "waiter," "salesgirl," "postman" or "stewardess") shall be taken to indicate an intention to discriminate unless the advertisement contains an indication to the contrary [Equal Opportunities Commission, 1977: 3].

In the Netherlands, although a few suffixes are available for the formation of feminine occupational terms—such as *-e* or *-ster,* as in *psychologe* (female psychologist) or *medewerkster* (female coworker)—women, including feminists, tend to prefer masculine terms, especially in the case of high-status professions. This tendency received official support when in 1980 the Dutch government decided that "M/V" (*man/vrouw*) must be added to masculine titles in job advertising to ensure that women would feel included.² This situation is also comparable to current changes in Scandinavia. In Norwegian, the few morphological markers for feminine nouns—like *-inne,* as in *laereinne* (female teacher), or *-trise,* as in *ekspeditrise* (female shop assistant)—are not generally used. Instead, the masculine form is claimed to be generic by the dominant group while women are working toward a change in the semantic structure of the masculine terms. Meanwhile, Norwegian women today may or may not feel included in *"laereren...han"* (the teacher...he).

In Swedish, while masculine titles such as *ingenjörer, lärare,* or *medarbeitare* (engineers, teachers, or co-workers) cannot yet be described as truly generic, the strategy of women has been to avoid the morphological marking of female referents. Rather, the few marked nouns—such as feminine *sjuksköterska* (nurse) or masculine *tjänsteman* (civil servant)—are used for both sexes. It is interesting to see that many Swedish employers, particularly in the technical fields, find it appropriate to stress the generic intention of their advertisements through explicit references to women. In an ad searching for "Ingenjörer (El-och Värmeteknik)," we find the following:

> Vi eftersträvar en jämnare könsfördelning,varför vi gärna ser att även kvinnor söker tekniska tjänster [*Svenska Dagbladet,* February 19, 1981: 30]. [We support a more equal distribution of jobs between the sexes; therefore we would like to see that women also apply for technical professions.]

Here is a similar announcement of a vacancy for a "VV-Inspektör":

> Både kvinnliga och manliga interesserade är därför välkomna med ansökan [*Dagens Nyheter,* February 19, 1981: 41]. [Both female and male interested persons are therefore welcome to apply.]

Such additions reflect current uncertainties about the semantic interpretations of Swedish occupational terms.

Reactions to the Generic Strategy

One may speculate on the chances of success for a semantic change of inherently masculine occupational terms in a patriarchal society. Judging from male reactions to language planning measures proposed by feminists, any substantial modification of the linguistic status quo must be expected to meet with strong opposition (Williams and Giles, 1978; Blaubergs, 1980).

On a surface level, in officially accepting the analysis of feminine marking as potentially discriminating, and in supporting the generic strategy (in its weak form), the dominant group appears to lose comparatively little, while retaining much. They lose the possibility, in certain registers, of identifying women as their lesser image, but will save the rule "male as norm" as long as women are unable to enforce corresponding changes in pronominal usage. However, aggressive reactions to feminist language planning suggest that on a deeper level males feel threatened by such measures. The use of unmarked terms in explicitly female-identified contexts will restructure the connotative setup of these terms so that the concept "feminine referent" will become more and more available psychologically. So the rule would be in danger of losing its associative force and—as a defensive device—pronominal changes are opposed violently in an effort to save the generic *he*.

Kramer et al. (1978: 648) have described one typical reaction to the implementation of the generic strategy:

> Strong action from a subordinate group will be met with strong action from the dominant group attempting to maintain its superiority and control. One strategy the dominant group might use is to accept, seemingly, the advances made but to redefine the situation so that the meaning of the change is diminished or lost (e.g., using "chairperson," but only in reference to women).

This has also happened in the use of Norwegian *-representant* (representative) and *-hjelp* (assistant) to replace *-mann* (man), as in *stortingsmann* (deputy to the Norwegian Parliament) and *-kone* (woman), as in *vaskekone* (charwoman). Thus, *stortingsrepresentant* (Parliamentary representative) and *reingjeringshjelp* (cleaning assistant) were created. However, the traditional association of "politician" with males was carried over to the new term so that it became possible to speak of "the representatives and their wives" (Blakar, 1975: 1691-70). Similarly, the term *sykepleier* (nurse) seems to have taken on primarily masculine connotations, so that some people have suggested the creation of the feminine *sykepleierske* to refer to women.

Other reactions of the dominant group include denying that a particular usage is in fact sexist, ignoring demands for changes or implementation measures, claiming that feminist language planning is a trivial and unnecessary concern since language will change automatically once society has changed, or ridiculing and demeaning the proponents of language planning strategies (Hellinger and Schräpel, 1983).

THE VISIBILITY STRATEGY

Members of a speech community exercise personal control through language, but they are also controlled by language. Therefore, in a language with grammatical gender, the automatic categorization of nouns as feminine, masculine, and perhaps neuter (especially human nouns, where grammatical gender will largely correlate with natural gender) may reinforce the concept of gender distinction in the speaker's mind.

If in such a language, morphological devices for the derivation of feminine nouns are still productive, then feminists are most likely to decide on the visibility strategy (that is, the consistent and systematic use of feminine terms) as a solution to the conflict outlined above. In English, because of the actual and potential semantic derogation linked with feminine marking, the goal of visibility has been placed second, whereas in German, visibility of the muted group has become the primary goal.

The benefits of morphological (and psychological) visibility are not without costs. On the one hand, the problem of semantic asymmetry between feminine and masculine occupational terms remains to be solved; on the other hand, masculine terms will become increasingly male-identified and thus lose even more of their alleged generic capacity. In other words, the fact that they are not really genuine generic terms will become more obvious. Finally, explicit naming of female referents requires conscious efforts from speakers and may lead to more complex—if nonsexist—constructions. An example of this is the following:

> Ich danke ... all meinen Studentinnen und Studenten, die mir jede und jeder auf ihre bzw. seine Weise geholfen haben, diese Arbeit zu schrieben [Trömel-Plötz, 1978: 49].
>
> [I thank ... all my students (feminine *and* masculine forms are expressed), who have each (feminine *and* masculine) helped me in her or his own way to write this paper.]

Feminist linguists argue that the achievement of nonsexist writing is well worth the cost of higher syntactic complexity, while some male linguists have described such usage as "bizarre," "uneconomical," "inelegant," and "ambiguous."

Neither strategy is revolutionary in the sense of discarding traditional asymmetric naming and creating new and truly generic terms (Pusch, 1980: 69ff). However, both are realistic in that they build on conventional, well-established patterns of usage, exploiting rules that are an integral part of the respective linguistic structure. In each case, feminists have developed a sharp sensitivity to those linguistic trends and changes that support the common goal of the muted group; rather than seeking to impose new norms on the speech community—with little, if any, hope for effective implementation—they advocate gradual innovation within the system.

Below I will briefly describe the situation in Italian and French, where feminist language planning has hardly begun to have an effect, and finally take German as an example of a relatively advanced stage of the implementation of the visibility strategy.

Proposing the Visibility Strategy in Italy and France

Italian has a number of productive morphological devices for the derivation of feminine terms: *cuoco/cuoca* (cook), *giardiniere/giardiniera* (gardener), *professore/professoressa* (professor), *il/la insegnante* (teacher). Masculine terms are supposed to be generic and include women, and although some women, especially in prestigious professions, still prefer the masculine terminology, the strategy of feminists is to make women visible by explicit and consistent reference.

Even a close look at Italian newspaper advertising reveals very few signs of equal linguistic treatment of the sexes. The professions and other traditionally male-dominated occupations use masculine terminology—*dottore, esperto, architetto, carpentiere, elettricista*—while the traditionally female fields show variability. *Addetto/a commessa/o,* and *portiere/a* are found next to *segretaria, domestica,* and *cucitrice (Corriere della Sera,* February 4, 1981: 12).

Variability is also a striking feature in French occupational terminology. There is a considerable number of feminine suffixes, the most important being *-e (assistente, présidente, politicienne, romancière), -euse (contrôleuse), -trice (aviatrice), -esse (poétesse),* and *-ine (laborantine).* Compounding also occurs, as in *femme soldat* or *femme peintre.* Conflicts in concord are common, as in "*Le* docteur Leclerc est *une* specialiste internationale."

However, the derivation of feminine nouns is neither generally acceptable (for example, neither *écrivaine* nor *médicine* occurs), nor are all acceptable forms used consistently. Apart from some cases in which the feminine noun denotes an occupational activity different from the masculine—as in *jardinier* (gardener) versus *jardinière* (kindergarten teacher)—the main reasons for such variability are (1) the rule "male as norm" and (2) negative connotations of many feminine nouns. Some suffixes, such as *-euse, -esse,* and *-ette,* "ont souvent une résonance un peu vieux jeu, un peu ridicule, même un peu péjorative" (Boel, 1976: 38). The masculine term frequently connotes authority and prestige, while the feminine term may denote a subordinate or less powerful activity. Compare, for example, "contrôleur des Finances" versus "contrôleuse de métro"; or "le président du Conseil, Mme Golda Meir" versus "Ingrid Bergman, Présidente du jury international" (Boel, 1976: 58).

The visibility strategy can follow different routes. In French it could simply involve a change of the article (and, of course, all subsequent gender-sensitive deictic references), to yield pairs such as *le chef/la chef, un médicin/une médicin, le professeur/la professeur.* Boel, in her empirical study of contemporary French usage of occupational titles, describes this step as "tout à fait inhabituel" and restricted to the spoken language or special registers. However, she leaves room for the hypothesis that combining a masculine term with a feminine article may mark the beginning of a genuine language change. In the framework of this chapter this might be called a "weak form" of the visibility strategy.

The strong form would involve overt morphological marking. Boel has observed an increase in the use of feminine occupational titles, predicting that

> au fur et à mesure que les postes importants dans la société seront couramment occupés par des femmes, l'emploi de la form féminine augmentera [p. 73].

Extensive variability remains, however, which certainly reflects current changes in linguistic as well as social patterns.[3] It is precisely the conflict between traditional male-centered usage and increasing female-identified usage that has prevented an easy decision on the "strong form" of the visibility strategy by women:

> [Il] éxiste un tendance à rester dans le masculin quant il s'agit de professions supérieures, bien rémunérées ou autrement prestigieuses. Inversement, on emploie le féminin pour désigner des occupations inférieures et moins bien payées [Boel, 1976: 71]

Thus, even very few members of the subordinate group perhaps advocate any form of the generic strategy, the decision on a specific form of the visibility strategy remains to be worked out in detail.

Implementing the Visibility Strategy in West Germany

German has the very productive suffice -*in,* which is used for the derivation of feminine occupational terms from masculine forms: *Arzt/Arzten* (doctor), *Lehrer/Lehrerin* (teacher), *Politiker/Politikerin* (politician). Occasionally, *-frau* (woman) is used as a compositional element, as in *Industriekauffrau* (industrial saleswoman) versus the masculine *Industriekaufmann* (industrial salesman). There are also a few non-native suffixes such as *-ess, -ice, -isse,* and *-euse* (as in *Stewardess, Directrice, Diakonisse, Friseuse*), which are no longer morphologically productive.

In publications on German word formation, feminine occupational terms are interpreted as gender-specific variants of the masculine forms (Fleischer, 1971; Brinkmann, 1971; Wellman, 1975). Again, a generic interpretation of masculine forms is assumed, but women may or may not feel included. The semantic asymmetry between masculine and feminine terms is reflected in the fact that the concept of genericness is associated only with masculine forms. Whereas *der Arzt* (masculine) or *die Arzte* (masculine plural) will be the only terms for males but may be used for females, as well, *die Arztin* (feminine) or *die Arztinnen* (feminine plural) can never refer to males. The use of the feminine plural in reference to a group of 99 women and 1 man would be ungrammatical, according to both current and past linguistic descriptions. Some women find this acceptable, preferring the masculine term because to them it carries more prestige than the feminine. Such women will identify themselves as *Arzt* rather than *Arztin,* a situation that has led to widespread variability in the use of -*in* in practically all registers.

Testing the Variability of -*in*

As a necessary step toward the analysis of present usage patterns in the area of occupational terminology in German, and subsequent decisions in language planning strategies, the variability of -*in* was empirically tested at the University of Hannover during the summer term, 1979. Female and male high school students (497) in the Hannover area (average age was 15), from 3 types of schools, were asked about their professional futures. The schools included an *Integrierte Gesamtschule,* a *Realschule,* and a *Gymnasium.* Since the goal was the elicitation of occupational titles, girls were asked for their first and second occupational choices. Information on the occupations of the informants' parents was also elicited. Information about the job or pro-

-fession their mother had been trained for and/or was currently practicing was recorded for girls and boys.[4]

In all types of schools there is a clear favoritism toward -*in*, that is, using the strategy of explicitly identifying women in the choice of a title. Combining the first and second occupational choices of the girls, we get an average of 54% of the terms having feminine markers. Information on the occupational background of the girls' mothers yielded 58% with -*in*, information on the boys' mothers' occupational background, 53%. Nevertheless, masculine terms occurred in 28% of the girls' first and second occupational choices.[5] The use of neutral terminology was so limited as to be of no significance.

The most unexpected and, in fact, shocking result was that more than 30% of both girls and boys of all school types were unable (or unwilling) to give any information on the occupational history or status of their mothers. In other words, work as a homemaker and mother is not recognized as a legitimate occupational activity by these students. The most obvious reason for this, presumably, is the lack of financial reward for homemaking.

When occupational terminology is used, women as well as men show considerable variability in their use of -*in* even, according to Oksaar (1976: 74), where the norm has been either the feminine term—*sie ist Lehrerin* (she is a teacher) for a traditionally female profession—or the masculine term—*sie ist Elektrikerin* (she is an electrician) for a traditionally male occupation.[6] The choice of either the feminine or the masculine form clearly depends on extra-linguistic factors. Possible parameters include the number of women and men practicing a given profession, the social status of that profession, the point of time when the career became accessible to women, and differing evaluations of feminine and masculine terms. It is this last point that I will take up in the next section in an attempt to provide an explanation for the variable use of -*in* in German.

Explaining the Variability of -*in*

In order to test empirically the hypothesis of a semantic asymmetry between feminine and masculine occupational titles in German, the semantic differential technique was used as an analytic instrument.[7] We expected to find evidence of stereotypical attitudes connected with selected occupational titles, which could hardly have been elicited from informants in any other way.

We asked 384 female and male informants, all of them students at the University of Hannover, to rate sixteen occupational titles on a seven-point scale with 25 polar adjectives. Each informant filled in one test sheet only, so that the pair *Pilot/Pilotin* (pilot) was evaluated by 48 informants (12 women and 12 men for each term). In addition, the data for *Frau* (woman) and *Mann* (man) were elicited from 48 informants in the same manner. Reactions from the total of 432 informants were represented in semantic profiles, which were the result of mean averages.

For *Frau* we received a profile that confirms many of the traditional stereotypes. I will mention only the most prominent: Women are very soft *(weich)*, helpful *(hilfsbereit)*, emotional *(gefühlvoll)* and fragile *(zart)*; they are cheerful *(heiter)*, playful *(verspielt)*, and dreamy*(verträumt)*; of course, they talk a lot *(redselig)*. Surprisingly, they are rather active *(aktiv)*, flexible *(beweglich)*, and fresh *(frisch)*. Men, on the other hand, are hard *(hart)*, rather than soft; they are strong *(stark)*, very active, orderly *(geordnet)*, calm *(nüchtern)*, vigorous *(robust)*, and very healthy *(gesund)*.

If we compare *Frau* and *Mann*, we find that the profiles differ in a number of respects. The most significant are the following: Women are a lot softer than men, more helpful, dreamy, much more emotional, talkative, and fragile. The profiles clearly reflect stereotypic judgments and thus confirm evidence presented by many other studies (Rosencrantz et al., 1968; Broverman et al., 1970).

Turning to occupational titles and comparing *Pilot* with *Mann*, we find that a number of features that are typically masculine are now even more pronounced: A pilot is harder, clearer, stronger, and more active than the "normal" male; he is also much more cool, calm, stern, flexible, and healthy. The profile for *Pilotin* and *Frau* shows much the same deviations. A female pilot is also much harder, clearer, and stronger than the "normal" woman; she is more active and cool and much more orderly, calm, stern, and healthy. On the whole, the profile for *Pilotin* seems to deviate more from *Frau* than *Pilot* from *Mann*. This suggests that features that are traditionally interpreted as masculine may be intensified in *Pilot*, while features that are described as stereotypically "feminine" may disappear in *Pilotin*. While a "normal" woman is soft, very emotional and dreamy, a female pilot is hard, cool, and calm—characteristics stereotypically associated with males.

The comparison between *Pilotin* and *Pilot* shows that, for some features, the woman is not quite as "good" as the man (hard, cool, calm, vigorous, flexible), whereas for others, she is even "better" (clear, active, orderly, fresh)—if, indeed, these are features that are relevant for the description of pilots. Other features—perhaps those that are not salient for pilots—remain close to the feminine stereotypes. This suggests that a female pilot is perceived as hard, cool, and calm, but not quite as hard/cool/calm as her male counterpart. On the other hand, she is more helpful, gentle, and peaceful than he is.

Looking at the deviations of all tested feminine and masculine occupational titles from the profiles for *Frau/Mann*, we can make an interesting observation: Without exception, all the deviations of the feminine terms from *Frau* run in the direction of *Mann*. This means that as soon as a woman performs one of the selected occupations, some of the associations linked with *Frau* will change in the direction of male stereotypes. On the other hand, 41% of the deviations of masculine terms from *Mann* run in the direction of *Frau*—away from the male stereotypes. In other words, while a profession will (in this study) never make a woman more "feminine," it may very well make a man less "masculine."

Occupational terms were then listed according to mere number of deviations from *Frau/Mann*. The list supports our initial intuitive classification into prestige (politician, lawyer) and middle-class occupations (cook, salesperson). The latter show fewer deviations, and these are less severe.

Finally, feminine and masculine occupational terms were compared. Prestige pairs differed slightly more from each other than middle-class pairs. Deviations of feminine terms from the masculine ones approached the profile for *Frau* more frequently (in 57% of all deviations counted) than the profile for *Mann* (only 43%). Thus, in the comparison of feminine occupational titles with *Frau*, all deviations were in the male direction. This tendency is somewhat neutralized in the comparison with masculine counterparts, where more than half of all deviations are again closer to the female profile. On the other hand, there are male features that women possess to a larger extent than men. Thus, a female politician is even more economical, clear, orderly, calm, and healthy than a male politician, and a female cook even more vigorous, wild, noisy, and domineering than a male cook. These observations cannot be generalized at this point, however tempting this may be.

Nevertheless, it seems reasonable to conclude this section with the following hypothesis that must be tested in future research. Qualities thought to be salient for certain occupations may be associated with women to a greater extent than with men (who possess many of these qualities "inherently"); in other words, women performing such occupational activities may be expected to be "better" than men. For other qualities, feminine stereotypes may prevail, causing an approximation of the respective occupational profile toward the profile of *Frau*.

Finally, the use of feminine terms by women seems to be related to at least two conflicting strategies:

(1) The desire for integration and participation in the man's world. Women then find themselves under pressure to achieve more than men.
(2) The desire to maintain the female identity. Then women must expect to be associated with traditional feminine stereotypes.

For German women the benefits of visibility seem to outweigh the cost of (some) stereotyping.

Changing the Semantic Structure of Occupational Terms

The hypothesis that feminist language planning strategies will have an impact on the semantic structure of occupational terms (which means, in the case of the generic strategy, that masculine terms will become generic, and in the case of the visibility strategy, that feminine terms will lose some of their stereotypic load) must also be approached on a diachronic level, i.e., comparing the profiles based on data from different points in time. Potential benefits of such a procedure may be illustrated by the following analysis.

The 1980 data for *Frau* and *Mann* were compared with data available from more than 20 years back (see Hofstatter, 1973: 259; Hellinger, 1981). The most remarkable result was that a number of female as well as male stereotypes were found to be considerably stronger in the older study. The woman of 1960 is softer, more passive, emotional, peaceful, lenient, and fragile than the woman of 1980; she is also more jovial, gentle, and submissive. Surprisingly, she is also more orderly, flexible, and healthy.

Even more pronounced are the differences between the two profiles for German *Mann*. The man of 1960 is harder, clearer, stronger, and more generous, active, and serious; he is also calmer, sterner, more vigorous, fresher, more domineering, and healthier than the man of 1980.[8]

Whereas the profiles for *Frau/Mann* of 1980 can be described as similar in that they differ quantitatively rather than qualitatively from each other, the profiles for *Frau/Mann* of 1960 show hardly any similarities at all.

The result of this comparison suggests that the associations linked with *Frau/Mann* (or, in linguistic terms, the connotative structure of these words) have changed considerably over the past twenty years.

Women of today are seen as harder, more active, more aggressive, and more vigorous as well as less emotional, less gentle, and less submissive. And, although stereotypic judgments are by no means based on empirical evidence experienced by individual speakers, this obvious modification of linguistic reality reflects important social changes. In changing current usage patterns, and encouraging and proposing further modifications, feminist language planners are changing social reality.

Implementing the Visibility Strategy in West Germany

Following a guideline by the European Community of 1976, legislative measures have been taken in the Federal Republic of Germany to establish equal rights for women and men in the area of their professional lives. (For example, equal pay has since that time been a legal, although by no means social, reality in West Germany.) The administration supports the visibility strategy: the extended use of feminine occupational titles.

In July 1979 the Bundesminister für Bildung and Wissenschaft announced that masculine *and* feminine occupational terms must be used in all regulations pertaining to job training. One example is the revision of the training regulations for *Reiseverkehrskaufmann* (male travel agent), which now explicitly addresses women by inclusion of the feminine form *Reiseverkehrskauffrau*.

In August 1980, in connection with a number of equal rights amendment regulations, the following was added to the German Civil Law Code "Bürgerliches Gesetzbuch" (§ 611b):

> Der Arbeitgeber [sic] soll einen Arbeitsplatz weder öffentlich noch innerhalb des Betriebes nur für Männer oder nur für Frauen ausschreiben.
>
> [The employer shall not advertise a vacancy for men or women only, either in public or internally.]

In effect, this means that women should be explicitly named in job advertising. However, support of the visibility strategy, even by the highest legislative authority, does not imply automatic acceptance by the dominant group on a lower level. Variability persists, even in the prestigious weekly newspaper *Die Zeit*, where sexist usage is found on the same page as neutral terminology: *Professor* or *Ingenieur* next to *Lektor/in* or *Erzieher(in)*. This practice may be explained by a variety of reasons: on a superficial level, by insecurity as to "correct" usage, concern over "cumbersome" expressions, uncertainty and/or reservations about new orthographic conventions, and so on; on a deeper level, by a desire to maintain the male-centered linguistic status quo. Early in 1981 a survey was carried out in the Federal Republic of Germany with newspapers that had not changed sexist practices in job advertising (*Informationen für die Frau,* 1981/6:13). Those newspapers offering any explanation at all said, for example, that they didn't know of the existence of the law or that they didn't approve of it.

To summarize, the visibility strategy—even if granted official approval and support—nevertheless poses a threat to large sections of the dominant group, who refuse to change their usage.

CONCLUSION

In the preceding sections two strategies were described that women of different language backgrounds have devised in attempts to contribute to changes in women's professional lives—more specifically, to achieve equal linguistic treatment of the sexes in this area. The strategies represent language planning on a sociolinguistic micro level, but must be interpreted as part of the macro level social and political upheaval marked by women's increasing power to name themselves and the world.

Both strategies have their costs, but each seems to be a genuine alternative to current practices in the given speech community. Follow-up devices must be sought to cope with remaining linguistic and social conflicts.

Both strategies increase women's prospects for wider acceptance in the future by defining new norms on the basis of changes already in progress in public and private interaction—changes that have most eminently emerged in feminist journalism, literature, and scholarship. To observe such a micro language change is important in that it may display mechanisms of support and rejection of a more general significance, with parallels to other social areas. Finally, it is of extreme importance to see women as a group publicly claiming their role in shaping their language, setting up their own norms of appropriate linguistic behavior:

> When women take steps to change the language structure and their own uses of language, they are in fact acting to change their status in society: they are challenging the legitimacy of the dominant group [Kramarae, 1980b: 65].

NOTES

1. Dennis Baron (1981) lists 35 proposals (from eighteenth- and nineteeth-century sources) for the third-person, singular, common, generic pronoun. Also see the extensive, annotated bibliography in Thorne et al. (1983).

2. I wish to thank Dédé Brouwer (Universiteit van Amsterdam), Marinel Gerritsen (Koninklijke Nederlandse Akademie van Wetenschappen), Else Ryen and Tove Beate Pedersen (both Universiteteti Oslo), Claire A. Forel (Université de Gèneve), and Luise F. Pusch (Universität Konstanz) for their helpful comments on professional terms in Dutch, Norwegian, French, and Italian.

3. It may be worth noting that the French and German versions of the European Guideline of 1976, whose goal is the equal treatment of the sexes in the area of professional life, speak of *travailleurs* (masculine) and *Arbeitnehmer* (masculine) and do not explicitly name women (see Guentherodt, 1979: 126).

4. For a more detailed description of this test, see Hellinger (1980: 39ff).

5. This is partly explained by the remarkable number of compounds with *-kaufmann* (salesman) as the second constituent. More than 50% of the masculine terms elicited for the Integrierte Gesamtschule were compounds of this kind.

6. For a further test of the variability of *-in*, which involves German translational items for English occupational titles, see Hellinger (1980: 41ff).

7. Developed in psychology, this method has also been applied in linguistics with very interesting results (see Oksaar, 1976). In West Germany, Hofstätter has refined the methodology, and all subsequent studies—most of them in the field of social psychology—are based on his work.

8. Surprisingly, the data elicited in 1980 for *woman/man* in the Liverpool (England) area, were much closer to the German profiles of 1960 than to 1980 results (see Helinger, 1981). This contrastive study suggests that cross-cultural female and male stereotypic judgments exist but that these show different quantitative values. Of course, such extra-linguistic factors as social background of informants, different school systems, and so forth must be considered in an interpretation of the results.

8

PLANNING FOR LANGUAGE CHANGE IN THE UNITED STATES
The Case of Monolingual Spanish Speakers

Joan Rubin

IT IS NO SECRET that in the last twenty years we have witnessed an increased public awareness of the communication needs of Spanish speakers in the United States. The subsequent action in this arena has been part of two decades of public demands for the rights of a wide variety of underserved groups (for example, Blacks, women, and other minorities). One can point to a wide variety of activities undertaken not only by the federal and state governments, but also by the Mexican-American Legal Defense Fund (MALDEF) and the Puerto Rican Legal Defense Fund (PRLDF), which identify some communication inadequacies and propose some sort of solution to them.

What I intend to do in this chapter is review how various communication issues vis à vis Spanish-only speakers have been dealt with, by considering the following questions:

(1) What language/communication *inadequacies* have been identified, and by whom?
(2) Who are the *planners* who have the authority and power to make and influence language-related decisions?
(3) What *plans* or *goals* have been set out to attend to the communication inadequacies identified?
(4) What attempts have been made at *planning*; that is, in what situations has a real effort been made toward implementation of or feedback to a plan?

My review will consider these problems in the following domains: health/medical, legal, employment, communication, citizenship,

*An earlier version of this chapter was keynote address at the El Español en Los Estados Unidos conference, Chicago, October 3, 1981, and was published in Eliás-Olivares et al. (eds.). I am indebted to Richard Baldauf for inspiration on the organization of the paper.

social welfare, and education. Through this analysis we will observe attempts to break through and redirect the focus of administrative agencies in serving limited-English speakers, as well as consider the role of private agencies in meeting the needs of limited-English speakers.

THE HEALTH/MEDICAL DOMAIN

In order to understand what might be identified as a communication inadequacy in health and medicine, it is helpful to remember that the main functions of this domain are to provide health care to its clients. For Spanish-only speakers, the question is whether patients have access to such services and whether the medical staff understands the patient's symptomatology well enough to make an accurate diagnosis and to negotiate an appropriate treatment with the patient. For example, MALDEF, in a brochure entitled *Chicanas and Mental Health* (1979), noted Hispanic underutilization of health and mental health services, finding as one of the contributing factors that "few mental health facilities provide bilingual services or employ a bilingual/bicultural staff." They note,

> A therapeutic relationship cannot be established when the client and the therapist cannot communicate. This can occur when the emotional experiences of the patient cannot be fully expressed in the patient's primary language:

Another study (Sternbach de Medina and Martinez, 1981) also suggests that language may indeed be a crucial barrier that discourages Hispanics from seeking services.

Until recently, identification of language/communication issues in the health domain has been largely ignored. However, this is in the process of change. A study undertaken by the California Department of Health Services regarding the lack of bilingual services in the emergency center of the San Francisco General Hospital had the following principal findings, noted by Aguirre (1980).

(1) Hospital employees in the emergency triage area try to communicate in English and in hand gestures with monolingual Spanish-speaking persons.
(2) In psychiatric emergency, a 24-hour unit with three shifts, only one of 46 people could speak Spanish, and this person worked the night shift only.

The medical domain is an area in which we are just beginning to recognize some of the important communication gaps. There is a strong need for further studies to detail how access to and effectiveness of medical care relate to communication barriers.

It is interesting next to ask who the planners in this domain might be: Who has the authority and power to make and influence language-related decisions? In public hospitals, the decision rests with the hospital authorities or with the state or federal department of health. Obviously, the public can also influence such decisions by complaining to the proper authorities. In the San Francisco General Hospital case mentioned above, the U.S. Office of Civil Rights (OCR) collaborated with the city and county of San Francisco. OCR stepped in and agreed that the failure to provide staff and services was a violation of civil rights.[1]

We can next ask what plans or goals have been set out to attend to these communication inadequacies. For San Francisco General, among a number of recommended solutions are the requirement that a minimum number of interpreters be provided, that the language competency of bilingual employees be tested, that bilingual signs be posted in the hospital, and that certain positions be designated as bilingual.

Other hospitals elsewhere in the country have provided the following services to meet the communication needs of monolingual patients:

(1) Signs are posted indicating, in Spanish, where particular offices are found.
(2) Textbooks have been published to train medical personnel in Spanish. Note, for example, *Medical Spanish: A Conversational Approach* (1981), *Communicating in Spanish for Medical Personnel* (1975), or *Basic Spanish for Health Personnel* (1973).
(3) The M. D. Anderson Hospital in Houston, Texas, provides Spanish translations of treatment explanations.
(4) Tarrant County in Texas now has Spanish speakers monitoring the Tel-Med system (a free health and medical information service available by telephone, sponsored by the Fort Worth Academy of Medicine, the Tarrant County Medical Society, and its auxiliary members). Spanish speakers are available every Tuesday from 9:00 a.m. until noon. The service also has 40 Spanish language tapes on such subjects as family planning, alcohol problems, mental health (from the *Arlington Texas News*, February 11, 1981).
(5) Kaiser Permanente, San Francisco, put together a book listing the second-language fluency of its employees and where speakers could be located in an emergency.

Finally, we can ask whether there has been much planning in the medical arena; that is, what attempts have been made to implement the goals or promote the use of the products suggested, and what information has been sought to evaluate the effectiveness of the implementation? Until recently, very little had been done in this area. However, at San Francisco General Hospital several steps have been taken to implement the goals established by OCB with the city and county of San Francisco. Most recently, the Civil Service Commission has completed and is administering a language skills test for the bilingual staff and is now administering it. For those passing the test there is a bonus increase per pay period.

Attention to language needs in the medical domain has been increasing in recent years and is beginning to be addressed in a much more systematic manner than it has been in the past, due to the collaborative efforts of community advocates and the OCR.

THE LEGAL DOMAIN

Most would agree that the main function of the law is "to provide justice for the members of the community." To the extent that the communication process prevents justice because the accused cannot follow the trial or understand the charges, we can note that there is a communication gap.

Within the legal domain, perhaps the major communication inadequacy for Spanish speakers (and others who do not speak English) has occurred in the courtroom, where it is critical that litigants understand the linguistic exchanges in which they are engaged. Until very recently, despite the critical importance of the interpreter in court cases, there were no measures (1) to require certification of the capabilities and training of an interpreter or to ascertain whether or not their understanding of the law and the interpretation process was adequate to the important assignment they were to carry out, or (2) to record the actual testimony of the witness so that the translation of the interpreter's version could be verified.

On October 18, 1978, the U.S. Congress, acting as a *language planner*, enacted Public Law 95-539 "to provide more effectively for the use of interpreters in courts of the U.S. and for other purposes." The goal/plan of this law is that the Director of the Administrative Office of the U.S. Courts (which becomes a language planner) shall establish a program to facilitate the use of interpreters in the courts. The law further specifies that the director's main goal shall be to prescribe, determine, and certify the qualifications of persons who may serve as certified interpreters in U.S. courts in bilingual proceedings and proceedings involving the hearing-impaired by considering the education, training, and experience of such persons. The law provides suggestions about how this plan is to be implemented: The director (1) shall maintain a current master list of all interpreters certified by the director and (2) shall report annually on the frequency of requests for and the use and effectiveness of interpreters. Here we see that some evaluation suggestions have been built into the plan by Congress.

The law further specifies when and under what conditions the plan is to be implemented:

> The presiding judicial officer...shall utilize the services of the most available certified interpreter...if the presiding judicial officer determines...that...such party...or a witness: 1) speaks only or primarily a language other than the English language; or 2) suffers from a hearing impairment.
>
> [If the problem is great enough] so as to inhibit such party's comprehension of the proceedings or communication with counsel or the presiding judicial officer, or so as to inhibit such witness' comprehension of questions and the presentation of such testimony [Public Law 95-539, 1978: 204].

Hence the law is quite specific as to its goals and more than a little specific about who is to carry out the plan and how they are to do so. It is less than specific about what is to be done with the evaluation it prescribes. That is, if there are more requests than interpreter services, they do not specify what action the Director of the Administrative Office of the U.S. Courts is to take. Arjona (forthcoming) details the complex procedure followed in developing an instrument for certifying Spanish/English interpreters to comply with the stipulations outlined in PL 95-539.

In this law we see clearly (1) how the linguistic inadequacy was defined; (2) who the planners are; (3) what the plan is; and (4) what implementation and evaluation procedures are envisioned. It is obvious that more work needs to be done on the problem of implementation and on the evaluation of the effectiveness of procedures instituted in meeting the perceived inadequacy. (For a more detailed discussion of the implementation process, see Arjona [1983], who has noted that a serious shortcoming of the act is the fact that it ignores issues of training.) Finally, we should note that no efforts have as yet been made to tape-record the witness' testimony.

California requires certification of interpreters, and the Circuit Court of Cook County trains and tests interpreters (Rodriguez and Ruiz, 1981). Given the powerful effect of the U.S. certification process, there are considerable endeavors to institute similar procedures in several of the states. To my knowledge, there are no standards for determining the language competence of witnesses, defendants, or plaintiffs in a court of law.

Sometimes private individuals perceive a need and prepare a product to try to meet it. Such an example is *A Spanish Manual for Law Enforcement Agencies* (Luna and Meneses, 1973). These men tried to provide a product that met an inadequacy that they perceived—namely, the need by law enforcement officers to be able to communicate more effectively with Spanish-speaking inhabitants. The only indication that we have that this product has been recognized as being suitable to meet that need is a memo from a park ranger in the U.S. Department of the Interior National Park Service to the superintendent of another park, suggesting that the volume may prove helpful to rangers in the second park. Clearly no planners (persons with authority to make or influence language-related decisions) were involved, nor is there a plan for the evaluation of this volume. It is possible that such a need exists and is perceived by others, and that the volume is an effective means of meeting this need, but in this case there has been no planning involved.

THE WORK DOMAIN

In the domain of work, there are a number of problems. The issues identified relate to (1) access to employment information by a consumer or client in relation to their language knowledge, and (2) certification as a bilingual for certain positions. What language inadequacies have been identified in the work domain and how have these been dealt with?

In its role as "influencer of language related decisions," the PRLDF brought suit in *Barcia v. Sitkin* in the state of New York. In this case, a Hispanic claimant's inability to understand English threatened to cost her hundreds of dollars in unemployment insurance benefits. The plan proposed was that the New York Appeal Board accord claimants elemental due process guarantees, such as the right of notice of the evidence considered against them. The PRLDF also sought to require the New York Appeal Board to consider the fact that in local unemployment insurance offices, claimants are often denied their rights to Spanish-language assistance, rights guaranteed by a

1976 court order in *Pabon v. Levine*. The perceived linguistic inadequacy is the Hispanic's inability to understand information in English about unemployment benefits. The planners here are the PRLDF and the courts. The plan requires that information be made available in Spanish to those who do not understand the English materials.[2]

The case is of interest because it begins to illustrate the problems connected with language planning when done by the courts. The court can issue a decision or an order. It may also provide for some guarantee of implementation. However, unless the court case is connected with a regular administrative procedure carried out by the executive branch of the federal or state government, the chances of its implementation are remote. Even more remote is the possibility of feedback for improving implementation. The PRLDF notes this difficulty in *Pabon v. Levine*, where although the U.S. Department of Labor has regulations similar to those involved in the Lau case, nonetheless, the court did not require an interpretive memorandum. Hence, in the case of employment benefits, it is necessary to prove a disparity of benefits, although in educational agencies, unequal benefits are presumed.

With the advent of state bilingual education acts, a need has been identified to specify the language skills of bilingual teachers. The perceived linguistic inadequacy is that monolingual English teachers by themselves cannot provide adequate educational services to limited-English-proficient or non-English-proficient (LEP/NEP) children. Bilingual teachers are needed as well. The planners in this instance vary from state to state. In California, authority to set goals and ensure compliance is vested in the State Commission on Teacher Credentialing. The plan is that all agencies granting educational credentials or certificates must assess the language competence of the prospective bilingual candidate, and in four language skills (speaking, reading, writing, and listening) the teacher must demonstrate competence and proficiency roughly equivalent to the Foreign Service Level 3, which is the professional proficiency level.[3]

Since implementation is vested in several different agencies, it is widely acknowledged that there is a great deal of variation in this implementation. However, a procedure for evaluation of these agencies does exist. In fact, the commission is constantly monitoring them, and if necessary, it can either close an assessor agency or withdraw credential approval; it has done so in two cases. In an effort to tighten up this assessment process, the state appointed a committee to provide clearer standards for the bilingual certificate of competence, and the committee issues a report.[4]

Florence Barkin (1981) described the model she and her committee are developing for a language assessment instrument, which will be the official Language Proficiency Examination for the State of Arizona, required of all teachers before receiving bilingual endorsement. In her paper, Barkin touches on some important problems of assessing language varieties and domains of usage—something that I understand has also been of concern to the California Committee on Standards[5]—and on the need to involve the educational staff in the preparation of the test. Some other states (Michigan and Texas, for example) also have similar procedures to certify the language competence of those involved in bilingual education. It is of interest that in the area of work where language is seen as a scarce resource, the procedures for planning are fairly well elaborated, though certainly there is room for improvement.

There should also be some perception of linguistic inadequacy among international business corporations, but not much has been done to date. That is, such corporations have not seen a need for their American employees to learn Spanish (or any other foreign language for that matter). According to three studies (Olympus Research, 1976; Inman, 1978; and Berryman et al., 1979), many U.S. companies require their overseas employees to learn English rather than have their executives learn Spanish. It is very hard to identify cases in which lack of Spanish knowledge has been perceived as negatively affecting marketing, contract confirmation, or the provision of service. However, increasingly there are individuals in specific companies who argue that language knowledge can make the difference in the sealing of a contract or the provision of a service.

THE COMMUNICATION DOMAIN

The issue here is one of access to information and/or service. In California the Hispanic Coalition has argued for the past ten years that Hispanic customers are not given services equal to that of English speakers. The linguistic inadequacy is the inability of the California Telephone Company to understand and provide services to its Spanish (and in some cases) Chinese customers. There are a variety of planners in this instance:

(1) The Hispanic Coalition, which has been pressing the California Public Utilities Commission (PUC) to see that services are provided for Spanish-speaking customers;

(2) The California PUC, which has compelled the Pacific Telephone Company to provide emergency services; and
(3) The Pacific Telephone Company, which has decided on the nature of the services.

The plan is a very complicated one. In 1976 the California PUC ordered Pacific Telephone to provide emergency telephone services in Spanish and Chinese to those areas where the population of Spanish speakers or Chinese speakers was more than 5%. In the same year, Pacific Telephone implemented this order by contracting with a telephone answering service in Los Angeles called Emergency Spanish Language Assistance Bureau (ESLAB). The Hispanic Coalition has questioned the effectiveness of this service. Although there is no documentation of the number of Spanish-language calls that are referred to it, in 1980 Pacific Telephone reported to the commission that 90% of the calls that go to ESLAB are handled satisfactorily. The coalition has questioned the definition of "satisfactory" for users in towns other than Los Angeles, since the problem of transmitting information is compounded by lack of direct interaction between the operator in the other town and the person reporting the emergency. They argue that Spanish-language operators should be part of the Pacific Telephone personnel, available in all cities where there are sufficient Spanish telephone users.

In 1979 the California PUC reopened the bilingual services case and held hearings to determine if the Pacific Telephone had complied with the order for bilingual emergency services and to discover if Pacific Telephone was providing the same services to non-English speakers as it was to English speakers. To answer these questions, Pacific Telephone contracted the services of Herman Gallegos, a member of the Pacific Telephone Board of Directors, to study the needs of the Spanish-speaking community. A MALDEF staff member reported that Mr. Gallegos had interviewed only Pacific Telephone customers. The PUC, recognizing that his study was biased, called for an independent survey of the telephone needs of the Spanish-speaking community, and a new contract was let and completed in 1983.

Further, in 1982 an independent study was conducted by Los Padrinos, an organization of Pacific Telephone employees, asking if monolingual speakers were being provided the same level of service as other customers and what the market potential would be if more services were rendered in Spanish. The study found that, although services were being provided in Spanish, since they were not being rendered in a standard manner, they were costing much more to provide and that, if fuller Spanish services were provided, the market potential would be considerable. Hence, the study concluded that better services can be provided for less money.[6] It now appears that through the efforts of several community interest groups, steps may be taken to provide standardized services to monolingual Spanish speakers.

What we can observe in this instance is a complex interaction among those who have the authority and power to make or influence language-related decisions. We can also note the problems that arise due to the lack of clear-cut specification of the implementation and evaluation process. Consequently, the only recourse of the pressure groups is to take every opportunity to reopen the issue.[7]

In the area of media the linguistic inadequacy identified is the need for Spanish language broadcast time. The Communication Act of 1934 stated that airwaves are public property and that stations are licensed to use these airwaves in the public interest. Therefore, the Federal Communications Commission (FCC) has ruled that stations are obliged to serve the needs and interests of the communities in which they are licensed. Since the FCC has had the authority to grant and suspend licenses (that is, it is the planner in this case), the commission has construed its responsibility to serve the interests and needs of *specific* communities as a basis for, at times, requiring broadcasting in languages other than English. (For us, this is the plan or goal.) Further, the FCC has interpreted the public interest to mean minority ownership of stations, since ownership influences station policies, and those in turn influence the way in which a population is served.

In Phoenix, American International Development (AID), which is owned and managed by a Chicana, proposed to bring Phoenix a 24-hour Spanish-language FM radio station. The applicant was, however, competing with two other (Anglo) applicants for Phoenix's last remaining FM channel. The case has gone through three review boards: (1) an FCC administrative law judge, who ruled in favor of the Chicana; (2) an FCC review board, which overturned that decision on technicalities; and (3) the FCC itself, which sustained the first decision in favor of the Chicana applicant. The case was appealed to the U.S. Court of Appeals, but in the opinon of the attorney for the Chicana,[8] the decision of the commission will most likely be sustained.

There is very little planning in the media domain. The commission does not monitor the number of non-English speakers in a community on a continuing basis to ascertain need, as it relates to the number of stations or other non-English media outlets. Rather, the issue is decided on a case-by-case basis. To date, at least, the commission has had a social policy—the 1934 law—which it could invoke to decide specific cases. However, if the law is ever revoked or drastically amended, issues of access to the media by Spanish-only inhabitants may be heard with less sympathy.

THE CITIZENSHIP PARTICIPATION AND REPRESENTATION DOMAIN

In the domain of citizenship participation and representation, there are two areas where language inadequacies (or related issues) have been identified: (1) the need for Spanish language forms in taking census counts and (2) the need for Spanish-language services connected with voting. Looking first at the census question, we can see that the linguistic inadequacy is of two kinds—(a) the need for Spanish language forms and (b) the question of what kind of Spanish should be used in such forms.

The 1980 census provided Spanish-language questionnaire forms. In the May 4, 1978, *Los Angeles Times*, Martinez (for MALDEF) indicated how pressures were brought and a rationale provided for this decision. She noted that an advisory committee was set up by the Census Bureau to identify the reasons for the 1970 census undercount of many language minority groups. The committee found that one of the reasons was the "inability of census takers to communicate with respondents speaking Spanish." They also found that in 1970 "Spanish-speaking families who could not read the forms often did not respond and, to compound the problem, non-Spanish speaking interviewers were frequently sent out to collect the missing information." In other words, at the insistence of various civil rights groups, acting as language planners, the Census Bureau investigated a problem that, it turns out, included a language inadequacy in their own administration of the census and, as we know, attempted to correct the problem by providing Spanish-language forms.

The question of what kind of Spanish to use in a census form has been answered in two ways. In 1975 the Bureau of the Census pilot-tested in Texas a Spanish-language form that was to be used in the 1980 census. In a letter to the Census Bureau, Troike (1981) identified this census translation as *inadequate*, and his observation motivated the bureau to give more serious consideration to the translation process. (I will describe that process below.) However, in 1976 the National Center for Educational Statistics contracted with the Center for Applied Linguistics (CAL) to provide a questionnaire in Spanish for the Survey of Income and Education to be administered in collaboration with the Bureau of Census count of the children of poverty. The goal was to provide a form that would be understandable to speakers of the several regional varieties of Spanish in the United States. Troike (1981) describes the process of implementation in the preparation of this form. CAL assembled four translators—one Puerto Rican, one Cuban, one Mexican-American from Texas, and another from California. Troike describes some of the language issues that emerged. For example,

> *employer* was translated as *Para quién trabaja?* rather than as *patrón*, since the English could refer to a company as well as a person. *Armed forces* was translated as *fuerzas armadas,* although several members preferred *ejército,* because the latter was too restricted; *el militar* was not accepted by any.

Troike expresses regret that there were neither time nor funds available to field-test this form, since no real evaluation of its effectiveness did in fact take place. The Census Bureau took a different tack in meeting the problem of a need for intelligible Spanish, given the several varieties of Spanish used in the United States. For the Commonwealth of Puerto Rico they prepared a form in Puerto Rican Spanish.[9] For the rest of the United States, the Decennial Census Division worked with an advisory committee in preparing a form that would accommodate the several varieties of Spanish. They used two strategies:

> (1) They provided two alternate forms side-by-side. For example, for "toilet" they said *inodoro (excusado),* and for "truck," *troca (camión).*
> (2) They gave a Spanish form along with the English equivalent: *bombas electricas* (heat pumps).

The plan was created by the Decennial Census Division working with an advisory committee. The bureau did attempt to get feedback (evaluation) on the validity of the translation by pretesting the questionnaire in Austin (Texas), New York City, and Oakland (California), where speakers of the three major Spanish-language varieties are concentrated.[10]

Even with a Spanish translation, the question of collecting data from Spanish-only inhabitants had to be dealt with. MALDEF expressed concern in a *Los Angeles Times* article (Martinez, 1978) about whether the implementation would be adequate, since at that time only English language forms were to be mailed to homes, even in areas where the population was predominantly Chicano. They noted that there would at least be a small notice in Spanish telling recipients that they could request a version in their own language. The Census Bureau did, in fact, have a fairly elaborate implementation plan to reach non-English speakers. They worked with community groups, which contacted people in the census and apprised them of the importance of the community; they also had spot notices on television in Spanish, telling of the forthcoming administration of the census. They also had similar notices in other media and informed the public through brochures of the importance of the 1980 census.[11] Their effectiveness can be measured by the enormous increase in the count of non-English speaking inhabitants.

Another language issue in the citizenship area is the perceived need for Spanish-language services for non-English-speaking citizens who participate in the voting process. This became a hotly contested issue, since many voting administrators have challenged the provision for bilingual voter services in the Voting Rights Act of 1975 (amended in June 1982). Nonetheless, it is helpful to understand some of the issues involved and to try to see how much we know about the planning process. Until 1975, the right to bilingual election procedures derived only from section 4(e) of the Voting Rights Act of 1965, in which it was noted that it was a manifest injustice to bar Puerto Ricans from voting because of illiteracy in English (Teitelbaum and Hiller, 1977). Section 4(e) was targeted to prohibit the application of New York's literacy test to Puerto Ricans residing in that state. But, as Teitelbaum and Hiller note,

> eradicating the use of literacy tests was not enough, since registration and voting was conducted in English, a language incomprehensible to the intended beneficiaries of section 4(e).

Consequently, beginning in 1973 a series of lawsuits were filed charging that English-only elections constituted a condition on the right of Spanish monolingual Puerto Ricans to vote. In the important case, *Puerto Rican Organization for Political Action v. Kusper*, the court determined that "the right to vote" meant the right to an effective vote, and that a Spanish monolingual could not cast an effective vote when confronted with election materials she or he could not understand.

All of these cases, and several others, provided the legal underpinning for the bilingual election provisions contained in section 203 of Title II and section 301 of Title III of the 1975 Voting Rights Amendments. The attorney general is charged with the implementation of the act. The law specifies that a jurisdiction is deemed in violation of the act if the attorney general determines that any voting or registration materials provided to voters are exclusively English when five percent of the voting age population within any state or political subdivision are members of a single language minority and the rate of illiteracy of the particular language minority exceeds the national average of voting-age citizens. We can note that while the court suits focused on the inability of speakers to vote because of a lack of knowledge of English, this law rested on figures indicating numbers of people belonging to the minority group rather than upon their knowledge of English. The 1983 amendment, however, limited the definition of language minority to members of each language group who cannot speak English well enough to use English-language registration and voting materials (Downing, 1983). The argument used was that for the first time the Census Bureau determined in 1980 which inhabitants were unable to speak English and what other languages they did speak. On the basis of census data, it is possible to allocate bilingual materials and assistance to those who really need them.

Only a little is known about the actual implementation of this law. The Federal Election Commission contracted with the University of New Mexico to survey creative ideas about how bilingual elections could be carried out (Department of Linguistics, 1978). Their survey considered Spanish, Chinese, and Native American language minorities in the United States. According to David Lopez, one of the principal investigators, the survey found that there was considerable hostility toward the legislation, but it was able to identify some exemplary procedures, most of which related to the *process of voting,* itself. However, Lopez considered this an inappropriate point of entry, since the first and most important barrier to voting was at the *point of registration.* Without Spanish-speaking officials at the registration sites, Spanish-speaking voters could not begin the voting process. The law is not very specific in identifying the services that the state, country, and local officials must provide. It is clear that there is no regular mechanism for evaluating the quality and quantity of these services.

THE SOCIAL WELFARE DOMAIN

In the domain of social welfare, we found a clear instance of the access to quality and quantity of services being dependent on meaningful communication. The issue has been most extensively debated in New

York City by PRLDF and others. Without going into the complexities of the planners and the plan, I think that there are a couple of interesting aspects of this domain to be considered. The PRLDF argued that because there were no Spanish employees or forms, persons speaking only Spanish did not have equal access to welfare benefits. They argued that Spanish-only applicants received fewer or no benefits and were unequally subjected to hardships because they were required to provide their own translators. This resulted in their having to return more frequently to the center, in their having to keep young children out of school so that they could serve as interpreters (hence exposing them to family traumas they perhaps should have been spared), or in violating their own privacy, when an acquaintance served as interpreter.

These complaints were subsequently substantiated by the Mendoza Report, commissioned by the U.S. Department of Health, Education and Welfare and issued in September 1978. Of particular interest is the fact that the PRLDF was unable to base its claims on language inadequacies, but rather had to rely on Title VI of the 1964 Civil Rights Acts, which prohibits discrimination on the basis of national origin. This case of social welfare is also of interest because it illustrates the complex interaction between the need for recourse to the many sources of authority for language-related problems.

In this case, in the first instance, in 1973, the complaint was made as an administrative one to the Office of Civil Rights (OCR). When nothing was done there, the complaint was filed in federal court, which required that the defendant prove that the complaint was incorrect. The OCR then did an in-depth study, which resulted in the Mendoza Report. In 1979 the OCR issued a letter of findings based on this report, which triggered the New York City Department of Social Services into submitting a plan in which the city agreed to hire provisionally 272 bilingual workers. These figures were then disputed by the PRLDF. The OCR replied that it would monitor the department and then make a decision.

In August, 1981, the OCR found that the city was still in violation of Title VI. The PRLDF was still not happy with the implementation of the law because

(1) there was no guarantee that Spanish-only speakers will be assigned to a bilingual worker (they argue against the current policy, which assigns applicants on a random basis without consideration of their langauge needs);
(2) they wanted the city to provide periodic reports on the actual number of bilingual workers; and

(3) they wanted the bilingual workers to be given civil service status so as to guarantee that the service will be available.

The PRLDF was successful in getting the city of New York to revise one of its practices: Bilingual employees are now being assigned exclusively to limited English-speaking applicants and recipients. This practice ensures that those persons will receive the benefit of the newly hired bilingual employees. The PRLDF was considering going back to the courts on some of the other items of implementation.

I have not here detailed all of the complexities of this case, but it illustrates some of the problems of not only seeing that a law applies in a particular instance but also, once having done so, seeing that the ruling/regulation is implemented in an effective manner and on a regular basis. Further, although the Civil Rights Act applies across the nation, there are considerable difficulties in seeing to it that the New York decision is brought to bear in other communities where there are non-English-speaking welfare applicants. In 1979 MALDEF petitioned the Department of Health, Education and Welfare to have this law apply across the nation. The PRLDF sent a similar petition in 1979 to the Department of Labor. The likelihood of a response is slim in an era of deregulation and less government coercion in all areas.[12]

THE EDUCATION DOMAIN

Finally, we come to the domain of education, which I have deliberately left for last because it is so complex. In the other domains we have considered, the correlation between language knowledge and access to or the quality of services provided is relatively straightforward. Further, although the process of ensuring implementation is complex in the other domains, it is overwhelmingly and extraordinarily diverse in the educational domain. This is in large part because of the complex relationship between federal and state regulations in the domain of education. Hence, one would have to investigate (and I hope that someone will do so on a statewide basis) who the planners are, what the plan is, and how planning is carried out.

Another continuing area of concern in planning is the problem communities have in agreeing on the proper functions of education: Should education provide for children's cognitive growth, socialize them, prepare them for work, make good citizens out of them, help in their self-image, or something else? Unlike the medical domain, where the function is relatively clear (although there are many hidden agendas among the medical personnel who prevent the satisfactory delivery of services) agreement on the functions of education is not common. Indeed, there has been continual debate regarding this issue. Most recently the debate about the functions of education has focused upon questions of the validity and justice of competency testing. A large part of the problem is that people have differing opinions about what education is supposed to achieve.

However, we do have several planners and plans that have agreed that LEP/NEP children are not being adequately served and that something other than the traditional English program must be provided for them. The legal cases in which this has been mandated are well known. *Lau v. Nichols* is the landmark case on the federal level. *Aspira of New York v. New York City Board of Education* is an important landmark case in the states. There are and continue to be many other cases specifying that limited English-speaking children must get special care.

How is this decision to be implemented? On the federal level, the OCR issued the Lau remedies, which spelled out how the *Lau v. Nichols* court decision was to be implemented. The remedies specified that only bilingual education was an acceptable program unless a school district could prove that another treatment was acceptable. These remedies were finally challenged by the state of Alaska on a technicality—that normal federal procedure, requiring a hearing before a regulation becomes law, had not been followed. The OCR attempted to provide new regulations that were more specific about the nature of the instruction, the certification of teachers, the process of entry and exit for these programs, and the nature of testing. Public hearings were conducted in six cities throughout the United States, and over 7000 depositions were taken. Secretary of Education Bell rejected these regulations in January 1981, striking down a federal means of ensuring bilingual education for LEP/NEP children. The OCR now uses an earlier memo (May 25, 1970) by then OCR director Pottinger, which requires school districts to address the deficient English-language skills of children and to take actions to rectify this deficiency.[13]

At the same time, the federal government still continues to provide monies toward the implementation of bilingual programs by supporting such services as materials development, technical assistance, teacher training, evaluation, research on bilingual education, as well as the National Clearinghouse for Bilingual Education. Many of the states have also enacted bilingual education laws that provide for limited-English speakers. That of California tries to spell out much of the implementation process in detail—how many children, what kind of treatment, how many teachers, what kind of competence teachers should have, and what sort of testing and placement. California Law AB507 took effect in September 1981; all of the regulations, guidelines and administrative directives associated with it are in place; however, administrators still look to the state for guidance in this area. They seek clarification or interpretation of regulations, they request approval of their plan as a response to the law, or in some cases they seek relief from certain provisions.

There are two other language-related issues in education that should be mentioned, both of them concerned with what could be called "corpus planning issues." The first relates to the testing of the children's knowledge of Spanish, and the second with the development of materials for Spanish-speaking children. Troike (1981) described how the Materials Development Center in Miami tried to serve children using different varieties of Spanish. He notes that they developed separate parallel curricula for Mexican-American, Cuban, and Puerto Rican Spanish in response to local demands. Further, he feels that most of the differences among these varieties for written purposes appear to lie in the names of objects (nouns, for example) and cites a few examples:

> the Southwestern *tortilla*, a flat, thin, circular, unleavened corn or wheat bread, is an omelette in the East, while an orange is a *china* in the East but a *naranja* in the West.

Keller (1983) has presented extensive information on the corpus planning issues in Spanish in the United States. He notes that the problem has been to decide which variety of Spanish to use in the classroom. He finds,

> The answer has been often made in the form of one or two extremes. There are those who exalt the ethnic form of their locality and denigrate what the American Association of Teachers of Spanish and Portuguese has called "world standard Spanish." Conversely, there are those who exalt "world standard Spanish" and denigrate the ethnic or folk form.

As a more specific example, Keller cites his experience in 1974 as linguist for a National Institute of Education project, which was to evaluate approximately 100 curriculum titles in Spanish bilingual education. The project found eight types of Spanish in existence in 1974 in Spanish bilingual education programs.

> (1) Programs that use "world standard Spanish." Some of the language is free of regionalisms. Some of the language may not be understood by United States Spanish speakers who use a regional or ethnic designation

instead of a standard one (e.g., these programs use *autobus,* but not *camión or guagua*).

(2) Programs that use language specific to particular regions or social groups of the Hispanic world outside of the United States, such as Spain, Bolivia, or Chile. For example, these programs may use *micro* (Chile) or *autocar* (Spain), but not *autobus, camión* or *guagua*.

(3) Programs that use language characteristic of all the regions and ethnic varieties of United States Spanish. That is, the programs use *guagua* and *camión,* but not *autobus*.

(4) Programs that use language characteristic of the eastern United States and the Caribbean; for example, they use *guagua,* but not *autobus* or *camión*.

(5) Programs that use language characteristic of the western United States and Mexico. For example, they use *Camión,* but not *guagua* or *autobus*.

(6) Programs that use nonstandard, non-Spanish (as in bad translations).

(7) Programs that use both the regional or ethnic varieties of language and the "world standard Spanish" variety. For example, they use *camión* and *guagua* in addition to *autobus*.

(8) Programs that use controlled "world standard Spanish," using only common language forms, for which there are no alternative regionalisms or ethnic varieties, hence eliminating *camión, guagua,* and *autobus* from instructional materials (Keller, 1983).

Keller argues that there needs to be appropriate compartmentalization. Type 1 he feels is best used in more advanced Spanish-language courses, particularly in the content areas such as math and the sciences. Types 4 and 5 should be used in the relevant regions in transitional bidialectal education. Type 8 feels he successfully deals with miscues that would otherwise crop up in teaching literacy. The complexities of language planning in education are fascinating and would require several volumes to discuss all of the issues, planners, plans, and processes of implementation and feedback.

SUMMARY

We have surveyed some of the major kinds of actors who have appeared and the activities they have undertaken in the United States in the last 20 years in an attempt to provide services to the Spanish-language community. We have focused largely on federal governmental planning activities, but have provided examples of state or nongovernmental attention to language inadequacies. All of the examples are ones in which the "instrumental" communicative function of language is clear.

We can note that in some cases the issues could be treated in terms of language, whereas in others it was necessary to use legal precedent to provide services for Spanish-only language clients. As a summary of cases from Teitelbaum and Hiller (1977: 96) notes,

> Accommodating non-English speakers in areas other than education requires a showing that without bilingual services, the protection of substantial rights is diminished. Thus, non-English-speaking plaintiffs must premise their language discrimination claim on the preservation of established rights, and not naked demands for bilingualism.

They note, further, that the greatest gains for non-English speakers have been where the rights at issue have been deemed to be of particular importance by the courts; for example, both voting rights and inequality in the criminal justice area are scrupulously probed, whereas the courts have given less favorable treatment to unequal delivery of social services.

The range of interaction of planners in the identification of problems and the making of a plan in any one domain is great. We have noted the extensive participation of the PRLDF and MALDEF, as well as others in influencing language-related decisions. At the federal level there is a very wide range of planners who have the authority and power to make language-related decisions; decisions can be made through judicial decrees, through congressional law. Although the PRLDF and MALDEF have thus far concentrated on litigation as a means of affecting policy, cases decided in a particular court are not automatically applied to other states without further litigation or executive regulation. Further, decisions made through litigation are difficult to implement, since the courts do not have the staff to ensure implementation and often appoint someone without much power to oversee the court order. When a decision is made in the courts and then implemented by an administrative branch of the executive, the possibilities for effective implementation are greater. For example, once the courts ruled in *Lau v. Nichols* that limited-English speakers needed more than "English only" treatment, the Office of Civil Rights had a strong basis for issuing regulations implementing bilingual education in all of the school districts. As we have noted, there are other planners on other levels; often these planners can be found in the private sector.

The plans occur in a wide variety of forms and products. In the federal case, as we have indicated above, they come most often in the form of court decisions, laws, or administrative regulations. But they can also consist of textbooks that contain specific kinds of language, or dictionaries that prescribe correctness or designate regionalisms, and so forth.

Finally, I would like to note that the area of planning is the one in which the actors are most diffuse. To the extent that the plan specifies who is to implement the plan in what way, who is to monitor the implementation process according to what sort of guidelines, and what they are to do with this monitoring, we can observe that the planning stage *can* be more effective. However, in most of the instances we have examined, the plan is not very specific, so that we find that there is a very disjointed, continual attempt to define the basis for an effective and appropriate implementation procedure. For example, the PRLDF in two separate cases in the educational domain brought suit to ensure adequate implementation. One suit related to the dispersal rather than the concentration of Hispanic children in Delaware (*Evans v. Buchanan*). Another related to the need to hire more Hispanic teachers (*Morgan v. McDonough*). Nonetheless, we can note that when regulations are too specific and the implementors do not agree with them, often because they do not suit their specific situation, then implementors may choose to ignore or violate them as long as they can. So, enlisting the participation of the implementors in the process of making a plan has been recognized as essential by some students of social planning (Webber, 1978).

We can conclude that over the past twenty years the United States has been deeply involved in defining language inadequacies that limited-English speakers may have in many public domains. Several of the issues have been carried out on behalf of Spanish-only speakers. Finally, I would like to note that scholars have a very important role to play in this process. First and foremost, they can be very influential in defining language-related difficulties experienced by Spanish-only speakers. Second, they have been and will continue to be important in providing information for making a plan and in the actual planning process, by helping to define adequate criteria for implementation as well as criteria for the evaluation of such plans. It is an extremely exciting and important area for the application of linguistic and sociolinguistic skills to monitor the ways in which attention to and solutions for language inadequacies arise and are resolved in the public domain.

NOTES

1. Personal communication, Lorenzo Avila, OCR, San Francisco.
2. This case was settled in January 1983. It provided, among other things, for automatic assignment of interpreters at hearings where requested or required, verbatim

translation of the entire proceedings including relevant parts of documents introduced in evidence, recognition that language difficulties may be a valid basis for reversing a denial of benefits, translation of all forms and notices at the administrative-law-judge and appeal-board levels, translation assistance in preparing written appeals to the appeal board and a periodic Spanish-language needs assessment to determine adequate staffing at the local offices where applications for benefits are processed (PRLDF, 1983: p. 7).

3. Level 3 means that the person can participate fully in conversations with native speakers of the language on a variety of topics, including professional ones, with relative fluency and ease. The person should have mastered most of the major grammatical features of the language and enough vocabulary to cover a large number of topics.

4. This information was obtained through the courtesy of Maria Ortiz, California Department of Education.

5. Personal communication, Concepción Valadez.

6. Personal communication, Henry Barnum.

7. According to information provided by attorney Ann Hill of MALDEF, one other state has looked into the language needs of its Spanish-speaking population: Connecticut. The Southern New England Telephone Company (SNETCO) has studied of the needs of the Hispanic community and held meetings to ascertain if their needs were met. This was done because in filing for a rate increase, SNETCO was required to demonstrate that it was satisfying its customers. Unfortunately, SNETCO has decided that the way to meet the needs of Hispanics is to provide an Emergency Spanish Assistance Lab modeled after that of Los Angeles.

8. Personal communicaton, attorney Margo Polivy.

9. Personal communication, Angel Landron, of the Census Bureau.

10. Personal communication, Carmina Young, Bureau of the Census.

11. Ibid.

12. I am indebted for this information to Robert Becker of the PRLDF and to Adalberto Aguirre (1980) for details on the Mendoza report.

13. However, unlike the remedies, under this memo there is more flexibility with respect to the range of possible remedies, and this now includes meaningful ESL programs.

9

THE ALCHEMY OF ENGLISH
Social and Functional Power of Non-Native Varieties

Braj B. Kachru

WHAT IS THE APPROPRIATENESS of the term "alchemy" to the functions of the English language today? In a metaphorical sense, this term captures the attitudinal reactions to the status and functions of English across cultures during our times. Competence in English and the use of this language signify a transmutation: an added potential for material and social gain and advantage. One sees this attitude in what the symbol stands for; English is considered a symbol of modernization, a key to expanded functional roles, and an extra arm for success and mobility in culturally and linguistically complex and pluralistic societies. As if all this were not enough, it is also believed that English contributes to yet another type of transmutation: It internationalizes one's outlook. In comparison with other languages of wider communication, knowing English is like possessing the fabled Aladdin's lamp, which permits one to open, as it were, the linguistic gates to international business technology, science, and travel. In short, English provides linguistic power.

One might, then, say that acquiring English is like going through a linguistic reincarnation. And from the perspectives of the Indian subcontinent, which is the main focus of this chapter, English initiates one into the caste that has power and, more important, that controls vital knowledge about the miracles of science and technology. Thus, as Cooper (1984) mentions specifically in the case of Israel, there is at present a "hunger" and an "indecent passion" for acquiring English. What is true of Israel applies to practically all other parts of the world as well.

This power of alchemy or transmutation was not always associated with English. The sociolinguistic context of the English language has been changing constantly from the sixteenth century to the present era (see, e.g., Baugh, 1935). However, this change has accelerated—and has been rather unexpected in some ways—during the post-Colonial period. (Various reasons for this change are discussed in Kachru, [1982e]).

The legacy of colonial Englishes has resulted in the existence of several transplanted varieties of English having distinct linguistic ecologies—their own contexts of function and usage. These nonnative varieties have, in turn, brought about changes in the native varieties of English and have also resulted in numerous sociolinguistic, linguistic, and literary questions being posed which have rarely been asked about English before. In recent years such questions have been discussed in several conferences and colloquia, in various types of publications, and in specialized journals devoted to English in the world context (Baily and Görlach, 1982; Greenbaum, 1984; King, 1980; Strevens, 1980; Smith, 1981; Kachru, 1982e).

I am concerned here with a small slice of this total time-span: the post-Colonial period since the 1940s and, in particular, three aspects of the colonial Englishes on the Indian subcontinent. First, I shall deal with the sociolinguistic consequences of the use of a Western language as a restricted code of communication that has rapidly become a symbol of power, authority, and elitism in the non-Western world. In such non-native contexts, English has become a vehicle of values not always in harmony with local traditions and beliefs. Second, I shall consider English as an "in-group" language, uniting elite speakers across ethnic, religious, and linguistic boundaries used for political change. Third, I shall examine the linguistic and cultural adaptation English has undergone in the process of maintaining various patterns of administrative, legal, educational, and professional power.

LANGUAGE AS POWER, LANGUAGE AND POWER

What does one mean by associating power with language? The term "power" is used here in an abstract sense, to refer to the control of knowledge and to the prestige a language acquires as a result of its use in certain important domains. The more important a domain is, the more "powerful" a language becomes. This, then, is reflected in the attitutude of native or non-native users toward a language or a specific variety of a language. In many societies language has traditionally been viewed as possessing intrinsically a mystic or superhuman power; one sees it in the word *śakhti* when attributed to *dev-vānī* (god's-language) referring to Sanskrit. (Ferguson [1982b] and

Samarin [1976] discuss language in the religious context.)

The mystic power attributed to a language, or the *mantra*[1] (verses or phrases believed to possess magical or religious efficacy) is as old as, for example, the Hindu tradition. In the case of Sanskrit, the relationship of language and power was subtly exploited for standardizing language and for maintaining its *śudda* (pure) form. In the *Aṣṭādhyāyī* (Eight Chapters), compiled by Pāṇini (fourth century B.C.), a prescriptive norm was established for Sanskirt. At that time Sanskrit was developing regional variations, which would eventually endanger intelligibility between speakers of its different varieties. A description of the language had to be made available that would provide a model for the learner and thus preserve, in an oral tradition, the sacred Hindu hymns. This prescriptive (and applied) motivation of the Indian grammarians, Pāṇini included, led to major theoretical and analytical breakthroughs in linguistics (Varma, 1929; Allen, 1953; Staal, 1975).

Of course at that time there were no organized academies to oversee the codification of language; therefore, divine wrath was threatened in various *sūtras*[2] (religious aphorisms), warning the reciter of the hymns of the consequences (psychologically severe and physically damaging) of any careless pronunciation or deviation from the prescribed text. The sūtras (Fremantle, 1974: 18-30) warned that

> [When a *mantra* is] deficient in a syllable it tends to diminish life, and [when it is] lacking in proper accent it makes the reciter troubled with illness, and the syllable (wrongly treated) will strike one at the head as a thunderbolt.
>
> A *mantra* [hymn] recited with incorrect intonation and "careless" arrangement of *varṇa* (letters) [reacts] like a thunderbolt and gets the reciter destroyed by God Indra [the chief vedic god, also the god of rain and thunder].
>
> The enunciation of *varṇa* should be perfect. The letters should be handled with the same care with which a tigress carries her cubs with her teeth. She is so careful that no cub is hurt, destroyed, or pained.

Pāṇini, the ancient Hindu grammarian, was seen as part of the divine scheme for codifying Sanskrit, and homage was paid to him "who having received the traditional lore of speech-sounds (*varṇa-samāmnāya*) from Siva [Hindu god of creation and destruction] has told us the entire grammar" (Fremantle, 1974: 30).

In such ancient texts, the power of the word is recognized as supreme. The first attempts toward prescriptivism in language (the supporting of a preferential model) were thus motivated by religion. Much later, the same purpose was served by the language academies (established, for example, in Italy in 1582, and France in 1635). The relationship of language *and* power (not in a superhuman sense) has also been well documented in the literature (Kramarae, 1981). But the language policies that the prolonged colonizers (e.g., British, French, America) or short-term colonizers (e.g., Japanese in Korea, Malaysia, and Indonesia) developed for control and stability have as yet to be discussed from linguistic, educational, and political perspectives.

The spread of English did not always entail the teaching and learning of a standard (or codified) variety prescribed by an authority such as an academy or by the sanctity of religion (Kachru, 1982a). In liturgical use, or as a symbol of Christianity, English was a minor linguistic tool, at best. The Christian missionaries and colonial administrators were not of one opinion about the role of English in proselytization: The controversy between the Orientalists and Anglicists (Occidentalists) is insightful concerning the role of English in the Indian subcontinent (Kachru, 1983: 68-69; for Africa see Chishimba, 1983). This contrasts with the association of Arabic with Islam, and Sanskrit with Hinduism. Ferguson (1982b: 104) rightly observes that

> all Brahmin priests, no matter what their sect or mother tongue, can make use of *some* Sanskrit if they meet together in Benaras, and all Muslim pilgrims to Mecca make some use of Arabic, but there is no common language for Buddhists or Christian clergy to recite the Three Treasures or Our Father.

ENGLISH AS A LANGUAGE OF POWER

The monarchy of Britain may have at one time claimed "divine rights," but those rights were never extended to the language of the monarchs. The power of English is, therefore, of a more worldly nature—in what Quirk et al. (1972: 2) have termed the "vehicular load" of a language, which English carries as the "primary medium for twentieth century science and technology." The other, equally important, markers of that power of English are its demographic distribution, its native and non-native users across cultures, its use in important world forums, and its rich literary tradition.

The power of English, then, resides in the domains of its use, the roles its users can play, and—attitudinally—above all, how others view its importance. On all these counts, English excels other world languages. One would not have foreseen this situation easily in the sixteenth century, though even in 1599 Samuel Daniel, a minor poet, fantasized about the "treasures of our language" going to "the strange shores." The questions Daniel asked (in his poem *Musothilus)* then have been fully answered and realized in the succeeding four centuries:

> And who, in time, knows whither we may vent
>   The treasures of our tongue, to what strange shores
>   This gain of our best glory shall be sent,
>   To enrich unknowing nations with our stores?
>   What worlds in the yet unformed Occident
>   May come refined with the accents that are ours?
> Or who can tell for what great work in hand
>   The greatness of our style is now ordained?
>   What powers it shall bring in, what spirits command,
>   What thoughts let out, what humours keep restrained,
>   What mischief it may powerfully withstand,
>   And what fair ends may thereby be attained?

Perhaps one could not take these rhetorical questions too seriously before the full impact of William Shakespeare, Ben Jonson, and others who made the Elizabethan period the glory of the English language. The exploits of the Raj had not yet unfolded; the "alien shores" were still not part of the Empire. As John Dryden lamented in 1693, the English language possessed "no prosodia, not so much as a tolerable dictionary or a grammar, so that our language is in a manner barbarous" (quoted in Baugh and Cable, 1978: 255). The picture had changed little for almost a century from 1582 when, in the words of Richard Mulcaster, English was "of small reach," extending "no further than this island of ours, nay not these over all" (quoted in Smith, 1981: xiv). But that cynicism was short-lived, as the following centuries were to prove.

Today the linguistic vision of Samuel Daniel has been realized, the English language is a tool of power, domination, and elitist identity, and of communication across continents. Although the era of the "White man's burden" has practically ended in a political sense, and the Raj has retreated to native shores, the linguistic and cultural consequences of imperialism have changed the global scene. The linguistic ecology of, for example, Africa and Asia is not the same. English has become an integral part of this new complex sociolinguistic setting. The colonial Englishes were essentially acquired and used as non-native second languages, and after more than two centuries, they continue to have the same status. The *non-nativeness* of such varieties is not only an attitudinally significant term, but it also has linguistic and sociolinguistic significance. (See Kachru [forthcoming] for a further dicussion.)

ENGLISH AS A COLONIAL LANGUAGE

The political power of the British (and Americans in the Philippines or Puerto Rico) gave to them as colonists a lot of political stature, requiring them to adopt a pose fitting their status. The white man's language became a *marker* of his power. Englishmen became different persons while functioning in Asia and Africa. The sahibs in the colonies underwent a change facilitated by the new-found prestige of their native language. What was true of the Indian scene was also true in other parts of the world, and E. M. Forster (1952 [1924]) captured it well in *A Passage to India*. Referring to the Englishmen in India, two of the novel's characters say,

India likes gods.

And Englishmen like posing as gods.

The English language was part of the pose and the power. Indians, Africans, and others realized it and accepted it. Therefore, it is not surprising that when a native tried to adopt the same pose—that is, to speak the same language—it made the sahib uncomfortable.

The term "non-native" Englishes is used here, following my earlier use of the term (Kachru, 1965, and later) for those transplanted varieties of English that are acquired primarily as second languages. In such a context, whatever other motivations there may be, English is used as a tool of power to cultivate a group of people who will identify with the cultural and other norms of the political elite. In India, T. B. Macaulay, in his often-quoted *Minute*, dreamt of developing a culturally distinct group who would form "a class who may be interpreters between us and those whom we govern, a class of persons, Indians in blood and colour, English in taste, in opinion, in morals and in intellect" (cited in Sharp, 1920-1922: I, 116).

Almost at the same time, another English-speaking nation, the United States, "set out to Americanize Puerto Rico with a vengeance during the first fifty years of its occupation" (Zentella, 1981: 219). The U.S. government's view, as Zentella observes, was presented by Victor Clark, the Commissioner of Education:

> If the schools became American and the teachers and students were guided by the American spirit, then the island would be essentially American in sympathies, opinions, and attitudes toward government.

The year 1898 saw American power extend in another direction as well—to the Philippines, where "the mock battle in Manila Bay marked the end of 300 years of Spanish and the beginning of American colonial domination." The U.S. atttitude toward this colony was no different from the one toward Puerto Rico. President McKinley is reported to have said the American duty toward the newly acquired colony should be "to educate the Filipinos and uplift and civilize and Christianize them to fit the people for the duties of citizenship" (quoted in Beebe and Beebe, 1981: 322).

Such views had been expressed a little earlier in South Asia by colonizers from the other side of the Atlantic. Charles Grant believed that

> the true curse of darkness is the introduction of light. The Hindoos err, because they are ignorant and their errors have never fairly been laid before them. The communication of our light and knowledge to them would prove the best remedy for their disorders [Grant, 1831-1832: 60-61].

In what was then known as Ceylon (now renamed Sri Lanka) the same pattern was repeated. In 1827 Sir Edward Barnes (the governor of Sri Lanka from 1824-1831) laid the foundation of a "Christian Institution":

> to give a superior education to a number of young persons who from their ability, piety, and good conduct were likely to prove fit persons in communicating a knowledge of Christianity to their countrymen [Barnes, 1932: 43]

In imparting such education, the governor, as Ruberu says (1962: 158-159), did not desire any association with or support from the American missionaries who were then present in Sri Lanka. Therefore, a letter was sent to the American missionaries on the island saying that "the means we possess in our own country for the conversion of our heathen subjects to Christianity are in the Lieutenant Governor's opinion fully adequate to all purposes" (quoted by Ruberu, 1962: 158). This was said much before Rudyard Kipling's call to "take up the White man's burden" (quoted in Shanks, 1970).

In these statements English is associated with a power more subtle than mere worldly success: It is considered to be a tool of "civilization" and "light." Provision of that tool is perceived as a colonizer's contribution—and duty—to the well-being of the inhabitants of newly acquired colonies. According to this view, then, language can open the gates for the emancipation of souls. And here we find a subtle parallel to the power attributed to the Sanskrit texts.

Along with its "other-worldly" reward, English also provided an earthly bonus as a medium for understanding technology and scientific development. For more pensive minds, it made available the literary treasures of the European languages. To newly "awakened" Asian and African minds, that literature in itself was a revelation. Macaulay had already warned the insecure among them that

> I have no knowledge of either Sanskrit or Arabic. But I have done what I could to form a correct estimate of their value. ... I am quite ready to take the Oriental learning at the valuation of the Orientalists themselves. I have never found one amongst them who could deny that a single shelf of a good European library was worth the whole native literature of India and Arabia [Sharp, 1920-1922].

The Industrial Revolution's technological impact and the cultural dimensions of the Renaissance clearly brought before non-Western intellectuals the accomplishments of the West. The ambitious among the colonized viewed English as their main tool with which to emulate such accomplishments.

Slowly the new political reality bestowed the socially and administratively dominant roles on the newly installed language. Ultimately the legal system, the national media, and important professions were conducted in English. The medium was associated with the message of medical miracles and of technology. There already existed an ambitious (albeit small) group who wanted to acquire English for "mathematics, natural philosophy, chemistry, anatomy, and other useful sciences, which the natives of Europe have carried to a degree of perfection" (Raja Rammohan Roy [quoted in Kachru, 1969,

1978]). For this purpose Roy was pleading that the "European gentlemen of talent and education" be appointed "to instruct the natives of India."

Eventually the small number of Indians, Africans, or Filipinos who became proficient in such professional roles became the symbols of what was termed "Westernization" (or, to use a neutral term, "modernization"). The "brown sahibs" seemed to feel solidarity, at least attitudinally, with the "white sahibs." Whether or not this feeling was reciprocated or exploited, the fact remains that a linguistic tool of power was steadily being shared. The domains of language use defined the power and prestige of language. English acquired a strong non-native base, and the local languages slowly lost the battle for prestige and power.

The elite language was eventually used against the Englishmen, against their roles and their intentions; it became the language of resurgence, of nationalism, and political awakening at one level. And now the colonized, like Caliban (Shakespeare, *The Tempest*), were sometimes heard to say,

> You taught me language and my profit on't
> Is, I know how to curse! The red plague rid you
> For learning me your language.

There are some who consider it a "grotesque perversion of the truth" that English "was imposed on a subject people by a set of foreign rulers for the sake of carrying on their alien government" (Chaudhuri, 1976: 89). The word "imposed" is tricky here, for what was attitudinally prestigious and pragmatically desirable and rewarding did not need imposition. Power seems to have a way of creating its linguistic base.

The linguistic and cultural pluralism in Africa and South Asia contributed to the spread of English, and helped foster its retention even after the colonial period ended. The nationalist awakening needed a pan-national medium for a resurgence; the medium chosen was, ironically, the "alien" language. And there were reasons, both cultural and linguistic, for that choice.

True, Indian leaders like Mohandas K. Gandhi were struggling to create consensus for a mutually acceptable native variety as the national language (Desai, 1964), but their message to the elite was expressed in English. By the 1920s, English had become the language of political discourse, intranational administration, and law, and it was associated with liberal thinking. These roles, and such an attitude toward English, maintained its power over local languages even after the colonial period ended.

ACQUIRING DOMAINS OF POWER

Ease in acquiring domains of power is not necessarily related to the number of a language's users. The number of bilinguals able to use English in non-native contexts has always been limited: in South Asia, for example, it has not exceeded 3% of the literate population.[3] However, that small segment of the population controls domains that have professional prestige; therefore, these people are considered worthy of emulation. One might say that they control certain types of knowledge that ambitious parents would like their children to possess. And whose parents are not ambitious?

In India, only Sanskrit, English, Hindi, and to some extent Persian have acquired pan-Indian intranational functions. The domains of Sanskrit are restricted, and the proficiency in it limited, except in the case of some professional pandits. The cause of Hindi was not helped by the controversy between Hindi, Urdu, and Hindustani. Support for Hindustani almost ended with independence; after the death of its ardent and influential supporter, Gandhi, very little was heard about it. The enthusiasm and near euphoria of the supporters of Hindi were not channeled in a constructive (and realistic) direction, especially after the 1940s. The result is that English continues to be a language both of power and of prestige (Kachru, 1976; K. Sridhar, 1982).

For governments, English thus serves at least two purposes. First, it continues to provide a linguistic tool for the administrative cohesiveness of a country (as in South Asia and parts of Africa). Second, at another level, it provides a language of wider communication (national and international). The enthusiasm for English is not unanimous, or even widespread. The disadvantages of using it are obvious: Cultural and social implications accompany the use of an external language. But the native languages are losing in this competition (Apte, 1976; Das Gupta, 1969, 1970).

English does have one clear advantage, attitudinally and linguistically: It has acquired a *neutrality* in a linguistic context where native languages, dialects, and styles sometimes have acquired undesirable connotations. Whereas native codes are functionally marked in terms of caste, religion, region, and so forth, English has no such "markers," at least in the non-native context. It was originally the foreign (alien) ruler's language, but that drawback is often overshadowed by what it can do for its users. True, English is associated with a small and elite group; but it is in their role that the *neutrality* of a language becomes vital (e.g., for Tamil speakers in Tamil Nadu, or Bengali speakers in the West Bengal). In India the most widely used language is Hindi (46%), and its different varieties (e.g., Hindustani, Urdu), have traditionally been associated with various factions: Hindi with the Hindus; Urdu with the Muslims; and Hindustani with the maneuvering political pandits who could not create a constituency for it. While these attitudinal allocations are not necessarily valid, this is how the varieties have been perceived and presented. English, on the other hand, is not associated primarily with any one faction.

Whatever the limitations of English, it has been perceived as the language of power and opportunity, free of the limitations that the ambitious attribute to the native languages.

ATTITUDINAL NEUTRALITY AND POWER

In several earlier studies it has been shown (Kachru, 1978, 1982c) that in *code-mixing,* for example, English is being used to *neutralize* identities one is reluctant to express by the use of native languages or dialects. "Code-mixing refers to the use of lexical items or phrases from one code in the stream of discourse of another. Neutralization thus is a linguistic strategy used to "unload" a linguistic item from its traditional, cultural, and emotional connotations by avoiding its use and choosing an item from another code. The borrowed item has referential meaning, but no cultural connotations in the context of the specific culture (Kachru, 1982c). This is not borrowing in the sense of filling a lexical gap, as the following examples show.

In Kashmiri the native word *mɔnd* ("widow") invokes the traditional connotations associated with widowhood. Its use is restricted to abuses and curses, not occurring in "polished" conversation. Vedvā (Hindi *vidhwā*) or English *widow* is preferred by the Hindus. In Tamil, as shown by Annamalai (1978) *maccaan* and *attimbeer* reveal the caste identity of the speaker—not desirable in certain situations. Therefore, one uses English *brother-in-law*, instead. English *rice* is neutral compared with *saadam* or *sooru* (purist) in Tamil. A lexical item may be associated with a specific style in the native language, as are *manaivi* (formal) and *peṇḍaṭṭi* (colloquial) in Tamil, but the English equivalent *wife* has no style restrictions.

In such contexts, then, the power of neutralization is associated with English in two ways. First, English provides—with or without "mixing"—an additional code that has referential meaning but no cultural overtones or connotations. Thus the types of linguistic features (especially lexicalization) that mark *granthika* (classical) versus *vyavahārika* (colloquial) in Telugu, *sādhubhaṣā* (literary) versus *calitbhāṣa* (colloquial) in Bengali, and Hindu versus Muslim Kashmiri, are obscured by using English or by lexicalization from English. English neutralizes discourse in terms of "identity," providing another identity. The bilingual (or multilingual) speaker can use codes for an identity shift: to obscure one identity and bring into the foreground another. Second, such use of English develops new code-mixed varieties of languages (Kachru, 1978). Lexicalization from English is particularly preferred in the contexts of kinship, taboo items, science and technology, or in discussing sex organs and death. What Moag (1982) terms the "social neutrality" of English in the case of Fiji is applicable in almost all the countries where English is used. In the Fijian context, Tongans and Fijians

> find English the only safe medium in which to address those of higher status. English not only hides their inability in the specialized vernacular registers, but also allows them to meet traditional superiors in a more or less equal footing [Moag, 1982].

VARIETIES AND STYLES: THEIR FUNCTIONAL POWER

The colonial Englishes, like any other variety of English, are not homogeneous. There is variation within each (Smith, 1981; Kachru, 1982b, 1983). As the range and depth of function increase, so does the variation of any language. The competence of speakers varies from the educated to the pidginized varieties. For example, in Nigeria, four varieties of English have been identified by their linguistic characteristics (Bamgboṣe, 1982). In Singapore, Malaysia (Platt and Weber, 1980; Wong, 1981; Tay and Gupta, 1983) and India (Kachru, 1965, and later) one notices the same cline of bilingualism. (See Kachru [1983: 4-5] for a discussion of variation and cline of bilingualism.)

The varieties are also distinguished on the basis of settings—formal or informal.

> In Singapore English, a final sentence particle *la*, probably of Hokkien origin, is extensively used when English is employed in informal settings

and where the speech event calls for solidarity, rapport, etc. [Richards, 1982].

In Malaysian English the situation is identical. Consider the following examples given by Wong (1983: 142).

Better you speak to him yourself *lah*.
He just sitting there and doing nothing *lah*.
I don't know *lah*.
I cannot move it *lah*.
Don't be stubborn *lah*.

It is, however, in the nativized communicative acts, and situationally dependent (non-Western) rhetorical styles, that one finds the subtle use of English. I shall not elaborate on this aspect, since it would take us into a detailed discussion of stylistic devices used in contact literatures in English (see Kachru [1983] for discussion and illustrations). I will only mention that a non-native writer of English faces a dilemma. On the one hand, Naipaul (1973: 12) is right when he says,

> It is an odd, suspicious situation: an Indian writer writing in English for an English audience about non-English characters who talk their own sort of English.... I cannot help feeling that it might have been more profitable for me to appear in translation.

On the other hand, several non-native writers in English have taken quite the opposite view (for example, poets A. K. Ramanujan and R. Parathasarthy, and fiction writers Mulk Raj Anand, R. K. Narayan, and Raja Rao). Narayan is "particularly fond of the language [English]...it is...very adaptable...and it's so transparent it can take on the tint of any country" (Walsh, 1971: 7). This view is almost identical to the view of the African creative writer Achebe (1965: 222) when he asks, "Can an African ever learn English well enough to be able to use it effectively in creative writing?" And he answers affirmatively, but qualifies his answer:

> If on the other hand you ask: "Can he ever learn to use it like a native speaker?" I should say, "I hope not. It is neither necessary, nor desirable for him to be able to do so. ...I feel that the English language will be able to carry the weight of my African experience. But it will have to be a new English, still in communion with its ancestral home but altered to suit its new African surroundings.

CONTACT LITERATURES IN ENGLISH: CREATIVITY IN THE OTHER TONGUE

The contact literatures in English have several characteristics, of which two may be mentioned here. In South Asia, to take one example, there are three more or less pan-South Asian literatures: Sanskrit, Persian, and Hindi. In terms of both style and content, Sanskrit has been associated with the native Hindu tradition. Persian (in its Indian form) and Urdu have maintained the Perso-Arabic stylistic devices, metaphors, and symbolism. It is this aspect of Urdu that alienated it from the traditionalist Hindus, who believe that in its formal experimentation, thematic range, and metaphor, it has maintained an "un-Indian" (Islamic) tradition, and continues to seek inspiration from such non-native traditions. This attitude toward Urdu tells only part of the story, and negates the contribution that the Hindus have made to the Urdu language, and the way it was used as the language of national revival. Indian English literature cuts across these attitudes. It has united certain pan-South Asian nationalists, intellectuals, and creative writers. It has provided a new perspective in India through an "alien" language.

In Indian English fiction (see, e.g., Mukherjee, 1971; Parameswaran, 1976) R. K. Narayan, Mulk Raj Anand, and Raja Rao (e.g., his *Kanthapura*) have brought another dimension to the understanding of the regional, social and political contexts. In the process, linguistically speaking, the process of the Indianization of English has acquired an institutionalized status (Kachru, 1983).

In a sociological sense, then, English has provided a linguistic tool and a sociopolitical dimension very different from those available through native linguistic tools and traditions. A non-native writer in English functions in two traditions. In psychological terms, such a multilingual role calls for adjustment. In attitudinal terms, it is controversial; in linguistic terms, it is challenging, for it means molding the language for new contexts. Such a writer is suspect as fostering new beliefs, new value systems, and even new linguistic loyalties and innovations.

This, then, leads us to the other side of this controversy. For example, what have been the implications of such a change—attitudinally and sociologically—for the Indian languages (and for African languages) and for those speakers whose linguistic repertoires do not include English? Additionally, we need to ask what are its implications for the creative writers whose media are "major" or "minor" Indian languages. (For further discussion, see Ansre [1979] for Africa, and Kachru [1982b] for South Asia.)

POST-COLONIAL PERIOD

Since independence, the controversy about English has taken new forms. Its "alien" power base is less an issue; so is its Englishness or Americanness in a cultural sense. The English language is not perceived as necessarily imparting only Western traditions. The medium is non-native, but the message is not. In several Asian and African countries, English now has national and international functions that are both distinct and complementary. English has thus acquired a new power base and a new elitism. The domains of English have been restructured. The result is that one more frequently, and very eloquently, hears people ask, Is English really a non-native ("alien") language for India, for Africa, and for Southeast Asia?[4]

In the case of India one wonders: has India played the age-old trick on English, too, of nativizing it and acculturating it—in other words, Indianizing it? The Indian writer and philosopher Raja Rao (1978) associates power with English, which in his mind is equal to if not greater than Sanskrit, when he says.

> Truth, said a great Indian sage, is not the monopoly of the Sanskrit language. Truth can use any language, and the more universal, the better it is. If metaphysics is India's primary contribution to world civilization, as we believe it is, then must she use the most universal language for her to be universal.... And as long as the English language is universal, it will always remain Indian.... It would then be correct to say as long as we are Indian—that is, not nationalists, but truly Indians of the Indian psyche—we shall have the English language with us and amongst us, and not as a guest or friend, but as one of our own, of our caste, our creed, our sect and our tradition.

These new power bases in Africa or in Asia have called into question the traditionally accepted, externally normative standards for the institutionalized varieties. The new varieties have their own linguistic and cultural ecologies or sociocultural contexts. The adaptation to these new ecologies have given non-native Englishes new identities. That the recognition of such an identity has implications for the local languages was pointed out by Halliday et al. (1964). In the case of India, for example, they felt that those who favor English as a model "should realize that in doing so they may be helping to prop up the fiction that English is the language of Indian culture and thus be perpetuating the diminished status of the Indian languages." The warning was too late. By 1964 English had already become a vital part of the Indian linguistic repertoire. What was "fiction" in the 1960s has now become a reality in the 1980s.

The wider implications of this change in the ecology of world Englishes are significant: The new nativized (non-native) varieties have acquired an ontological status and developed localized norms and standards. Purists find that the situation is getting out of hand (Prator, 1968); they are uncomfortable that the native speakers' norms are not universally accepted. There are others who feel that a pragmatic approach is warranted and that a "monomodel" approach for English in the world context is neither applicable nor realistic. (Kachru [1984] provides a detailed discussion of this topic.)

The extended non-native uses of English also raise serious theoretical issues, both in sociolinguistic and linguistic research. These are not necessarily related to the questions of "power," but to language analysis and description. It seems that linguists' traditional preoccupation with the monolingual "native speaker" is now being questioned—and rightly so. Does one need a new perspective and a new theoretical and descriptive technique for writing bilinguals' or multilinguals' grammars? Such probing questions are the result of the spread of English, and of the alchemy that English uses for changing itself, and for "Englishizing" the non-Western languages with which it has prolonged contact (discussed by Ferguson, 1978, 1982a; Kachru, forthcoming.) What we see here is that the "power" of English has deeper implications, going beyond what we see on the surface.

One might say that contemporary English does not have just one defining context but many—across cultures and languages. This is also true of the growing new literatures in English. The concepts of "British literature" or "American literature" represent only a part of the spectrum. The new traditions—really not so new—must be incorporated into the tradition of "literatures in English" (Narasimhaiah, 1978).

The power bases for English today exist on almost all continents. This unprecedented linguistic situation, therefore, needs new understanding and pragmatics. In each context the English language is manipulated differently, as a medium of power, control, authority, and cohesion. English has therefore acquired intranationally and internationally most important roles. In each English-using country, these roles are in the hands of a small portion of the total population. If this linguistic power is wielded without sensitivity, without understanding, English becomes a language for oppression (Ansre, 1979).

The alchemy of English (present and future) then does not only provide social status, it also gives access to attitudinally and materially desirable domains of power and knowledge. It provides a powerful linguistic tool for manipulation and control. In addition, this alchemy of English has left a deep mark on the languages and literatures of the non-Western world. English has thus caused transmutation of languages, equipping them in the process for new societal, scientific, and technological demands. The process of Englishization has initiated stylistic and thematic innovations, and has "modernized" registers. The power of English is so dominant that a new caste of English-using speech communities has developed across cultures and languages. It may be relatively small, but it is powerful, and its values and perspectives are not necessarily in harmony with the traditional values of these societies. In the past, the control and manipulation of international power have never been in the hands of users of one language group. Now we see a shift of power from the traditional caste structure; in the process, a new caste has developed. In this sense, English has been instrumental in a vital social change, and not only in that of languages and literatures.

One might ask, does one see signs of change in the international power of English? We have seen that legislation or educational planning in, for example, Africa or Asia, has failed to accomplish this change fully. One reason for failure is that such a change entails changing attitudes toward a language and initiating effective policies to provide a power base for other languages. This has not happened, and the consequences are that in many respects the roots of English are deeper now than they were during the period of political colonization. English continues to be used as an alchemy for language modernization and social change. It continues to provide unprecedented power for mobility and advancement to those native and non-native users who possess it as a linguistic tool.

But there are murmurs that cannot be ignored. These are not necessarily heard from the purists or from traditional anti-English groups. An appropriate question is often heard now: How does one "domesticate modernization"? Perhaps one answer is that there is a need for "a circumscription of domestic use of English" (Jernudd, 1981: 50). Such an approach, Jernudd believes, will "liberate English for use as a truly international language, a role that today is tarnished by the misuse of English to prevent the economic, sociopolitical, and cultural advancement of those who do not possess it."

In more and more countries, as in India, English is also perceived by some as the language of oppression, as yet another way to exclude large populations from participation in vital national decision-making processes, and from various educational, political, and scientific domains. In other words, the argument goes, English has introduced a "language bar" in regions that are still fighting against the traditional "caste bar" or "tribal bar." This reaction to English is particularly reflected in the non-English-language press, political pamphleteering, party manifests, and in uncontrollable language riots that take place in different parts of the world.

In India, as elsewhere, politicians of different hues exploit the language issues and invariably paralyze the educational and administrative systems. However, the more pragmatic among them see to it that their own children, and other loved ones, are able to get an English education. Is this, then, a case of linguistic schizophrenia? The answer is, Yes. Thus, in anti-English circles, there is one policy for the home and another for outside; the language policy is designed for specific consumers. (For further discussion and references see Apte [1976], Brass [1974], and Das Gupta [1970].)

However, for the present this fact remains: As Quirk et al. (1972) observe, the real power of English is in its "vehicular load," in the attitude toward the language, and in the deep and increasing belief in its power of alchemy linguistically to transmute an individual and a speech community.

NOTES

1. *Mantra* means "an instrument of thought." In literature it is also used as a general term for a sacred text, syllable, word, or verse, which if repeated, has a spiritual or a temporal effect.

2. Aphorisms compiled mainly between the sixth and second centuries B.C., *sūtras* provide instruction concerning human conduct, domestic ritual, and scriptural interpretation.

3. This percentage is misleading, since in actual numbers it includes over 28 million people—indeed, a large segment of the world's population. The number of English speakers in South Asia is greater than the English speaking population of three English-speaking countries: Australia, Canada, and New Zealand.

4. For a detailed discussion on each area see, for South Asia, Lal (1969), Rao (1978), Kandiah (1981), and Kachru (1982e, 1983); for Africa, see relevant chapters in Kachru (1982a); for Southeast Asia, see Llamzon (1969, 1983) Marasigan (1981), Platt and Weber (1980), Tay and Gupta (1983), Wong (1981, 1983), and Richards (1982). For a discussion of American English and other Englishes, see Kachru (1981).

10

DEFINING REALITY
A Powerful Tool

Dale Spender

FOR REASONS I EXPLORE in this essay, too little attention has been paid to the role of language in the construction of inequality. This reluctance on the part of many to consider language and power issues is itself worth attention. As evidenced by the essays in this collection, there are many ways of approaching the topic of language and power; the one I am going to use is that of sketching my own route to the intersection of language and power. It is an idiosyncratic route, but one that helps map out the terrain, and leads to some of the reasons for the long tradition of separating questions about language from questions about power—a separation that has implications for every speaker in every conversation.

To attempt to itemize the properties of language in terms that would be satisfactory to all those who focus on *language* as an area of research would be to take on an impossible task; to attempt to categorize definitively the properties of *power* would be to assume an equally impossible task; at the very least this makes language and power an area of debate and contention. However, despite the many differences of opinion that may exist about the nature of language and the nature of power, it may be possible to arrive at a consensus that will help formulate the parameters and permit discussion.

For example, it is likely that, regardless of one's background or interest, there would be little disagreement with the statement that language is a means of organizing and structuring the world. It is also likely that most people would accept both Suzanne Langer's thesis (1942, 1976) that language is a means of symbolizing and representing experience, and Peter Berger and Thomas Luckman's thesis (1972) that it is the vehicle for constructing reality. And perhaps there would be little quarrel with a broad definition of power as the capacity of some persons to produce effects on others, effects sometimes contrary to their interests. If these claims can be accepted, then there is a basis for bringing language and power together and for formulating the focus of this chapter: I will consider how some people affect others through the means of organizing and structuring the world, through symbolizing and representing experience, through the construction of reality.

To begin, I am going to address myself to the issue of men having the capacity to have effects on women, through language. I am going to discuss the negation of women's experience in a male-dominated society *from inside that framework*, from within the context of male domination. As a woman, I am going to describe the experience of women in a society where women's experience is frequently denied or dismissed. If I were a man, speaking for women, or if I were describing men's experience, then my case would probably be seen as representative, but because I am a woman, describing women's experience, I confront the very problem I am attempting to address. I am involved with—as distinct from detached from—my data, and within our socially constructed schemata this is in itself problematic, because convention suggests that I should be reporting on previously acquired data and that this essay should not of itself constitute data. For many reasons—which will emerge later—I challenge that convention and those who are responsible for it.

My initial interest in language and power was broadly with the realm of meaning. I began with the attempt to find an explanation for sexually differentiated meanings in the language: Why did the English language possess fewer meanings for women (see Nilsen [1977] for documentation of the fewer lexical items for women); why were so many of these meanings negative (see Schulz [1975] for evidence of the semantic derogation of women); and why were so many of these negative meanings concentrated in a few specific areas (see Stanley [1973] for the discussion of promiscuous terms for women, terms that outnumber the promiscuous terms for men by ten to one)? What were the implications of this in terms of organizing and symbolizing experience, for the construction of reality?

I was conscious that language does not spring forward into the world, ready made, but that it is invented, and I was interested in finding out if explicit reasons had ever been given for these sexually differentiated meanings. That male grammarians and politicians had specifically stated that the term "man" should be used for woman, on the grounds that the masculine gender was more worthy and comprehensive (Snowden, 1913: 143-144; Bodine, 1975), seemed to me a rather unusual pronouncement, given their data, but it also helped me to focus on the sexually differentiated participation that has occurred in the making of the language. I began to suspect that, while both sexes used the language, it was men who had created the English that is codified in our textbooks and dictionaries.

However, it was not just these single units of meaning that interested me; I was also interested in "available sets of meanings," which is the terminology that Michael Young (1975) uses to designate knowledge. Within the available sets of meanings that constitute such disciplines as anthropology, history, philosophy, psychology, and sociology, I found patterns comparable to those manifested in the language; women were negated, absent, or noted in a derogative or negative manner. I began to appreciate that codified knowledge, and the codified language, had been constructed primarily by men, that men considered themselves representative of humanity, and that this has had numerous consequences for women.

At this stage I became familiar with the work of Shirley Ardener (1975) and Edwin Ardener (1975). Edwin Ardener, for example, had noted the propensity among male anthropologists for going off to other cultures and consulting only males about the way the world worked. He concluded that "Those trained in ethnography evidently have a bias towards the kinds of models that men are ready to provide (or to concur in) rather than towards any that women might provide" (E. Ardener, 1975: 2). This helped to explain for Ardener why it was that "no one could come back from an ethnographic study of 'the X' having talked only *to* women and *about* men, without professional comment and some self-doubt [but that the] reverse can and does happen constantly" (p. 3). That ethnographers should seek out males when trying to "crack the code" of a particular culture was understandable, however, according to Ardener. The male version of reality, he argues, is more readily accessible to anthropologists, because males are more articulate, more experienced at bridging the kind of gap between themselves and ethnographers than are women, and tend "to give a bounded model of society such as ethnographers are attracted to" (p. 2). This represents an analytical problem for Ardener, who says that

> if the models of a society made by most ethnographers tend to be models derived from the male portion of society, how does the symbolic weight of that other mass of persons—half or more of a normal human population, as we have accepted—express itself [E. Ardener, 1975; 3]?

This was certainly a question that attracted me; but it is not the only way the problem can be conceptualized. Ardener assumes that the men in societies studied by ethnographers actually do have a more developed and accessible version of reality, to which ethnographers from our society are *attracted;* there is an assumption that ethnographers from our society are neutral and value free, and no attempt is made to analyze the reasons for their attraction to the male version of reality in other societies. The problem of getting women's experience into anthropology, of giving women a voice to articulate the symbolic weight of their experience is, as he sees it, a problem of getting women into the data of Western anthropologists; it is about making *their* version of reality more accessible. But perhaps it is the anthropologists who need to have their behavior modified.

One thing that Edwin Ardener does not do is examine the frames of meaning that Western anthropologists bring with them to the societies they study. He assumed that the invisibility of women in anthropological explanation and interpretation is a product of the women's behavior, but I would want to ask whether it might be the product of the values of Western anthropologists. For it seems to me that English-speaking anthropologists, at least, have a language that negates women's experience, and they have codified bodies of knowledge that negate women's experience (see Spender, 1981), and it is therefore "understandable" that they should impose this pattern of invisibility or negation on women *outside*, as well as *inside*, their own society. Whereas E. Ardener assumes that the superiority of male models of the world is a product of their particular construction of reality, I would want to ask if it might not be a product of their cultural maleness. Perhaps he was not pointing to a methodological problem in anthropology, but to a problem that has its origins in male dominance—a problem of language and power.

It was Shirley Ardener who articulated the concept that women's meanings were blocked at the level of expression in a male-dominated society. In my own work on language as the vehicle for the construction of reality, I have encountered repeatedly the negation of women's experience and the possibility that when it comes to language, it is men who have the power, for, although the evidence is to some extent circumstantial, it seems unlikely that it has been women who have been the producers, the originators, of these devalued meanings about women and their experience of the world.

When I began to undertake more systematic research in this area I found that the problem of expressing the symbolic weight of women's experience was not confined to other societies (which anthropologists might study) but was a problem consistently encountered by women within our own society (and which anthropologists have not studied). That it has never been the central focus of any discipline, that it has been rendered invisible or trivial, that it has been negated, despite the fact that it has been consistently expressed for centuries by representatives of half the human population, was data in itself. There is a long, varied tradition of women's protest against male power (see Spender, 1982, 1983a, 1983b), and the fact that it is not part of the conventional set of meanings, that it is not readily accessible, is more an indication of the way women's voice is "denied, dismissed, distorted"[1] than it is evidence that women have not protested. From Christine de Pisan in the fifteenth century, through Aphra Benn, Mary Astell, Mary Wollstonecraft, Frances Wright, Harriet Martineau, to Matilda Joslyn Gage, Charlotte Perkins Gilman, Mary Ritter Beard, and Simone de Beauvoir (to name but a few), women have been encoding an experience as women—as subordinated women—an experience that men do not have; and men have been denying the authority and significance of that experience, on the precise grounds that it is an experience they do not have. After all, they are ostensibly representative of humanity!

Between the sexes there has been no parity, no exchange of experience, no dialogue; on the contrary, the limited experience of one sex has been legitimated as the complete human experience, so that those who do not endorse it are marked as not fully human, as the deviants from humanity.

By such means is a significant segment of human experience deemed not to count; it is categorized as nondata. And the experience of reality of those who dominate, of those who have power, dominates. It is men who are the arbiters of convention, said Virginia Woolf (1929), and when a woman presents her version of experience,

> she will find that she is perpetually wishing to alter the established values—to make serious what appears insignificant to a man, and trivial what is to him important and for that, of course, she will be criticized: for the critic of the opposite sex will be genuinely puzzled and surprised by an attempt to alter the current scale of values, and will see in it, not merely a difference of view, but a view that is weak, or trivial, or sentimental, because it differs from our own [Woolf, 1972: 146].

Women have experience of the world that men do not have; this is not just the experience associated with the biological condition of being woman, it is the experience of having one's life and values constantly negated. It is the experience of being permanently, and by definition, in the wrong. Individual men can make use of this negation of women's experiences, in order to discredit women's arguments. Few women writers/philosophers have not commented on this fundamental denial of their experience and the implications it has for their dialogue; in 1949, Simone de Beauvoir summed it up when she said,

> In the midst of an abstract discussion it is vexing to hear a man say: "You think thus and so because you are a woman"; but I know my only defence is to reply: "I think thus and so because it is true," thereby removing my subjective self from the argument. It would be out of the question to reply: "And you think the contrary because you are a man," for it is understood that the fact of being a man is no peculiarity. A man is in the right being a man; it is the woman who is in the wrong [de Beauvoir, 1972: 15].

Contemporary feminist writers describe the same phenomenon, although they may use different terminology. Mary Daly (1973) for example, has declared that women have had the power of naming stolen from them, that they have no names that accurately symbolize their experience of the world, but are obliged to use the names that men have produced. And the names that men have produced describe a world from a position women do not occupy; women's perceptions are often "precisely those perceptions that men, because of their dominant position, could *not* perceive" says Jean Baker Miller (1976: 6). But because men's partial view of the world is decreed to be the whole, men's terms are inadequate and false (Daly, 1973).

It would appear that *both* sexes generate models of the world, but where there is a discrepancy between the two, the issue is resolved in favor of men (S. Ardener, 1975). By this process, women's experience is negated, declared to be nondata, decreed as nonexistent, as unreal. Were both sexes to enjoy the power to legitimate their own meanings, then there could be a multiplicity of symbols to represent the different views of the sexes on substantive issues, but while only *one* sex possesses the power to legitimate meanings, its meanings become the totality, its partial meanings are accepted as complete. By such means does one sex have the capacity to produce an intended effect on the symbolizing and structuring activities of the other sex; by such means is sexual inequality constructed, reinforced, and perpetuated. Men have defined themselves as more central, as more worthy, more comprehensive (and so on), *and they have checked only with other men to validate and authenticate their meanings.*

The exclusion of women is structural; the negation of their experience is probably the inevitable outcome of such a structure. No matter what women do or say, no matter how they represent their experience, in these terms, if it is not also the experience of men, it will be consigned to the realm of nondata. I can still remember my rage (hardly an acknowledged virtue among researchers) when I understood the implications of the then-fashionable questions and answers, in relation to "tag questions" and "women's language deficiency." Briefly, the belief was that there was something wrong with women's language, and this was reflected in the lack of confidence and in the hesitancy and tentativeness of the way women used language. Robin Lakoff (1975) has suggested that the source of this "deficiency" was in women's use of tag questions. Now apart from the linguistic problem of identifying a tag question,[2] I was open to the possibility that there might be something in this hypotheses. So were others. Dubois and Crouch (1975) tested women and men for tag questions in a conference setting and found that, far from women's being the culprits in the ostensibly deviant usage, it was men whose language was prone to such productions. I waited—as a reasonable researcher—for the discussion of the findings. I waited—with great glee—for the logical development and the finding that as it was men who used more tag questions than women, perhaps it was men who had the hesitant and tentative speech. But no. Instead of a discussion about the deficiencies in male language, I was entertained with the "sweet reason" that obviously the source of women's lack of self-confidence was not contained in the tag question. Men's language, once more, went on its way unchallenged, while the primary task of locating the source of women's deficiency continued—in another place, of course. This is the bias of the discourse.

American, Australian, British, Canadian, and French women have all attested to this phenomenon; they have been describing it for centuries (it is present in Mary Wollstonecraft's *Vindication of the Rights of Women* [1792]), but because it has not been the experience of men, it is not part of the tradition—which is supposedly *our* tradition but which is more accurately described as *men's* tradition. (Had it been the experience of men, feminists have argued, it would have been a central philosophical issue, as would menstruation have been the locus for glorification had it been the experience of men).

Women have been excluded "from a full share in the making of what becomes treated as *our* culture" says Dorothy Smith (1978: 283), with the result that women's meanings and experience have been omitted or excised from the culture's meanings, and thus from conversations. What consequences does this have for women? In part, it helps to construct their inequality and dependency, to convince them of their own "inferiority." It is possible, for example, for women to feel strong and autonomous but with no means of representing this concept through language (there are no words for women's strength;

see Miller and Swift [1976]); they cannot *voice* that strength and autonomy. They may even begin to doubt the validity of the concept for women; if women *can* feel strong and autonomous, why has there been no need to encode words to represent this state of existence? Women might feel sexually healthy—and autonomous—but again, there are no words that can carry the weight of this meaning.

Men have validated their own sexuality with *virility* and *potency*, but there are no equivalents for women; women are offered a choice between the equally offensive terms "frigidity" and "nymphomania" (and it is significant that there are no semantically equivalent terms for men). With no means of symbolizing a positive, healthy sexual existence, why should women not doubt their own authenticity, particularly when almost every aspect of social organization reinforces their lack of authority. The list could go on and on.

It is not an accident that I have chosen to include *autonomy* in both the examples cited; this is a fundamental aspect of the negation of women, for they are defined in our society, in relation to men, as a derivative of men (even to the extent of deriving from Adam's rib). Linguists have categorized them in this way; in his componential analysis of the English language Geoffrey Leech (1969) divides nouns into (+male) and (-male) indicating the semantic dimensions of the language, as he sees them. As Julia Stanley (1977: 48) says, women are defined negatively:

> [O]ur behaviour is that *which is not masculine*. The definition of the word *mannish* explains to us that women who possess such attributes as strength, fortitude, honesty, courage, directness and bravery are "aberrant."

Women can only aspire to be as good as man; there is no point in trying to be as good as a woman.

Shirley Ardener (1975) has used the terms "dominate" and "muted" to designate the different relationship of the sexes to language and reality. Males, as the dominant group, can impede the free expression of alternative models of the world which women, as the muted group, may express; she suggests that males may even inhibit the generation of models from the muted group, who, for example, may become so convinced of their *dependence* that they cease to generate any notions of *independence* for themselves. It may be, says Shirley Ardener, that the muted group is even relatively less articulate because they are required to express themselves through an idiom not of their own making; it may be that they "are silent on matters of special concern to them for which no accommodation has been made" in the idiom of the dominant group (S. Ardener, 1975: xii).

For women to speak on the issue of women's silence in language and culture is to invoke many of those penalties that have helped to keep women silent on this matter; for, while this representation of experience may "ring true" for many women, it may remain "meaningless" for men. Within the legitimated frame of reference in which we operate, it would be perfectly consistent for men to dismiss this issue as nondata, as trivial or insignificant. It would be predictable if they were to claim that the substance of this argument escapes them for, as Joan Roberts has said,

> Because of female exclusion from thought systems, the hardest thing for a man to know *is* what a woman thinks. But it is harder still for him to listen and to accept her thoughts because they are certain to shake the foundation of his beliefs [Roberts, 1976: 19].

What are the implications for a male when a woman asserts that there is "something *wrong* with a man" who cannot accept the authenticity of a woman's view of the world? What are the implications for men when women insist that men and male power are a problem; when to men it does not feel as though their sex and their power are a problem? They may be discomfitted by this assertion, they may be confused, they may even feel that they are being confronted with a double bind; for, if they accept the authenticity of women's experience, then they accept that their sex and their power constitutes a problem. Yet, if they deny the validity of women's assertions and dispute that their sex and power is a problem, they are doing nothing other than demonstrating that they are the precise problem that women's experience encodes; they are acting as the dominant group incapable of granting legitimation to experience outside their own.

A no-win situation? Certainly—and one constructed when someone with experience other than their own assumes the right to name the world. And if men feel the constraints of this double bind, if they feel damned if they disagree, then I am sure that the sympathy of many women will be with them. For let me assure them that, while this may be an isolated and novel experience for men, it is the daily reality of women's lives. Women can know what it is like to be damned if they agree with the prevailing definitions of womanhood, and damned if they disagree.

This is the unfortunate outcome of a structure that permits only one perceptual order. I could stop here. I could say that for centuries men have imposed their view on women; now it is time for women to have a turn and impose their view on men so that we can retain a uniform perceptual order but simply change the sexual origin of the world view. But I have reservations about this stance.

I have no compunction about using such reversals to make a point, no reluctance when it comes to providing a learning experience for men. But replacing the tyranny of one sex with the tyranny of the other is not for me a long-term solution: I do not want to insist that equality between the sexes depends on women's meanings predominating; I do want to insist that women's meanings should be allowed to coexist, that they should be accorded equal validity. In other words, I am seeking a radical solution: I want a woman's word to count as much as a man's, no more and no less. Then neither sex will have their reality circumscribed by the experience of the other; neither will have their existence structured into a double bind.

What I want to do now—very briefly—is to (a) acknowledge the partial nature of my view, and (b) suggest appropriate generalizations that might be made from it. I think the marginality of women can be productive; I think this experience of women as a negated, deviant, deficient group can be utilized to provide insights into the operation of language and power in society and can help to eliminate those divisions between dominant and muted groups. It is my contention that tyranny emerges only when one sex (or group) has sole access to the legitimation of experience and that (at the risk of oversimplification), if it could be accepted that there is more than one way of looking at the world, the current male monopoly could be undermined. It is a multiplicity of meaning rather than *monodimensional* meaning (Daly, 1978) that needs to be cultivated. Perhaps because they have had more experience in dealing with multiple realities (their own as well as that of men), women are in a more advantageous position in this respect and can help to lead the way.

Gender, of course, is not the only dimension along which we divide the world into unequal parts; class and ethnicity are also used in this way. The case for the negation of experience could be equally applicable for working-class or Black people who are also outside the white, middle-class, male, legitimating circle. (The coinage of "Black is beautiful" was surely an attempt to subvert the legitimated meanings.) But the list is not complete with the nomination of sex, class, and ethnicity; they are not the only bases for the criteria for entry to that circle in which reality is defined. "Others" are those who—to name but a few characteristics—are *not* white, middle- or upper-class, middle-aged, heterosexual, able-bodied, or male. It would seem that those who are the legitimators have indeed only a partial view of the world!

Frequently it is the context that determines the structuring of dominant and muted groups. In my own work within education, for example, I can characterize teachers as the dominant group with the power to define the reality of the classroom, and students as the muted group who consistently have their experience negated. The spectacle of teachers as decreeing that their view of the world is *the* view of the world—while the experience that the students have (and that is different from the teacher's) is declared nondata—is not an uncommon one. I have listened to tapes in which teachers have systematically constructed the dependence of their students by insisting that they deny their own experience and accept as valid only that which the teacher presents. I have listened to myself doing this!

Obviously, in a hierarchical society, people find ways of constructing stratification. But there has been no extensive work undertaken on the part played by language in the *construction* of inequality,[3] and on the ways that the negation of women's experiences and words differentially structures women's and men's linguistic resources and arguments for the expression of *personal power*. Terms such as "role playing," "internalization of oppression," and "conditioning" have been coined to label this phenomenon whereby people come to believe in and accept their own inferiority/superiority, dependence/independence, but there has been no real focus on how this process works. If this had been an issue in language study, then it is possible that language researchers would be displaying great interest in women who are involved in the modern women's movement, that they would be looking to such women as a source of data and would be inspecting the cultural factors that enhance or suppress the power of individual speakers. I think it highly significant that virtually no research has been undertaken on consciousness-raising, despite the fact that it has been an activity in which thousands of women have been engaged, and in which many of the conventions of language and power, as they have been outlined here, have been repudiated.

Joan Cassell (1977) has stated that through consciousness-raising, women "switch world"; Mary Daly (1973) has stated that they begin to recycle the symbols for the structuring and ordering of experience; Jo Freeman (1975) has stated that they experience a growth in self-esteem and confidence. I would argue that they cease to operate as a muted group, that they begin to validate and authenticate their own meanings, which frequently contradict and subvert the legitimated meanings. They cease to role play, to internalize their oppression; they become "resocialized" (Cassell, 1977). They begin to define themselves and to negate the negation of their experiences. The "effects contrary to their interests" can no longer be relied upon to take place.[4] That this change is occurring at the moment is incontestable; that it is not the substance of "serious" research in language and power is unfortunate—but understandable. To start looking at women as a source of data in this way could well begin to establish them as representative of humanity.

NOTES

1. A forthcoming issue of *Women's Studies International Forum* devoted to this topic is entitled "Gatekeeping: The Denial, Dismissal and Distortion of Women."

2. While "I'll be home after supper, all right?" *is* a tag question, the British "We don't want any women in the club, all right?" is *not* a tag question, despite the fact that they possess comparable linguistic features.

3. There have of course been *descriptions* of language and inequality. See particularly the work of Labov (1972a, 1972b).

4. There is still a long way to go, and women frequently acknowledge the resistance of the language to their efforts to change it; there is still no word in general circulation for women's strength, for example. But there are new words that do "alter the balance of power" and that women have coined (see Daly, 1978; Spender, 1981).

11

MINORITY WRITERS
The Struggle for Authenticity and Authority

Muriel Schulz

We all know that the development of a consciousness of self within any people, first and foremost, deals not only with the identity of said people—nationally and internationally—but also speaks to the power—or lack of it—of that people [Haki Madhubuti, 1978: 35].

In addressing the central problem of the poet—the problem of finding a personal voice—Erica Jong (1972) links the words *authenticity* and *authority* as being crucial to the development of the writer. An author achieves authenticity through the use of a generalized persona with which all readers can identify. She must also have the authority to say, "I am important, and what I have to say is important." If the writer's voice lacks authenticity, readers will dismiss the work as failing to express universal experience. If it lacks authority, readers will dismiss it as trivial or peripheral.

Minority writers find it difficult to develop an authentic voice that both dominated and dominant groups will accept as expressing the best that they, themselves, might think or say. The problem is similar for all minority writers, but it is vividly illustrated by two dominated groups in the United States: women and Blacks.[1] Both have well-established literary traditions in English; both have tried to move into the mainstream of literature; and both have attempted, when those efforts failed, to forge independent literary traditions. Women who are Black belong to, and share the problems of both groups; however, their experiences are more complex than those described here. Black women were at first ignored both by feminists and by Black male writers: their work was overlooked by women publishing collections of female writers and by males publishing collections of Black writers. Ironically, in attempting to establish a new canon of writers deserving greater recognition, minority groups have often disregarded minorities within their own ranks (Fisher, 1980).

In a literate society, the power to name rests largely with writers whose work is widely known. However, as Catharine Stimpson (1979) points out, the power to name the namer is even more potent than is the power to name. We may think that the literary canon comes into being by natural selection—a cultural equivalent of the survival of the fittest—but, in fact, it owes its existence to human selection. It survives not entirely on its own merits, but because an educational establishment accepts it, curries it (translating what is thought worthy, annotating what is thought obscure), and transmits it (teaching subsequent generations what it means and why it is worthy). Members of the literary establishment take for granted the superiority of the tradition, using the existing canon as a model against which new works are measured. Thus, the literary tradition exemplifies the most insidious and impregnable form of power, one so well-entrenched that it is unaware of any alternatives (Lukes, 1974). And that power is held by the literary establishment; those who control the presses and journals have the power to decide who will be printed and who will be valued. Stimpson suggests that their resistance to pressure from outside reflects a "psychic and social version of a law of inertia: bodies in power tend to stay in power, unless external forces disturb them" (1979: 71). During the 1960s and 1970s, minority writers have attempted to disturb the power of the literary establishment. The successes, failures, and frustrations they have experienced illustrate something of the dynamic nature of power.

An immediate problem is that minorities have been defined by the culture as lacking the very qualities necessary to enable them to interpret their own experience. Before they can begin, members from the dominated group must redefine themselves, finding within their own lives a replacement for the false and diminished identities created for them by the dominant culture. Yet, these writers too are products of that culture, and many of them tacitly subscribe to its values, even including its denigration of the group to which they belong. Instead of having challenged its values, minorities have frequently perceived the gap between the cultural definition of their group and the reality of their own lives as a peculiar sign of their inadequacy, if they are women (Cornillon, 1972), or of their deviation from the norm, if they are Blacks (Billingsley, 1975). Thus, when their own realities have not matched those of the "majority," women have tended to feel guilty and Blacks to feel alienated.

Developing an authentic voice is difficult for minority writers because their experience has for so long been interpreted for them by others. They have been trained to read the literature of their culture as though they were its representatives and have come to associate the authentic literary voice with the white dominant male. Black writers have spoken of their difficulty in terms of finding an identity and of defining themselves (Wright, 1957; Brown, 1975; Billingsley, 1975; Amini, 1975). In this passage from *The Autobiography of Miss Jane Pittman,* Ned Douglass is explaining to his children the importance of self-definition, but his words could just as well be addressed to Black writers:

> Look inside yourself. Say, "What am I? What else beside this Black skin that the white man call nigger?" Do you know what a nigger is? ... First, a nigger feels below anybody else on earth. He's been beaten so much by the white man, he don't care for himself, for nobody else, and for nothing else. He talks a lot, but his words don't mean nothing. He'll never be American, and he'll never be a citizen of any other nation. But there's a big difference between a nigger and a Black American. A Black American cares, and will always struggle. Every day that he gets up he hopes that this day will be better. The nigger knows it won't [Gaines, 1971: 110].

Women have often spoken of their difficulty in terms of the problems of speaking authoritatively with the first person pronoun (Woolf, 1953 [1941 entry]; Johnson, 1978; Sontag, 1978). They have been muted by their inability to take for themselves the cultural *I*.[2] Adrienne Rich, in tracing her development as a writer, expresses the difficulty as follows:

> I had been taught that poetry should be "universal," which meant, of course, non-female.... I hadn't found the courage yet to do without authorities, or even to use the pronoun "I"—the woman in the poem ["Snapshots of a Daughter-in-Law"] is always "she" [1975: 97].

The attempts by feminists and by Blacks to forge a new literary tradition have sometimes split the ranks of both. There is a tension, even within a single writer, between the wish to reject Western, white, male cultural values and the necessity to draw upon the cultural tradition founded on those values. Lloyd Brown (1975: 8) says of the dilemma,

> The Western heritage is deeply suspect but its influence is pervasive precisely because it is the source of so many of the referents that are available to the Black Artist who is attempting to define his own sense of identity and tradition.

Not all writers can break free of the literary tradition, and not all want to. To write in a new idiom is to risk obscurity, and writers do not wish to be unread. As a result, some—especially those who have been taken up to some degree by the establishment—adopt the attitudes of the establishment toward the new traditions:

> [In the 1950s and 1960s] Negro intellectuals began to talk about how the national aspect of Afro-American writing had to be cooled out, lessened; that Black writers wrote too much about Black people, which sounds like the straight-out bourgeoisie. Did anyone ever run that on O'Casey or Joyce, that they leaned on Irishmen too much, or get to Dostoevsky and his Russian self [Baraka, 1980: 7]?

Some members of the dominated group reject the very notion that an alternative tradition might (or should) exist:

> I'm not interested in the "woman's world" or the assertion of a "female viewpoint." This is often rather an artificial ideal and can in fact injure the promotion of equal rights. We want to join the human race, not invent a new separatism. This self-conscious separation leads to rubbish like "Black studies" and "women's studies." Let's just have studies [Iris Murdoch, quoted in Biles, 1978: 119].

Women who have chosen not to confront the traditional values have engaged in this sort of civil war since the nineteenth century, with the result that they have developed "self-deprecation...humility... coy assurance seeking...and self-hatred" as strategies for competing for the few literary rewards the establishment is willing to distribute among women (Showalter, 1977: 21).

> *Flush* will be out on Thursday, and I shall be very much depressed, I think, by the kind of praise. They'll say it's charming, delicate, ladylike.... I must not let myself believe that I'm simply a ladylike prattler: for one thing it's not true. But they'll say so [Woolf, 1953 (February 10, 1933 entry)].

> There's a certain kind of woman writer who's a capital W. Virginia Woolf certainly was one, and Katherine Mansfield was one, and Elizabeth Bowen is one [Mary McCarthy, quoted in Veebuhr, 1981].

> I don't like to defend myself against Miss McCarthy's opinions or anybody else's. I think Miss McCarthy is often brilliant and sometimes even sound. But, in fiction, she is a lady writer, a lady magazine writer [Lillian Hellman, quoted in Phillips and Phillips, 1967].

Of such remarks Pauline Kael said (in a review noting antifeminism in Mary McCarthy's *The Group*),"We try to protect ourselves as women by betraying other women. And, of course, women who are good writers succeed in betrayal but fail to save themselves" (1968: 96).

A second problem arises because any opposition to cultural stereotypes is, in fact, opposition to a tradition that has served the political-ideological ends of the dominant group. Both racism and sexism have contributed to the maintenance of differentials in economic privileges and rewards (Staples, 1979: 31; Storey, Crouch, and Storey, 1981), advantages not readily abandoned:

> [T]here's a very strong element of power play in [literary criticism], you know. Critics have a vested interest in the survival of art as economics [Morrison, 1974-1975: 91].

The cultural devaluation of dominated groups helps to excuse and sustain their exploitation by those in power. It is clear, for example, that the concept of the American Indian in Western culture represents myth-making necessary to the view white Americans have chosen to take of their conquest of North America. It has been

> shaped not by the Indian and not even by his translator but by the white American writer or moviemaker. The dime novels, the Saturday afternoon westerns, and, on a different level, the poems of a Longfellow and the novels of a Cooper have done their work, have themselves become a part of the American tradition [Levitas et al., 1974: xxiv].

Similarly, the cultural presentation of the Black has long served to justify to the establishment its inhumane and selfish treatment of them. As a result, as Blacks have achieved literacy, they have been "doubly burdened" by a society that provides *"implicitly* negative materialistic definitions of value which America offers...her citizens" (but which most Blacks cannot hope to share), and *"explicitly* negative definitions of color and race, definitions which proclaim the inherent worthlessness of Black people" (Billingsley, 1975: 11). And, while women have adquately demonstrated that the domestic and physical virtues attributed to the ideal woman have contributed to the exploitation of her unpaid labor and of her body, we are less aware that strong heroines may function to support masculine, rather than feminine, ideologies, as well. Elizabeth Janeway (1979: 393) points out that even heroines like Antigone and Lysistrata serve primarily to support masculine ideals, reflecting a "male need to value women as equal and worthy, in order to authenticate an order where honor and dignity rule."

The difficulty with such mythologies is not only that they serve the psychic needs of the dominant culture, but also that they become the mythologies of the minority. If new realities are to be made available to members of the dominated group, these must be accompanied by new mythologies. Writers must create a body of literature that speaks authentically about the experiences of the dominated, not only so that the dominant can hear their voices, but also so that other minority members can take strength from them.

The creation of a new identity in literature, because it opposes existing values, leads to writing that is more openly political than the literary tradition is accustomed to. Writers redefining their experience often become enraged at the cultural model they are renouncing, and their writing is likely to be negatively characterized as being shrill—said of the feminists (Woolf, 1953 [Oct. 23, 1929 entry]; Scruton, 1982)—or strident—said of the Blacks (Zatlin, 1976: 21). However it is characterized, the tone sets such writing apart from that of the established writers.

Writing from members of the dominated group is also likely to handle themes unpopular with the white male establishment, and theme is often chosen by establishment critics to demonstrate the limitations of a minority author. For instance, Robert Moss, in the *Saturday Review* (1975: 12) criticizes Black writers for being "restricted to the narrow focus of racial injustice," arguing dismissively that the "overriding theme of most Black-American art remains the denial of the black man's humanity by white America." And critics have been impatient with the topics of women who, as Erica Jong (1980: 4) puts it, have "raged and mocked and menstruated through whole volumes of prose and poetry." Elizabeth Janeway (1979: 393) points out, however, that women *had* to do this, if they were to destroy the old myths, to speak authentically:

> If we assume that these women [Antigone and Lysistrata] typify existing reality, we are guilty of a literary blunder; we are falsifying what exists. The impulse of women writers to immerse their characters in a soup of everyday annoyances is an effort to avoid this falsification.

Another problem awaits the minority writers who overcome all of these problems and write honestly about their experiences. The desired audience may not be there to read their works. Authenticity may be developed by the writer during the creative process, but authority—like any form of power—requires the consent of another (in this case an *acknowledgment* of the writer's authority). Should an audience be sought within the dominated group or within the mainstream? Many writers want both. They are creating new mythologies for the dominated and, often, new, positive self-images for its members. It is essential to their goals that members of their group read the works. But if the writing never reaches the mainstream, the author's deeper political intent (to change cultural values) will be thwarted. Most minority writers wish to be read by mainstream readers because they wish both to reach a large audience and to speak authentically to those readers about the minority experience.

Sooner or later such authors must send their work out to the establishment publishers, where they encounter a new obstacle. Both women and Blacks have found it difficult to get into print. Editors tend to devalue their work and to recommend for publication only those authors who fit in with the established tradition. Women have occasionally attempted to overcome this resistance by assuming male-sounding names (Erica Jong [1972: 66] wonders whether there is any woman writer who has not toyed with the idea of submitting her work under a male name). Both women and Blacks have tailored their work to fit the attitudes and beliefs of the dominant class, saying what it wants to hear (Myers, 1974-1975; Gayle, 1975).

Even if the writer reaches print, the work may be ignored or misunderstood. Reviewers often misread (Ellmann, 1968; Stimpson, 1978; Baraka, 1980); or they devalue a work, simply because it is written by someone outside the tradition. Literature is, after all, whatever the dominant culture decrees that it is. If literary theorists decide that a different tradition is inferior, it is very difficult to persuade anyone otherwise. From Aristotle to Hardwick, critics have joined voices in dismissing writing by women as being less universal than that by men (see Shapiro [1980], who traces this tradition; Elizabeth Hardwick [1962], who contributes to it). So it is that *The Portrait of the Artist as a Young Man* can stand as a metaphor for the human condition, but *The Bell Jar* is said to deal with a woman's problems. John Berryman can write about childbirth and produce a work of general interest; Adrienne Rich writes about childbirth and produces a book for women. Saul Bellow can characterize a woman's novel as being

> about a woman who is miserable because her lover has ditched her, dismissing it by saying that "it was very nice, considering its limited female subject," and then go on to produce a novel about a man whose wife has ditched him (*Herzog*) and have it accepted as making a universal statement [Johnson, 1978: 156].

The problems encountered by Black writers are somewhat different from those of women. Black writers have also suffered dismissiveness and neglect. But the white dominant male establishment is presently (overtly at least) eager to bring Blacks into the literary mainstream— that is, writers whose work is harmonious with the white values (Gayle, 1975; Myers, 1974-1975; Baraka, 1980). In the process some worthy writers have been ignored, while others have been elevated above their worth. Those who fit in with the culture's values disappear into the tradition:

> One of the basic weapons imperialism uses is absorption, to absorb sections of the oppressed, usually bourgeoisie, so that they uphold the oppressor's culture, and therefore the ideas of the oppressor, a central one of which is that the oppressed need to be oppressed! ... And certainly in official U.S. literary history, they usually raise the most conservative, the backward, or so mix them with the progressives that the radical or revolutionary trend is obscured. And the Blacks, Latinos, Native Americans, Asians, and women are in distorted minority if they are represented at all [Baraka, 1980: 11].

Ironically, then, the writer who is taken up by the establishment feels compromised. Simone de Beauvoir says of this problem,

> The question arises always: do you have to join the system or not? If you do not, you risk being ineffectual. If you do, you place your feminism at the service of a system which you want to take apart [quoted in Jardine, 1979: 227].

And Jean Genet (1970: 5-6) writes,

> It is perhaps a new source of anguish for the Black man to realize that if he writes a masterpiece, it is in his enemy's language, his enemy's treasury which is enriched by the additional jewel he has so furiously and lovingly carved.

As a result, many women and Blacks have rejected the establishment, refusing to be published by white males and (in the case of Blacks) preferring not to be reviewed by them (Stern, 1974; Fox, 1977). Separatists have attempted to forge a new tradition, one not subject to the imprint of dominant values. And while the motives are admirable, the results are problematic. Artistic freedom has not followed from the creation of independent printing faciltiies. Minority journals and presses have, like their white, male-dominated models, proved reluctant to print writing lacking the correct ideological content[3] (Tuttleman, 1971; Gates, 1978; Jong, 1980).

Also in imitation of the establishment, minority critics have taken their own dominated group as a norm. At first this meant male writers to the Blacks, and white female writers to the feminists. Consequently, Black feminist writers—initially, at least—were ignored by feminists and dismissed by Black males, remaining outsiders to both groups (McDowell, 1980).

Even more serious for the Blacks (though not for women at the moment), is that the audience for their work is not growing as they hoped it would. Haki Madhubuti (1978: 35) writes,

> Even though there may be a greater percentage of Black high school graduates within the general population in 1978 than there was in 1968, this does not mean that the basic life support skills (reading, writing and computation) have increased accordingly within the Black community. Indeed, all this actually says is that more Black people are involved in an "education" or "training" process. The negative results of that process are not being debated openly. In fact, if one looks at the educational system of a city like Chicago what is common knowledge is that its $1.5 billion education machine is actually turning out Black students who not only cannot read (or write), but even more serious, is producing young men and women who actually fear and hate books.

For all these reasons, women and Blacks find it difficult to flourish outside the mainstream. When the caterpillar asked Alice, "What's the good of having names for things if the things do not answer to their names?" he posed a question that plagues minority writers today. The power to define reality for the mainstream has not yet been conferred upon them. Such readers continue to refuse to acknowledge that an important reality is being named and defined by most feminist or Black writers. In speaking of "masculine power," Tillie Olsen (1975: 40-41) says, "Power is seldom recognized as the power it is at all, if the subject matter is considered woman's: it is minor, moving, evocative, instinctive, delicate." In a similar vein, Ralph Ellison complains of the white establishment: "American criticism has so thoroughly excluded the Negro that it fails to recognize some of the most basic tenets of Western democratic thought when encountering them in a Black skin" (quoted by Zatlin, 1976: 22).

White males choose not to accept the female or Black perspective as universal, or they are unable to. But they project their limitations as readers upon the material itself. They insist that *it* lacks some quality necessary to their enjoyment of literature. They do not say that they are unable imaginatively to participate in the experiences of a woman or a Black. They say that such experiences lack universality. But, as Robert Fox (1977: 22) points out, "the far-flung catchword 'universality' is in fact a euphemism for Western [male] values, which by implication are the only *significant* values." If the themes treated are not those of the white male establishment, the writers are considered to lack universality. They do not speak authoritiatively to the dominant group. Writers may claim the authority to name and define reality. However, that authority comes not only from their own power, but from the conventions within which they write, and if those conventions negate their interpretations of reality, they are in the position described by the caterpillar: naming things that refuse to respond to their names.

What can they do?

They can acknowledge defeat, renounce the attempt to forge an independent tradition, and try once more to "pass" into the dominant one. Or they can continue to write out of their own experience and pay the price of separateness—the inability to reach more than a limited audience. Certainly the minority audience has been warmly supportive of its writers and minority writing has flourished with that audience. But can it endure?

At the December 1979 annual meeting of the Modern Language Association (MLA), the Women's Studies Division celebrated its ten-year anniversary. The speakers might have congratulated themselves on their accomplishments of the previous ten years. They might have exulted in the number of female artists, writers, and musicians who have been rescued from obscurity through the conscientious and painstaking research of feminists. They might have gloated about the number of women who attend the women's meetings at MLA, at the numbers of sections of courses with a woman's focus currently being taught throughout the United States. They might have been content to count the number of poems, novels, and plays by women currently being published. Those numbers attest to one success of the women's movement: Attitudes have been changed, creativity has been liberated, and lives have been enriched.

What the speakers in San Francisco expressed, however, was uneasiness and dismay at their continued separatism, at the failure of male mainstream readers to accept them. Women comprised 99% of the audience at MLA meetings devoted to women's literature,[4] as they do for such courses taught throughout the United States, and as they do for the readership of literary works by women. The indifference of the literary establishment to anything smacking of women's concerns struck many of these speakers as an ominous sign that all still might be lost. In the introductory address to the MLA panel, "Changing: Ten Years of Women's Studies in the MLA," Florence Howe (1981: 13) said,

> I was relatively trusting of the meritocracy a decade ago. I assumed that, once it was apparent that the literature women had written was worth studying and teaching, all members of our profession, male and female alike, would rush into action. Just as women had spent academic lifetimes studying the culture of men so as to be able to read the literature they had written—from their points of view—so, I imagined naively, would men begin to read women writers.... I was wrong.

Women writers continue to be taught chiefly by women in ghettoized courses endangered now by economic cutbacks (Showalter, 1981). Black studies courses, too, are threatened by a shortage of funds for so-called peripheral courses. Indeed, financial problems jeopardize the Black literary separatist movement as well (Johnson and Johnson, 1979; Yarborough, 1981). In the twentieth century, 64 journals have been founded by and for Black readers. Of these, 40 failed in the first year, another 13 failed in the next four years, and only 3 have lasted 20 years. Money has usually been the reason for failure. Money is a problem for any artist not in the mainstream, as Baraka (1980: 10) has said (with bitterness, since he favors separatism),

> To *use* us is the term of our stay in this joint, but left out of the mainstream means that Bird died of scag, Jellyroll had to play in a whorehouse, Duke played one-night stands till he died, the Beatles make millions and cite some Blood running an elevator in Jackson.

Minority literature continues to occupy a place outside of the mainstream. Its writers may name their literary output "authoritative" and "authentic," but if mainstream readers refuse to accept it as such, their attempt at naming misfires. Members of the dominated class have succeeded in writing in their own, authentic voices, but we may yet need to find a way to confer authority upon these voices.

NOTES

1. Paredes (1978) and Oaks (1978) discuss the literary problems of Chicanos and Native Americans and report problems similar to those discussed here. See also the Summer 1981 edition of *Melus* devoted to problems of minority writers.

2. Noëlle Bisseret Moreau in this volume suggests an explanation for the difficulty. The persona of the author is not that of an individual speaker but, rather, of a spokesperson for the culture; historically the cultural *I* has an unstated male referent.

3. Nina Baym points out that aesthetic values are inevitably linked with political ones, that traditional standards also require "a correct ideological content": "I cannot avoid the belief that 'purely' literary criteria, as they have been employed to identify the best American works, have inevitably had a bias in favor of things male" (1978: 14).

4. Despite the small number of meetings involved, the executive director of the MLA, Joel Conarroe, found it necessary to defend the MLA against a charge that a "feminist takeover" of the MLA was under way (*MLA Newsletter*, Spring 1980, p. 2).

12

STUDYING POWER IN LITERARY TEXTS

Jean F. O'Barr

POLITICAL SCIENTISTS typically study power by examining attitudes and behaviors in the public arena. In doing so, we frequently puzzle over the sources of beliefs and actions and must stretch our abilities to explain how these phenomena arise. Our search for the antecedents of what we are observing might be characterized more as a scramble to say something useful than as an organized and thorough exercise in which we have some confidence. This is particularly characteristic of those of us who work on non-Western cases, where we lack sophisticated and reliable survey data.

In this chapter I argue that literary texts provide a wealth of material for political scientists interested in the study of power, its origins, and its use. The literary works of Kenyan women authors provide an opportunity to study the distribution of power between men and women in that society. Such an analysis is indicative rather than exhaustive; other researchers will find literary texts to be a rich data source *if* the texts are approached from the point of view of asking what they say about social, political, and economic relationships. In this analysis I illustrate the use of literary texts as sources for political analysis by focusing on what the texts say about the kind and amount of power men, as compared to women, possess.

These novels, poems, and short stories show men and women locked into a social framework that disadvantages women and that women generally believe cannot be changed. As a result, women use a wide range of devices to gain political influence in personal as well as public forums when direct power (i.e., actual control over resources that can command action) is denied to them. Literary texts allow us to see how women conceptualize power issues and how they act in accordance with those understandings long before they translate their views into the public acts chronicled in accounts of politics. It is this ability of literary texts to convey and analyze the dynamics of power at their inception that makes the study of literary texts a valuable tool in the study of power. The emphasis on speech in the social sciences generally, and in this volume in particular, can be, I will argue, usefully augmented by a consideration of written language as a means of understanding power relationships.

LITERARY SOURCES AND THE STUDY OF POLITICS

Before turning to the main part of the analysis and examining the ways that the study of language in literary texts can contribute to the study of power distributions in society, a word of background is in order on the more conventional use of literary sources in the study of politics. It is common for an essay or a book in the discipline to be decorated with a literary quotation or to incorporate literary references as examples of political interaction. Political scientists rarely take a set of research questions to literary texts and use the texts as data.[1] Rather, political scientists more typically discuss the fact that literary works can have political impact in society at large and that writers are members of the intelligentsia who assume public political roles (Kurzweil and Phillips, 1983). Nonetheless, to go to literature to ask what is being said about power in society is a new undertaking.

The more typical data sources for political scientists are documents and survey materials. Historical documents, both of a primary and secondary nature, are written by social commentators, not artists; they describe events and ideas that governments undertake, organizations pursue, or elite figures describe, and that become part of public discourse in the larger political process. Survey and statistical materials are enumerations of the characteristics of people's material conditions, political and social behaviors, and psychological states. When one's interests are in the kinds of power men and women possess in contemporary Africa, historical documents and survey data are almost useless. Women's control over societal resources and the distribution of that control with men are issues rarely discussed in historical documents and collections of survey data.

New research addressing the questions of power distribution is obviously desirable, but the difficulties of conducting such research are familiar problems. Short of undertaking new research efforts, are there other sources of information available for answering questions, testing hypotheses, and exploring policy issues? The literature of a nation—its novels, poems, and stories that are already written and available—is a particularly useful alternative source. These materials are created by individuals who have grown up in and participate in the society they describe in fiction. In contrast to most anthropological case studies, which are limited in time and place, works of fiction can draw on experiences at all points in the life cycle and can cross barriers of time and space with a freedom unavailable to social scientists. Unlike the quantitative work of people in politics, sociology, and economics, literary works describe the private, psychological states of people, not just their public institutional behavior. And unlike the material being written by foreign aid experts in the field of women and technological change, novels are able to interpret action in terms of cultural information, giving a more comprehensive picture of how and why people behave as they do.

Literature, in short, is a useful complement to the conventional data of political scientists and merits a more systematic exploration. It has the potential to contribute new information, to correct biases in existing knowledge, and to modify and refine the understandings arrived at by other methods. With the caveat that one cannot jump freely from what is said in imaginative literature to objective statements of fact, literary sources are strong candidates for the study of the distribution of power in society, especially in areas like gender relationships, where so little data are available through any other means.

GENDER AND POWER IN THE WRITINGS OF KENYAN WOMEN

The relationships between men and women are dominant themes in the literary works by Kenya's women authors. The novels analyzed here constitute all the currently published works of English fiction by Kenyan women writers. The works demonstrate that Kenyan women are experiencing a social situation fraught with contradictions and that they respond with a mixture of initiative and passivity. These sources document the facts that structural constraints on women's exercise of options are severe and that the individual solutions that women work out can be no more than temporary coping mechanisms. They suggest that the next decade may see increasingly tense political policy debates if women move from a personal awareness of difficulties to a collective stance on remedies and how to implement them through public policies. The writings provide information not otherwise available about how women conceptualize power issues and how they deal with these issues when the changing social milieu works against any consensus on alternatives.

By and large, the novels are stories of how individuals and communities react to changing conditions. Some plots describe power struggles between men and women (Likimani, 1974b; Were, 1972, 1980) or between individuals and the larger society (Likimani, 1974a; Njau, 1975). Some expose the dilemmas of modernization (Ogot, 1966, 1968, 1980a, 1980b), others are remembrances of the past (Waciuma, 1969; Nguya, 1975), and one discusses a Kenyan living in another society—Britain (Mugot, 1971). It is not necessary to know the plots in detail in order to understand what the literary works say about women's views of their powerlessness and how the distribution of power affects their participation in contemporary society.

For purposes of analysis, I make the assumption that what the authors say about the distribution of power in male-female relationships reflects their personal experiences and professional observations of contemporary Kenya. This assumption is based on both the close parallels between the situations described in the literary works and social analyses of Kenya (Strobel, 1982; Wipper, 1975) and the comments several of the authors offered during recent interviews.[2]

All of the authors are professional people who are relatively young and hold positions in their society as public relations officers, doctors, development officers, teachers, and the like. None defines herself primarily as a writer; none makes her livelihood exclusively from writing; and none claims to have been trained as a writer. Indeed, the authors write because they "have to." One maintains that stories come into her head and that if she doesn't "let them out," they "torment" her. Most write over a period of years and do not pursue the possibility of publication with much determination. In addition, the authors claim that the people, situations, and ideas they write about come out of their own experiences. They are unanimous in their belief that there is little difference between what they write about and what they experience. These are realist works, written by people who eschew esoteric debates about the relationship of literature to life.

Two issues dominate the theme of male-female relationships that runs through all of the literary works cited here. The first is that the distribution of power between men and women is unequal, and the second is that women are powerless to change that basic inequality. The authors present women as either ignored or abused by contemporary social arrangements. Their view of men is quite different; they see men as being able to use both the traditional and modern systems of prestige and resources, as appropriate, to advance their goals. The authors go on to illustrate the idea that women are powerless to alter this basic inequality. Some of the characters they create attempt to escape the constraints common to women by becoming "stars"; yet these women are doomed to pay for their successes at some personal cost (Ogot, 1968; Njau, 1975). Other characters assert their independence from men, yet they constantly fall back on both their cultural and personal needs for male protection (Likimani, 1974a, 1974b; Ogot, 1980a, 1980b). Many women in the novels rely on their children rather than their husbands as the means of linking them to society. Frequently in the stories, women ridicule men's foibles as a means of exercising their influence indirectly (Were, 1972). Above all, most characters in the novels seek personal accommodation, not a collective response to difficulties (Were, 1980). The authors illustrate women's powerlessness by choosing characters and situations in which women never bond together nor demand of men (individually or collectively) control over their own destinies.

The study of literary texts contributes to an understanding of power relationships between men and women in at least four ways.[3] First and foremost, literature allows exploration of the very early stages of political consciousness, even before people formulate clear ideas and opinions about what is happening to them, and before they are thinking and acting in ways that can be recorded by the conventional methods of political science. Literary works describe the conflicting claims, the difficulties of operating in systems with contradictory standards, and the feelings of confusion that are present long before people are moved to write letters to newspapers, join organizations, and support public policy positions. Thus literature can be a fertile source of information for political scientists seeking to understand the basis of power equations.

Unlike political scientists, whose training and conventions demand that only established patterns be reported, the authors are not afraid of confusion, are willing to tolerate overlapping and contradictory ideas, and are able to piece together the outline of a stiuation before patterns are set and trends are observable in the public domain. Because authors deal with political consciousness at the individual level, they do not need to wait for its public manifestation before recording and discussing it. In this way, understanding how men and women view each other provides a basis for looking at public power struggles that is much more informed than is usually available in political science.

Second, writers reflect how women search for ways to manage personal and social problems outside the formal groups that propose limited views of the options for women in contemporary Kenya. Political scientists almost always look to group behavior, or to the leaders of groups, for explanations about why things happen the way they do. Likimani (1974a) demonstrates the limits of group analysis for understanding how and why things happen when she describes how young girls were denied access to their traditional age sets and forced to become Christians.

The primary focus of Likimani's *They Shall Be Chastised* is evident when a character makes the statement, "one had either belong to the community, or to be a Christian" (1974a: 18). The unyielding quality of Christianity as taught by the local missions rendered an assimilationist stance nonviable. The book portrays the major conflict inherent in the position of women in transitional generations. Traditional stability is denied to these generations of women, as are the Eurocentric ideals of modernization and Christianity. The dismissal of ancient beliefs without providing an adequate or efficient substitute serves to undermine the basic stability of society. The women frequently encounter the most extreme pressure in their families and local communities, especially in situations where sexual mores are extremely divergent. Women are expected to be both virgin and whore. In most social situations described in Likimani's book, the male position contains more intrinsic prerogatives. Women are subject to the vagaries of both men and society. Denied outlets for sexual and emotional energies in European society, the women experienced guilt and retaliation when they practiced the traditional rituals that were designed to enhance the small amount of power they could yield. Traditional practices were considered evil by African missions, but they were the only way an African Christian could attain recognition in his or her village.

Women more frequently than men are placed in this no-win situation. They develop their manipulative skills simply to survive, culturally as well as economically. It is almost impossible to develop legitimate, recognized power structures if one is regarded either as a nonentity or as inhabiting a stereotypical role, such as the Eve/Mary role illustrated in Likimani's novel. Productivity means power; women, such as the mission girls who are trained in European skills to the exclusion of all things African, are not adequately prepared to function within an African society. A narrow base of knowledge limits productivity and consequently limits power. Likimani writes of the interlocking nature and frequently open conflict between two types of cultures, both fighting for supremacy, although neither side would be seen as a "group" in the terminology of political science and, hence, subject to analysis in it. Literature, in contrast, encourages observers to follow the development of alternate points of view in diverse settings and to find the origins of positions in the social structure.

Third, the literature being examined here describes the support networks and coping mechanisms that sustain women in view of the limited ability of formal organizations to provide assistance. Political scientists tend to look only at the public domain—not at the private domain that undergirds it. By analyzing neither relationships in the private domain nor the link between the public and private domains, political scientists often miss a critical aspect of power relationships. In almost every literary work, women describe how the support of female kin groups sustains them through various life tasks.

In *Daughter of Mumbi* (Waciuma, 1969), young women model themselves on the older women who are in charge of their initiation into adulthood. In *What Does a Man Want?* (Likimani, 1974b), women rely on their children, especially their female children, for the help and support it takes to maintain themselves emotionally and economically in a society fraught with contradictory messages about what roles women should play. In *Ripples in the Pond* (Njau, 1975) and in *Land Without Thunder* (Ogot, 1968), women working in the contemporary economy attempt to fashion support groups from among their co-workers and are only partially successful in doing so. The basis of support—shared values and a community membership— is missing, and a new basis—common difficulties—is weakened by the growing male-female competitiveness that develops out of the changing conceptions of gender roles. In *Black Night of Quiola* (Mugot, 1971), it is the absence of female support that is the most difficult aspect of life for the central character. None of the support networks—be they emotional, economic, or political—are public in the sense that they would be seen by political scientists to be formal organizations amenable to study. Yet all of them provide substantial encouragement for individuals experiencing change in their relationships, encouragement crucial to understanding how they function as actors in the public domain.

Fourth, these writers demonstrate that action is not always possible for contemporary Kenyan women. For these authors, literature is a surrogate for personal action. Yet their literary works simultaneously may serve as a call to action for others. In contrast, social science assumes that the inevitable outcome of political consciousness is action. The works of Ogot best illustrate this immobility. Ogot's female characters analyze their dilemmas with some clarity, but they are unable to move beyond analysis to action. In order for collective action to take place, people must not only perceive their own deprivation, they must understand their disadvantaged situation to be unfair and believe it to be amenable to alteration.

The study of the way in which women discuss their inability to act illustrates how and why they have been moved to no action other than talking and writing. For Ogot the transitional generations of women are caught in an inescapable flux of mores and expectations. Men regard women as passive reactors, objects for manipulation, while in reality women are struggling protagonists. Assuming many guises, they attempt to satisfy all male needs. At some point, the stress becomes unbearable. Rage, directed inward (as suicide) or outward (as violence toward society), explodes. In attempting to conform to the rapidly developing structures of modernized society, women are denying the structures that gave them power while attempting to adhere to divergent social expectations. The combination creates social and personal chaos. Denied male prerogatives, they seek to manipulate their surroundings to maximize their situations within male-defined parameters. What are generally considered vanity, promiscuity, or piousness can be explained as female reactions to protect their most desired and saleable assets in the male sphere. In "Elizabeth," one story in *Land Without Thunder* (Ogot, 1968), the title character commits suicide as a last desperate gesture against male domination when she is raped. An analysis of Ogot's work reveals the dependence of women upon men for basic security. A woman's major, and in many cases only, asset is her body, which can be bartered for this security. Until women are recognized as legitimate productive members of society, they will continue to rely on manipulation and sexual exploitation for survival. It is not clear how this recognition will eventually be attained or even if any form of progress has been made. What is clear is the intrinsic dependence and weakness of the female as portrayed in these literary works by Kenyan women.

CONCLUSION

To recapitulate briefly, this Chapter has presented the argument that we as political scientists can learn a great deal about political phenomena through the analysis of literary texts. I have illustrated that proposition by describing what a particular set of literary texts says about the distribution of power between women and men in Kenya. The ideas raised by this analysis of gender and power are applicable to a wider range of political questions, and they demonstrate the contribution made by the study of women, their experiences, modes of expression, and situations to the study of social and political phenomena more generally.

NOTES

1. Marxist literary criticism deals with a similar issue from its own perspective, looking beyond the correlation of literary and social facts to an analysis of ideologies through the study of forms, styles, and meanings as products of a particular history (Eagleton, 1975, 1976).
2. Interviews were held with Muthoni Likimani, Rebeka Njau, and Miriam Were in March 1983 in Nairobi. The interviews ranged over a large number of topics, including the question of the relationships of their writing to their life experiences. All three agreed that they wrote out of their personal experiences, drawing in characters and situations they had encountered in their own lives.
3. The four points made in the following pages can be interpreted at two levels. First, I am arguing that literature is a rich source of data for political analysis generally. Second, I am saying that these particular literary texts are a good data base from which to analyze male-female relationships in modern Kenya.

13

FRANCOPHONIE
Language Planning and National Interests

Brian Weinstein

FOR FOUR CENTURIES government decisions concerning the status and development of the French language have affected patterns of communication within France and between France and other countries. Kings, emperors and democratically chosen prime ministers and presidents recognized that control of communication helped reach political, economic, and social goals among which French national unity and a presence in the world were most important. Obstacles to these goals were the use of Latin in world affairs and intellecutual life, and the use of regional, local tongues such as Provençal and Breton in areas of France; these obstacles were overcome in the first case by the mid-seventeenth century and in the second during the Third Republic. (This history has been described by Gordon [1978] and condemned by Calvet [1974].)

Today language is a key link between France and all its former colonies and protectorates in Africa, Haiti, Canada, and Southeast Asia as well as between France and French-speaking populations in western Europe. Elites in these countries wish to maintain close ties across national frontiers for the social, economic and political benefits they facilitate. Cooperation and mutual dependence give France prestige in world affairs and a relatively secure source of certain raw materials, as well as a small but lucrative market for exports. The relationship gives political elites in Africa vital political and military support along with economic assistance and trade. For French-speaking minorities in Louisiana, Canada, Italy, Belgium, and elsewhere, cultural contacts outside their countries strengthen their identity, influence, and even survival.

New challenges to the position of French threaten these relationships. American power and technological predominance in the mid- and late twentieth century have convinced many that English is a better instrument than French for working in the modern world. The fact that American English is widely used in space technology, communications, and popular culture has meant the absorption of American English words and expressions into French. French cultural elites view excessive borrowing as a threat to the integrity and autonomous development of their language, and because Quebec borrowing, for example, is different from Paris borrowing, many French speakers feel that the unity of the language around the world is threatened. A second challenge comes from the increasing demand to use regional mother tongues or what are called "community languages" in France itself, or national languages in countries such as Senegal, Haiti, and Morocco. None of the proponents of local languages wishes to remove French completely from schools or government, but many appear to wish to develop national tongues by modernizing their lexicons and introducing them as media of instruction as steps toward officialization. In these countries, as in areas where French is the mother tongue, the inclusion in speech and writing of locally invented terms—albeit French in form rather than English— is perceived as another challenge to standard international French defined as the language of "the cultured Parisian bourgeoisie" (Valdman, 1983).

It is not yet clear what the relative position of standard French, national mother tongues, and local varieties of French or "regional French" will be by the end of the century, but some French-speaking elites in all countries fear that any weakening of the position of standard or "central" French in the schools, literature, science, and government will inevitably weaken political and economic ties and interests. Because the language and French culture are also valued for their own sakes, their decline would be viewed as a loss for the world.

Educators, intellectuals, linguists, scientists, journalists, politicians, civil servants, and writers have reacted to these challenges and threats. They have created their own organizations to act within national frontiers and across borders, and they have called on governments and world organizations to act. Thus, nongovernmental and governmental actions are directed toward an effort to protect the status of French and its particular body of words, sounds, and structures. After a decade of alarmist predictions and exaggerated efforts to suppress any perceived threats—which often included heavy-handed struggles to prevent any recognition of the mother tongues of Africans, Haitians, and Southeast Asians—supporters of "Francophonie" are now carefully and thoughtfully studying the place of French alongside other languages in multilingual societies in a multilingual world.

Central authorities in France, African states, Belgium, Quebec, and elsewhere have not come to an agreement on one clear and comprehensive policy, however. In Africa, in particular, political elites hesitate to enter the cultural realm in a decisive way because they fear unexpected results will break their fragile regimes. Culture is even less controllable than economies, and it is known that confused efforts in Morocco and Madagascar have created problems in schools and tensions between ethnic groups. Cultural elites outside government are not in agreement among themselves either. Writers and intellectuals do not present a united front because they represent different ethnic, ideological, and regional interests and because they, too, are unsure of the long-term effects of language decisions.

Planning within states and across national frontiers is one solution to the growing issue of language and particularly the respective places of French and mother tongues other than French in educational and political systems. Planning is also a possible pathway to solving the problem of standardization or maintaining norms. In some countries planning has begun. The increasingly likely outcome is officially recognized bilingualism, where French is not the mother tongue, despite almost worldwide ambivalence about bilingualism. A second outcome is a much broader and imprecise definition of what constitutes standard French.

FRANCOPHONIE

Francophonie or the Francophone movement is a loose coalition of about 100 governmental, intergovernmental, and nongovernmental organizations that, since the late 1960s, has attempted to preserve and expand the status of a mutually comprehensible and mutually respected French language within all countries where it is spoken and written as a mother tongue or learned as an official language and in all interstate organizations where it is currently used. As such, Francophonie provides quite openly a cultural basis for maintaining and expanding political, economic, and military cooperation (Weinstein, 1983).

Key initiators of the movement have been Senegalese, Quebecois, and Tunisians as well as the French, but France has inevitably played the key role financially and intellectually. Great Britain, Spain, and Portugal no longer dominate the evolution of their national languages because of the rise of larger and richer countries, such as the United States of America, Mexico, and Brazil, which also use them as national and official tongues. France, on the other hand, has always been and will remain the largest, richest, and most influential French-using state. Paris is the capital of the French-speaking world.

The Paris-based but multinational or intergovernmental Agence de Coopération Culturelle et Technique (ACCT or AGECOP) is the single most visible organization of Francophonie. African heads of government and state founded it in 1970. It has been headed first by a Quebecois, then a Nigerien, and then a Gabonese. ACCT has about 20 members and a modest budget of somewhat over $20 million, 46% of which comes from France. Canada supplies about 35% of its revenues and Belgium 12%. All other states contribute 7%, which means that their financial support is largely symbolic. ACCT has run a managerial school in Bordeaux, directed multilateral aid programs in education, helped support research into methods of language teaching (French and other languages), sponsored conferences on French and other languages, and has introduced audiovisual equipment and techniques into schools. Most of its activities are in Africa.

Other components of Francophonie include the nongovernmental Association des Universités Partiellement ou Entièrement de Langue Française (AUPELF), which links universities by coordinating work on French studies and facilitating mobility of students. AUPELF also encourages the publishing of original and translated university textbooks in disciplines with a marked dependence on English language materials. The Association Internationale des Parlementaires de Langue Française provides a forum for exchanges of communication and visits among legislators.

Several linguists belong to the Conseil International de la Langue Française (CILF). Until the mid-1970s the CILF concerned itself exclusively with the modernization of a single standard French language through the introduction of neologisms, replacement of English words that had entered the language with French words and preaching the necessity of a single Paris-based standard. In 1975 Dankoulodo Dan Dicko, then leader of ACCT, redefined and broadened the goals of Francophonie to include the promotion of national cultures and languages of all members within a more varied French context. The CILF followed, and it considers the place of other languages in Africa, Asia, and the Caribbean, admitting that French cannot and should not replace the mother tongues of millions of black and brown peoples.

Results of the new orientation of Francophone multilateral organizations such as CILF include new support for the use of the Wolof language in educational television programs in Senegal, money for research into African languages in Ivory Coast and Niger, and sponsorship of meetings of Centers of Applied Linguistics for the purposes of redefining the concept of standard French and debating the role of language in the process of economic and political development.

In 1983 the socialist government of François Mitterand announced the unilateral creation of three governmental organizations with an international membership to promote the ideals of Francophonie. Because they are French organizations, no other country can challenge the members chosen to run them. The first is the Haut Conseil de la Francophonie. Its president is the French head of state; its vice-president is the former president of Senegal, Léopold Sédar Senghor; and its other ten members come from Quebec, Africa, the Middle East, and elsewhere. The council's role is to set forth and redefine when necessary the basic principles of the movement, its goals, and the means to reach the goals in France and in the rest of the world. The second organization is the Commissariat Général de la Langue Française, whose specific purpose is to coordinate all French government activities for the strengthening and expansion of the French language within France and outside of France. The third is the Comité Consultatif pour la Francophonie to advise the French prime minister. The French government has promised considerable financial support (Péroncel-Hugoz, 1983: 22).

These three organizations are concrete evidence of the firm commitment to Francophonie by the French socialists. There are other signs. The 1983 budget of the Ministry for Cooperation and Development showed a sharp increase in funds for social and cultural projects, for example. The amount of money increased by 63.25% compared with the budget of 1982 ("Budget" 1983: 51). The single most important organization promoting the ideas of Francophonie from within the French government is the Direction Générale des Relations Culturelles, Scientifiques et Techniques (DGRCST) of the Ministry of Foreign Affairs. About 40% of the ministry's budget goes to the DGRCST, which means more than $500 million annually. In 1980 this money supported 274 French schools outside France with 5,000 teachers, as well as 1000 cultural missions, 164 cultural centers, and 7600 scholarships (Rigaud, 1980: 19). Total French expenditures on what is called "public diplomacy" (because it is openly aimed at the publics of other countries) exceed that of any other non-Communist country, and in terms of percentages of national budgets, France is probably number one in the world (Comptroller General of the United States, 1979). An important aspect of these programs is specific and explicit support for the French language. In the last decade the amount of money designated exclusively for the language has risen from $53 million in 1971 to about $200 million in 1984 (see *Le Monde* Sept. 7, 1983, p. 6), or about ten times the budget of the ACCT. Without the bilateral programs, which give France considerable leverage and influence, Francophonie as a movement would be insignificant.

This is not to say that others have not taken important initiatives. For many years the Quebec government, Quebec private organizations, and the French-speaking Roman Catholic hierarchy in Canada have taken a special interest in the survival of French-speaking communities in the United States. For example, a decade ago French teachers traveled south of the border to the state of Louisiana and the flow has continued to the present. The government of Quebec opened an office in the town of Lafayette, and provincial cabinet members have traveled there as a sign of solidarity. Belgians have also joined Quebecois and French teachers in the state. Although there have been highly charged debates about which variety of French should be promoted—a standard, internationally understood variety or the local "Cajun"—Gold believes the ethnic and linguistic consciousness of all participants has been sharpened: "the international alliance is seen as a useful one for the first stages of the state-wide revival of a French language presence in public institutions." The visits and presence of Belgian and other teachers has made Louisiana "part of international francophonie" and may help speakers of different varieties of French in Louisiana form "a single ethnic consciousness" (Gold, 1980: 19, 13, 29).

Not everyone agrees that these efforts—the multilateral programs of ACCT and the bilateral programs of France or Quebec—are succeeding. The masses of people in Africa and Haiti do not know French, although they appear to want to learn it. The French used in former colonies is giving way in some domains to local languages, while English retains its popularity for high school students and other young adults (Fishman et al., 1977: 16). Further, a survey has revealed that "more than 50% of researchers feel obliged to express themselves in English," even at scholarly meetings in France itself (de Chambrun and Reinhardt, 1980: 28). In French popular culture there seems to be no way to stop the inflow of Anglo-American expressions. In 1983, for example, a new magazine was launched in Paris with the decidedly "franglais" title of *Magazine Hebdo: Le News d'Aujourd'hui*.

A more general problem is the weakness of the economic underpinning for Francophonie. The major investors and trading partners of Quebec are in the United States. France's major trading partner is

West Germany. Haiti is in the American sphere of economic and political influence. Morocco is increasing its economic ties with the Soviet Union. Vietnam, Laos, and Cambodia are also tied to the Soviet Union in various ways. Undaunted, the French are making an effort to strengthen economic ties within the Francophone community. A newly nationalized French aluminum company will build a huge $1.5 billion smelter in Quebec; the French have associated African states with the Common Market; and they continue to maintain a presence in Haiti, Lebanon, and elsewhere.

Proponents of Francophonie refuse to admit they are swimming against an inexorable tide, and many believe language planning, particularly in Africa, is a way to coordinate and strengthen their efforts. African states that emerged from the French empire have the closest economic and political ties with France, and their largely illiterate populations offer the most promising areas for the expansion of French speakers. Increasing demands for the use of African languages alongside French are a challenge to the ingenuity of the emerging planners.

LANGUAGE PLANNING

In my view, language planning means "a government-authorized, long-term sustained and conscious effort to alter a language's function in a society for the purpose of solving communication problems." It is important to add that the "communication problems are themselves the result of nonlinguistic socio-economic or political changes." And, although government bodies are usually the "major agents of language planning, private or semiprivate specialized organizations and groups of writers, printers and other communication specialists play an essential role, too, with or without government approval" (Weinstein, 1980: 57).

Kloss (1969: 81-82) has broken down planning into two distinct but interdependent forms. "Status planning" involves decisions about a language's function in a society and then an implementation of those decisions by law or decree. Should a language be taught as a subject or should it be the medium of instruction im primary school, for example? "Corpus planning" is the decision to develop and then the actual development of a language by writing it down, standardizing it, and modernizing its lexicon so that it can be used for the purposes the society desires. Obviously each form of planning depends on the other for success. A language cannot serve as a medium of instruction in modern public schools unless it is written down and modernized, but if there is no chance it will be adopted for education, what is the point of developing it? Without a general plan including both facets, efforts will be wasted and confusion will grow.

In the years since the independence of former French colonies, where French was not the mother tongue, pressures have steadily grown to change the status of languages that had little or no role in education or government during the colonial period. In Moroccan primary schools prior to independence, children spent "80 percent of their school time...either studying French or using it as a medium of learning" (Hammoud, 1982: 40). Obviously this situation provided a convenient target for the nationalist movement that promised Arabicization. While, as late as 1978, students were required to show skill in the French language in order to continue their education into secondary school (Hammoud, 1982: 59), Arabic is now the language of instruction throughout the primary cycle of studies, and Arabic is the "official state language" according to the constitution.

Algeria, Tunisia, Mauritania, Burundi, Rwanda, and Madagascar have also declared an African language (or Malagasy) official and have reduced the importance of the French examinations. What this means in part is that local languages are now used in these countries as media of instruction at least in the primary schools, but even without officialization they have been declared "national" languages, thus raising their prestige. Similarly, Creole has been declared a "national" language in Haiti, and Senegal has chosen Diola, Malinke, Poular, Sérère, Soninke, and Wolof as national. During the 1983 elections the leaders of one political party in Senegal called for the upgrading of these national languages into official languages (Ndiaye, 1983: 5).[1]

Many educators have called for a change in the status of mother tongues. In 1982, 250 Nigerien teachers and political leaders meeting at Zinder decided that during the first two years of primary school mother tongues will serve as media of instruction, depending on local needs. Beginning in the third year, one Nigerien language will be used throughout the country while the others are taught as subjects ("La déclaration de Zinder," n.d., p. 22). Experimental programs had already been using African languages in Niger, and by the school year 1982-1983, twenty experimental schools were assigned one African language as a medium of instruction (Hutchison, 1983). It is important to note that no laws or decrees were written to permit this experimentation. Decisions taken at low and medium levels are responsible here in Upper Volta, Togo, and Guinea. Ten experimental classes in Senegal were taught through Wolof in 1979 with support from the Francophone ACCT, and I have heard that over 100 schools in the Central African Republic have introduced Sango, although recent instability in that country may have closed the schools. The government of Congo has promised changes in the future, but there is some hesitation.

Governments hesitate to engage in open discussions such as the one held in Niger about the future of education. Because many tend to make decisions in all domains without consultation with the people most concerned, there is widespread ignorance about language planning goals, interests, and means. Therefore, teachers and students in Morocco who are committed to Arabicization are nonetheless worried about how it is carried out (Hammoud, 1982: 202-205). In 1979 the government of Haiti permitted public schools to teach through the medium of Creole and supported a general effort at status and corpus planning paid for by the World Bank. French, Quebec, and Haitian, and American linguists and educators were involved in the effort. In 1982 the government arbitrarily froze efforts to implement proposals. It was widely believed that French-speaking elites feared a future challenge to their positions with the rise of a large Creole literate population. Another reason, here as in Africa, is that people are confused about the utility of literacy in their mother tongues. They perceive that the best positions in their societies require French literacy and a French-style education; they also observe that elites send their own children to private schools where French is the medium of instruction. These elites continue to preach about the *patrimoine*, about the richness of African or Haitian culture, but most of the pressure to engage in rational status planning for African languages comes from outside government.

Unesco, the World Bank, American foundations, Francophone organizations, and French and African linguists and teachers are increasingly certain African and other mother tongues must have a role in the educational process. At least intitial literacy should be in these languages. From the Francophone point of view, children will be better able to learn French once they are already literate. In the words of Jacques Champion (1974: 12),

> The best way to ensure the progress of French as a language of culture and its international diffusion (francophonie) is to have local African languages taught first at the elementary level.

With respect to corpus planning or language development, a less coordinated and more unofficial effort has been increasing. In only a few cases has the government openly given its support. Committees of linguists and teachers in pedagogical centers, missionaries, institutes of applied linguistics, and informal clubs and cultural organizations have taken the initiative; they discuss language questions, write down previously unwritten languages, prepare newspapers and other publications in them. They also encourage a public discussion of the language issue by presenting plays, films, and public readings of poetry to urban audiences of students, workers, and others (Weinstein, 1983: 62-78).

In Madagascar a Service de la Logistique Pédagogique in the Ministry of Education engages in corpus planning by preparing books for teachers and "finding Malagasy equivalents for French technical and scientific terms" (Turcotte, n.d.: 243-246). The Center for Applied Linguistics in Dakar is working on neologisms and spelling Wolof, and linguists there believe they have successfully standardized the language. Cameroun, Ivory Coast, and other countries are now trying to put in effect a standardized spelling system for all African languages spoken within their borders. Conferences sponsored by Unesco have suggested methods and a system for several languages. But some countries such as Guinea prefer to develop their own orthographies. The Institut Pédagogique National in Port-au-Prince, Haiti, proposed a standard spelling for Creole, which is now accepted in exile communities in New York as well as in Haiti (Weinstein and Segal, 1984).

Efforts to modernize and standardize the many varieties of spoken Arabic are the responsiblity of several institutes, but the most interesting is the Institut d'Etudes et de Recherches pour l'Arabisation (IERA) in Morocco. Its director, Ahmed Lakhdar-Ghazal, studied printing technology as well as language planning and developed a method to reduce the number of Arabic characters to facilitate the printing of this language. He is also "stocking" his computer with all the French and Arabic dictionaries available, and he hopes to put English words in it also. When his task is finished, he plans to ask the computer for an Arabic-French lexicon that will help the IERA choose the best Arabic equivalents for French words. Where there are no Arabic equivalents, he and his colleagues will create them. Professor Lakhdar-Ghazal has been a member of the Conseil International de la Langue Française, and this affiliation permits him to keep abreast of work on French elsewhere in the world. He sees no incompatibility between the development of French and the development of Arabic in Morocco.[2] There is even a section of the IERA where work on French continues.

Most research into the problems of French in African schools takes place in African pedagogical institutes, in African institutes of applied linguistics in Senegal, Ivory Coast, Congo, and in France. For several years the Bureau pour l'Enseignement de la Langue et de la Civilisation Francaise à l'Etranger (BELC) and the Centre de Recherche de d'Etude pour la Diffusion du Français have been studying errors made in pronunciation and writing by African children due to what linguists call "interference" from their mother tongues. Beginning with this effort to remedy what for some was a type of "creolization" threatening the standard as they perceived it, they developed a simple basic French *Français Fondamental* particularly for adult education. They also began to advise teachers to teach French no longer as if it were the mother tongue of children, but rather to start from the language sounds and structures they know and move toward French pronunciation and grammar. The technique emphasized oral French, which created problems in the spelling of French and, in the opinion of some African educators, helped create the impression that African sounds were inferior and African pronunciation inadequate. The BELC techniques were denounced at general education meetings in Senegal and eliminated from the French program there.

The Office de la Langue Française (OLF) in Quebec has undertaken a massive program in corpus planning. In 1961 the provincial government created the first OLF in order to draw Quebec closer to the French of France. In 1977 passage of Law 101, the Charter of the French Language, recreated the Office de la Langue Française to direct francization programs in the public and private sectors, to standardize terms in French and to improve the French used. The second Office is larger than the first and does not necessarily condemn all Quebec usage. Its annual budget is over $14 million (Canadian), and about 380 employees work for the OLF.[3]

The Banque de Terminologie of the OLF is an important contribution to corpus planning and standardization of French around the world. The banque stores an acceptable French terminology in its computers and disseminates it to governments and private enterprises. Computer terminals linked with the main computers have been set up in educational institutions, provincial offices, and private companies to facilitate consultation. In 1982 the French set up a computer terminal at their own terminological institution, FRANTERM, and they linked it with the Quebec Banque de Terminologie, which greatly assists coordination and standardization (Daoust, 1983: 59-61). A Commission de Terminologie recommends specific terms that may include purely Quebec French words. Proponents of local varieties of French are no longer intimidated by educated Parisian French. For example, the Senegalese rejected French efforts to eliminate African phonology or Senegalese pronunciantion of French words. In Louisiana, due to the work of planners and linguists, local varieties of French are now respected (Rapp, 1983: 17; Bourhis, 1982). International respect for Cajun music, which is broadcast over Louisiana radio and in Parisian radios, has grown. Radio announcers refuse requests to use educated Parisian French and instead prefer local words, such as *aéroplane* instead of *avion* for airplane. In 1977 James Faulk published his book *Cajun French I* for use in high schools in Louisiana, thus giving the local variety more prestige, and state universities have given further support to the local language (Gold, 1982: 231-238). In Quebec, Aléong found in his study of technical schools that, although students learn the French words for automobile parts, they prefer to continue using the "Vernacular automotive terminology" which he defines as a "mixture of English and French terms set in a French linguistic structure" (Aléong, 1982: 47, 68). In Ivory Coast Partmann found that about 5.3% of the Ivorian population uses what she calls a "Standard Ivorian French" differing from educated Parisian French in pronunciation. Educated Ivorians regard this as correct and resent efforts to change it (Partmann, 1979). The French-born American linguist, Albert Valdman, believes the proponents of Francophonie should build on these variations rather than try to destroy them. An effort should be made to maintain a shared and standard grammar, but variations in lexicon and pronunciation should be recognized as inevitable because of the different experiences of French-speaking peoples. The variation will doubtless increase as education extends to the masses (Valdman, 1983: 699-700). Respect for local varieties of French has grown along with respect for community and national languages. Corpus planners must decide how to incorporate these variations in a mutually comprehensible international French or at least to show the required respect for them.

Another debate will continue about the relative positions of French and other languages in education and government. Pierre Alexandre, a well-known French linguist specializing in African languages, has helped force planners to focus on the means to make French and African or Asian or Creole languages compatible: "The question is now the respective domains of usage of mother tongues and the language of the ex-colonizer and from that, the method of teaching them (Alexandre, 1974: 7). The answer is clearly bilingual education.

BILINGUALISM

Francophonie as a world movement and language planning efforts are both moving rapidly toward the support of bilingualism for pedagogical and political reasons. The French, African, Haitian and other supporters of teaching in community languages or mother tongues in primary schools and then switching to French believe there will be an improvement in the learning process, a decline in the presently high rate of failures and dropouts, and an extension of the French language to the masses. The ultimate contribution of such a policy should then be a more productive, mobilized population and close ties among all countries where French is the major means of communication. Some of these elites also believe the African states will continue to follow and support French positions in world affairs, thus ensuring an important French presence in the decades to come, no matter how many people speak and write English.

Although schools in France are not bilingual, the provisions of the Deixonne Law of January 1951—which allowed brief study of Breton, Basque, Catalan, Occitan, and then Corsican—have been enlarged. It is now possible for students to study what are courteously called "regional languages" for three hours a week in secondary school. Other provisions are giving these languages a place in the university program if students desire.

Bilingualism is clearly more important as an issue in Quebec, situated as it is in a massive English-speaking North America. An ambivalence toward bilingual education is evident among planners who are suspicious that French-English bilingualism actually means that French speakers will learn English while English speakers will not learn French. On the other hand, some planners believe that Law 101, which made French official in Quebec, has stopped the assimilation of French speakers and new immigrants into the English-speaking community. This law, along with a higher self-confidence in their identity as Quebecois, should mean that a stable bilingualism may be possible.

In Africa, Haiti, Lebanon, and (perhaps) Vietnam, studies show that the loyalty to French as an instrument of the modern world is intense, and the suggestion that English is superior to French is viewed suspiciously as a form of Yankee imperialism. Abdelâhi Bentahila found in a survey of language attitudes in Morocco that bilinguals have a high degree of loyalty to Arabic and French. They wish to retain French for specific functions and to retain Arabic for (more) specific functions (Bentahila, 1983: 165). The place of French in Morocco, as in many other countries, will probably be more sharply restricted to formal domains, however. During the colonial period African mother tongues were forbidden from the classroom and the school playground. Now they are widely used in informal settings as well as for explanatory purposes in formal settings (Hammoud, 1982: 216-217). This will continue and expand, but French will always have a place, and where French is openly threatened, as in Belgium, efforts to preserve and expand its domains will increase.

New tensions between supporters of bilingualism are emerging. Planners in France and elites in power in most African states and Haiti support what in America is called transitional bilingualism, meaning that students should study through the medium of French soon after achieving literacy in their first languages. Many African intellectuals, as well as political opponents of African regimes in search of issues, support another approach, namely the maintenance and extension of mother tongue competency. They say their goal is use of African languages as media of instruction throughout the educational system and introduction of African tongues into the day-to-day operations of government, spoken and written. They believe French should be taught as a subject to secondary school and university students. The result would be a diminished role for French, and practically no role for French among the masses. The debate will continue.

CONCLUSION

The material results of Francophonie are not obvious. Some of the reasons are historical and goegraphical. Several of the mineral-poor and landlocked states of Africa happen by historical events to be Francophone states. Haiti is poor because of rapacious local elites. Chad is torn apart by competing elites. French, Quebec, Canadian, Belgian, and other assistance, given partly in the name of Francophonie (which is naturally tied to national interests), has helped the poorest survive.

A problem for future results is that Francophone organizations such as the ACCT may be unable to analyze and solve problems of a political and economic nature between France and other Francophone states if there is a risk of embarrassment for France. For example, Paris wishes to discourage immigration of workers and, because of unemployment, has begun to reduce illegal foreign-worker populations. This issue came before the 1979 meeting of the Association Internationale des Parlementaires de Langue Française, but after what must have been a very timid discussion the matter was deferred for further study. Members were satisfied to pass yet another resolution in favor of workers and their relatives in France and Africa who would like nothing better than to use and improve the French that helps them obtain jobs. Increasing attacks on foreigners in 1983 in France prompted a warning from the president of Algeria, a warning delivered in the framework of bilateral relations between France and Algeria and not through the framework of Francophonie.

The strengths of Francophonie should not be underestimated. Loyalty to French need not be translated as disloyalty to other communities. The loyalty serves local interests and serves as a basis for political, economic, and military cooperation across frontiers. Haiti uses French to affirm its separate identity in a Spanish- and English-speaking Caribbean, and it is used similarly in Belgium, Switzerland, Canada, and West Africa. Within West African states French retains its vitality as a means of upward mobility. In a survey conducted at the University in Togo, Sedlak found that although many students had spent years in Anglophone Ghana, a mere "four percent wanted their children educated in English." A very high percentage of 62% expressed a desire that their children be educated only in French or in Franco-African bilingual programs (Sedlak, 1980: 10).

Another strength is the fact that although French cannot be viewed as a "neutral" language in any multilingual society—since it must be associated with a local class, region or ethnic group, or internationally with France—it is still preferable in several societies to one local language, partly because it is also more developed than these languages. Finally, the growth of a rich literature in varieties of French outside France helps support those who claim there can be a Francophone world to which all contribute and in which we all share. The election of Léopold Sédar Senghor to a seat in the Académie Française is a symbol of this position.

In short, a change in attitudes in the Francophone world, reflecting a recognition of local differences and interests; an effort to improve the economic and political benefits of the cultural links; a commitment to planning; the openness of the movement to differing professional, class, regional, and ethnic interests; increasing concern about the masses' ability to learn and use French; and a broader definition of what is standard international French all mean that Francophonie is a vital cultural movement affecting the lives of thirty states and tens of millions of people in the years to come. Through planning and through the reinforcement of political and economic links, a French language, more open to change than in the past, retains its position as a world language. As in the past, such a status helps France preserve its political prestige and pursue its national interests. What is different about the future is that a strong French language, accepted and used alongside other languages, also helps other states pursue their national interests.

NOTES

1. It was Ndiaye who suggested the term "community language" to me.
2. Professor Lakdar-Ghazad's views were obtained in an interview at the IERA, May 16, 1979.
3. This information was obtained in interviews at the OLF, May 20, 1983.

14

DISCOURSE, CONSCIOUSNESS, AND LITERACY IN A PUERTO RICAN NEIGHBORHOOD

Adrian T. Bennett and Pedro Pedraza, Jr.

IN A RECENT REPORT on the American high school, Ernest Boyer (1983: 90) suggests,

> Clear writing leads to clear thinking; clear thinking is the basis of clear writing. Perhaps more than any other form of communication, writing holds us responsible for our words and ultimately makes us more thoughtful human beings.

It is not uncommon for such general surveys of education to present the connection between literacy and thinking as relatively direct, even to the point of assuming that good writing produces critical awareness (e.g., Adler, 1982; Illich, 1971; National Commission of Excellence in Education, 1983). This view might be considered part of a prevalent ideology in U.S. society, one that began to take shape in the last three decades of the nineteenth century, as Heath's (1981b: 35) survey of grammar and composition texts of the period indicates:

> The strong implication was that those who wrote and criticized well had more intelligence, morality, and industry than did their fellow students. A class consciousness was developing on the basis of the language used and the standards of writing perpetuated in the classroom.

Nevertheless, recent research on literacy in anthropology, linguistics, cognitive psychology, history, and other fields seems to validate the claim that writing and thinking are causally related. Many scholars have argued that literacy in Western industrial societies has played an important role in facilitating the development of "modern" forms of consciousness, social behavior, and cultural life, which contrast with those found in oral traditions and in most other literature traditions (Havelock, 1963; Goody and Watt, 1968; Ong, 1977). In Western literate societies, so the argument goes, knowledge can be treated as if it were independent of those who produce and use it. Because knowledge can be rather precisely recorded in written form, it can be treated as sets of self-contained concepts or propositions that can be examined critically according to value-free principles of logic that operate independent of specific social contexts. Statements judged valid according to such criteria can then pass into the growing stock of recorded knowledge.

The technologies of writing and print (and now of computer "literacies"), according to this view, have produced societies vastly different from more "traditional" societies, such as the tribal and agrarian societies that were on the peripheries of expanding Western empires. For example, education moved away from such personally involving relationships as master and neophyte, or equally powerful ritual experiences, such as puberty rites, in which what is learned is carefully integrated with the very being of the learner. This is replaced with a "separation of the knower from the known," and an "autonomous, self-governing personality" is constructed, "symbolized as the power to think, to calculate, to cogitate, and to know, in total distinction from the capacity to see, to hear, and to feel" (Havelock, 1963). The job of education, certainly in modern times, becomes the transmission of a body of objective knowledge by first teaching the young the "basics" of literacy, then guiding them through the appropriate written texts that contain that knowledge, and finally—for an elite few at least—encouraging the development of critical (text-analytical) skills.

As literacy spread in Western societies, new forms of oral communications influenced by literacy evolved that also affected education. As Cook-Gumperz and Gumperz (1981: 106) suggest,

> With the growth of mass communication and the increasing need for communicating with individuals who differ in culture and home background, culturally neutral styles of speaking have evolved for use in instruction giving, public lectures, broadcasting and classroom lectures and similar instrumental tasks. These oral styles have taken on many of the characteristics of . . . modern written descriptive prose and have thus become distinct from the home languages.

Formal education in Western societies thus involves a gradual inculcation of such "culturally neutral styles" along with the criteria of truth, clarity, and impersonal social relations that go with developing skills in what Scribner and Cole (1978) have dubbed "essayist literacy." Much of the social science research on literacy, which has grown prodigiously in the last ten years, has concerned itself with describing differences between "home" and "school" cultures. Recognizing that learning to read and write involve acquiring new communicative skills, Cook-Gumperz and Gumperz (1981: 106) suggest,

> The transition from the child's culture at home . . . where the child has learnt to make sense and achieve social actions within his/her own communicative system, requires a change of communicative understanding for all children.

Anthropological research has shown that oral styles, as well as the uses, forms, and functions of literacy, can vary socially and culturally. (See for example, Gumperz and Hymes, 1972; Bauman and Sherzer, 1974; Blount and Sanches, 1975; Goody, 1968; Whiteman, 1981.)

It has been argued that for certain social groups such differences can clash with the demands of schooling. For example, Heath (1983) found considerable variation in the forms and uses of literacy in a ten-year study of three Carolina Piedmont communities. "Maintowners," consisting largely of middle-class white professionals, had high skills in essayist literacy. The working-class whites of "Roadville" valued literacy skills highly, yet they did not use the written word very much for communicative purposes more complicated than shopping lists, telephone messages, or reading storybooks to very young children. The working-class Blacks of Tracton did not place the same high value on essayist literacy skills as did their white counterparts in the other two communities, and they disapproved of those who consumed print in isolation from others. On the other hand, they often used written materials—e.g., letters, recipes, directions for operating and repairing appliances—as a basis for interpersonal, oral interaction.

Heath suggests that these differences help account for differential school success of children from the three communities. Maintown children are comparatively successful. Roadville children start out well, but begin to lag in the intermediate grades, and Tracton Black children tend to do poorly from the beginning. Heath argues that these differences are accounted for by different communicative patterns revolving around the uses of literacy. In particular, Roadville children have been carefully instructed by parents in skills that are emphasized in the first few grades—naming things and providing factual information in response to questions. Tracton children, on the other hand, have fairly well-developed skills in comparing, analyzing, and making inferences from limited sources of information, but are not given a chance to use these skills until the middle grades. The emphasis on minutiae and on providing factual responses in early literacy training in the early grades turn them off from formal instruction. On the other hand, Roadville children find it difficult to make the transition from these "basic" skills to the more "sophisticated" inferential skills called upon in the later grades.

Heath and others who have focused on descriptions of cultural and communicative differences between the school and home communities (e.g., Scollon and Scollon, 1981; Michaels, 1981) suggest that educators need to be aware of such differences in designing curricula and in developing classroom practices that can mediate between the expectations children form at home and the demands of schooling.

In carrying out research on the discourse of Puerto Ricans in East Harlem, New York, we expected to uncover communicative patterns that might be sources of conflict in schooling and that could help account for a dropout rate of 80 percent by grade 12 (Aspira, 1983). Our previous work in this community, known as "El Barrio" among residents, involved several years of study and included ethnographic observations, attitude surveys, and sociolinguistic studies (Language Policy Task Force, 1983). Communicative networks of the residents in a one-block area were delineated; members' interactions in a variety of formal and informal situations were observed and taped; attitudes toward language, ethnicity, schooling and other concerns were surveyed; and sociolinguistic studies of codeswitching and other linguistic variables were conducted.

The community dates back to the 1920s and extends over a thirty-block area on the upper east side of Manhattan. There are about 180,000 residents, of which over half are Hispanic (mostly Puerto Rican), while most of the remainder are Black. El Barrio is an important cultural and political center for the 1,400,000 Hispanics in the city. It is a viable community, both culturally and linguistically, despite extensive poverty and a consistently high unemployment rate of about 25 percent. Puerto Ricans value their ethnic identity highly and have high aspirations for their children's education.

Language use is highly variable, involving Spanish, English, and codeswitching, but there is no evidence that Spanish is dying out or being "taken over" or "corrupted" by English. It has been maintained, notably by Fishman (1971), that bilingual situations are unstable when separation of the two languages into separate domains of usage—such as home versus public settings—is not maintained.

> Without separate though complementary norms and values to establish and maintain functional separation of the speech varieties, that

language or variety which is fortunate enough to be associated with the predominant drift of social forces tends to displace the other [Fishman, 1971: 298].

Yet we found that many speakers use both languages for all types of communication:

> It is even the case that for many the simultaneous use of both languages in the same discourse setting, conversation, and utterance is not unusual. In fact, it may be the most appropriate type of speech behavior a member of the community can exhibit in very informal public settings.... It is obvious to us, therefore, that the lack of functional compartmentalization of the language of a bilingual community can coexist with language maintenance. In fact, language shift (in terms of changing relative proficiency) and language maintenance are found together in this Puerto Rican neighborhood...but no diglossia [Pedraza et al., 1980: 36-37].

Thus, it is evident from our studies that language and other cultural practices could not be explained in terms of individual psychology but, rather, must be "understood as a reflection of the social history and conditions of the community" (Language Policy Task Force, 1980), and as the community's response to that history and those conditions.

This work has given direction for our current research on the communicative patterns of Puerto Ricans in El Barrio. But, in addition to communicative patterns, we have become increasingly interested in the relationship between these patterns and consciousness. We are exploring ways of understanding language use as communicative *practices* that Puerto Ricans have evolved in response to changing social, political, and economic conditions. Puerto Rican ways of speaking may well pattern differently than "school language," yet viewing them as practices constructed in response to historical forces might provide better insight into such chronic and pervasive social problems as school failure. From this perspective, an understanding of Puerto Ricans' own understandings of historical conditions may be critical.

We did in fact find interesting features of Puerto Rican communicative patterns, which seem to reflect different standards of reasoning and truth and which reflect forms of social relationships other than those fostered by the pedagogy of essayist literacy in the schools. But having found such differences, we were not sure how to interpret them. We were unconvinced of the adequacy of the cultural and communicative differences theory of school failure and of other forms of social oppression. To illustrate our reasons for drawing these conclusions, and at the same time to exemplify our approach to discourse analysis as it has evolved to this point, we discuss a brief segment of tape-recorded conversation involving three male residents, one a researcher, engaged in casual talk as they sit on a stoop watching the street scene. The appended transcript (translated from Spanish into English) contains certain interesting differences in the talk of two of the men, "Edmundo" and "Carlos," relating to essayist literacy. We will indicate some differences in their communicative patterns as revealed by preliminary analysis, then discuss the limits of that analysis, and finally attempt a reanalysis that raises questions about the consciousness of Edmundo and Carlos by considering their discourse as practices that respond to historical conditions.

We focus first on Edmundo's and Carlos' argument styles. They can be seen countering one another's viewpoints in turns 7-19 and 35-44 over two focal issues: (1) What makes a person worth something, and (2) how mothers are to be defined or categorized.

Their methods of argument differ. Carlos repeatedly uses *dichos* ("sayings") that have symbolic implications. With Raymond Williams (1977) we might call this strategy a "cultural residue," as it makes reference to a bygone era when Puerto Rico was primarily an agrarian society, and uses a communicative strategy associated with that society. An example is turn 36, when he says, "Even the *yautía* plant loves her children," to support his point that mothers have a special relationship to their children grounded in nature. Therefore, it can be taken for granted that when he says "Damn all women," (T.28) he does not intend to include mothers. Again, Carlos often identifies himself with aspects of the natural world. For example, in turn 19 he compares himself to the *morivivi* plant of Puerto Rico, which when touched droops and seems to die, but gradually revives itself: "I always live like the morivivi." Carlos uses symbolic expressions like this to make points, to bolster arguments, and to evoke a personal identification with traditional aspects of Puerto Rican society.

In each of these examples, the speaker relies on the listener to make the right connections to shared cultural knowledge in order to draw the correct inferences. These inferences are steps in an argument, but their propositional content is left implicit, while the dicho is used to foreground an image, a metaphor, or a story.

Edmundo also sometimes evokes the authority of tradition through the use of dichos, as when he says "Even Christ said 'Why do you cry, woman?'" (T. 42), to support his contention that mothers are women too. That is, even Christ called his own archetypal mother a woman.

Therefore, if you say "Damn all women," you are saying "Damn mothers" too. (It is, incidentally, at such points that the tongue-in-cheek, almost facetious quality of the argument becomes evident.) But Edmundo exhibits another mode of argument in his response to Carlos' reference to the yautía plant: "Well then, if a mother can be like that, how can you say 'Damn all women'?" (T.38). Here his approach is to quote Carlos' earlier statement in order to foreground a logical inconsistency with a later proposition that Edmundo makes explicit in turn 40: "Look what an avocado you are, they loved you, watched over you, when you were little." This use of logical analysis, supported by the rule that two contradictory statements cannot be true, is a feature of Edmundo's argument repertoire that Carlos does not resort to in this interaction.

The extent to which these differences represent differences in the communicative repertoires of Edmundo and Carlos cannot be adequately determined from one small segment of talk such as this. However, Pedraza's interaction over a long period of time with Edmundo and Carlos suggests that such differences persist over many kinds of interactional situations.

How can we interpret and understand these differences? We can note that Edmundo has some command of the same criteria of logic and impersonal evaluation of assertions that researchers have reported as characteristic of essayist literacy. When we compare his background with that of Carlos we are not surprised to find important differences: Edmundo has lived in New York since he was a young child, attended school up to twelfth grade, is bilingual, and is employed in a skilled job in a hospital. Carlos came to New York in his teens, has had several kinds of unskilled labor jobs, and had been unemployed for over a year. His education was limited to primary school, and he is Spanish-dominant. This type of information, if supplemented by more ethnography and analysis, can be very useful to teachers. Several specific insights that emerge from our research could assist teachers in understanding communicative and other cultural differences between Puerto Ricans and "mainstream" or middle-class Anglos:

(1) We could show teachers that some Puerto Ricans use metaphoric, personal, and symbolic styles of expressing ideas and supporting points of view. We could add, from our other work, that personal narratives (a form Carlos uses later on in the tape) are also an important resource because they imply access to the authenticity of having "been there."

(2) We could also show teachers that there is important variation in the community; there is not one "Puerto Rican," as the differences between Edmundo and Carlos demonstrate, and teachers should be aware of the dangers of stereotyping.
(3) We could demonstrate too that literacy can influence oral styles, and that Puerto Ricans show differential access, or at least reliance on, essayist literacy styles in their spoken discourse.
(4) Finally, we could inform teachers that these are not so much phenomena of code—e.g., Spanish versus English—but of discourse, and of communicative practices that can occur in either language.

We feel it is valuable for teachers to have such information. We also feel it is not enough.

There are two main problems with the cultural differences approach to the explanation and correction of school failure and social inequality. First, there are theoretical problems in the absence of explanatory theories. If literacy has taken different forms in different social groups—many of which have been in direct and frequent contact—how did this come about? How are particular relations between written and oral modes developed? How are certain configurations of form, function, means of transmission and reproduction, and social uses of literacy produced in different societies over time? How is this process of production related to other social and historical processes, such as the production and maintenance of particular divisions of power, labor, economic resources, knowledge, skills, ideology, and interests?

Second, there is a practical problem regarding the application of research on cultural and communicative differences to specific social problems, such as educational inequities. In a society in which certain social groups exert power over and exploit certain other social groups, how can the awareness of cultural differences result in changes in power relations between exploiters and exploited? Those who have treated the cultural contexts of literacy have tended to portray societies as homogeneous, self-maintaining, and independent systems, and they have portrayed cultures—to quote Eric Wolf (1982)—"As integrated totalities in which each part contributes to the maintenance of an organized, autonomous, and enduring whole." This cultural relativism has its counterpart in a political practice that fosters pluralistic idealism. The basic social structure dividing haves and have-nots can remain untouched, although a few individuals of high skill will be able to move up the social scale.

There is, however, an alternative view of culture as an ongoing social process of constructing, dismantling, and reconstructing meanings in response to developing social, political, and economic conditions. The ability to bestow meanings—to construct the categories through which we perceive, understand, and evaluate social reality—is itself a source of power. Patterns of culture and the communicative symbolic practices by means of which culture is reproduced, can be explained only if we see them in their connections to economic and political processes. Cultural practices are in fact potential weapons in the clash of social interests in societies where differentiations of power between classes are sustained and embedded in institutions.

If we take this view of culture and communication, the description of cultural and communicative practices needs to be supplemented by asking such questions as the following:

- To what extent are these practices part of processes of accommodation or resistance to structural inequalities?
- To what extent do they reveal members' critical awareness of social contradictions that members themselves live out in their daily lives?
- What possibilities might there be for concerted political action among community members?

How can the community address social problems as a community? To answer such questions we need to know more than that certain patterns of expression and reasoning reflect essayist literacy traditions while others reflect oral traditions. We use the discourse data in the transcript to illustrate how such data can help answer questions like these.

We will consider now some aspects of content. Edmundo argues that mothers are like all women. For example, in turn 34 he says, "No, she is the same woman, she has the [inaudible], she has the same, no more or no less than any other woman." Edmundo's classification of mothers is based on a modern, secular view of nature, and supercedes categorizations based on tradition, family, or community values. By contrast, Carlos argues that mothers are a special category by virtue of a special relationship through love to their children. Carlos portrays this special relationship as a natural one, characteristically using an agrarian metaphor to make his point: "Listen, even the yautía plant loves her children" (T. 37).

The views that Edmundo and Carlos express about mothers and their relationships to the superordinate category of women thus reflect different views of the natural world. Edmundo's argument depends on separating the natural from the social realms, excluding, for the purpose of his argument, the special relationship of mothers to children, or subsuming this relationship under the more general category of woman as the female of the human species. Carlos, on the other hand, builds an argument that depends on seeing nature, not independent of the social and family realms but rather as their foundation. Even the yautía loves her children. The biological relationship gives a special meaning to the social-familial one.

These alternative views of the social and natural worlds are expressed in other parts of the conversation. For example, Edmundo and Carlos also express different perspectives on the basis of human worth. Edmundo expresses, again, a more urbanized, modern view in Turns 11-13: "As for me, I'm worth a lot, my life has no price." This presupposes that one's value can be asserted on the basis of individual autonomy. Carlos, on the other hand, expresses a more complex view. First he maintains that he is worth nothing. For example, in Turn 16 he says, "If I were worth anything I would have sold myself; nobody wants to buy me." That is, in American society one's value is as a commodity that can be exchanged for money. But a few moments later, Carlos expresses a rather different viewpoint, more similar to his view of motherhood, when he says, that, although he has not been able to "do business" in selling himself, his wife, or his son, he always comes back to life and survives, like the morivivi plant, which when touched seems to collapse and die, yet springs back to life again later: "I always like like the morivivi" (T. 19). Just as motherhood is grounded in the natural world, so too is his own identity as a resilient survivor. Here again we find differences between Edmundo and Carlos, which is more information that we could pass on to teachers and other professionals who deal with Puerto Ricans as clients of institutions of various kinds.

However, Carlos is not simply expressing values, but is talking about his own social and economic positioning as a person without value. He is also providing a response that, despite being positioned as powerless to earn a living, he has a resilience grounded in the close association of personal, social, and natural worlds. The social positioning to which Carlos is responding is expressed in his ironic characterization of himself as valueless yet capable of surviving. This is a contradiction he lives out in his daily life. His awareness of this contradiction reflects a critical view of the commodity system in which even one's wife and children are potential commodities. Yet he also expresses his resistance through the image of the morivivi plant in his symbolic identification with nature.

Edmundo, on the other hand, asserts his individual autonomy, implying an independence from the social. Yet Edmundo is not critical of society; in fact, his individualism has certain parallels in the individualism of what many have characterized as bourgeois ideology (e.g., Gould, 1978; Ollman, 1971).

At this point, we might ask whether Edmundo or Carlos exhibits more critical awareness and potential for resistance. The answer is certainly not obvious. From our own point of view Edmundo appears to buy into the dominant ideology more than Carlos, but he has also been more successful than Carlos in participating in the market economy by selling his labor. By contrast, Carlos shows critical awareness and even resistance. But even in his resistance there are contradictions. His identification with nature may be be adequate to cope with his peripheral position in a market economy, any more than the agrarian idealism exemplified by Tolstoy, William Morris, or Zeno-Gandía (Puerto Rican author of the novel *La Charca*), stopped capitalism from spreading all over the world in the last 100 years. It is even possible that Carlos's recourse to a precapitalist agrarian ideology while providing a refuge from the modern world, may limit his ability to participate as an active agent in that world and thereby help sustain his peripherality, politically and economically. Edmundo may, in fact, be better equipped to deal with the dominant ideology in that his readiness to use logical criteria of truth and validity could, at least theroretically, be as easily applied to a critical analysis of dominant ideologies—as they encroach on Puerto Ricans through mass media, schooling, the job market, and so on—as to the values Carlos expresses.

As for potential resistance, we should note that Edmundo's and Carlos's ability to engage in this kind of dialogue, mixing humor and seriousness in an egalitarian relationship governed by *respeto* (respect), and called *bromavera* (joking truth) by some Puerto Ricans, could itself be seen as a form of resistance, at least potentially. It certainly provides an alternative to relations based on *negocios* (business) and commodity exchanges. Their skillful and thoughtful dialogue encompassing complex issues certainly goes far beyond that with which most middle-class people would be likely to credit them.

CONCLUSION

It would be difficult to say the relationship of literacy to consciousness and critical thinking is simple and direct or that a certain technological base simply results in a particular kind of awareness. Rather, we suggest that there is a relationship between literacy and thinking, and that this relationship is socially constituted. It is produced through historical processes involving struggles of ideology, power, and interest. This means that human beings decide how literacy and thinking are to be related. If the relationship between essayist literacy and modern consciousness is today as researchers have reported, it is because the way we conceptualize literacy in the schools and other public institutions is also an ideological manifestation of capitalist society. We believe there should be workable alternatives.

What we have argued touches upon issues concerning the literacy instruction of Puerto Rican children within our schools. Our understanding of what literacy entails needs to be altered from that of a set of mechanical skills to that of a social/cultural phenomenon related to other political and economic processes. Literacy always occurs within a social context. It is neither ahistorical nor static; and, more than likely, it is variable. Whenever literacy activity occurs, in learning or as performance, it must be comprehended as an accomplishment embedded in other cultural processes.

Therefore, we must ask ourselves not only if the way we teach literacy contradicts, or ignores, community practices, but if we are furthering the development of critical thinking, self-awareness, and community needs. The liberal model of pluralist education that is supported by the linguistic relativism of sociolinguistic theory has some very progressive features that distinguish it from conventional American pedagogy. Sociolinguists and anthropologists have significantly improved public awareness of social and cultural differences and have provided an empirical basis for demanding (sometimes through litigation) greater accountability from public institutions such as the schools for provision of equitable services to minority and other disadvantaged populations (Labov, 1982). The equal treatment of all students in terms of resources, curriculum, testing, and social relations is a laudable ideal that social scientists should continue to support. However, from the point of view of Puerto Ricans living in El Barrio, and in similar communities both on the U.S. mainland and in Puerto Rico, some problems remain.

Just one example: A report recently released by the National Center for Educational Statistics (NCES, 1983) indicated that Puerto Rican high school dropouts are just as likely (or maybe even more likely) to get jobs as are Puerto Rican high school graduates. How are schools preparing students for a situation of increased competition for fewer jobs? A better understanding of communicative sources of cross-cultural misunderstanding in all public sectors is certainly needed (Gumperz, 1982); yet improving communication will not automatically lead to dissolution of the kinds of social, political, and economic inequities that Puerto Ricans have suffered since their island was invaded by U.S. marines in 1898 (Bonilla and Campos, 1981). Such inequities have been a constant in Puerto Rican life, despite numerous economic programs and attempts at social, educational, and political reform (History Task Force, 1979).

We suggest that sociolinguists should expand their concern with communicative patterns to explore the hypothesis that the phenomena of unequal distribution of societal resources and cultural and communicative misunderstanding are part of the same general political and economic processes. However, an understanding of these processes and of how they impinge on communicative practices cannot be adequately developed without attention to how access to society's resources is controlled through the deployment of power and the legitimation of that deployment through subtle ideological processes. It is interesting that those who advocate making teachers and other professionals more sensitive to cultural differences, and to providing minority students with opportunities to expand their communicative repertoires, rarely address the question of how power is distributed within educational institutions or of how these institutions are themselves caught in a tissue of power relations that extends throughout U.S. society (Apple, 1982; Giroux, 1981).

To include a consideration of power as it is structured into institutions and into the interpersonal relations within those institutions' domains would be to expand considerably the notion of context as it has been developed in sociolinguistic and anthropological studies of communication so far. We consider the analysis provided above to be only a beginning step in this direction. We need to look more closely at how community members construct particular forms of consciousness through their ongoing daily communications with each other. We need to understand better how that consciousness, in its variability, provides members with responses to particular sociohistorical conditions as they experience them. But more than that, we need to find ways, as Labov (1982) advocates, to build commitment into all stages of research.

We suggest that the best way to do this is to develop better ways to work cooperatively with those who participate in such institutional processes as schooling. Anthropologists have recently made considerable efforts to work cooperatively with professionals (Gilmore and Smith, 1982; Heath, 1983). We believe that, if the interests of the community are to be served, we must in addition find ways to work within the community, basing our conceptions of education and literacy in the needs and interests of the community as defined through cooperative efforts between researchers and community members. If researchers engage in such a process through their research itself, they may well find themselves committed to using their knowledge to help change existing structures of power.

APPENDIX

Transcript—Tape B14

1. Pablo: and, and, and of and those five feet three inches how much do you think its worth
   /3 sec./

2. Edmundo: (three) P. (laughs)

3. Carlos: To myself, to myself I'm not worth anything. The purpose is that after I die they bring me back to life.
   /2 sec./

4. C: ⎡And⎤
5. E: ⎣Live⎦ in the eyes, in the eyes of another person in a kidney . . . a heart.

6. C: But I'll live

7. P: But how much of this guy do you think is even worth the trouble

8. E: About that ⎡I don't know⎤
9. C: ⎣not worth anything⎦ not worth anything
   ⎡not worth anything⎤
10. E: ⎣I don't tease⎦
    anyone so that they don't tease me

11. C: The truth is that its not worth ⎡anything, the head⎤ (of a
12. E: ⎣for (   )⎦ as
    for me, I'm worth a lot

13. C:		No, I'm not worth anything because if I were valuable I would have sold ⎡myself⎤
14. E:		⎣(my)⎦ my life has no price
15. E:		Eh?
16. C:		If I were worth something I would have sold myself, nobody wants to (buy me)
17. P:		⎡(laughs)⎤
18. E:		⎣Not even⎦
19. C:		I I was selling my wife and child and no one wanted to buy. I sell myself and even less are they willing to buy...so what am I to do if I can't sell. If I can't sell I can'd do business but even though I ⎡always⎤ live like the "morivivi."
20. ?:		⎣( )⎦
21. E:		Oh Damn
22. P:		He's hurt, he's hurt
23. E:		Oh, he hit his chest when he fell.
24. C:		Well check him to make sure he hasn't broken his chest or heart.
?:		No, his heart he didn't break because . . .
25. E:		No, he needs a woman.
26. C.		Eh?
27. E:		When the heart is broken it has to be a woman.
28. C:		Damn all women, man.
29. E:		Man, what do you mean, if it wasn't for a woman I wouldn't be here.
30. P:		That's true, _____.
31. C:		Yes, but that's a different type of woman . . .
32. E:		She's ⎡a woman like any other.⎤ No, she's the same type of woman, she has
33. C:		. . . from ⎣the type of woman I'm referring to⎦ ( )

34. E: ... ⎡She has ⎤the same, she has no more or ⎡no less ⎤than
            ⎣ (   )⎦   any other woman   ⎣its not⎦ its
35. C: not
    :   its not the same because a, a, a mother
36. E: only, only, a label
           a title tells you ⎡mother⎤
37. C: ⎣listen⎦ even the "yautía" loves her children
38. E: Well then, if a mother can be like that how can you say damn
           all women.
39. C: Because when you ⎡take   ⎤
40. C: ⎣Look what⎦ an avocado you are they
           loved you, ⎡watched over you⎤
                      ⎢   ⎥ when you were little (right)
41. C: ⎣listen listen   ⎦   to me   listen yes but,
    :   that, that is a different type of woman, one's mother
42. E: ( ) she's a
           woman
    :   ⎡even, even,⎤ Christ said to his mother, "Why do you cry
           ⎢   ⎥   woman?"
43. C: ⎣compared to⎦ the others
                                   /3 sec./
44. C: (   ) she had to cry, right, it was her son.
54. E: ⎡But ⎤ she was a woman
46. C: ⎣Now ⎦   now if it were a lover.
47. E: Perhaps ⎡she'll still cry⎤
48. C: ⎣or if it were ⎦
49. E: ⎡Maybe she'd cry anyway⎤
50. C: ⎣ Or if it were   ⎦   a husband she didn't love, she'd cry
           out of ⎡hypocrisy⎤
51. E: ⎣Ahhh   ⎦
           If it's a husband she would be happy because she would get
           the pension
52. C: Haven't you ever been in a situation where a woman who has
           lost a husband has her lover next to her and the guy tells her
           but let me submit the name and those papers and she crying

		tells him (mimics crying) "thirty-three, fourty-four, fifty-six."
53.	E:	No I've never been in such a situation.

Key

[ ]	= overlapping speech
( )	= not transcribable
(words)	= unclear, transcriber's guess

15

ASKING THE RIGHT QUESTIONS ABOUT LANGUAGE AND POWER

William M. O'Barr

THE CONTRIBUTORS TO THIS volume have addressed the relation of language and power in various ways. Some have focused on the relation of whole languages to the power structures of communities, nation-states, and even the international order. Others have considered language varieties and styles as these intersect with the distribution of power. But whatever the level of context, a single and important conclusion can be drawn from them all: The issues considered here are not so much linguistic as political ones. Language is the mirror, the vehicle, and the means for expression of many political relations. Seldom is it the basic issue itself, and to assume that it *is* only diverts attention from the fundamental phenomenon described in some manner in all the preceding papers—the power structure in society.

This perspective on the relation between language and power requires us to look beneath the surface to ask questions about the relations among the parts of society, especially how power is distributed with regard to the social structure. When we begin to understand this, we also begin to see more clearly how language serves as a major means of expressing, of manipulating, and even of transforming power relations. This chapter is intended not as a review of what has been said in the various contributions to this volume, but as a stimulus to thinking about further aspects of language-power relations toward the goal of a more complete understanding of them. In the first part, language and power are discussed in relation to social situations and cultural contexts. In the second, language and power are examined in interaction. In the third section, the social and political concomitants of literacy are discussed. In the fourth section, the question of a world language is considered with regard to the political issues it reflects. Each of these issues in turn shows how situations or issues involving language are appropriately analyzed as situations or issues about language and power.

LANGUAGE AND POWER: SOCIAL SITUATIONS AND CULTURAL CONTEXTS

A classic paper about language and power focuses on the political significance of pronouns. Its authors (Brown and Gilman, 1960) argue that so simple a part of language as which pronoun a speaker chooses in referring to another person reflects patterns of social hierarchy or equality. The specific case they describe is the use of *tu* as opposed to *vous* in French, and the similar patterns that occur in most Indo-European languages. Three basic patterns are posited for dyadic relationships: reciprocal familiar pronouns (tu/tu) which reflect equality and solidarity within the dyad, reciprocal formal pronouns (vous/vous) which also mirror equality and solidarity within the dyad, but one more formally and distantly, and nonreciprocal pronouns (tu/vous), which indicate inequality and hierarchy.

It would be naive to assume that English, which lacks a specific tu/vous type of alternation between second-person pronouns, is somehow more egalitarian in its basic orientation than French, Spanish, German, and others. It takes only a little effort to find a similar reflection of inequality in the ways speakers address one another. Brown and Ford (1961), writing about the patterns of first- and last-name usage, have shown a related phenomenon at work: When male speakers of American English call one another by first names, they similarly reflect the equality and familiarity of their relationship. Titles with last names (e.g., Mr. Smith/Mr. Jones) indicate a more formal and distant relationship, whereas inequality is indicated by nonreciprocal usages (as in Mr. Smith/John). Whatever the specifics of the particular patterns, language is taken in these instances to mirror social relationships, and the study of language patterns a means toward understanding them.

A more comprehensive description of language as a reflection of social relationship that takes into consideration situational and contextual variation is provided by Varenne (1978). Investigating the memoranda written by a high school principal to his faculty, the researcher was able to note several different relationships expressed beneath the overt surface of a memorandum. For instance, the principal wrote frequently in a "personal" style (characterized by phrases like "let me take this opportunity to thank each of you" and "keep up the good work and I certainly look forward to the many ideas and future changes which each of you are discussing and attempting to implement") and employed usages that differentiate and separate him from his audience (conceived of as separate individuals rather than a collectivity). On another occasion, the principal referred to himself as "the principal" and to his audience as "the teacher." This memorandum, composed in what Varenne terms "administrative talk," sets out formal relations between the writer and those to whom the message is directed. In this instance, the teacher is an anonymous individual who is, along with the principal, a part of the administrative hierarchy of the high school, in which roles are conceived as rather formal and inflexible. In another memorandum, the principal wrote to his faculty as follows:

> There is something intriguing about a teacher surplus which now exists in our country today. It permits us to be very selective in education. It enables us to assign teachers better. It even lets us replace some teachers we should not have hired in the first place.

The relationship in this memorandum is again conceived differently, but the message communicated by its form can hardly fail to be heard by those to whom it is addressed.

Once we are into this mode of analyzing the relation between language and power, we can easily extend it to a wide range of social situations that reflect social relationships in language. But is the relation between language and power only that of a mirror for society? Many current theorists think not. The choices we make—whether in the pronouns or titles we use to address someone or in other markers of social relations—are recursive upon the situations that generate them. For example, if one elects to use *Ms.* in lieu of other possibilities, a political statement is made. Similarly, any other alternative would also carry important information, including the possibility that the speaker or writer is attempting to minimize political connotations by selecting the most neutral term (i.e., the one with the least associated political information). What particular message is intended or heard as a result of a particular choice will not always be the same; it very likely depends on such factors as the speakers, their relationship, the context, the situation, and so on.

Language and power are related at other levels of society as well. A national language policy reflects the power structure and social hierarchy of the nation's population. And the cultural and linguistic preferences or requirements embodied in such public institutions as schools, courts, and the mass media are those of the dominant group(s) or class(es) in the society (see Mueller, 1973).

The respective statuses of English vis-à-vis other immigrant languages in the United States, and of the French and English languages in Canada, illustrate this. The similarity between the two countries, when considered in global perspective, makes a comparison of their language policies especially instructive. European immigrants founded both nations at about the same time, and the descendants of these original immigrants have become the most powerful segments of each country, greatly outnumbering both the Amerindian populations and the much smaller groups of immigrants from non-European backgrounds. Despite these and other similarities, the two countries differ greatly with regard to their policies concerning language diversity. The demand for cultural and linguistic assimilation in the United States has generally been so great that the country has been called a "melting pot," while greater toleration of diversity has resulted in Canada's being termed a "mosaic" of peoples, language, and cultures.

The Constitution of the United States of America is mute on the matter of a national language. Nonetheless, it is possible to see patterns suggesting that a de facto policy regarding English and other languages has operated since the early years of American independence (Liebowitz, 1976). Toleration for linguistic diversity during the first century was replaced by a period, from about 1880 to World War II, when English language requirements were blatantly used to exclude and discriminate. Following World War II, the civil rights movement and accompanying social changes culminated in tolerance and even encouragement for the use of languages other than English. Current conservatism reversing this trend questions the cost of recent language policies to both the nation's budget and unity.

Canada, by contrast, has had an official language policy since it was granted independence under the terms of the British North America Act in 1867: equality of English and French in many areas of national life. Despite official equality, actual practice made English dominant over French in most situations. Political violence and a rising consciousness among francophone Canadians led in the mid-1960s to the appointment of a Royal Commission on Bilingualism and Biculturalism to investigate the status of the country's two official languages. The commission's reports and studies revealed and documented great inequality between the languages. To reduce continuing conflict, the Canadian Parliament reaffirmed the officially bilingual status of Canada and embarked on a series of specific changes designed to rectify inequalities in services and opportunities available to francophone Canadians. At about the same time, the province of Quebec conducted its own study of the status of French within Quebec.

As Quebec took steps to establish greater cultural and linguistic autonomy within provincial affairs and pressed for greater equality in national life for both French and English Canadians, the 1970s continued to be a period of turbulence over language. Official bilingualism was questioned in the 1970s by other disenfranchised groups (i.e., non-native speakers of either English or French, including both immigrants and Amerindians.). By the end of the decade, national concern with bilingualism and biculturalism had shifted to discussions of the appropriateness of multilingualism and multiculturalism. The 1980s, although different in their specifics, have witnessed no abatement of the concerns about language rights among the Canadian population.

In both Canada and the United States, persons who have felt disenfranchised because they are not speakers of the society's dominant language(s) or dialect(s) have been responsible for political movements intended to shift the balance of political power through a realignment of linguistic advantages, preferences, and requirements. In these two countries, efforts have for the most part been peaceful, depending heavily on legislative machinery to effect changes. Elsewhere in the world, perhaps most notably in India, expressions of concern have frequently been violent ones.

As social relations can be reflected covertly in language at varying levels (ranging from the interpersonal uses of pronouns and titles to the de facto or de jure language policies of nation-states), so too is overt politicking with and about language a phenomenon limited to no specific level of social organization. The language issues of Canada have their interpersonal counterparts in daily interactions among the population of the nation, as the following excerpt from a paper on French-English bilingualism shows. Monica Heller (1978) reports the following encounter about language from her studies at Montreal.

> The other day I walked into a department store and had a conversation which made me feel foolish. It was also frustrating.... It's the same kind of conversation I have an awful lot of nowadays.... The conversation always goes something like this:
>
> I walk up to the counter, intent on buying some socks. "Bonjour," says the woman behind the counter, smiling. "Est-ce que je peux vous

aider?" "Qui," I smile back. "Je voudrais acheter des bas comme ça." I point to some socks on display in the showcase. "En beige, s'il vous plaît." "Yes, of course, Madame," she responds in English. "What size?" "Er," I pause, "nine and a half, please."

Our transaction continues smoothly and I thank her and leave the store. But inwardly, the whole time this pleasant bilingual woman is fishing my socks out of the showcase and putting them in a bag and taking the money, I am cursing. Dammit, I want to say. Dammit, lady, why do you always switch to English? [Does] my French sound so terrible that you'd rather not converse in it with me? [Do you] recognize an anglophone ... and presume I'd prefer to use my own language? Could it even be that... you're telling me... that you're a federalist? (This happened once, in such a conversation. I stopped in a garage... that my windshield wipers were *congelé* and I wanted to make them *fonctionner*. The man listened in mild amusement and then said: "You don't have to speak French to me, madame. I'm not a separatist.")

In attempting to understand the relations between language and power, it is important to keep in mind that there is no simple, single way in which the two are connected, nor is the connection limited to particular portions of the spectrum of social organization. Rather, the evidence points to the conclusion that language is both a mirror of society and a major factor influencing, affecting, and even transforming social relationships. To choose among possibilities for addressing another person in a relationship indeed mirrors the type of relationship that the speaker considers it to be. Yet, once selected, the very form of language used also affects by defining and concretizing the conceptions that may not have yet been spelled out. Similarly, national languge policies reflect the ideals and realities of the power structure and social structure of a nation-state. And even when they exist only informally and in practice (as well as when they are clearly articulated statements), these policies in turn affect access to public institutions, economic success, and overall social welfare in the socity.

Further, language can be used as a means of control across the range of social relationships. At the interpersonal level for example, attitudes about language operate to define and reify systems of social categorization that are also related to political and economic opportunities. Giles and Powesland (1975) review a large number of studies that point to this conclusion. Although the specifics vary as to which language is favored and what particular attitudes are generally associated with speakers of specific languages or dialects, studies in the United States, Canada, Britain, and many European countries show that most people hold strong beliefs about particular speech patterns and that these in turn affect judgments about individuals and opportunities granted to them.

Between the interpersonal and the governmental levels, language and control can be seen as closely connected in a variety of situations. For example, interest groups that focus on language rights typically emerge to champion the rights of those whose language abilities may limit their opportunities in society. The francophone movement (in Canada and in other nations as well) exhibits this concern, as do the minority language interest groups in the United States. The two basic options open to such interest groups appear to be assimilation to the majority or dominant languages, or mobilization to transform the language policies of the society. Both situations can be seen in contemporary language movements, and it is frequently the case that a particular movement will alternate between the poles of assimilation and transformation at different points in its history.

At governmental levels, language control is more obvious. Most of the world's nations have specific language policies that specify which language or languages shall be used in which situations. These policies directly influence the lives of all individuals in the society by controlling access to economic, political, and social opportunities. And when changes in national language policies are made, massive shifts in language use frequently follow (as often do resistance movements by those for whom the new requirements may mean reduced access and opportunities). Even those nations, like the United States, lacking specifically defined policies are not immune to these issues. De facto national language policies are as consequential politically as de jure ones.

Finally, at the international level, language and control are also related. In much the same way as a national language policy enfranchises or disenfranchises individuals, so too do the patterns of language use articulate with the international social and political order. At this point in human history, nations whose speakers know English are necessarily advantaged over ones like Brazil and Portugal, for instance, where the national language is simply not useful in a variety of international contexts. Whether one likes it or not, knowledge of English does allow an individual or a nation to manage quite effectively internationally, without bothering to learn other languages. The same is not true for speakers of Portuguese, Hindi, and most of the world's other languages.

THE POLITICS OF LANGUAGE IN INTERACTION

Considerations of language and power often lead to issues concerning languages or varieties of languages and their relation to power in society. Also important, but much less studied, are links between language and power in interactions between individuals. The development of systematic inquiry into turn-taking in conversation over the past two decades provides a basis for discussing the issues that might be studied at the interactional level of analysis.

The study of conversation has progressed to the point at which a model of how turns-at-talk involving orderly changes among speakers has been proposed, generally accepted by other researchers, and provided basis for even more detailed investigations of the intricacies of the "grammar" of conversational interaction (Sacks et al., 1974; Levinson, 1983: Chap. 6).

The basic model for the mechanics of turn-taking in ordinary conversations was described by Sacks, Schegloff, and Jefferson (1974), who noted that turn-taking is not merely limited to conversation, but is a general characteristic of social interaction. By implication, findings about turn-taking should clarify processes of interaction more generally. Whether the focus is on conversation or other forms of social interaction involving exchanges, Sacks et al. noted that turn-taking must be learned; that much effort is devoted to instructing children about turn-taking; and that there are probably many similarities across cultures regarding the essential characteristics of speech and other exchange systems.

In considering the first and second of these observations, it should be noted that the capacity for learning turn-taking is much like the capacity for learning language generally. It is not an innate human characteristic to take turns, but rather a fundamental quality of human social organization that turns are necessary and that they can and must be taught. Observations of persons with learning disabilities suggest that the capacity to learn turn-taking appears to be an all-or-nothing phenomenon. Individuals either have the capacity to learn to take turns or they do not. For the vast majority of humans who do have the capacity, socialization involves complex long-term instruction in turn-taking, primarily—but not only—in childhood. The third observation is based on general observation, logical deductions, and some limited field studies. Although the specific mechanics for turn-taking may vary by language and culture, there is agreement that the phenomenon of turn-taking itself seems to be a general characteristic of all human societies and that the model proposed for English by Sacks et al. appears to hold for other languages as well.

The proposed model is straightforward and relatively simple. It appears complex on first acquaintance because of the many details and fine points that the theorists have added. Among the most general characteristics of conversational turn-taking are its orderliness (i.e., speakers take turns at talk with rather minimal confusion over turns, and they regularly exchange opportunities to talk); the fact that most conversations have relatively little gap or overlap between turns (i.e., changes among speakers occur without long periods of silence or simultaneous speech); and the fact that everyday conversations, where no referee oversees turn-taking, are managed by the speakers themselves (i.e., relatively little confusion occurs over whose turn it is in conversation, even though there are no specific rules allocating a specific order to turns, length of turns, and so on). The model is intended to account for everyday, non-administered conversation (termed "natural conversation" by Sacks et al.). Interactions occurring in formal settings or having additional considerations regarding turns would, of course, be different. (See, for example, Atkinson and Drew [1979] on turn-taking in courts of law.)

Specific characteristics of the model include these factors: Speaker changes occur throughout a conversation; usually only one person talks at a time; simultaneous speech does occur, but its duration is typically brief; and transitions between turns are remarkably orderly, with little or no apparent gaps and overlaps. Order of speakers, length of turns, contents of particular turns, duration of conversations, proportion of turns per speaker, number of speakers per conversation, and the units from which turns are constructed vary and are not fixed in any way external to the conversation itself. Further, techniques for allocating turns are employed by speakers. Two of the most common occur when the current speaker shows a preference for a particular person to speak in a multiparty conversation and when a person elects to speak when no one else has been previously selected. A final critical observation about turn-taking is that errors, violations of conventions, and misjudgments do occur, as when two people find themselves talking at once, or when an interruption occurs. A variety of mechanisms exist to deal with these problems.

In order to consider the political aspects of turn-taking in conversation, it is necessary to discuss two aspects of the model in more detail. First, we consider the nature of turn constructional units. Normally speakers in conversations are granted by the other parties to the conversation only a single turn at a time. This turn can be made of an astoundingly large variety of phenomena, including single words, whole sentences, grunts, gestures, or even silence. Upon completion of each turn, a critical moment recurs throughout the conversation. This is the moment of transition between turns. Whenever a speaker's utterance may be construed to be syntactically complete (as indicated by relevant grammatical, intonational, and gestural aspects), another turn must begin or the conversation will cease. For convenience, Sacks et al. refer to these points in conversations as "transition relevance places" (or TRPs). I shall have more to say about them shortly.

Second, we consider more fully the procedures for the allocation of turns among speakers. Sacks et al. discuss the two especially common techniques of the current speaker selecting or showing a preference for the person he or she wishes to speak next and of self-selection. In the first instance, a current speaker may indicate preference for a particular person to speak next by mentioning his or her name, or by directing a question or remark to a particular person. Self-selection is the likely possibility for speaker selection at a TRP if the previous speaker has not designated whom he or she wishes to speak next. This amounts to a person's simply *volunteering* to speak when it appears to be no one else's turn.

Against this background of a model of how nonadministered, everyday conversations work, it is now possible to consider a different question: Can the model be manipulated; that is, can it be used politically? In posing this question, innumerable instances come to mind of persons who monopolize conversations, whether on the telephone, at the dinner table, or in groups of any sort. It is quite possible that monopoly is sometimes gained through using the structural rules of the situation in which interaction occurs. In classrooms, for instance, teachers normally direct interactions, do more talking than students, and decide who shall and who shall not speak. But it must be remembered that in all situations in which referees are incorporated into the structure of the speech exchange situation, different rules will apply. Our discussion of the politics of turn-taking is, like the model summarized above, focused on the everyday conversations in which no unusual rules apply and no referees, except those engaged in interaction with one another, are involved.

Scrutiny of verbal interactions shows a number of instances of situations in which the basic rules of interaction are manipulated to the advantage of one party over another. Some examples show the wide range of possibilities that exist for skillful manipulation of the game plan for conversation.

One possibility is that a speaker may construct a turn so as to postpone the occurence of a TRP for a very long time, especially until basic points are made. This possibility emerges from the fact, as described in the model, that each speaker normally has the right to *complete* a turn before the issue arises as to whether he or she shall have an additional turn or the next turn shall go to another speaker. An instance of this principle at work comes from courtroom interaction, where the constraint for a single turn per speaker and strict management is even greater than in everyday situations. It often happens that witnesses in court wish to qualify their answers to specific questions. In response to a question, "Did you or did you not do X?" many witnesses will reply either "Yes' or "No" and attempt to qualify their answers by continuing with "but...". However, attorneys satisfied with the unqualified answer frequently restrict the witness by maintaining that the question has been answered. One way around this situation is for the witness to invert the affirmation/negation and the qualification, as in "Well, if (qualification), wouldn't anybody do X? Yes, of course, I did X." Everyday conversations also contain instances of this type of manipulation where one speaker manages to get a longer-than-usual turn by virtue of the manner in which the turn is constructed. Thus, one way to manipulate the model is through the units used to construct turns.

A second means of manipulation is to hold the floor in conversation by "owning" periods of silence. Gaps between turns, as noted earlier, are minimal, but they do occur. In such positions, silence is up for grabs. Whoever elects to begin talking through self-selection gains the next turn. There is, however, a different kind of silence —that which occurs within turns, not between them. By pausing after a turn has begun and not at a TRP (where it might be logically assumed that one has finished), speakers may hold the floor without actually saying anything. Compare what is likely to happen in the two following instances:

> I [pause] went to [pause] town yesterday to [pause] get my [pause] mother some [pause] milk because [pause] she [pause] was sick and asked [pause]
>
> I went to town [pause] yesterday [pause] to get my mother some milk [pause] because she was sick [pause] and asked [pause]

The intuition of any native speaker of English leads to the quick conclusion that the first speaker is far more likely than the second to hold the floor through the several pauses. The only difference of significance here is that pauses occur in the first instance at non-TRPs and in the second at TRPs. Thus, a second technique for manipulation involves the skillful placement of pauses.

A third method of manipulating the model comes through the control of who talks next. Note these two instances of how, in the first, the current speaker selects another person and, in the second, herself:

(1) Bill, what do you think?
[Now it is clearly Bill's time to answer.]

(2) Do you know what I think?
[Unless this technique has been abused by the speaker, some other party in the conversation is quite likely to respond with "What?", in which case the previous speaker has set up a sequence that will select him or her to speak again in the next-but-one-turn.]

A fourth technique is for a speaker to interrupt the current speaker and to stop short of a full turn. Under such circumstances, it typically happens that this technique leads to the one who interrupted and who stopped being granted a turn by other parties to the conversation. This amounts to a preselection of the next speaker *before* arriving at a TRP in the current speaker's turn or without necessitating selection by the current speaker. In ordinary conversations, this might take the form of another party to the conversation, including the previous speaker, asking, "Were you trying to say something?" or "What did you say?" Again, if not abused, this can be a subtle technique for preselection before the usual turn allocation moment arises.

Like all techniques, any of these may be overused and are typically successful only under appropriate circumstances. They do show, however, how the model of what we ordinarily do in everyday conversations can be manipulated to advantage. Fuller knowledge of techniques of this sort may help show how it is that some people manage to hold the floor when others seldom seem able to do so, how others seem to get turns to talk when competition is fierce, and so on. Aside from these specific insights, consideration of such issues calls squarely to attention the fact that politicking with language is not limited to national or international arenas, nor does it necessarily occur within our usual range of conscious attention.

POWER AND THE WRITTEN WORD

The question of what life is like in a society without writing intrigues us today, as it has many of our intellectual forebears for at least two millenia. Ironically, we know of their interest only through the records that have outlived them. Socrates, for instance, noted that a consequence of writing is the transformation of our relationship with the past itself. We may seek, but possibly never find, an author's intent.

> [W]ritten words seem to talk to you as though they were intelligent, but if you ask them anything about what they say, from a desire to be instructed, they go on telling you the same thing forever [*Phaedrus*, quoted in Goody and Watt, 1968: 51].

More recently, anthropologist Jack Goody and historian Ian Watt pondered the social consequences of literacy in a collection of essays that Goody (1968) edited. Linguist Walter J. Ong (1982) has reflected on the social transformations accompanying shifts from preliterate to literate to postliterate civilizations. Whether literacy is conceived as the determinant of social transformation or as a consequence of some other change or changes, the essential issue of what it is like to live without literacy concerns modern writers as it did those of previous generations.

Two ways of answering emerge from the puzzlings of those who share their thinking with us through what they have written about literacy. One way is to reflect on earlier periods of human existence when systems of writing were either nonexistent or minimally present. This method presents itself as a conundrum out of which it seems impossible to emerge satisfactorily. Since the dead can neither speak to us directly nor through records, because they lacked any means to leave them, we must piece together as well as we can the puzzle of how writing emerged in the first instances and of what its existence apparently meant for those who discovered it. Even so, much is forever lost. For example, the motives, feelings, and thoughts of our nonliterate ancestors are unknowable. The debris of their lives can be sifted for clues, but it seems we can go only so far in speculating what some object might have been used for, what its maker may have had in mind, or how those who used it may have responded. The aggravations a reader faces in confronting a written text which Socrates noted are felt even more acutely when we attempt to comprehend those persons from the past who left no texts at all.

A second way of deriving some answers was employed by Goody (1968) in inviting contributors to his collection to assess the consequences of the acquisition of literacy during the nineteenth and twentieth centuries by peoples who had, until then, lived without writing. While there are many differences between the rapid transformations that have taken place this historical period and the emergence of systems of writing in more pristine contexts, these studies do have the signal advantage of being based on fuller documentation and far less speculation. Some of the contributors are anthropologists who base their views on first-hand field experiences, whereas others are historians whose conclusions are drawn from an array of documents, including journals, government records, and even writings by members of the societies who have themselves lived through and experienced directly the consequences of the transformation to literacy.

One may read all these considerations about the shift along the preliterate-postliterate continuum from the perspective of asking what is gained and what is lost in social life at the various junctures. In doing so, one must reckon with the positive values that seem almost inevitably to be associated with such discussions where literacy is adjudged as a major acquisition in the development of human culture or, alternatively, when life without the burdens attendant to literacy is romanticized. The fascination with those who are not like us is great for those of us entwined in the linearity of a literate history of our past, either because we view them as free of the bonds of literacy or because we view them as deficient in a critical necessity of social life as we know it. The possibilities for knowing directly those who would wish to speak to us and of being free of confrontations with written words, of remodeling without apologies our cultural histories to suit the needs of each succeeding day, and of face-to-face relations with those to whom we communicate, or at least with their interlocutors, bedazzle and excite our imaginations. By the process of asking how their lives differ from ours, we admit our conviction that literacy does make a difference.

Many social concomitants of literacy are political ones. The emergence of stratification in association with literacy is noted for both pristine and recent acquisitions of literacy in society. Whatever the specifics of the pattern, it is unlikely that anything approaching an entire society becomes literate at once or that degrees of literacy are ever common throughout. More typically, the earliest literates constitute an elite by virtue of possessing so unique a skill unto themselves, if not for other reasons. This skill is the essence of many kinds of power, for it allows the past to be recalled, the present to be recorded, records to be kept, complex accounts to be tallied, and—above all—knowledge to be encoded and managed.

In conjunction with the emergence of literate people in a society, a category of brokers frequently develops. This includes the scribes of ancient civilizations; the educated who sell their letter-writing skills in West African markets to their illiterate countrymen; the lawyers of Western society, who command a code unintelligible to illiterates and highly educated people alike; and the programmers of computers, whose skills (termed *computer literacy*) are now deemed so necessary a part of modern life.

The power that obtains for those who command literacy (when it is not shared by all) and for those who may assist in communicating between groups of persons (who, although they may be literate in some codes, lack competency in essential ones) is unparalleled in societies that lack systems of writing. For example, there are those who, like the Girots of Senegal, know and recite oral texts ordinarily inaccessible to the rest of the citizenry. They too derive prestige and power from their linguistic skills. It is not the presence or absence of literacy, per se, that makes the difference, but the degree to which societies that use literacy in very many aspects of life differ from those that do not. What is really a matter of degree gives rise to what appears as a matter of kind, and it is on this essential difference between the nonliterate and the literate that so much of our attention focuses. Perhaps we shall never know much more about life before or without literacy than we have already discovered, but those who have pondered the issue concur in the conclusion that it is in fact very different.

Another political aspect of literacy is reflected in the widespread assumption that equates literacy (especially widespread literacy) with democracy. The basis for this equation is the belief that the opening of communication channels represented by widespread literacy either breaks down or eliminates restrictions that may otherwise limit participation in the political process to only a segment, perhaps only a very small segment, of the total population. It was this view of the relation between literacy and democracy that apparently concerned the framers of the American Constitution, who considered the electoral college to be a solution to the voting problems of a population with limited knowledge, restricted communication channels, and widespread illiteracy.

By contrast, the East African country Tanzania, which also had a high adult illiteracy rate when it gained independence in 1964, found a different solution to the problem—one that interestingly and somewhat paradoxically points toward the futuristic visions of many who are concerned about the new illiteracy's emerging as a result of the shift from writing to other media for mass communication. Tanzania's solution was startlingly simple. The two candidates standing for office were assigned symbols, either a *jembe* (hoe) or a *nyumba* (house), and illiterate voters were instructed in marking their preferences on ballots that did not require voters to know how to read or write in order to participate in democratic elections.

Further, radio communications and political rallies took the place of the written word for many Tanzanians. These represented an innovative solution when immediate literacy was not possible for the entire society; similar alternatives to reading and writing in American society are frequently viewed as portending the downfall of culture and even democratic institutions as we know them. There is no pejorative equivalent for "idiot box" to refer to a newspaper as a means of communicating the daily news or a book for entertaining. The advent of signs in public buildings and on highways that communicate through symbols rather than words is viewed by many as a necessary evil, not a step forward toward more efficient mass communication. Those who do view these changes more positively see much that is regained through the new media, especially much of the nonverbal information that is lost when spoken communications are transformed into written ones.

As literacy and power are intricately related in contemporary society, it is apparent that technological changes of the future will bring with them even greater possibilities for stratification based on differential access to the various literacies that will be available for dealing with an increasingly complex world. While it may be exciting to entertain the joys of virtually instantaneous access to libraries via computer terminals located in homes and offices, such potential portends new opportunities for restricting access and censorship, as well as increasing access and making information more widely available. As technology provides more opportunities, the potential for politics through control of language and communication expands.

A WORLD LANGUAGE?

The possibility of a single language serving the communicative needs for the entire world arises in the consideration of the social and political difficulties associated with language diversity. Is it possible that a single language could serve in worldwide communication, either in addition to or instead of the many different languages now spoken? Examination of the facts shows that this is a political, rather than a linguistic question.

History reveals that the particular languages used most for international communication have varied considerably. In ancient times and throughout the Middle Ages, Latin served as the major vehicle for universal communication in much of Europe and the nearby territory. Its association first with the Roman Empire and later with Catholicism provided the base upon which its acceptance was predicated. By the eighteenth century, French had emerged as the language associated with feudal power and had become the language of international communication, of diplomacy, and of social elitism. The Industrial Revolution and the rise of capitalism helped elevate the language used by the British and the Americans to the status of the most significant international language by the mid-twentieth century. The emergence of the Soviet Union as a major world power has elevated Russian to one of the world's most important languages during the latter part of the century. Similarly, the economic rise of the OPEC countries, most of whom are located in the Middle East, and of Japan, have raised Arabic and Japanese to more than regional languages. These shifts in the statuses of particular languages are closely linked to the economic and political contexts in which they are used.

In considering the possibility for a single world language, it is instructive to consider how international communication actually works today. The most public arena in which international communication must be facilitated, despite significant language barriers, is the United Nations. Under its present structure, the United Nations uses five official languages, English, French, Chinese, Russian, and Spanish. Interpretation is provided among these languages and, when required, between them and the large array of national languages spoken by member nations. Publications and record keeping in the United Nations is limited to English and French, the two "working" languages. Since the facilities, resources, and effort put into managing international communication at the United Nations is not practicable in most other situations, international communications usually take place in one of a small number of major world languages, such as English, Spanish, or Russian.

Fifteen languages have more than 50 million speakers each. However, number of speakers alone is no guarantee that a language will achieve international status. The data in Table 15.1 show that number of speakers alone is insufficient to make a language one of the most important for world communication. The fifteen most widely known languages include some that are indeed used in international communications (for example, English, Spanish, Russian, and French) and others that are almost entirely restricted to particular world regions (Mandarin, Hindi, Bengali, Telugu, and Punjabi). The evidence supports the thesis that the status of a language is more a function of its political and economic associations than the number of speakers it has.

Some people who have been concerned about the problems of international communication have argued that an artificial language would be a better choice for a world language than any of the hundreds of natural ones. Over the past one hundred years, various individuals and groups have proposed several constructed languages as candidates and claimed as advantages both their simpler structures and vocabularies, and their lack of strong associations with particular interest groups.

Among the better-known artificial languages are Esperanto (based on Romance and Anglo-Saxon languages), Interlingua (based on Latin), and Basic English (a simplified version of the language).Yet, all these have significant problems as candidates for a world language. All do in fact favor speakers of related languages over those who speak languages with which there are no cognates and little or no structural similarities; and all lack the richness of literary traditions, history, and culture associated with natural languages. It seems to those who have tried to learn and use them that such languages can, in fact, be used, but that artificial languages tend to lack much interest and commitment on the parts of large numbers of people. Few people, it seems, are willing to set aside their own language in favor of

TABLE 15.1 The World's Most Commonly Spoken Languages

Rank	Language	Millions of Speakers
1	Mandarin	387
2	English	300
3-4	Spanish	200
	Russian	200
5	Hindi	180
6	Bengali	110
7-10	Arabic	100
	Japanese	100
	Portuguese	100
	German	100
11	French	75
12	Italian	60
13-15	Indonesian	50
	Telugu	50
	Punjabi	50

NOTE: Data in this table are based on Fromkin and Rodman (1978).

another, whether it is someone else's natural language or one specially constructed to facilitate interlingual communications.

The inevitable conclusions that emerge from serious consideration of these possibilities for a single world language are that speakers show strong ties to their own languages and exhibit a general unwillingness to learn another language in its place or to use another in addition to it. Rather, it seems that people most often learn languages when there are significant advantages to doing so, as shown by the changing interests in Latin, French, English, Russian, and Arabic. It is simply too early in human history to know the degree to which one language may actually become the basis for most human communications. Certainly, if it does happen, whichever language actually emerges will not depend on the internal characteristics of that language itself. Rather, it will depend on the political and economic associations of the language. People have a remarkable ability to learn languages when it is to their advantage to do so, and an equally remarkable ability to refuse to do so when no apparent advantages are present.

ASKING THE RIGHT QUESTIONS ABOUT LANGUAGE AND POLITICS

The diverse situations and issues associated with linguistic interaction, literacy, and a world language show how consideration of the political and economic underpinnings illuminate, sharpen, and even serve to focus questions about language and power. What may appear as questions about language are often better comprehended as questions about language *and* power.

For example, most studies of the functions of language take the communicative role as one of language's most basic functions and proceed to elaborate specific details and particulars of language's facilitation of human communication. Yet it is also true that language is one of the major barriers to communication. Because humans speak not one but many languages, actual patterns of communication are restricted to those persons speaking the same language or even at times to those speaking the same variety of a particular language. Those individuals who command more than one language or variety can often find roles for themselves as translators or interpreters—roles that may entail significant political advantages. Likewise, in many instances those who know only a single language or a nonstandard variety (that is, a variety not associated with the major power factions in the society) find themselves politicallly disadvantaged. Such evidence suggest that language may also be important in erecting barriers that limit communication, in reinforcing social and political inferiority or superiority, and in helping distribute political resources and rewards in society. How we formulate questions about issues of concern defines and limits what we shall admit as evidence and what we are willing to accept as answers. Only by asking about the relation of language to power are we likely to find out much about the political and economic bases on which it is predicated.

The materials considered in this chapter also serve to remind us that language-power relations are limited to no particular contexts or levels of society. Attitudes about languages can be as effective as de jure national language policies in influencing how people behave with regard to one another's language. And language politics can occur at the dinner table as well as in the international arena. What is critical to the understanding of the interrelation of language and power is that we ask questions that do not ignore the fact that language and politics are closely connected. Questions that do not presume language to be a closed system, but rather a political phenomenon, lead us in the right direction.

REFERENCES

ACHEBE, CHINUA. 1965. English and the African writer. *Transition*. Kampala. 4, 18.
ADLER, MORTIMER. 1982. *The Paideia Proposal: An Educational Manifesto*. New York: Macmillan.
AGUIRRE, ADALBERTO. 1980. The political economy context of language in social service delivery for Hispanics. Discussion paper, Conference on Ethnicity and Public Policy, May 30-June 1, 1980.
ALATIS, JAMES E., Ed. 1969. *Monograph Series on Languages and Linguistics*, No. 22. Washington, DC: Georgetown University Press.
ALATIS, JAMES E. and G. RICHARD TUCKER, Eds. 1979. *Language and Public Life*. Washington, DC: Georgetown University Press.
ALÉONG, STANLEY, 1982. The role of the technical school in the knowledge and use of prescribed automotive terminology among students in Quebec, Canada. *International Journal of the Sociology of Language*. 38, 45-70.
ALEXANDRE, PIERRE. 1974. Foreword. In J. Champion, ed. *Les Langues Africaines et la Francophonie*. Paris: Mouton.
ALLEN, W.S. 1953. *Phonetics in Ancient India*. London: Oxford.
ALLEYNE, MERVYNE C. 1980. *Comparative Afro-American: An Historical-Comparative Study of English-Based Afro-American Dialects of the New World*. Ann Arbor, MI: Karoma Press.
AMINI, JOHARI M. 1975. Statement of the Black arts. *Black World*. 24 (February), 80-81.
ANDERSEN, ELAINE. 1977. Learning to speak with style. Unpublished doctoral dissertation. Stanford University.
ANNAMALAI, E. 1978. The anglicized Indian languages: A case of code-mixing. *International Journal of Dravidian Linguistics*. 7, 239-247.
ANSRE, GILBERT. 1979. Four rationalisations for maintaining European languages in Africa. *African Languages/Langues Afraicaines*. 5(2), 10-17.
APPLE, MICHAEL. 1982. *Education and Power*. London: Routledge & Kegan Paul.
APTE, MAHADEV L. 1976. Language controversies in the Indian Parliament (Lok Sabha): 1952-1960. In W. M. O'Barr and J. F. O'Barr, eds. (pp. 213-234) *Language and Politics*. The Hague: Mouton.
ARDENER, EDWIN. 1975. Belief and the problem of women. In Shirley Ardener, ed. (pp. 1-28) *Perceiving Women*. London: Malaby.
ARDENER, SHIRLEY, Ed. 1975. *Perceiving Women*. London: Malaby.
ARJONA, ETILVIA. Forthcoming. The court interpreter's act: A look at minimal competency testing for certifying interpreters for the U.S. Federal courts. In L. Elías-Olivaras et al., eds. *Spanish Language Use and Public Life in the United States*. The Hague: Mouton.

ARJONA, ETILVIA. 1983. Language planning in the judicial system: A look at the implementation of the U.S. Court Interpreters Act. *Language Planning Newsletter.* 9(1), 1-6.

ASPIRA. 1983. Racial and ethnic high school dropout rates in NYC: Summary report. New York: Aspira of New York, Inc.

ATKINSON, J. M. and P. DREW. 1979. *Order in Court.* London: Macmillan.

ATWOOD, MARGARET. 1975. A reply [to Carol P. Christ and Judith Plaskow]. *Signs.* 2, 340-341.

BAILEY, RICHARD W. and M. GORLACH, Eds. 1982. *English as a World Language.* Ann Arbor: University of Michigan Press.

BAKER, HOUSTON A., Jr. 1981. Generational shifts and the recent criticism of Afro-American literature. *Black American Literary Forum.* 15(1), 3-21.

BALDWIN, JAMES. 1979. If Black English isn't a language, then tell me what is? *New York Times.* July 29.

BAMGBOṢE, AYỌ. 1982. Standard Nigerian English: Issues of identification. In B. Kachru, ed. *The Other Tongue: English across Cultures.* Urbana: University of Illinois Press.

BARAKA, AMIRI. 1980. Afro-American literature and class struggle. *Black American Literature Forum.* 14, 5-14.

BARKIN, FLORENCE. 1981 Testing bilingual language proficiency: An applied approach. In L. Eliás-Olivares et al., eds. *Spanish Language Use and Public Life in the United States.* The Hague: Mouton.

BARNES, J.A. 1954. Class and committees in a Norwegian Island parish. *Human Relations.* 7, 39-58.

BARNES, SIR EDWARD. 1932. *The History of Royal College.* Colombo.

BARON, DENNIS. 1981. The epicene pronoun: The word that failed. *American Speech.* 56, 83-97.

BASS, J. A. 1972. *Porgy Comes Home: South Carolina After Three Hundred Years.* Columbia, SC: R. L. Bryan.

BATE, BARBARA. 1978. Nonsexist language use in transition. *Journal of Communication.* 28, 139-149.

BATES, ELIZABETH. 1976. *Language and Context: The Acquisition of Pragmatics.* New York: Academic Press.

BAUGH, ALBERT C. 1935. *A History of the English Language.* New York: D. Appleton-Century.

BAUGH, ALBERT C. and THOMAS CABLE. 1978. *A History of the English Language,* revised edition. Englewood Cliffs, NJ: Prentice-Hall.

BAUMAN, RICHARD and JOEL SHERZER. 1974. *Explorations in the Ethnography of Speaking.* London: Cambridge University Press.

BAYM, NINA. 1978. *Woman's Fiction: A Guide to Novels by and About Women in America, 1820-1870.* Cornell, NY: Cornell University Press.

BECKER, HOWARD S., BLANCHE GEER, EVERETT C. HUGHES, and ANSELM STRAUSS. 1961. *Boys in White: Student Culture in Medical School.* Chicago: University of Chicago Press.

BECKER, JUDITH. 1982. Children's strategic use of requests to mark and manipulate social status. In S. Kuczaj, ed. *Language Development: Language, Thought, and Culture.* Hillsdale, NJ: Erlbaum.

BÉDARD, EDITH and JACQUES MAURAIS, Eds. 1983. *La norme linguistique.* Quebec: Conseil de la Langue Française.

BEEBE, JAMES and MARIA BEEBE. 1981. The Filipinos: A special case. In C. Ferguson and S. Heath, eds. *Language in the U.S.A*. New York: Cambridge Univeristy Press.
BENDIX, LUDWIG. 1968. *Zur Psychologie der Urteilsfahigkeit des Berufsrichters*. Berlin: Luchterhand.
BENSTON, M. 1969. The political economy of women's liberation. *Monthly Review*. 21(4).
BENTAHILE, ABDELÂLI. 1983 *Language Attitudes among Arabic-French Bilinguals in Morocco*. Clevedon, Avon: Multilingual Matters.
BERGER, PETER and THOMAS LUCKMANN. 1972. *The Social Construction of Reality*. Harmondsworth: Penguin.
BERNSTEIN, BASIL. 1973. *Class, Codes and Control*. Vol. 1. St. Albans, Herts.: Paladin.
BERNSTEIN, BASIL. 1970A. Familiales Rollensystem, Kommunikation und Sozialisation. In B. Bernstein, ed. (pp. 117-113) *Soziale Struktur, Sozialisation und Sprachverhatten*. Amsterdam: De Munter.
BERNSTEIN, BASIL, Ed. 1970B. *Soziale Struktur, Sozialisation und Sprachverhalten*. Amsterdam: De Munter.
BERNSTEIN, BASIL. 1962. Social class, linguistic code and grammatical elements. Language and Speech. 5, 221-240.
BERRYMAN, SUE E., PAUL F. LANGER, JOHN PINCUS, and RICHARD H. SOLOMON. 1979. *Foreign Language and International Studies Specialists: The Marketplace and National Policy*. Santa Monica, CA: Rand Corporation. (Prepared for the National Endowment for the Humanities.)
BILES, J. 1978. An interview with Iris Murdoch. *Studies in the Literary Imagination*. 12(2), 115-125.
BILLINGSLEY, R. G. 1975. Forging new definitions: The burden of the hero in modern Afro-American Literature. *Obsidian*. 1(3), 5-21.
BISSERET, NOËLLE, 1979. *Education, Class Language and Ideology*. London: Routledge & Kegan Paul.
BISSERET, NOËLLE. 1974. *Les inegaux ou la selection universitaire*. Paris: Presses universitaires de France.
BISSONET, LISE. 1984. De Voltaire à Godin. *Le Devoir*. September 19.
BLAKAR, ROLV MIKKEL. 1975. How sex roles are represented, reflected and conserved in the Norwegian language. *Acta Sociologica*. 18, 162-173.
BLAUBERGS, MAIJA S. 1980. An analysis of classic arguments against changing sexist language. In Cheris Kramarae, ed. *Women's Studies International Quarterly*. 3, 135-147.
BLAUBERGS, MAIJA S. 1978. Changing the sexist language: The theory behind the practice. *Psychology of Women Quarterly*. 2, 244-261.
BLOUNT, BEN and MARY SANCHES. 1975. *Sociocultural Dimensions of Language Use*. New York: Academic Press.
BLUMER, HERBERT. 1969. *Symbolic Interaction: Perspective and Method*. Englewood Cliffs, NJ: Prentice-Hall.
BLUMER, HERBERT. 1966. Sociological implications of the thought of George Herbert Mead. *American Journal of Sociology*. 71, 534-544.
BODINE, ANN. 1975. Androcentrism in prescriptive grammar: Singular *they*, sex indefinite *he*, and *he* or *she*. *Language in Society*. 4, 129-156.
BOEL, ELSE. 1976. Le genre des noms designant les professions et les situations féminines en française moderne. *Revue Romane*. 11, 16-73.

BOKAMBA, EYAMBA G. 1982. The Africanization of English. In B. Kachru, ed. *The Other Tongue: English across Cultures.* Urbana: University of Illinois Press.

BOLINGER, DWIGHT. 1980. *Language: The Loaded Weapon.* London: Longman.

BOND, HORACE MANN. 1966. *The Education of the Negro in the American Social Order.* New York: Octagon Books.

BONILLA, FRANK and RICARDO CAMPOS. 1981. A wealth of poor: Puerto Ricans and the new economic order. *Daedalus* 110 (2), 133-176.

BOSK, CHARLES. 1979. *Forgive and Remember: Managing Medical Failure.* Chicago: University of Chicago Press.

BOTT, ELIZABETH. 1956. Urban families: Conjugal roles and social networks. *Human Relations.* 8, 345-384.

BOURDIEAU, PIERRE and L. BOLTANSKI. 1975. Le fetichisme de la langue. *Actes de la Recherche in Sciences Sociales.* 4, 2-32.

BOURHIS, RICHARD Y. 1982. Language policies and language attitudes: Le monde de la francophone. In Ellen B. Ryan and Howard Giles, eds. (pp. 34-62) *Attitudes Towards Language Variation.* London: Edward Arnold.

BOYER, ERNEST L. 1983. *High School: A Report on Secondary Education in America.* New York: Harper & Row.

BRASS, PAUL R. 1974. *Language, Religion and Politics in North India.* London: Cambridge University Press.

BRINKMAN, HENNIG. 1971. *Die deutsche Sprache: Gestalt und Leistung.* 2nd. ed. Düsseldorf.

BROVERMAN, INGE K. et al. 1970. Sex-role stereotypes and clinical judgments of mental health. *Journal of Consulting and Clinical Psychology.* 34, 1-7.

BROWN, LLOYD. 1975. Jones (Baraka) and his literary heritage in *The System of Dante's Hell. Obsidian.* 1(1), 5-17.

BROWN, PENELOPE. 1980. How and why are women more polite: Some evidence from a Mayan community. In Sally McConnell-Ginet et al., eds. *Women and Language in Literature and Society.* New York: Praeger.

BROWN, PENELOPE and LEVINSON, STEPHEN. 1978. Universals in language usage: Politeness phenomena. In E. Goody, ed. (pp. 56-389) *Questions and Politeness.* Cambridge: Cambridge University Press.

BROWN, ROGER, COURTNEY B. CAZDEN, and URSULA BELLUGI. 1969. The child's grammar from I to III. In J.P. Hill, ed. (pp. 28-73) *Minnesota Symposium on Child Psychology*, Vol. 2. Minneapolis: University of Minnesota Press.

BROWN, ROGER and M. FORD. 1961. Address in American English. *Journal of Abnormal and Social Psychology.* 62, 375-385.

BROWN, ROGER and A. GILMAN. 1960. The pronouns of power and solidarity. In T. A. Sebeok, ed. *Style in Language.* Cambridge, MA: MIT Press.

BRUNER, JEROME. 1971. *Studien zur Kognitiven Entwicklung.* Stuttgart: Klett.

BUCHER, RAE and J. STELLING. 1977. *Becoming Professional.* Beverly Hills, CA: Sage.

Budget 1983 du Ministere de la Cooperation et du Developpement. *Afrique-Contemporaine (Paris).* 127 (July-August-September), 50-57.

BUTTERS, RONALD R. 1983. Can I ax you about that arruh? *New York Times Magazine.* August 21.

CALVET, LOUIS-JEAN. 1974. *Linguistique et colonialisme: Petit trait de glottophagie.* Paris: Payot.

CAPITAN PETER, COLETTE. 1981. Racisme, sexisme et ideologie liberale. Paper presented at the Third Conference of the NWSA, Storrs, Connecticut, May-June.

References

CARRILLO, C., G. GIBSON, and C. A. ESTRADA. 1979. *Chicanas and Mental Health*. San Francisco: MALDEF.

CASSELL, JOAN. 1977. *A Group Called Women: Sisterhood and Symbolism in the Feminist Movement*. New York: David McKay.

CHAMPION, JACQUES, Ed. 1974. *Les langues africaines et la francophonie*. Paris: Mouton.

CHAUDHURI, NIRAD C. 1976. The English language in India—past, present and future. In Alastair Niven, ed. *The Commonwealth Writer Overseas: Themes of Exile and Expatriation*. Bruxelles: Librairie Marcel Didier S.A.

CHISHIMBA, MAURICE M. 1983. African varieties of English: Text in context. Unpublished doctoral dissertation, University of Illinois, Urbana.

CHOMSKY, NOAM. 1972. *Language and Mind*. New York: Harcourt Brace Jovanovich.

CHOMSKY, NOAM. 1966. *Cartesian Linguistics*. New York: Harper & Row.

CICOUREL, AARON. 1970. *Methode und Messung in der Soziologie*. Frankfurt: Suhrkamp.

CICOUREL, AARON. 1968. *The Social Organization of Juvenile Justice*. New York: Academic Press.

COLLINS, RANDALL. 1975. *Conflict Sociology: Toward an Explanatory Science*. New York: Academic Press.

Comptroller General of the United States. 1979. *The Public Diplomacy of Other Countries: Implications for the United States*. Washington, DC: General Accounting Office.

CONLEY, J. M., W. M. O'BARR, and A. E. LIND. 1978. The power of language: Presentation style in the courtroom. *Duke University Law Journal*. 6, 1375-1399.

CONRAD, ANDREW W. and JOSHUA FISHMAN. 1977. English as a world language: The evidence. In J. A. Fishman et al., eds. *The Spread of English: The Sociology of English as an Additional Language*. Rowley, MA: Newbury House.

COOK-GUMPERZ, JENNY and JOHN GUMPERZ. 1981. From oral to written culture: The transition to literacy. In M. Farr Whiteman, ed. *Variation in Writing: Functional and Linguistic-Cultural Differences*. New York: Erlbaum.

COOPER, ROBERT L. 1984. Fantisti! Israeli attitudes toward English. In S. Greenbaum, ed. *The English Language Today*. London: Pergamon Press.

COOPER, ROBERT L. ed. 1982.*Language Spread: Studies in Diffusion and Language Change*. Bloomington: Indiana University Press.

CORNILLON, SUSAN K. 1972. The fiction of fiction. In S. Cornillon, ed. (pp 113-130) *Images of Women in Fiction*. Bowling Green University Press.

DAHRENDORF, RALF. 1959. *Class and Class Conflict in Industrial Society*. Palo Alto, CA: Stanford University Press.

DALBY, DAVID. 1972. The African element in American English. In T. Kochman, ed. (pp. 170-186) *Rappin' and Stylin' Out: Communication in Urban Black America*. Chicago: University of Illinois Press.

DALBY, DAVID. 1969. *Black through White: Patterns of Communication in Africa and the New World*. Bloomington: Indiana University Press.

DALY, MARY. 1978. *Gyn/ecology: The Metaethics of Radical Feminism*. Boston: Beacon Press.

DALY, MARY. 1973. *Beyond God the Father*. Boston: Beacon Press.

DAOUST, DENISE. 1983. La planification linguistique au Québec: Un aperçu des lois sur la language. *Revue Québécoise de Linguistique*. 12, 59-61.

DAS GUPTA, JYOTIRINDRA. 1970. *Language Conflict and National Development: Group Politics and National Language Policy in India*. Berkeley: University of California Press.

DAS GUPTA, JYOTIRINDRA. 1969. Official language problems and policies in South Asia. In T. Sebeok, ed. (pp. 578-596) *Current Trends in Linguistics*, Vol. 5. The Hague: Mouton.

De BEAUVOIR, SIMONE. 1972. *The Second Sex*. Harmondsworth: Penguin.

De CHAMBRUN, NOËLLE and ANNE-MARIE REINHARDT. 1980. La Science en patois. *La Monde Diplomatique*. August.

DELPHY, C. 1980. The main enemy. *Feminist Issues*. Transaction Periodicals Consortium. 1(1), 23-40.

Department of Linguistics. 1978. *Provision of Bilingual Registration and Election Services*. Final Report for the Federal Election Commission. December. Albuquerque: University of New Mexico.

DESAI, M(AGANBHAI) O. 1964. *The Problem of English*. Ahmedabad: Navajivan.

DILLARD, J. L. 1977. *Lexicon of Black English*. New York: Seabury Press.

DILLARD, J. L. 1972. *Black English*. New York: Random House.

DiLORENZO-KEARON, M. A. and T. P. KEARON. 1981. *Medical Spanish: A Conversational Approach*. New York: Harcourt Brace Jovanovich.

DINNERSTEIN, LEONARD and MARY DALE PALSSON, Eds. 1973. *Jews in the South*. Baton Rouge: Louisiana State University Press.

DOWNING, PAUL M. 1983. The Voting Rights Act of 1965: Historical and policy aspects. Issue Brief Number IB81079. The Library of Congress Congressional Research Service. January 14, 1983. Mimeo.

DRESSLER, WOLFGANG, RUTH LEODOLTER, and EVA CHROMCE. 1973. Phonologische Schnellsprechregeln in der Wiener Umgangssprache. *Wiener Linguistische Gazette*. 1, 1-20.

DuBOIS, BETTY LOU and ISABEL CROUCH. 1975. The question of tag questions in women's speech: They don't really use more of them, do they? *Language in Society*. 4, 289-294.

DuBOIS, WILLIAM E. B. 1903. *Souls of Black Folk*. New York: Fawcett Edition, 1961.

EAGLETON, TERRY. 1976. *Marxism and Literary Criticism*. Berkeley: University of California Press.

EAGLETON, TERRY. 1975. *Myths of Power*. New York: Barnes and Noble.

EAKINS, BARBARA W. and R. GENE EAKINS. 1978. *Sex Differences in Human Communicatons*. Boston: Houghton Mifflin.

EDELMAN, MURRAY. 1964. *The Symbolic Uses of Politics*. Urbana: University of Illinois Press.

EHLICH, K., Ed. 1980. *Erzahlen im Alltag*. Frankfurt: Konrad.

ELIÁS-OLIVARAS, L., E. A. LEONE, R. CESNEROS, and G. GUTTIÉREZ, Eds. Forthcoming. *Spanish Language Use and Public Life in the United States*. The Hague: Mouton.

ELLIS, J. and J. N. URE. 1969. Language varieties: register. In A. R. Meetam, ed. *Encyclopedia of Linguistics, Information and Control*. London: Pergamon Press.

ELLISON, RALPH. 1953. *Shadow and Act*. New York: Random House.

ELLMANN, MARY. 1968. *Thinking About Women*. New York: Harcourt Brace Jovanovich.

ELZAS, BARNETT A. 1905. *The Jews of South Carolina: From the Earliest Times to the Present Day*. Philadelphia: J. B. Lippincott. (Reprinted 1972. Spartanburg, SC: The Reprint Company.)

ENGEL, GEORGE L. 1977. The need for a new medical model: A challange for biomedicine. *Science* (April 8) 129-136.
EQUAL OPPORTUNITIES COMMISSION. c. 1977. *Guidance on Employment Advertising.* Manchester.
ERVIN-TRIPP, SUSAN M. 1979. Children's verbal turn-taking. In E. Ochs and B. Schieffelin, eds. (pp. 391-412). *Developmental Pragmatics.* New York: Academic Press.
ERVIN-TRIPP, SUSAN M. 1977. Wait for me, roller-skate! In C. Mitchell-Kernan and S. Ervin-Tripp, eds. (pp. 165-187). *Child Discourse.* New York: Academic Press.
ERVIN-TRIPP, SUSAN M. 1976. Is Sybil there? The structure of some American English directives. *Language in Society.* 5, 25-66.
FANON, FRANTZ. 1970. *Wretched of the Earth.* Harmondsworth: Penguin. (First edition in French, 1961.)
FANON, FRANTZ. 1967. The Negro and language. *In Black Skin, White Masks.* New York: Grove Press.
FANON, FRANTZ. 1952. *Peau noire, masques blancs.* Paris: Seuil.
FASOLD, RALPH W. and ROGER W. SHUY. 1970. *Teaching English in the Inner City.* Washington DC: Center for Applied Linguistics.
FERGUSON, CHARLES A. 1982a. Foreword. In B. Kachru, ed. *The Other Tongue: English Across Cultures.* Urbana: University of Illinois Press.
FERGUSON, CHARLES A. 1982b. Religious factors in language spread. In R.L. Cooper, ed. (pp. 95-106) *Language Spread: Studies in Diffusion and Language Change.* Bloomington: Indiana University Press.
FERGUSON, CHARLES A. 1978. Multilingualism as object of linguistic description. In B. Kachru, ed. (pp. 97-105) *Linguistics in the seventies: Directions and prospects.* Special issue of *Studies in the Linguistic Sciences.* Urbana: Department of Linguistics, University of Illinois.
FERGUSON, CHARLES A. 1959. Diglossia. *Word.* 15, 325-340.
FERGUSON, CHARLES A. and SHIRLEY B. HEATH, Eds. 1981. *Language in the U. S. A.* New York: Cambridge University Press.
FERGUSON, CHARLES A. and DAN L. SLOBIN, Eds. 1973. *Studies of Child Language Development.* New York: Holt, Rinehart and Winston.
FISHER, DEXTER, Ed. 1980. *The Third Woman: Minority Woman Writers of the United States.* Boston: Houghton Mifflin.
FISHER, SUE and ALEXANDRA DUNDAS TODD, Eds. 1983. *The Social Organization of Doctor-Patient Communication.* Washington DC: Center for Applied Linguistics.
FISHMAN, JOSHUA A., Ed. 1974. *Advances in Language Planning.* The Hague: Mouton.
FISHMAN, JOSHUA. 1972. *The Sociology of Language.* Rowley, MA: Newbury House.
FISHMAN, JOSHUA. 1971. *Advances in the Sociology of Language.* The Hague: Mouton.
FISHMAN, JOSHUA A., ROBERT L. COOPER, and ANDREW W. CONRAD, Eds. 1977. *The Spread of English: The Sociology of English as an Additional Languages.* Rowley, MA: Newbury House.
FLEISCHER, WOLFGANG. 1971. *Wortbildung der deutschen Gegenwartsprache,* 2nd edition. Tubingen: Niemeyer.
FORSTER, E. M. 1924, 1952. *A Passage to India.* New York: Harcourt Brace and World.

FOUCAULT, MICHEL. 1980. *Power-Knowledge: Selected Interviews and Other Writings. 1972-77.* C. Gordon, Ed. C. Gordon, L. Marshall, J. Mepham, and K. Soper, translators. New York: Pantheon.
FOUCAULT, MICHEL. 1975. *The Birth of the Clinic: An Archaeology of Medical Perception.* New York: Vintage.
FOUCAULT, MICHEL. 1973. *Madness and Civilization. A History of Insanity in the Age of Reason.* R. Howard, translator. New York: Vintage Books.
FOUCAULT, MICHEL. 1972. *The Archaeology of Knowledge.* A. Sheridan, translator. New York: Harper Torchbooks.
FOX, ROBERT E. 1977. The logic of the white castle: Western critical standards and the dilemma of black art. *Obsidian.* 3(2), 18-37.
FRANKEL, RICHARD M. Forthcoming. Talking in interviews: A dispreference for patient-initiated questions in physician-patient encounters. In George Psathas and Richard Frankel, eds. *Interactional Competence.* New York: Irvington.
FRANKEL, RICHARD M. and HOWARD B. BECKMAN. 1982. IMPACT: An interaction-based method for preserving and analyzing clinical transactions. In Lloyd Pettegrew et al., eds. (pp. 71-85) *Straight Talk: Explorations in Provider and Patient Interactions.* Nashville: Humana, Inc., in conjunction with the International Communication Association.
FREEMAN, JO. 1975. *The Politics of Women's Liberation.* New York: David McKay.
FREIDSON, ELIOT. 1970. *Profession of Medicine.* New York: Dodd & Mead.
FREMANTLE, ANN. 1974. *A Primer of Linguistics.* New York: St. Martin's Press.
FRIEDAN, BETTY. 1965. *The Feminine Mystique.* New York: Norton.
FROMKIN, VICTORIA and R. RODMAN. 1978. *An Introduction to Language.* New York: Holt, Rinehart and Winston.
GAINES, ERNEST. 1972. *The Autobiography of Miss Jane Pittman.* New York: Bantam Books.
GAL, SUSAN. 1979. *Language Shift: Social Determinants of Linguistic Change of Bilingual Austria.* New York: Academic Press.
GARFINKEL, HAROLD. 1967. Some rules of correct decisions that jurors respect. In Harold Garfinkel, ed. (pp. 104-115) *Studies in Ethnomethodology.* Englewood Cliffs, NJ: Prentice-Hall.
GATES, HENRY-LOUIS. 1978. Preface to Blackness: Text and pretext. In D. Fisher and R. B. Stepto, eds. (pp. 44-69) *Afro-American Literature: The Reconstruction of Instruction.* New York: Modern Language Association.
GAYLE, ADDISON, JR. 1975. Strangers in a strange land. *Southern Exposure.* 3 (Spring/ Summer), 4-7.
GELPI, BARBARA C. and ALBERT GELPI, Eds. 1975. *Adrienne Rich's Poetry.* New York: Norton.
GENET, JEAN. 1970. Introduction. *Soledad Brother: The Prison Letters of George Jackson.* New York: Coward-McCann.
GERHARDT, UTE. 1971. *Rollenanlyse als kritische Soziologie.* Neuwied: Luchterhand.
GILES, HOWARD. 1970. Evaluative reactions to accents. *Educational Review.* 22, 211-227.
GILES, HOWARD, RICHARD Y. BOURHIS, and D. M. TAYLOR. 1977. Towards a theory of language in ethnic group relations. In H. Giles, ed. *Language, Ethnicity and Intergroup Relations.* London: Academic Press.

GILES, HOWARD and P.F. POWESLAND. 1975. *Speech Style and Social Evaluation*. New York: Academic Press.
GILES, HOWARD, PETER ROBINSON, and PHILIP M. SMITH. 1980.*1st International Conference on Social Psychology and Language*. Oxford: Pergamon Press.
GILES, HOWARD, KLAUS R. SCHERER, and D. M. TAYLOR. 1979. Speech markers in social interaction. In K. R. Scherer and Howard Giles, eds. *Social Markers in Speech*. Cambridge: Cambridge University Press.
GILES, HOWARD and PHILIP M. SMITH. 1979. Accommodation theory: Optimal levels of convergence. In H. Giles and R. St. Clair, eds., *Language and Social Psychology*. Oxford: Blackwell.
GILES, HOWARD and ROBERT ST. CLAIR, Eds. 1979. *Language and Social Psychology*. Oxford: Blackwell.
GILES, H., D. TAYLOR, and R. BOURHIS. 1973. Towards a theory of interpersonal accommodation through language: Some Canadian data. *Language in Society*. 2, 177-223.
GILLIGAN, CAROL. 1982. *In a Different Voice: Psychological Theory and Women's Development*. Cambridge, MA: Harvard University Press.
GILMORE, PERRY and DAVID M. SMITH. 1982. A Retrospective Discussion of the State of the Art in Ethnography and Education. In P. Gilmore and A. Glatthorn, eds. *Children In and Out of School: Ethnography and Education*. Washington DC: Center for Applied Linguistics.
GIROUX, HENRY. 1981. *Ideology, Culture and the Process of Schooling*. Philadelphia: Temple University Press.
GOFFMAN, ERVING. 1959. *The Presentation of Self in Everyday Life*. Harmondsworth: Penguin.
GOLD, GERALD. 1982. The Cajon French debate in Louisiana. In B. Hardford et al., eds. *Issues in International Bilingual Education: The Role of the Vernacular*. New York: Plenum Press.
GOLD, GERALD. 1980. *The Role of France, Quebec and Belgium in the Revival of French in Louisiana Schools*. Québéc: Centre International de Recherche sur sur le Billinguisme.
GOLDMAN, L. 1966. *Sciences humaines et philsophie*. Paris: Gontheir.
GOLDMAN, L. 1964. *Hidden God*. London: Routledge & Kegan Paul.
GOODY, JACK, Ed. 1968. *Literacy in Traditional Societies*. Cambridge: Cambridge University Press.
GOODY, JACK and IAN WATT. 1968. The consequences of literacy. In J. Goody, ed. *Literacy in Traditional Societies*. Cambridge: Cambridge University Press.
GORDON, DAVID C. 1978. *The French Language and National Identity*. The Hague: Mouton.
GOULD, CAROL C. 1978. *Marx's Social Ontology: Individuality and Community in Marx's Theory of Social Reality*. Cambridge, MA: MIT Press.
GRANT, CHARLES. 1831-1832. Observations on the state of society among the Asiatic subjects of Great Britian, particularly with respect to morals, and on the means of improving it. (Written chiefly in 1792. Ordered by the House of Commons to be printed, 15 June 1832.) London: *General Appendix to Parliamentary Papers* 1831-1832. Vol. 10. No. 282.
GREENBAUM, SIDNEY, Ed. 1984. *The English Language Today*. London: Pergamon Press.

GRICE, HERBERT. 1968. The logic of conversation (Mimeo).
GUENTHERODT, INGRID. 1980. Behördliche Sprachregelungen gegen und für eine sprachliche Gleichbehandlung von Frauen und Männern. *Linguistische Berichte.* 69, 22-36.
GUENTHERODT, INGRID. 1979. Berufsbezeichnungen für Frauen. Problematik der duetschen Sprache im Vergleich mit Beispielen aus dem Englischen und Französischen. *Osnabrücker Beiträge zur Sprachtheorie.* 3, 120-132.
GUILLAUMIN, C. 1981. The practice of power and belief in nature. Part 1, The appropriation of women. *Feminist issues.* 1(2), 3-38.
GUILLAUMIN, C. 1972. *L'Ideologie raciste, genese et langage actuel.* Paris: Mouton.
GUMPERZ, JOHN. 1982. *Discourse Strategies.* London: Cambridge University Press.
GUMPERZ, JOHN and DELL HYMES, Eds. 1972. *Directions in Sociolinguistics: The Ethnography of Communication.* New York: Holt, Rinehart and Winston.
HABERMAS, JURGEN. 1970. *Zur Logic der Sozialwissenschaffen.* Frankfurt: Subrkamp.
HALL, ROBERT A. 1966. *Pidgin and Creole Languages.* Ithaca, NY: Cornell University Press.
HALLIDAY, MICHAEL A. K., ANGUS McINTOSH, and PETER STREVENS. 1964. *The Linguistic Sciences and Language Teaching.* London: Longman.
HAMMAUD, MOHAMED SALAH-DINE. 1982. Arabicization in Morocco: A case study in language planning and language policy attitudes. Unpublished doctoral dissertation, University of Texas, Austin.
HARDWICK, ELIZABETH. 1962. The subjection of women. *A View of My Own.* New York: Farrar, Strauss & Giroux.
HARRISON, JAMES A. 1884. Negro English. *Anglia.* 7, 232-279.
HARTFORD, BEVERLY, ALBERT VALDMAN, and CHARLES FOSTER, Eds. 1982. *Issues in International Bilingual Educaton: The Role of the Vernacular.* New York: Plenum Press.
HAVELOCK, E. A. 1963. *Preface to Plato.* Cambridge, MA: Harvard University Press.
HEATH, CHRISTIAN. 1982. Preserving the consultation: Medical record cards and professional conduct. *Sociology of Health and Illness.* 4(1), 56-74.
HEATH, SHIRLEY BRICE. 1983. *Ways with Words: Language, Life and Work in Communities and Classrooms.* Cambridge: Cambridge University Press.
HEATH, SHIRLEY BRICE. 1981a. English in our language heritage. In C. Ferguson and S. Heath, eds. (pp. 6-21) *Language in the U.S.A.* New York: Cambridge University Press.
HEATH, SHIRLEY BRICE. 1981b. Toward an ethnography of writing in American education. In M. Farr Whiteman, ed. *Variation in Writing: Functional and Linguistic-Cultural Differences.* New York: Erlbaum.
HEATH, SHIRLEY BRICE. 1979. The context of professional languages: An historical overview. In J. Alatis and R. Tucker, eds. (pp. 102-118) *Language and Public Life.* Washington, DC: Georgetown University Press.
HELLER, M. S. 1978. "Bonjour, hello?": Negotiations of language choices in Montreal. Sociolinguistic Working Paper No. 49. Austin, TX: Southwest Educational Development Laboratory.
HELLINGER, MARLIS, Ed. In prep. *Sprachwandel und feministische Sprachpolitik (Language Change and Feminist Language Policy).*
HELLINGER, MARLIS. 1981. Wissenschaftler (in f) m — (f a. woman) scientist, man of science: Zur Semantik weiblicher und männlicher Berufsbezeichnungen in Deutschen und Englischen. Paper presented at the Symposium on Lexical Semantics at the University of Hannover.

HELLINGER, MARLIS. 1980. Zum Gebrauch weiblicher Berufsbezeichnungen im Deutschen. Variabilität als Ausdruck aussersprachlicher Machtstrukturen. *Linguistische Berichte.* 69, 37-58.
HELLINGER, MARLIS and BEATE SCHRÄPEL. 1983. Über die sprachliche Gleichbehandlung von Frauen und Mannern. *Jahrbuch fur Internationale Germanistik.*
HERSKOVITS, MELVILLE. 1941. Myth of the Negro Past. Boston: Beacon Press.
History Task Force. (Center for Puerto Rican Studies.) 1979. *Labor Migration under Capitalism.* New York: Monthly Review Press.
HOFFMAN, LUTGER. 1979. Zur Pragmatik von Erzählformen bei Gericht.
HOFSTATTER, PETER R. 1973. *Einführung in die Sozialpsychologie,* 5th edition. Stuttgart: Kroner.
HOLLY, WERNER. 1977. Gesprachstteuerung und Imagearbeit. Unpublished doctoral dissertation. University of Heidelberg.
HOWE, FLORENCE. 1981. Those we still don't read. *College English.* 43, 12-16.
HUGHES, ARTHUR and PETER TRUDGILL. 1979. *English Accents and Dialects: An Introduction to Social and Regional Varieties of British English.* London: Edward Arnold.
HUTCHINSON, JOHN. 1983. Language policy for education in Niger. Paper prepared for Delaware Symposium on Language Studies: Language in National Policies and International Relations, University of Delaware, October.
HYMES, DELL. 1980. *Language in Education.* Washington, DC: Center for Applied Linguistics.
HYMES, DELL. 1974. *Foundations in Sociolinguistics.* Philadelphia: University of Pennsylvania Press.
HYMES, DELL. 1971. *Pidginization and Creolization of Languages.* Cambridge: Cambridge University Press.
ILLICH, IVAN. 1971. *Deschooling Society.* New York: Harper & Row.
INMAN, MARGARET E. P. 1978. An Investigation of the Foreign Language Needs of U.S. Corporations Doing Business Abroad. Unpublished doctoral dissertation. University of Texas at Austin.
JACOMY-MILLETTE, ANNEMARIE, Ed. 1978. *Francophonie et Commonwealth: Mythe ou réalité.* Quebec: Choix.
JAMES, SHARON. 1978. Effect of listener age and situation on the politeness of children's directives. *Journal of Psycholinguistic Research.* 7, 307-317.
JANEWAY, ELIZABETH. 1980a. Women and the uses of power. In H. Eisenstein and A. Jardine, eds. (pp. 327-344) *The Future of Difference.* Boston: G. K. Hall.
JANEWAY, ELIZABETH. 1980b. *Powers of the Weak.* New York: Knopf.
JANEWAY, ELIZABETH. 1979. Women's literature. In Daniel Hoffman, ed. (pp. 342-395) *Harvard Guide to Contemporary American Literature.* Cambridge, MA: The Belknap Press of Harvard University.
JARDINE, ALICE. 1979. Interview with Simone de Beauvoir. *Signs.* 5, 224-236.
JERNUDD, BJORN H. 1981. Planning language treatment: Linguistics for the Third World. *Language in Society.* 10, 43-52.
JOHNSON, ABBY A. and RONALD M. JOHNSON. 1979. *Propaganda and Aesthetics: The Literary Politics of Afro-American Magazines in the Twentieth Century.* Amherst, MA: University of Massachusetts Press.
JOHNSON, DIANE. 1978. What women artists really talk about. In Jeannette L. Webber and Joan Grumman, eds. (pp. 155-156) *Woman as Writer.* Houghton Mifflin.
JOINER, CHARLES W. (Judge, U.S. Eastern District Court). 1979. *Memorandum Opinion and Order.* Civil Action No. 7-71861, July 12, 1979.

JONG, ERICA. 1980. Blood and Guts: The Tricky Problems of Being a Woman Writer in the Late 20th Century. In J. Sternburg, ed. (pp. 169-179) *The Writer on Her Work*. New York: Norton.

JONG, ERICA. 1972. The artist as housewife. *Ms. Magazine*. December, 64-66.

JOSEPH, JOHN. 1983. "Superposed" languages and standardization. Paper presented at the Modern Language Association Convention, December.

JOYNER, CHARLES W. 1983. A community memory: The Jews of Georgetown, S.C., 1761-1904. In Samuel Proctor and Louis Schmier, eds. *The Jewish Experience in the South*. Macon: Mercer University Press.

KACHRU, BRAJ B. Forthcoming. The Bilingual's Creativity. To appear in Proceedings of the Conference on English as an International Language: Discourse Patterns Across Cultures, East-West Culture Learning Institute, Honolulu, June 1-7, 1983.

KACHRU, BRAJ. B. 1984. Institutionalized second language varieties. In Sidney Greenbaum, ed. *The English Language Today*. London: Pergamon Press.

KACHRU, BRAJ B. 1983. *The Indianization of English: The English Language in India*. New Delhi: Oxford University Press.

KACHRU, BRAJ B. 1982a. Models for non-native Englishes. In B. Kachru, ed. (pp. 31-57) *The Other Tongue: English across Cultures*. Urbana: University of Illinois Press.

KACHRU, BRAJ B. 1982b. South Asian English. In R. Bailey and M. Gorland, eds. (pp. 353-386) *English as a World Language*. Ann Arbor: University of Michigan Press.

KACHRU, BRAJ B. 1982c. The Bilingual's Linguistic Repertoire. In B. Hartford and A. Valdman, eds. (pp. 25-52) *Issues in International Bilingual Education: The Role of the Vernacular*. New York: Plenum Press.

KACHRU, BRAJ B. 1982d. Meaning in Deviation: Toward Understanding Non-native English Texts. In B. Kachru, ed. (pp. 325-350) *The Other Tongue: English across Cultures*. Urbana: University of Illinois Press.

KACHRU, BRAJ B., Ed. 1982e. *The Other Tongue: English across Cultures*. Urbana: University of Illinois Press.

KACHRU, BRAJ B. 1981. American English and other Englishes. In C. A. Ferguson and S. B. Heath, eds. (pp. 21-43) *Language in the U.S.A*. New York: Cambridge University Press.

KACHRU, BRAJ B. 1978. Code-mixing as a communicative strategy in India. In J. Alatis, ed. (pp. 107-124) *International Dimensions of Bilingual Education*. Georgetown Monographs on Languages and Linguistics. Washington, DC: Georgetown University Press.

KACHRU, BRAJ B. 1976. Models of English for the Third World: White man's linguistic burden or language pragmatics? *TESOL Quarterly*. 10, 221-239.

KACHRU, BRAJ B. 1969. English in South Asia. In T. Sebeok, ed. (pp. 627-678) *Current Trends in Linguistics*, Vol. 5. The Hague: Mouton.

KACHRU, BRAJ B. 1965. The *Indianness* in Indian English. *Word*. 21. 391-410.

KAEL, PAULINE. 1968. *Kiss Kiss Bang Bang*. Boston: Little, Brown.

KAHANE, HENRY. 1982. American English: From a colonial substandard to a prestige language. In B. Kachru, ed. *The Other Tongue: English across Cultures*. Urbana: University of Illinois Press.

KALLENBERG, A. and L. J. GRIFFIN. 1980. Class, occupation, and inequality in job rewards. *American Journal of Sociology*. 85, 731-768.

KANDIAH, THIRU. 1981. Lankan English schizoglossia. *English World-Wide: A Journal of Varieties of English.* 2(1), 63-81.
KAZIN, ALFRED., Ed. 1967. *Writers at Work.* Third Series. New York: Viking.
KELLER, GARY D. 1983. What can language planners learn from the Hispanic experience with corpus planning in the United States. In J. Cobarrubias and J. Fishman, eds. *Progress in Language Planning: International Perspectives.* The Hague: Mouton.
KENDON, ADAM. 1967. Some functions of gaze direction in social interaction. *Acta Psychologica.* 26, 1-47.
KIDRON, MICHAEL and RONALD SEGAL. 1981. *The State of the World Atlas.* New York: Simon and Schuster.
KING, BRUCE. 1980. *The New English Literatures: Cultural Nationalism in the Changing World.* New York: St. Martin's Press.
KLEINMAN, ARTHUR. 1983. The cultural meanings and social uses of illness. *Journal of Family Practice.* 16, 539-545.
KLOSS, HEINZ. 1969. *Research Possibilities on Group Bilingualism: A Report.* Quebec International Center for Research on Bilingualism.
KOCHMAN, THOMAS, Ed. 1972. *Rappin' and Stylin' Out: Communication in Urban Black America.* Chicago: University of Illinois Press.
KRAMARAE, CHERIS. 1981. *Women and Men Speaking.* Rowley, MA: Newbury House.
KRAMARAE, CHERIS, Ed. 1980a. *The Voices and Words of Women and Men* (Special Issue of *Women's Studies International Quarterly*). 3(2-3).
KRAMARAE, CHERIS. 1980b. Proprietors of language. In Sally McConnell-Ginet et al., eds. (pp. 58-68) *Women and Language in Literature and Society.* New York. Praeger.
KRAMARAE, CHERIS and PAULA A. TREICHLER. Forthcoming. *In Our Own Words.* London: Routledge & Kegan Paul.
KRAMER, CHERIS, BARRIE THORNE, and NANCY HENLEY. 1978. Perspectives on language and communication. *Signs.* 3, 638-651.
KRAPPMAN, LOTHAR. 1972. *Soziale Dimensionen von Identität.* Stuttgart: Klett.
KURZWEIL, EDITH and WILLIAM PHILLIPS, Eds. 1983. *Writers and Politics: A Partisan Review Reader.* Boston: Routledge & Kegan Paul.
La declaration de Zinder. n.d. Copy from Embassy of Niger. Washington, DC.
LABOV, WILLIAM. 1982. Objectivity and commitment in linguistic science: The case of the Black English trial in Ann Arbor. *Language in Society.* 11, 165-201.
LABOV, WILLIAM, Ed. 1972a. *Sociolinguistic Patterns.* Philadelphia: University of Pennsylvania Press.
LABOV, WILLIAM, Ed. 1972b. *Language in the Inner City.* Philadelphia: University of Pennsylvania Press.
LABOV, WILLIAM. 1969. The Logic of Nonstandard English. In James E. Alatis, ed. (pp. 225-261) *Monograph Series in Languages and Linguistics,* No. 22. Washington, DC: Georgetown University Press.
LABOV, WILLIAM. 1966. *The Social Stratification of English in New York.* Washington, DC: Center for Applied Linguistics.
LABOV, WILLIAM and DAVID FANSHEL. 1977. *Therapeutic Discourse: Psychotherapy as Conversation.* New York: Academic Press.
LABOV, WILLIAM and JOSHUA WALETZKY. 1967. Narrative analysis: Oral versions of personal experience. Unpublished manuscript.

LAKOFF, ROBIN. 1975. *Language and Woman's Place.* New York: Harper & Row.
LAL, P. 1969. *Modern Indian Poetry in English.* Calcutta: Writers Workshop.
LAMBERT, WALLACE and R. GARDNER. 1972. *Attitudes and Motivation in Second Language Learning.* Rowley, MA: Newbury House.
LAMBERT, WALLACE, H. GILES, and D. PICARD. 1975. Language attitudes in a French American community. *International Journal of the Sociology of Language.* 4, 127-152.
LAMBERT, WALLACE E., R. C. HODGSON, R. C. GARDNER, and S. FILLENBAUM. 1960. Evaluational reactions to spoken languages. *Journal of Abnormal Social Psychology.* 60, 44-51.
LANE, ANN J., Ed. 1977. *Mary Ritter Beard: A Source Book.* New York: Schocken Books.
LANGER, SUZANNE. 1942, 1976. *Philosophy in a New Key: A Study of the Symbolism of Reason, Rite, and Art.* Cambridge: Harvard University Press.
Language Policy Task Force. 1983. *Integenerational Perspectives on Bilingualism from Community to Classroom.* Final report on NIE, Grant No. NIE-G-78-0091. New York: Hunter College, City University of New York.
Language Policy Task Force. 1980. *Social Dimensions of Language Use in East Harlem.* Working Paper No. 7. New York: Centro de Estudios Puertorriquenos.
LARSON, MAGALL SARFATTI. 1977. *The Rise of Professionalism: A Sociological Analysis.* Berkeley: University of California Press.
LEECH, GEOFFREY. 1969. *Toward a Semantic Description of English.* Bloomington: Indiana University Press.
LEMERT, CHARLES C. and GARTH GILLAN. 1982. *Michel Foucault: Social Theory as Transgression.* New York: Columbia University Press.
LEODOLTER, RUTH (Wodak). 1975a. *Das Sprachverhalten von Angeklagten bei Gericht.* Kronberg: Scriptor.
LEODOLTER, RUTH (Wodak). 1975b. Die Sprechsituation. *Grazer Linguistische Studien,* 1, 142-149.
LEVINSON, S. C. 1983. *Pragmatics.* Cambridge: Cambridge University Press.
LEVITAS, GLORIA, FRANK R. VIVELO, and JACQUELINE J. VIVELO, Eds. 1974. *American Indian Prose and Poetry: We Wait in the Darkness.* New York: Putnam.
LIEBOWITZ, A. 1976. Language and the law: The exercise of political power through official designation of Language. In W. M. O'Barr and J. F. O'Barr, eds. *Language and Politics.* The Hague: Mouton.
LIKIMANI, MUTHONI. 1974a. *They Shall Be Chastised.* Nairobi: East African Literary Bureau.
LIKIMANI, MUTHONI. 1974b. *What Does a Man Want?* Nairobi: Kenyan Literary Bureau.
LIND, E. A. and W. M. O'Barr. 1979. The social significance of speech in the courtroom. In H. Giles and R. St. Clair, eds. *Language and Social Psychology.* College Park, MD: University of Maryland Press.
LIPS, HILARY. 1981. *Women, Men, and the Psychology of Power.* Englewood Cliffs, NJ: Prentice-Hall.
LLAMZON, TEODORO A. 1983. Essential features of new varieties of English. In R. B. Noss, ed. (pp. 92-109) *Varieties of Language in Southeast Asia: Singapore.* SEAMEO Regional Language Centre.
LLAMZON, TEODORO A. 1969. *Standard Filipino English.* Manila: Ataneo University Press.
LUHMANN, NIKLAS. 1969. *Legitimation durch Verfahren.* Berlin: Luchterhand.
LUKÁCS, GEORG. 1971. *History and Class Consciousness: Studies in Marxist Dialectics.* (First edition, 1923.) Cambridge, MA: MIT Press.

LUKES, STEVEN. 1974. *Power: A Radical View.* New York: Macmillan.
LUNA, LARRY and ADALBERTO MENESES. 1973. *A Spanish Manual for Law Enforcement Agencies.* Las Vegas, NV: Latino Languages Enterprises, Inc.
MacKAY, DONALD G. and TOSHI KONISHI. 1980. Personification and the pronoun problem. In Cheris Kramarae, ed. (pp. 149-163) *Women's Studies International Quarterly.* 3(2-3).
MacKAY, DONALD G. and DAVID FULKERSON. 1979. On the comprehension and production of pronouns. *Journal of Verbal Learning and Verbal Behavior.* 18, 661-673.
MADHUBUTI, HAKI. 1978. Black writers and critics: Developing a critical process without readers. *Black Scholar.* 10(1), 35-40.
Maher, Joseph E., Judge, vs. Cockrel, Kenneth V. 1969. Recorder's Court Miscellaneous No. 133882. Detroit, Michigan.
MAJOR, CLARENCE. 1970. *Dictionary of Afro-American Slang.* New York: International Publishers.
Making Health Care Decisions. 1982. Report of the President's Commission for the Study of Ethical Problems in Medicine and Biomedical and Behavioral Research. Washington, DC: Government Printing Office.
MALDEF. 1981. *Docket.* San Francisco: MALDEF Litigation Department.
MALDEF. 1979. *Chicanas and Mental Health.* San Francisco: MALDEF.
MANIGAT, LESLIE F. 1978. Reflexions sur la fonction politique du Commonwealth et de la Francophonie. In Annemarie Jacomy-Millette, ed. (pp. 241-250) *Francophonie et Commonwealth: Mythe ou Realite.* Quebec: Choix.
MARASIGAN, ELIZABETH. 1981. Creolized English in the Philippines. Paper presented at the sixteenth regional seminar on varieties of English. SEAMCO Regional Language Centre, Singapore. April 20-24, 1981.
MARTINEZ, VILMA S. 1978. Uno, dos, tres . . . will the next census again skip millions? *Los Angeles Times.* May 4. (Distributed by MALDEF.)
MARTYNA, WENDY. 1980. The psychology of the generic masculine. In Sally McConnell-Ginet et al., eds. (pp. 69-78) *Women and Language in Literature and Society.* New York: Praeger.
MARTYNA, WENDY. 1978. What does "HE" mean? *Journal of Communications.* 28, 130-138.
MATHIEU, N. C. 1979. Biological paternity, social maternity: On abortion and infanticide as unrecognised indicators of the cultural character of maternity. In Chris Harris et al., eds. *The Sociology of the Family: New Directions for Britain.* University of Keele, Sociological Review Monographs. 28, 232-240.
MAZRUI, ALI. 1975. *The Political Sociology of the English Language.* The Hague: Mouton.
McCONNELL-GINET, SALLY, RUTH BORKER, and NELLY FURMAN, Eds. 1980. *Women and Language in Literature and Society.* New York: Praeger.
McCORMACK, WILLIAM C. and STEPHEN A. WURM, Eds. *Language and Society: Anthropological Issues.* The Hague: Mouton.
McDOWELL, DEBORAH. 1980. New directions for Black feminist criticism. *Black American Literature Forum.* 14(4), 153-159.
McGINNIS, JAMES and GENEVA SMITHERMAN. 1978. Sociolinguistic conflict in the schools. *Journal of Non-White Concern.* American Personnel and Guidance Association. January, 87-95.
McWORTER, GERALD. 1969. Ideology of a Black social science. *Black Scholar.* December, 28-35.
MEAD, GEORGE HERBERT. 1934. *Mind, Self, and Society.* (Charles W. Morris, ed.). Chicago: University of Chicago Press.

MEAD, MARGARET. 1971. *Male and Female.* Harmondsworth: Penguin.
Mendoza Report. 1978. *Access of Non or Limited English Speaking Persons of Hispanic Origin to the New York City Department of Social Services.* U.S. Department of Health, Education and Welfare: Office of Civil Rights.
MICHAELS, SARAH. 1981. Sharing time: Children's narrative styles and differential access to literacy. *Language in Society.* 10, 423-442.
MILLER, CASEY and KATE SWIFT. 1976. *Words and Women: New Language in New Times.* New York: Anchor Press.
MILLER, JEAN BAKER. 1976. *Toward a New Psychology of Women.* Harmondsworth: Pengiun.
MILROY, LESLIE. 1980. *Language and Social Networks.* Oxford: Basil Blackwell.
MITCHELL, HENRY. 1975. *Black Belief.* New York: Harper & Row.
MITCHELL, HENRY. 1970. *Black Preaching.* Philadelphia: Lippincott.
MITCHELL-KERNAN, CLAUDIA. 1969. *Language Behavior in a Black Urban Community.* Berkeley: University of California.
MITCHELL-KERNAN, CLAUDIA and S. ERVIN-TRIPP, Eds. 1977. *Child Discourse.* New York: Academic Press.
MITCHELL-KERNAN, CLAUDIA and KEITH T. KERNAN. 1977. Pragmatics of directive choice among children. In C. Mitchell-Kernan and S. Ervin-Tripp, eds. (pp. 189-210) *Child Discourse.* New York: Academic Press.
MOAG, RODNEY F. 1982. The life cycle of non-native Englishes: A case study. In B. Kachru, ed. (pp. 270-288) *The Other Tongue: English across Cultures.* Urbana: University of Illinois Press.
MORISSET, PAUL. 1983. Josette Rey-Debova: Il ne faut pas mêler français et québécois. *Le Devoir.* June 4.
[MORRISON, TONI.] 1974-1975. [Anon.] A conversation with Alice Childress and Toni Morrison. *Black Creation.* 6, 90-92.
MOSS, ROBERT F. 1975. The arts in Black America. *Saturday Review.* November 15, 1975.
MUELLER, C. 1973. *The Politics of Communication.* Oxford: Oxford University Press.
MUGOT, HAZEL. 1971. *Black Night of Quiloa.* Nairobi: East African Publishing House.
MUKHERJEE, MEENAKSHI. 1971. *The Twice-born Fiction: Themes and Techniques of the Indian Novel in English.* New Delhi: Arnold-Heinemann.
MYERS, WALTER. 1974-1975. From a Black editor in a white industry. *Black Creation.* 6, 93-94.
NAIPAUL, V. S. 1973. *The Overcrowded Barracoon.* New York: Knopf.
NARASIMHAIAH, C. D., Ed. 1978. *Awakened Conseience: Studies in Commonwealth Literature.* New Delhi: Sterling Publishers.
National Commission on Excellence in Education. 1983. *A Nation at Risk: The Imperative for Educational Reform.* Washington, DC: Government Printing Office.
NCES. 1983. *The Condition of Education for Hispanic Americans 1980.* National Center for Educational Statistics. Washington, DC: Government Printing Office.
NDIAYE, BABACAR. 1983. Senegal: A framework for a national policy of language allocation. Unpublished M.A. thesis, University of Lancaster.
NGWYA, LYDIA. 1975. *The First Seed.* Nairobi: East African Literary Bureau.
NICHOLS, PATRICIA C. Forthcoming. *Language and Dialect in South Carolina.*
NICHOLS, PATRICIA C. 1983. Black and white speaking in the rural South: Difference in the pronominal system. *American Speech.* 58, 201-215.

NICHOLS, PATRICIA C. 1980. Women in their speech communities. In Sally McConnell-Ginet et al., eds. *Women and Language in Literature and Society*. New York: Praeger.
NICHOLS, PATRICIA C. 1977. A sociolinguistic perspective on reading and Black children. *Language Arts*. 54, 150-157.
NICHOLS, PATRICIA C. 1976. Linguistic change in Gullah: Sex, age, and mobility. Unpublished doctoral dissertation, Stanford University.
NILSEN, ALLEEN PACE. 1977. Sexism as shown through the English vocabulary. In A.P. Nilsen et al., eds. (pp. 27-42) *Sexism and Language*. Urbana: N.C.T.E.
NILSEN, ALLEEN PACE et al., Eds. 1977. *Sexism and Language*. Urbana: N.C.T.E.
NJAU, REBEKA. 1975. *Riples in the Pond*. London: Heinemann.
NOSS, R. B., Ed. 1983. *Varieties of English in Southeast Asia: Singapore*. SEAMEO Regional Language Centre.
OAKS, PRISCILLA. 1978. The first generation of Native American novelists. *Melus*. 5(1), 57-65.
O'BARR, WILLIAM. Forthcoming. Continuity and change in the functions of Swahili and vernacular languages in rural East Africa. In J. Maw and D. Parkin, eds. *Swahili Language and Society*. Vienna: Afropub.
O'BARR, WILLIAM. 1982. *Linguistic Evidence: Language, Power, and Strategy in the Courtroom*. New York: Academic Press.
O'BARR, WILLIAM. 1976. Boundaries, strategies, and power relations: Political anthropology and language. In W. M. O'Barr and J. F. O'Barr, eds. *Language and Politics*. The Hague: Mouton.
O'BARR, W. M. and J. F. O'BARR, Eds. 1976. *Language and Politics*. The Hague: Mouton.
OEVERMANN, ULRICH. 1973. *Sprache und Soziale Herkunft*. Frankfurt: Suhrkamp.
OGOT, GRACE. 1980a. *The Graduate*. Nariboi: Uzima.
OGOT, GRACE. 1980b. *The Island of Tears*. Nairobi: Uzima.
OGOT, GRACE. 1968. *Land without Thunder*. Nairobi: East African Publishing House.
OGOT, GRACE. 1966. *The Promised Land*. Nairobi: East African Publishing House.
OKSAAR, ELS. 1976. *Berufsbezeichnungen im heutigen Deutsch*. Dusseldorf: Schwann.
OLLMAN, BERTELL. 1971. *Alienation: Marx's Conception of Man in Capitalist Society*. Cambridge: Cambridge University Press.
OLSEN, TILLIE. 1975. *Silences*. New York: Dell.
Olympus Research. 1976. *Language for the World of Work*. Salt Lake City, UT: Author.
ONG, WALTER J. 1982. *Orality and Literacy*. London: Methuen.
ONG, WALTER J. 1977. *Interfaces of the Word*. Ithaca, NY: Cornell University Press.
PARAMESWARAN, UMA. 1976. *A Study of Representative Indo-English Novelists*. New Delhi: Vikas.
PAREDES, RAYMUND A. 1978. The evolution of Chicano literature. *Melus*. 5(2), 71-110.
PARSONS, TALCOTT. 1968. *The Social System*. Glencoe, NY: Free Press.
PARTMANN, GAYLE H. 1979. National identity and the Ivorization of French. Paper delivered at meeting of the African Studies Association, Los Angeles, California.

PEDRAZA, PEDRO, JOHN ATTINASI, and G. HOFFMAN. 1980. Rethinking diglossia. In R. Parilla, ed. *Ethnoperspectives in Bilingual Education Research: Theory in Bilingual Education.* Ypsilanti, MI: Eastern Michigan University.

PÉRONCEL-HUGOZ, J. P. 1983. La relance de la francophonia. *Le Monde.* August 25.

PHILLIPS, JOHN and ANNE PHILLIPS. 1967. Interview with Lillian Hellman. In A. Kazin, ed. *Writers at Work.* New York: Viking.

PIAGET, JEAN. 1977a. *Grasp of Consciousness: Action and Concept in the Young Child.* London: Routledge & Kegan Paul.

PIAGET, JEAN. 1977b. *Origin of Intelligence in the Child.* Harmondsworth: Penguin.

PIAGET: JEAN. 1967. *Psychologie der intelligenz.* Zurich: Huber.

PICARD, JEAN-CLAUDE. 1980. Le sommet de Dakar n'aura pas leiu. *Le Devoir (Montreal).* November 29, 1980.

PITTINGER, ROBERT E., CHARLES F. HOCKETT, and JOHN J. DANEHY. 1960. *The First Five Minutes.* Ithaca, NY: Paul Martineau.

PLATT, JOHN and HEIDI WEBER. 1980. *English in Singapore and Malaysia: Status: Features: Functions.* New York: Oxford University Press.

PRATOR, CLIFFORD H. 1968. The British heresy in TESOL. In J. A. Fishman, C. A. Ferguson, and J. P. Gupta, eds. *Language Problems of Developing Nations.* New York: Wiley.

PRIDE, J. B. 1979. A transactional view of speech functions and code-switching. In W. C. McCormack and S. A. Wurm, eds. *Language and Society: Anthropological Issues.* The Hague: Mouton.

PRLDF. 1983. *Litigation Report.* January 14, 1983. Mimeo.

PRLDF. 1981. *Docket of Cases.* June 1981. Mimeo.

Public Law 95-539. 1978. *Court Interpreters Act.* October 28, 1978.

PUSCH, LUISE F. 1980. Das Deutsche als Männersprache. Diagnose und Therapievorschläge. *Linguistische Berichte.* 69, 59-74.

QUIRK, RANDOLPH, SIDNEY GREENBAUM, GEOFFREY LEECH, and JAN SVARTVIK. 1972. *A Grammar of Contemporary English.* London: Longman.

RAO, RAJ. 1978. The caste of English. In C.D. Narasimhaiah, ed. *Awakened Conscience: Studies in Commonwealth Literature.* New Delhi: Sterling.

RAPP, LINDA LORETTO. 1983. French in the New World: Linguistic Response to Cultural Patterns. *Language Problems and Language Planning.* 7(a), 1-20.

REDDY, MICHAEL. 1979. "Frame Conflict in our Language about Language." In Andrew Ortony, ed. *Metaphor and Thought.* London: Cambridge University Press.

RICH, ADRIENNE. 1976. *Of Woman Born.* New York: Norton.

RICH, ADRIENNE. 1975. When we dead awaken: Writing as re-vision. In B. Gelpi and A. Gelpi, eds. (pp. 90-98) *Adrienne Rich's Poetry.* New York: Norton.

RICHARDS, JACK C. 1982. Singapore English: Rhetorical and communicative styles. In B. Kachru, ed. *The Other Tongue: English across Cultures.* Urbana: University of Illinois Press.

RIGAUD, JACQUES. 1980. *Rapport au Ministre des Affaires Etrangères sur les relations culturelles extérieures.* Paris: La Documentation Française.

ROBERTS, JOAN, Ed. 1976. *Beyond Intellectual Sexism: A New Woman, a New Reality.* New York: David McKay.

RODRIGUEZ, M. and C. RUIZ. 1981. *Interpreters Manual.* Circuit Court of Cook County. Office of the Chief Judge. Mimeo.

ROSECRANTZ, PAUL et al. 1968. Sex-role stereotypes and self-concepts in college students. *Journal of Consulting and Clinical Psychology.* 32, 287-295.

ROSS, JOHN R. 1979. Sampling, elicitation, and interpretation: Orleans and elsewhere. In W. C. McCormack and S. A. Wurm, eds. (pp. 231-247) *Language and Society: Anthropological Issues.* The Hague: Mouton.

ROYER, JEAN. 1980. Leándre Bergeron—Qu'est-ce qu'un dictionnaire de la language québécoise? *Le Devoir.* December 6.

RUBERU, RANJIT. 1962. *Education in Colonial Ceylon.* Kandy: Kandy Printers.

RUBIN, J. and B. JERNUDD, Eds. 1975. *Can Language Be Planned?* Honolulu: University Press of Hawaii.

RYAN, ELLEN BOUCHARD. 1979. Why do low-prestige language varieties persist? In H. Giles and R. St. Clair, eds. *Language and Social Psychology.* Oxford: Blackwell.

SABOURIN, LOUIS. 1978. Dimensions politiques de la Francophonie: De la problematique culturelle a la dynamique internationale. In Annemarie Jacomy-Millette, ed. (pp. 221-226) *Francophonie et Commonwealth: Mythe ou réalité.* Quebec: Choix.

SACK, FRITZ and RENE KONIG, Eds. 1968. *Kriminalsoziologie.* Frankfurt: Suhrkamp.

SACKS, HARVEY. 1966. Unpublished lectures, University of California at Los Angeles.

SACKS, HARVEY, E. SCHEGLOFF, and G. JEFFERSON. 1974. A simplest systematics for the organization of turn-taking in conversation. *Language.* 50, 696-735.

SAMARIN, WILLIAM J., Ed. 1976. *Language in Religious Practice.* Rowley, MA: Newbury House.

SANKOFF, DAVID and SUZANNE LABERGE. 1978. The linguistic market and the statistical explanation of variability. In D. Sankoff, ed. *Linguistic Variation: Models and Methods.* New York: Academic Press.

SCHMITZ, WOLFGANG and HERBERT RICHTER. 1979. Zur Analyse von Aushandlungsprozessen in polizeilichen Vernehmungen von Geschadigten und Zeugen. In H. Soeffner, Ed. (pp. 24-38) *Interpretative Verfahren in der Sozial-und Textwissenschaften.* Stuttgart: Metzler.

SCHNEIDER, GILBERT D. 1966. West African Pidgin English. Unpublished doctoral dissertation. Hartford Seminary.

SCHULZ, MURIEL R. 1975. The semantic derogation of women. In B. Thorne and N. Henley, eds. (pp. 64-75) *Language and Sex: Difference and Dominance.* Rowley, MA: Newbury House.

SCOLLON, R. and B. K. SCOLLON. 1981. *Narrative, Literacy, and Face in Interethnic Communication.* Norwood, NJ: Ablex.

SCOTT, MELVIN and SCOTT LYMAN. 1968. Accounts. *American Sociological Review.* 33, 46-62.

SCRIBNER, SYLVIA and MICHAEL COLE. 1978. Unpackaging literacy. *Social Science Information.* 17(1), 19-40.

SCRUTON, ROGER. 1982. Doing without gender. *Times Literary Supplement.* January 1, 1982, p. 6.

SEBEOK, THOMAS, Ed. 1969. *Current Trends in Linguistics,* Vol. 5. The Hague: Mouton.

SEDLAK, PHILIP A. S. 1980. Francophones and francophiles: Ewe elite language attitudes. Unpublished manuscript. Lomé, Togo.

SEYMAN, M. R. 1973. *Basic Spanish for Health Personnel.* Garden Grove, CA: Trainex Press.

SHANKS, EDWARD. 1970. *Rudyard Kipling: A Study in Literature and Political Ideas.* New York: Cooper Square.

SHAPIRO, ANN R. 1980. The woman reader and the male critical establishment. *Reader*. Newsletter from the Department of French and Italian, University of Iowa.

SHARP, SIR HENRY, Ed. 1920-1922. *Selections from Educational Records*. Calcutta: Bureau of Education, Government of India.

SHERIDAN, ALAN. 1980. *Michel Foucault: The Will to Truth*. London: Tavistock.

SHOWALTER, ELAINE. 1981. Responsibilities and realities: A curriculum for the eighties. *ADE Bulletin*. 70 (Winter), 17-21.

SHOWALTER, ELAINE. 1977. *A Literature of Their Own*. Princeton, NJ: Princeton University Press.

SHUY, ROGER. 1976. The medical interview: Problems in communication. *Primary Care*. 3(3), 365-86.

SKOLNICK, JOSEF. 1966. *Justice without Crime*. New York: Academic Press.

SMITH, ARTHUR, Ed. 1972. *Language, Communication and Rhetoric in Black America*. New York: Harper & Row.

SMITH, ARTHUR. 1969. *Rhetoric of Black Revolution*. Boston: Allyn and Bacon.

SMITH, DOROTHY. 1978. A Peculiar Eclipsing: Women's Exclusion from Man's Culture. *Women's Studies International Quarterly*. 1(4), 281-296.

SMITH, LARRY E., Ed. 1981. *English for Cross-Cultural Communication*. London: Macmillan.

SMITHERMAN, GENEVA. 1981. *Black English and the Education of Black Children and Youth: Proceedings of the National Invitational Symposium on the King Decision*. Detroit: Center for Black Studies, Wayne State University.

SMITHERMAN, GENEVA. 1979. Toward educational linguistics for the First World. *College English*. 41, 202-211.

SMITHERMAN, GENEVA. 1977. *Talkin and Testifyin: The Language of Black America*. Boston: Houghton Mifflin.

SMITHERMAN, GENEVA. 1973a. The power of the rap: The Black idiom and the new Black Poetry. *Twentieth Century Literature*. 19, 259-274.

SMITHERMAN, GENEVA. 1973b. White English in Blackface, or who do I be? *The Black Scholar*. 4(8-9), 32-39.

SMITHERMAN, GENEVA and JACK L. DANIEL. 1979. Black English and Black identity: Message to the "talented tenth." *Journal of Educational and Social Analysis*. 1, 20-30.

SMITHERMAN, GENEVA and JAMES McGINNIS. 1977. Black language and Black liberation. *Black Books Bulletin*. 5(2), 8-14.

SNOWDEN, ETHEL. 1913. *The Feminist Movement*. London: Collins' Clear Type Press.

SOEFFNER, HANS, Ed. 1979. *Interpretative Verfahren in den Sozial-und Text-wissenschaften*.Stuttgart: Metzler.

SONTAG, SUSAN. 1978. *I, et cetera*. New York: Farrar, Strauss & Giroux.

SPENDER, DALE. 1983a. *Feminist Theorists: Three Centuries of Women's Intellectual Traditions*. London: The Women's Press.

SPENDER, DALE. 1983b. *There's Always Been a Women's Movement This Century*. London: Pandora Press.

SPENDER, DALE. 1982. *Women of Ideas and What Men Have Done to Them*. London: Routledge & Kegan Paul.

SPENDER, DALE, Ed. 1981. *Men's Studies Modified: The Impact of Feminism on the Academic Disciplines*. Oxford: Pergamon Press.

SPENDER, DALE. 1980. *Man Made Language*. London: Routledge & Kegan Paul.

SRIDHAR, KAMAL K. 1982. English in a South Indian Urban Context. In B. Kachru, ed. (pp. 141-153) *The Other Tongue: English across Cultures*. Urbana: University of Illinois Press.

SRIDHAR, S. N. 1982. Non-native English literatures: Context and relevance. In B. Kachru, ed. (pp. 291-306) *The Other Tongue: English across Cultures*. Urbana: University of Illinois Press.
STAAL, J. F. 1975. *A Reader in the Sanskrit Grammarians*. Cambridge, MA: MIT Press.
STANLEY, JULIA P. 1977. Gender-marking in American English: Usage and reference. In A. Nilsen, ed. (pp. 43-74) *Sexism and Language*. Urbana: N.C.T.E.
STANLEY, JULIA. 1973. Paradigmatic woman: The prostitute. Paper presented at South Atlantic Modern Language Assn. Linguistic Society of America.
STAPLES, ROBERT. 1979. The myth of black macho: A response to angry black feminists. *The Black Scholar*. 10(6-7), 24-33.
STARR, PAUL. 1983. *The Social Transformation of American Medicine*. New York: Basic Books.
STERN, FREDERICK C. 1974. Black Lit, white crit? *College English*. 35, 637-658.
STERNBACH de MEDINA, J. and D. C. MARTINEZ. 1981. Ethnicity and language. Barriers to health care. Presented at El Español en los Estados Unidos Conference at Chicago Circle Center, October 2-3, 1981.
STIMPSON, CATHARINE R. 1979. The power to name: Some reflections on the avante-garde. In J. Sherman and E. Beck, eds. (pp. 55-77) *The Prism of Sex: Essays in the Sociology of Knowledge*. Madison: University of Wisconsin Press.
STIMPSON, CATHARINE R. 1978. Ad/d feminem: Women, literature, and society. In E. W. Said, Ed. (pp. 174-192) *Selected Papers from the English Institute*. New Series, No. 3. Baltimore: Johns Hopkins University Press.
STOREY, ANNE, HENRY CROUCH, and ANN STOREY. 1981. "The little woman" syndrome: An analysis of some cultural determinants of pay differentials. *International Journal of Women's Studies*. 4(3), 289-303.
STRANG, BARBARA M. H. 1970. *A History of English*. London: Methuen.
STREVENS, PETER, 1980. *Teaching English as an International Language*. Oxford: Pergamon Press.
STROBEL, MARGARET. 1982. African women. *Signs*. 8 (Autumn) 109-131.
SULLEROT, E. 1968. *Histoire et sociologie du travail feminin*. Paris: Gonthier.
SUTTON-SMITH, BRIAN. 1979. The play of girls. In C. Kopp, ed. (pp. 229-258) *Becoming Female: Perspectives on Development*. New York: Plenum Press.
TABERY, J. J., M. R. WEBB, and B. V. MUELLER. 1975. *Communicating in Spanish for Medical Personnel*. Boston: Little, Brown.
TAJFEL, HENRI, Ed. 1978. *Differentiation between Social Groups: Studies in the Social Psychology of Intergroup Relations*. European Monographs in Social Psychology, No. 14. London: Academic Press.
TAY, MARY W.J. and ANTHEA F. GUPTA. 1981. Toward a description of standard Singapore English. In R. B. Noss, ed. (pp. 173-189) *Varieties of English in Southeast Asia: Singapore*. SEAMEO Regional Language Center.
TAYLOR, ORLANDO. 1975. Black language and what to do about it: Some Black community perspectives. In R. L. Williams, ed. (pp. 28-39) *Ebonics: The True Language of Black Folks*. St. Louis: Institute of Black Studies.
TEITELBAUM, HERBERT and R. J. HILLER. 1977. The legal perspective. *Bilingual Education: Current Perspectives*. Vol. 3. Arlington, VA: Center for Applied Linguistics.
THORNE, BARRIE and NANCY HENLEY, eds. 1975. *Language and Sex: Difference and Dominance*. Rowley, MA: Newbury House.
THORNE, BARRIE, CHERIS KRAMARAE, and NANCY HENLEY, Eds. 1983. *Language, Gender and Society*. Rowley, MA: Newbury House.

TODD, ALEXANDRA DUNDAS. 1983. A diagnosis of doctor-patient discourse in the prescription of contraception. In S. Fisher and A. Todd, eds. *The Social Organization of Doctor-Patient Communication.* Washington, DC: Center for Applied Linguistics.
TREICHLER, PAULA A. and KATHY ZOPPI. 1983. Professional socialization and medical discourse: Students and power. Paper presented at the annual meeting of the Speech Communication Association, Washington, DC.
TROIKE, RUDOLPH. 1981. Language problems and language planning of Spanish in the United States. *Language and Development.* 3-7.
TRÖMEL-PLÖTZ, SENTA. 1978. Linguistik und Frauensprache. *Linguistische Berichte.* 57, 49-68.
TRÖMEL-PLÖTZ, SENTA et al. 1981. Richlinien zur Vermeidung sexistischen Sprachgebrauchs. *Linguistische Berichte.* 71, 1-7.
TUCKER, G. RICHARD and WALLACE E. LAMBERT. 1969. White and Negro listeners' reactions to various American-English dialects. *Social Forces.* 47, 463-468.
TURCOTTE, DENIS. n.d. La politique linguistique en Afrique francophones: Une étude comparative de la Côte d'Ivoire et de Madagascar. Unpublished manuscript.
TURNER, LORENZO DOW. 1949. *Africanisms in the Gullah Dialect.* Chicago: University of Chicago Press.
TUTTLEMAN, JAMES. 1971. The Negro writer as spokesman. In C. Bigsby, ed. *The Black American Writer.* Harmondsworth: Penguin.
U.S. Department of Labor. 1975. *Job Title Revisions to Eliminate Sex- and Age-referent Language from the Dictionary of Occupational Titles,* 3rd edition. Washington, DC.
VALDMAN, ALBERT. 1983. Normes locales et francophonie. In E. Bédard and J. Maurais, eds. *La norme linguistique.* Quebec: Conseil de la Langue Francaise.
VALDMAN, ALBERT, Ed. 1977. *Creole and Pidgin Linguistics.* Bloomington: Indiana University Press.
VALIN, ROCH. 1983. Reflexions sur la norme. In E. Bédard and J. Maurais, eds. *La norme linguistique.* Quebec: Conseil de la Langue Francaise.
VARENNE, H. 1978. Culture as rhetoric: Patterning in the verbal interaction between teachers and administrators in an American high school. *American Ethnologist.* 5, 635-650.
VARMA, SIDDHESHWAR. 1929. *Critical Studies in the Phonetic Observations of Indian Grammarians.* London: Royal Asiatic Society.
VEEBUHR, ELIZABETH. 1963. Interview with Mary McCarthy. In Van Wyck Brooks, ed. (pp. 283-315) *Writers at Work.* Second Series. New York: Viking.
WACIUMA, CHARITY. 1969. *Daughter of Mumbi.* Nairobi: East African Publishing House.
WALSH, WILLIAM. 1971. *R. K. Narayan.* Writers and Their Work 224. London: Published for the British Council by Longman Group.
WATSON, ROD. 1983. Goffman, talk, and interaction: Some modulated responses. *Theory, Culture and Society.* 2(1), 103-107.
WEBBER, MELVIN. 1978. A difference paradigm for planning. In R. Burchell and G. Sternlieb, eds. *Planning Theory in the 1980's: A Search for Future Directions.* New Brunswick, NJ: Rutgers University Press.
WEEDON, CHRIS, ANDREW TOLSON and FRANK MORT. 1980. Theories of language and subjectivity. In *Culture, Media, Language: Working Papers in Cultural Studies* (pp. 194-216). 1972-1979. London: Hutchinson. In association with the Centre for Contemporary Cultural Studies, University of Birmingham.
WEINREICH, URIEL. 1963. *Language in Contact.* The Hague: Mouton.

WEINREICH, URIEL, WILLIAM LABOV, and MARVIN I. HERZOG. 1968. Empirical foundations for a theory of language change. In W. P. Lehmann and Y. Malkiel, eds. *Directions for Historical Linguistics*. Austin: University of Texas Press.
WEINSTEIN, BRIAN. 1983. *The Civic Tongue: Political Consequences of Language Choices*. New York: Longman.
WEINSTEIN, BRIAN. 1980. Language planning in francophone Africa. *Language Problems and Language Planning*. 4(1), 55-77.
WEINSTEIN, BRIAN and AARON SEGAL. 1984. *Haiti: Political Failures and Cultural Successes*. New York: Praeger.
WEIR, ANN LOWRY. 1982. Style range in New English literatures. In B. Kachru, ed. (pp. 307-322) *The Other Tongue: English across Cultures*. Urbana: University of Illinois Press.
WELLMANN, HANS 1975. *Deutsche Wortbildung: Typen und Tendenzen in der Gegenwartssprache*. Düsseldorf.
WERE, MIRIAM. 1980. *Your Heart Is My Altar*. Nairobi: East African Publishing House.
WERE, MIRIAM. 1980. *The Eighth Wife*. Nairobi: East African Publishing House.
WERLICH, EGON. 1975. *Typologie der Texte*. München: UTB.
WEST, CANDACE. 1983. "Ask me no questions . . . ": An analysis of queries and replies in physician-patient dialogues. In S. Fisher and A. Todd, eds. (pp. 75-106) *The Social Organization of Doctor-Patient Communication*. Washington, DC: Center for Applied Linguistics.
WHITEMAN, MARCIA FARR. 1981. *Variation in Writing: Functional and Linguistic-Cultural Differences*. New York: Erlbaum.
WILLIAMS, JENNIFER A. and HOWARD GILES. 1978. The changing status of women in society: An intergroup perspective. In Henri Tajfel, ed., *Differentiation between Social Groups: Studies in the Social Psychology of Intergroup Relations*. London: Academic Press.
WILLIAMS, RAYMOND. 1977. *Keywords*. London: Fontana.
WIPPER, AUDREY. 1975-1976. The Maendeloya Wanawahe Movement in the Colonial Period: The Canadian connection, Mau Mau, embroidery and agriculture. *Rural Africana*. 29, 195-214.
WIPPER, AUDREY. 1975. The Maendelo ya Wanawake Movement: Some paradoxes and contradictions. *African Studies Review*. 3 (December), 99-120.
WIPPER, AUDREY. 1971. Equal rights for women in Kenya? *Journal of Modern African Studies*. 9, 3 (September), 429-442.
WITTGENSTEIN, LUDWIG. 1969. *Philosophical Investigations*. 3rd edition. Translated by G.E.M. Anscombe. New York: Macmillan. (First published, 1953.)
WITTIG, MONIQUE. 1981. One is not born a woman. *Feminist Issues*. 1(2), 47-54.
WITTIG, MONIQUE. 1980. The straight mind. *Feminist Issues*. 1(1), 103-111.
WODAK, RUTH. 1981. *Das Wort in der Gruppe. Linguistische Studien zur Therapeutischen Kommunikation*. Wein: Akademie der Wissenschaften.
WODAK-LEODOLTER, RUTH. 1980. Problemdarstellungen in gruppen-therapeutischen situationen. In K. Ehlich, ed. (pp. 179-208) *Erzahlen im Alltag*. Frankfurt: Konrad.
WODAK-LEODOLTER, RUTH and WOLFGANG DRESSLER. 1978. Phonological variation in colloquial Viennese. *Michigan Germanic Studies*. 4(1), 30-67.
WOLCK, W. 1972. Attitudes toward Spanish and Quechua in bilingual Peru. Unpublished manuscript.
WOLF, ERIC R. 1982. *Europe and the People without History*. Berkeley: University of California Press.

WOLFRAM, WALT. 1969. *A Sociolinguistic Description of Detroit Negro Speech.* Washington, DC: Center for Applied Linguistics.

WOLFRAM, WALT and RALPH W. FASOLD. 1974. *The Study of Social Dialects in American English.* Englewood Cliffs, NJ: Prentice-Hall.

WOLLSTONECRAFT, MARY. 1792. *A Vindication of the Rights of Women.* London: Joseph Johnson.

WONG, IRENE F.H. 1983. Simplification features in the structure of colloquial Malaysian English. In R. B. Noss, ed. (pp. 125-149) *Varieties of English in Southeast Asia: Singapore.* SEAMEO Regional Languages Centre.

WOOD, BARBARA and ROYCE GARDNER. 1980. How children get their way: Directives in communication. *Communication Education.* 29, 264-272.

WOODSON, CARTER G. 1936, 1969. The education of the Negro. In *The African Background Outlined, or Handbook for the Study of the Negro.* New York: New American Library.

WOODSON, CARTER G. 1933. *The Mis-Education of the Negro.* Washington, DC: Associated Publishers.

WOOLF, VIRGINIA. 1972. Women and fiction. In Leonard Woolf, ed. (pp. 141-148) *Collected Essays: Virginia Woolf,* Vol. 2. London: Chatto and Windus.

WOOLF, VIRGINIA. 1953. *A Writer's Diary,* 2nd edition. New York: Harcourt Brace Jovanovich.

WOOLF, VIRGINIA. 1929. *A Writer's Diary.* New York: Harcourt Brace Jovanovich.

WRIGHT, RICHARD. 1957. The literature of the Negro in the United States. In *White Man, Listen!* Garden City, NY: Anchor Books.

WRONG, DENNIS H. 1979. *Power: Its Forms, Bases, and Uses.* Oxford: Blackwell.

WURM, STEPHEN A. 1977. Pidgins, creoles, lingue franche, and national development. In A. Valdman, ed. (pp. 333-357) *Creole and Pidgin Linguistics.* Bloomington: Indiana University Press.

YARBOROUGH, RICHARD. 1981. The crisis in Afro-American letters. *College English.* 43, 773-778.

YOUNG, MICHAEL F.D., Ed. 1975. *Knowledge and Control: New Directions for the Sociology of Education.* London: Collier Macmillan.

ZATLIN, LINDA. 1976. Paying his dues: Ritual in LeRoi Jones' early dramas. *Obsidian.* 2(1), 21-31 and 159-187.

ZENTELLA, ANA CELIA. 1981. Language variety among Puerto Ricans. In C. Ferguson and S. Heath, eds. *Language in the U.S.A.* New York: Cambridge University Press.

ZIMMERMAN, DON and CANDACE WEST. 1975. Sex roles, interruptions and silence in conversation. In B. Thorne and N. Henley, eds. *Language and Sex: Difference and Dominance.* Rowley, MA: Newbury House.

INDEX

Academie Francaise, 242
Academies, language, 177-178
Achebe, Chinua, 188
Adler, Mortimer, 243
Africa, 18-19, 26-28, 102, 104-105, 107, 179, 184, 185, 188, 190, 218-226
Afro-American, 209
Age, 26, 32, 40, 116-135
Agence, de Cooperation Culterelle et Technique, 230
Aguirre, Adalberto, 155, 175
Alaska, 170
Aleong, Stanley, 238
Alexandre, Pierre, 238-239
Algeria, 234, 241
Ali, Mohammad, 103, 104
Allen, W. S., 178
Alleyne, Mervyne C., 102
Allusion, 118-135 passim
American colonialization, 182
American-International Development, 163
American South, 23-42, passim
Americo-Liberians, 110
Amerindian, 27, 263, 264
Amini, Johari, M., 208
Anand, Mulk Raj, 188, 189
Andersen, Elaine, 122, 123
Anglo, 154-175 passim
Ann Arbor (Michigan), 23-24, 103
Annamalai, E., 186
Ansre, Gilbert, 190
Anthropologists, 196, 197
Apple, Michael, 255
Apte, Mahadev L., 185, 193
Arabic, 234, 235, 236, 277
Ardener, Edwin, 196, 197
Ardener, Shirley, 196, 197, 199
Argument style, 248
Arizona, 161
Arjona, Etilvia, 158, 159
Artificial language, 277

Asia, 18, 20, 190, 230
Aspira, 170, 246
Assertiveness training, 24
Atkinson, J. M., 268
Attention forms, 124, 128
Attinasi, John, 246
Attitudes toward language varieties, 177
Austin (Texas), 165
Austria, 39
Authenticity, 194-205, 206-217
Authority, 11, 206-217
Authors, 206-217, 218-226; see Literary traditions

Bailey, Richard W., 177
Baldwin, James, 105
Bamgboṣe, Ayọ, 187
Baraka, Amiri, 209, 212, 213, 216
Barcia v. Sitkin, 159-160
Barkin, Florence, 161
Barnes, J. A., 39
Barnes, Sir Edward, 182
Barnum, Henry, 175
Baron, Dennis, 153
Basic Engish, 278
Basque, 239
Bass, J. A., 27
Bate, Barbara, 136
Bates, Elizabeth, 118, 134
Baugh, Albert C., 176
Bauman, Richard, 245
Baym, Nina, 217
Becker, Howard S., 88
Becker, Judith, 123
Becker, Robert, 175
Beckman, Howard B., 62-88
Beebe, James, 182
Beebe, Maria, 182
Belfast, 39
Belgium, 227, 229, 230, 232, 240, 241
Bellow, Saul, 212
Bengali, 186, 187, 277

Bennett, Adrian T., 243-259
Benston, M., 45
Bentahila, Abdelâli, 240
Berger, Peter, 194
Bernstein, Basil, 90
Berryman, Sue E., 161
Bilingual education, 169-172, 239
Bilingual speakers, 187
Bilingualism, 25, 113, 154-175 passim, 160, 166, 167, 185, 227-242 passim, 243-259 passim, 246-247, 264
Billingsley, R. G., 207, 208, 210
Bisseret Moreau, Noëlle, 25, 37, 43-61, 217
Black, 22, 23, 101-115, 206-217, 245
Black English, 23, 28, 101-115, 245
Black Studies, 216
Blaubergs, Maija S., 136, 141
Blount, Ben, 245
Blumer, Herbert, 38
Bodine, Anne, 195
Boel, Else, 145
Bokamba, Eyamba G., 102
Bolinger, Dwight, 21
Boltanski, L., 36
Bond, Horace, Mann, 110
Bonilla, Frank, 255
Bosk, Charles, 88
Bott, Elizabeth, 39
Bourdieau, Pierre, 36
Bourhis, Richard Y., 238
Boyer, Ernest L., 243
Boys, 120-135 passim, 136-147
Brass, Paul R., 193
Brazil, 229, 267
Breton, 227, 239
Brinkmann, Hennig, 146
Broadcasting, 163, 164
Brouwer, Dédé, 153
Broverman, Inge K., 148
Brown, Lloyd, 208
Brown, Penelope, 24, 116, 121
Brown, Roger, 134, 261
Bucher, Rae, 88
Burundi, 234
Butters, Ronald R., 25

Cajun, 232, 238
California, 154-175 passim

Calvet, Louis-Jean, 227
Cambodia, 233
Cameroun, 236
Campos, Ricardo, 255
Canada, 25, 26, 227, 230, 240, 241, 263, 264, 266
Capitan Peter, Colette, 43
Caribbean, 230, 241
Cassell, Joan, 204
Caste, 176, 186, 192
Catalan, 239
Census Bureau (U.S.), 164-166
Center for Applied Linguistics, 165
Chad, 240
Champion, Jacques, 235
Chaudhuri, Nirad C., 184
Chicana, 154-175 passim
Chicano, 154-175 passim, 217
Children, 112-115, 116-123
Chinese, 162, 166, 277
Chishimba, Maurice, 179
Chomsky, Noam, 105
Christianity, 26, 179, 182, 183, 223
Civil Rights Acts (U.S.), 168, 169
Civil Rights, Office of (U.S.), 156, 168
Civil War (American), 109
Class 21, 23-42 passim, 43-61 passim, 89-100, 101-115, 138, 241, 245
Classroom, 21, 169-172, 204; see Education
Code-mixing, 186
Code-switching, 246, 247
Cole, Michael, 245
Collins, Randall, 37
Colonialization, 18, 108, 109, 176-193
Colonizers, 179
Comité Consultatif pour la Francophile, 231
Communicaton Act, 163
Community language, 228
Compliance, 117-120
Computer literacy, 244, 274
Conarroe, Joel, 217
Congo, 235, 237
Congress (U.S.), 157, 158
Consciousness-raising, 204
Conseil International de la Langue Française, 230
Control acts, 116-135

Index

Conversation analysis, 15, 89-100
Cook County, 159
Cook-Gumperz, Jenny, 244, 245
Cooper, Robert L., 176
Cornillon, Susan K., 207
Corsican, 239
Cost factors, 120, 121
Courtroom, 89-100, 157-159, 160, 166, 173, 270
Creativity, 189, 190, 206-227
Creole, 16, 23-42 passim, 138, 234-236
Crouch, Henry, 210
Crouch, Isabel, 200
Cultural elite, 227

Dahrendorf, Ralf, 36
Dakar, 236
Dalby, David, 115
Daly, Mary, 136, 139, 199, 203-205
Danehy, John J., 65
Daniel, Jack L., 114
Daniel, Samuel, 180
Daoust, Denise, 238
Das Gupta, Jyotirindra, 185, 193
De Beauvoir, Simone, 199-213
De Chambrun, Noelle, 232
Defendants, 89-100
Deference expressions, 118-135 passim
Deixonne Law (France), 239
Delaware, 174
Delphy, C., 45
Democracy, 102, 275
Desai, Maganbhai O., 184
Dialects,13, 23-42 passim, 95, 101-106, 110, 113-114
Diaspora, 109
Dicko, Dankouludo Dan, 230
Dictionary, 18, 174, 196, 236
Dillard, J. L., 102, 115
Dinnerstein, Leonard, 27
Diola, 234
Directives, 116-135 passim
Discourse analysis, 89-100
Douglass, Frederick, 109, 111
Downing, Paul M., 167
Drew, Paul, 268
Dryden, John, 180
Dubois, Betty Lou, 200
DuBois, William, E. B., 108, 111

Eagleton, Terry, 226
Eakins, Barbara W., 139
Eakins, R. Gene, 139
Edelman, Murray, 16
Education, 21, 43-61 passim, 101-115, 168-172, 204, 234, 241, 243-259 passim; bilingual, 160
Elaborated code, 90
Election, bilingual, 166, 167
Elections, 275
Elite language, 176-193
Ellis, J., 26
Ellison, Ralph, 108, 214
Ellmann, Mary, 212
Elzas, Barnett A., 27
Engel, George, 73
English, 19, 20; as man-made, 194-205; in India, 176-193; international language, 176-193, 228, 267, 276; language of oppression, 192 et passim; varieties, 23-42 passim, 109, 176-193
Equal Opportunities Commission (Great Britain), 140
Ervin-Tripp, Susan M., 116-135
Esperanto, 277
Esteem, 118, 131
Ethnic, 27
Ethnographers, 196, 197
Evans v. Buchanan, 174

Fabio, Sarah Webster, 114
Family, 22, 51; interaction, 90, 91, 116-135
Fanon, Frantz, 61, 108, 109
Fanshel, David, 118
Fasold, Ralph W., 23, 111
Father, 122, 124, 131
Faulk, James, 238
Federal Communications Commission (U.S.), 163
Feminine occupational titles, 136-153 passim
Feminine terminology, 144
Feminism, passim
Ferguson, Charles A., 17, 23, 25, 177, 191
Fiji, 187
Fisher, Dexter, 206
Fishman, Joshua, A., 14, 232, 246, 247
Fleischer, Wolfgang, 146
Floor, 124

Force, 11
Ford, M., 261
Forel, Claire A., 153
Forster, E. M., 181
Foucault, Michel, 12, 15, 21, 63
Fox, Robert E., 213, 215
Français Fondamental, 237
France, 36, 43-61 passim, 227-242 passim
Francophone movement, 266
Francophonie, 227-242 passim
Frankel, Richard M., 62-88
Frau/Mann, 146, 149, 152
Freedom, artistic, 213
Freeman, Jo, 204
Freemantle, Ann, 178
Freidson, Eliot, 88
French, 25, 36, 43-61, 108, 227-242 passim, 276, 277
Fulkerson, David C., 136

Gaines, Ernest, 208
Gal, Susan, 39
Gallegos, Herman, 162
Gandhi, 184, 185
Gardner, Royce, 129, 134
Gates, Henry-Louis, 214
Gayle, Addison, Jr., 212, 213
Gender, 23-42, 43-61 passim, 96, 119-135 passim, 136-153, 194-205, 206-217, 218-226
Gender, grammatical, 143-153 passim
Generic strategy, 139
Generics, 140, 142, 153
Genet, Jean, 213
German, 39, 136-153 passim
Germany (West), 146-152
Gerritsen, Marinel, 153
Ghana, 241
Giles, Howard, 21, 41, 42, 63, 141, 266
Gillan, Garth, 12
Gilligan, Carol, 11
Gilman, A., 261
Gilmore, Perry, 256
Girls, 120-135 passim, 146, 147
Giroux, Henry, 255
Gold, Gerald, 232, 238
Goldman, L., 45
Goody, Jack, 244, 245, 272

Gordon, David C., 227
Gorlach, M., 177
Grant, Charles, 182
Great Britian, 140, 179, 229
Greenbaum, Sidney, 177
Griffin, L. J., 36
Guentherodt, Ingrid, 140, 153
Guillaumin, C., 43, 45
Guinea, 235, 236
Gullah, 28, 107
Gumperz, John, 244, 245, 255
Gupta, Anthea F., 187, 193

Haiti, 227-229, 232, 234, 235, 236, 239, 240, 241
Hall, Robert A., 102
Halliday, Michael A.K., 190
Hammoud, Mohammed Salah-Dine, 234, 235, 240
Hannover, 146
Hardwick, Elizabeth, 212
Harlem, 246
Harrison, James A., 102
Haut Conseil de la Francophonie, 231
Havelock, E. A., 244
Health 155; see Medical setting
Health, Education and Welfare, Department of, 169
Heath, Shirley Brice, 20, 63, 69, 243, 245, 246, 256
Heller, Monica S., 264
Heller, R. J., 173
Hellinger, Marlis, 136-153
Hellman, Lillian, 209
Henley, Nancy, 136, 142
Heterosexuals, 203
High language, 17-18, 21, 23
Hill, Ann, 175
Hiller, R. J., 166
Hindi, 178, 179, 185-187, 189, 277
Hindustani, 185, 186
Hints, 118-135 passim
Hispanic, 154-175 passim
Hispanic Coalition, 161-162
History, literary, 213
History Task Force, 255
Hockett, Charles F., 65
Hoffman, Lutger, 100

Hofstatter, Peter R., 150, 153
Hokkien, 188
Holly, Werner, 94
Home, 116-135 passim, 245, 246
Hospital, 155-157
Howe, Florence, 216
Hughes, Arthur, 26
Hungarian, 39
Hutchinson, John, 234
Hymes, Dell, 14, 16, 19, 105, 245

Identity, 43-61 passim; literary, 206-217
Ideology, 43-61 passim
Illich, Ivan, 243
Immigrant workers, 241
India, 176-193, 264
Indonesia, 179
Industrial Revolution, 183
Influence, 11
Inman, Margaret E.P., 161
Insurance claims, 160
Intelligence, 50
Interlingua, 277
Interpreter, courtroom, 157
Interruptions, 25, 124, 129, 271
Israel, 176
Italian, 144
Italy, 227
Ivory Coast, 236-238

James, Sharon, 118
Janeway, Elizabeth, 11, 24, 210, 211
Japan, 277
Japanese, 179
Jardine, Alice, 213
Jefferson, Gail, 79, 267-269
Jernudd, Bjorn H., 192
Johnson, Abby A., 216
Johnson, Diane, 208, 212
Johnson, Ronald M., 216
Joiner, Charles W., 112, 113
Jong, Erica, 206, 211, 212, 214
Jonson, Ben, 180
Joseph, John, 18
Joyner, Charles W., 27
Judges, 89-100
Justifying, 118-135 passim

Kachru, Braj B., 176-193
Kael, Pauline, 210
Kaimowitz, Gabe, 112
Kallenberg, A., 36
Kandiah, Thiru, 193
Kashmiri, 186
Keller, Gary D., 171, 172
Kendon, Adam, 70
Kenya, 218-226
Kernan, Keith T., 116, 122
Kidron, Michael, 16
King (federal court case), 101-115
King, Bruce, 177
King, Martin Luther, school, 111-115
Kleinman, Arthur, 73
Kloss, Heinz, 233
Kochman, Thomas, 111
Konishi, Toshi, 136
Korea, 179
Kramarae, Cheris, 9-22, 24, 62-88, 152, 153
Kramer, Cheris, 136, 142
Kurzweil, Edith, 219

Laberge, Suzanne, 36
Labor, Department of (U.S.), 140
Labov, William, 23-26, 35, 90, 95, 118, 205, 254, 255
Lakdar-Ghazad, 242
Lakoff, Robin, 200
Lal, P., 193
Lambert, Wallace, 25
Landron, Angel, 175
Langer, Suzanne, 194
Language Policy Task Force, 247
Language, definition, 4, 5, 15, 20, 23; varieties, 21;
Language brokers, 274
Language loyalty, 17
Language planning, 136-153 passim, 154-175 passim, 176-193 passim, 227-242 passim, 265
Laos, 233
Larson, Magell Sarfatti, 88
Latin, 18, 227, 276
Lau v. Nichols, 160, 170, 174
Law, 101, 157-159, 239; see Courtroom
Lebanon, 239

Leech, Geoffrey, 201
Legal, 157-159
Lemert, Charles C., 12
Leodolter, Ruth, 91
Levinson, Stephen, 24, 116, 121, 267
Levitas, Gloria, 210
Lewis, Kenneth, 112
Liberia, 110
Liebowitz, A., 263
Likimani, Muthoni, 221-226 passim
Lincoln, Abraham, 109
Linquistic push-pull, 108
Linguistics, 89-114
Linguists, 236
Lips, Hilary, 11
Literacy, 26, 110-113, 143-259 passim, 272
Literary establishment, 206-217
Literary separatism, 206-217 passim
Literary texts, 218-226
Literary traditions, 18, 176-193 passim, 198, 206-226, 241
Literature, 218-226
Liverpool, 153
Llamzon, Teodoro A., 193
London, 39
Lopez, David, 167
Los Angeles, 162
Los Pardinos, 162, 163
Louisiana, 232, 238
Low language, 17-18, 21, 23
Luckman, Thomas, 194
Luhmann, Niklas, 93
Lukács, Georg, 45
Lukes, Steven, 207
Luna, Larry, 159

Macaulay, T. B., 181-183
MacKay, Donald G., 136
Madagascar, 229, 234, 236
Madhubuti, Haki, 206, 214
Major, Clarence, 115
Malagasy, 234, 236
Malaysia, 179, 187, 188
Male as norm, 136-153, 194-205 passim
Malinke, 234
Mandarin, 277
Mandingo, 115

Manipulation, 11
Manthieu, N. C., 49
Marasigan, Elizabeth, 193
Marriage, 55-58
Martinez, D. C., 155
Martinez, Vilma S., 164, 166
Martyna, Wendy, 136
Marxist literacy criticism, 226
Masculine terminology, 136-153 passim
Mauritania, 234
Mazrui, Ali, 19
McCarthy, Mary, 209
McDowell, Deborah, 214
McGinnis, James, 107, 110, 114
McWorter, Gerald, 111
Mead, George Herbert, 38
Mead, Margaret, 111
Meaning, 194-205
Media, 112, 160-164, 207, 213, 275
Medical setting, 22, 154-157
Mendoza Report, 168
Meneses, Adalberto, 159
Merskovits, Melville, 102
Mexican-America Legal Defense Fund, 154-175 passim
Mexico, 229
Miami, 171
Michaels, Sarah, 246
Michigan, 161; see Ann Arbor
Middle East, 231
Miller, Casey, 136, 201
Miller, Jean Baker, 11, 199
Milroy, Leslie, 39-40
Minimizers, 130
Minority languages definition, 167
Minority writers, 206-217
Missionaries, 179, 182, 183, 236
Mitchell, Henry, 111
Mitchell-Kernan, Claudia, 106, 116, 122
Mitigations, 118-135 passim
Mitterand, François, 231
Moag, Rodney F., 187
Modeling behavior, 121, 122
Modern Language Association, 215-217
Montreal, 36
Morgan v. McDonough, 174
Morocco, 229, 233-235, 240
Morrison, Toni, 105, 210

Moss, Robert F., 211
Mother, 120, 122, 131, 133, 135
Mother tongue, 228, 229, 237
Ms., 262
Mueller, C., 263
Mugot, Hazel, 221-226 passim
Mukherjee, Meenakshi, 189
Mulcaster, Richard, 180
Murdoch, Iris, 209
Muted group, 201, 202
Myers, Walter, 212, 213

Naipaul, V. S., 188
Nairobi, 226
Naming, power of, 199, 207
Narasimhaiah, C. D., 191
Narayan, R. K., 188, 189
National Center for Educational Statistics, 165
National Clearinghouse for Bilingual Education, 171
National Commission of Excellence in Education, 243
National Institute of Education, 172
National languages, 227-242 passim
Nationalist movement (India), 184
Native Americans, 28, 167, 217, 263
Ndiaye, Babacar, 234, 242
Netherlands, The, 140
Neutralization, 185, 186
New York, 166
New York City, 35, 165, 168, 236, 246
Ngwya, Lydia, 221-226 passim
Nichols, Patricia C., 23-42, 93
Niger, 234, 235
Nilsen, Alleen Pace, 136, 195
Nommo, 104
North America, 227, 228
Norway, 39
Norwegian, 141, 142
Novels, 218-226

O'Barr, Jean F., 218-226
O'Barr, William M., 9-22, 260-279
O'Connor, Mary Catherine, 116-135
Oakland (California), 165
Oaks, Priscilla, 217
Occitan, 239

Occupation, 28, 34, 35, 37, 40, 48, 49, 94, 147; see Work
Occupational titles, 136-153 passim
Oevermann, Ulrich, 93
Ogot, Grace, 221-226 passim
Oksaar, Els, 153
Olsen, Tillie, 214
Olympus Research, 161
Ong, Walter J., 244, 272
Oral tradition, 104
Ortiz, Maria, 175

Pabon v. Levine, 160
Palsson, Mary Dale, 27
Parameswaran, Uma, 189
Parathasarthy, R., 188
Paredes, Raymond A., 217
Parents, 116-135 passim
Paris, 230, 238, 241
Partmann, Gayle H., 238
Pedersen, Tove Beate, 153
Pedraza, Pedro, Jr., 243-259
Péroncel-Hugoz, J. P., 231
Persian, 185, 189
Persuasion, 10, 11
Peru, 25
Philippines, The, 182
Phillips, Anne, 209
Phillips, John, 209
Phillips, William, 219
Phoenix, 163
Paiget, Jean, 45
Pidgin, 42
Pittinger, Robert E., 65
Planners; see Language planning
Platt, John, 187, 193
Play groups, 130
Politeness, 118-135 passim
Political scientists, 218, 219
Politics, 10, 11
Polivy, Margo, 175
Portugal, 229, 267
Poular, 234
Power, definition, 2-4, 14, 15, 37, 63, 64, 118, 177, 194, 195, 214
Power relationships, 12, 37, 63
Powesland, P. F., 21, 266
Prator, Clifford H., 191

Prescriptivism, 179
Prestige language, 17, 25, 227
Pride, J. B., 14
Professional terms, 136-153
Pronouns, 261
Provençal, 227
Psychoanalytic theory, 49, 50
Public Law 95-539, 158-159
Public Utilities Commission (California), 162
Publishers, establishment, 212
Publishing, 206-217
Puerto Rican Legal Defense Fund, 154-175 passim
Puerto Ricans, 243-259
Puerto Rico, 165, 166, 182
Punjabi, 277
Puppet play, 121, 135
Pusch, Luise F., 143, 153

Quebec, 228, 229, 232, 235, 237-240, 264
Questions, 68, 116-135 passim
Quirk, Randolph, 179, 193

Race, 27, 101-115; see Ethnic
Racism, 206-217; see Slavery
Raj, 180
Ramanujan, A. K., 188
Rao, Raj, 188-190, 193
Rapp, Linda Loretto, 238
Reality, construction of, 194-217; defining, 214
Reddy, Michael, 15
Reinhardt, Anne-Marie, 232
Religion, 177-179; see Christianity
Requests, 116-135
Researchers, 33, 76, 121, 194-217, 219
Restricted code, 90
Rich, Adrienne, 11, 208
Richards, Jack. C., 187, 188, 193
Riguad, Jacques, 231
Roberts, Joan, 202
Rodriguez, M., 159
Roman Catholic, 232, 276
Rosenberg, Jarrett, 116-135
Rosencrantz, Paul, 148
Ross, John R., 14
Roy, Raja Rammohan, 183, 184

Ruberu, Ranjit, 183
Rubin, Joan, 154-175
Ruiz, C., 159
Russian, 277
Rwanda, 234
Ryan, Ellen Bouchard, 42
Ryen, Else, 153

Sacks, Harvey, 68, 79, 267-269
Samarin, William J., 177
Sanders, Mary, 245
Sango, 235
Sankoff, David, 36
Sanskrit, 178, 179, 183, 185, 189, 190
Schegloff, E., 267-269
Scherer, Klaus R., 63
Schneider, Gilbert, 102
Schools, 169-172, 240, 243-259 passim; see Education
Schulz, Muriel, 9-22, 138, 195, 206-217
Scollon, B. K., 246
Scollon, R., 246
Scribner, Sylvia, 245
Scruton, Roger, 211
Sedlak, Phillip A. S., 241
Segal, Aaron, 236
Segal, Ronald, 16
Segregation (U.S.), 28
Semantic derogation, 139, 140
Senegal, 229-231, 234, 235, 237, 238, 274
Senghor, Léopold Sédar, 231, 241
Serere, 234
Sex, 43-61, 119-135 passim, 194-205, 206-217, 218-226; see Gender
Sexism, 136-153 passim, 206-217
Sexist language, 136-153 passim, 194-217
Shakespeare, William, 180, 184
Shanks, Edward, 183
Shapiro, Ann R., 212
Sharp, Sir Henry, 182, 183
Sheridan, Alan, 12
Sherzer, Joel, 245
Showalter, Elaine, 209, 216
Shuy, Roger, 111
Signifyin, 104
Silence, 60, 202, 271
Singapore, 187, 188
Slavery, 27, 101-115

Index 313

Slobin, Dan L., 25
Smith, Arthur, 106, 111
Smith, David M., 256
Smith, Dorothy, 200
Smith, Larry E., 177, 187
Smith, Philip M., 42
Smitherman, Geneva, 23, 97, 101-115
Snowden, Ethel, 195
Social class, 89-100; see Class
Social linguistics, 13, 89
Social networks, 38-41
Social stratification, 13, 23-42 passim; see Class
Social welfare, 168, 169
Sociolinguistics, 15, 33, 175, 191
Sociology, 38, 51
Soninke, 234
Sontag, Susan, 208
South Asia, 176-193
South Carolina, 23-42 passim
Southeast Asia, 227, 228
Soviet Union, 233, 276
Spain, 229
Spanish, 154-175 passim, 277; varieties, 165, 171, 172
Spelling, 237
Spender, Dale, 136, 139, 194-205
Sri Lanka, 182, 183
Sridhar, Kamal K., 185
Staal, J. F., 178
Standard English, 23-42 passim, 179
Standard language, 13, 17, 21
Stanley, Julia Penelope, 139, 195, 201
Staples, Robert, 210
Starr, Paul, 63
Status, 116-135 passim
Stelling, J., 88
Stereotypes, 89-100; of occupational titles, 147
Stern, Frederick C., 213
Sternbach de Medina, J., 155
Stimpson, Catharine R., 207, 212
Storey, Ann, 210
Strevens, Peter, 177
Stroebel, Margaret, 221
Sutton-Smith, Brian, 130
Swedish, 141
Swift, Kate, 136, 201

Switzerland, 241
Symbolic payment, 120-135 passim

Tag questions, 200, 205
Tamil, 186
Tanzania, 103, 275
Tay, Mary W. J., 187, 193
Taylor, D. M., 63
Taylor, Orlando, 111
Technology, 276
Teitelbaum, Herbert, 166, 173
Telephone service, 161-163
Telugu, 187, 277
Texas, 161, 164; see Austin
Textinguistics, 89-100
Thorne, Barrie, 136, 142, 153
Threat, 130
Titles, 65, 261
Todd, Alexandra Dundas, 73
Togo, 235, 241
Treichler, Paula A., 62-88
Trials, 89-100
Troike, Rudolph, 164, 165, 171
Trömel-Plötz, Senta, 136, 143
Trudgill, Peter, 26
Tucker, G. Richard, 25
Tunisia, 229, 234
Turcotte, Denis, 236
Turn-taking, 267-272
Turner, Lorenzo Dow, 102, 107
Tuttleman, James, 214

Unesco, 235, 236
United Nations, 277
United States, 154-175 passim, 229; dialects of, 25
Upper Volta, 235
Urdu, 185, 186, 189
Ure, J. N., 26

Valadez, Concepción, 175
Valdman, Albert, 102, 228, 238
Varenne, H., 261, 262
Varma, Siddheshwar, 178
Veebuhr, Elizabeth, 209
Videotaping, 65, 123
Vienna, 91
Vietnam, 233, 239

Visibility strategy, 139, 143-146
Voting, 166, 167
Voting rights (U.S.), 26, 166; amendments, 167

Waciuma, Charity, 221-226 passim
Waletzky, Joshua, 95
Walsh, William, 188
Watson, Rod, 15
Watt, Ian, 244, 272
Webber, Melvin, 174
Weber, Heidi, 187, 193
Weedon, Chris, 12
Weinreich, Uriel, 26, 105, 109
Weinstein, Brian, 227-242
Welfare, 168, 169
Wellman, Hans, 146
Were, Miriam, 221-226 passim
West Africa, 241
West, Candace, 25, 68
White, 22, 105-115, 206-217, 245
White English, 101-115
White man's burden, 180, 183
Whiteman, Marcia Farr, 245
Williams, Jennifer A., 141
Williams, Raymond, 248
Wipper, Audrey, 221
Wittgenstein, Ludwig, 23
Wittig, Monique, 61

Wodak-Engel, Ruth, 89-100
Wolck, W., 25
Wolf, Eric R., 250
Wolfram, Walt, 23, 111
Wollstonecraft, Mary, 200
Wolof, 230, 234, 235
Women's studies, 216
Wong, Irene F.H., 187, 188, 193
Wood, Barbara, 129, 134
Woodson, Carter G., 110, 111
Woolf, Virginia, 198, 208, 209, 211
Work, 159-161; see Occupation
World Bank, 235
Wright, Richard, 208
Writers, 198, 206-217, 218-226; see Literary traditions
Writing, 15, 160, 206-217, 228, 233, 245, 272
Wrong, Dennis H., 11
Wurm, Stephen A., 136, 137

Yarborough, Richard, 216
Young, Carmina, 175
Young, Michael F.D., 196

Zatlin, Linda, 211, 214
Zimmerman, Don, 25
Zoppi, Kathleen, 62-88

ABOUT THE CONTRIBUTORS

HOWARD B. BECKMAN, M.D., is assistant professor at Wayne State University School of Medicine, and residency coordinator for Primary Care Internal Medicine Program. He has a special interest in research and teaching that focuses on the psychosocial aspects of patients' medical problems. With Richard Frankel he has published articles on patient-physician encounters.

ADRIAN T. BENNETT is research associate and project director at the Centro de Estudios Puertorriquenos, Hunter College, City University of New York. He has published articles on discourse analysis, cross-cultural communication, psychotherapeutic interaction, language assessment of linguistic minority children, nonverbal communication, and literacy. He is currently writing a book on literacy research and the ideology of educational policy making as it relates to writing in the schools.

SUSAN ERVIN-TRIPP is professor of psychology at the University of California, Berkeley. Her research has focused upon the acquisition of language by children, upon the pragmatics of language use, and upon the relationships between the social context of an interaction and the form and content of the communicative event. Most recently she has been studying the symbolic expression of power in face-to-face interaction, through the analysis of requests and related acts, including the development of strategic skills in second languages.

RICHARD M. FRANKEL is assistant professor at Wayne State University School of Medicine. He is trained as a sociologist and became interested in medical interactions as a result of studying service encounters for his dissertation. He is especially interested in the use of patient expertise in teaching and health promotion. With Howard Beckman, he has developed a research and training program in which physician and patient review and comment on their videotaped interaction in order to share points of view.

MARLIS HELLINGER is professor in English linguistics and head of the English Department of the University of Hannover. She has published in contrastive linguistics, creole studies, and feminist language politics. Within the latter field her main interest is in language change under the impact of the women's movement, in particular, syntactic and semantic conflicts of reference. She is co-author of the first German guidelines for nonsexist language use.

BRAJ B. KACHRU is professor of linguistics in the Department of Linguistics at the University of Illinois, Urbana, and the coordinator of the Division of Applied Lingustics. Born in Kashmir, India, he received his early education in Srinager, Allahabad, and Pune, and his Ph.D. from Edinburgh University. He has published extensively on non-native varieties of English; his latest books on the topic include *The Other Tongue: English Across Cultures* (ed., 1982), *The Indianization of English: The English Language in India* (1983), and *The Alchemy of English: The Spread, Functions and Models of Nonnative Englishes* (1984). He is co-editor of *English World-Wise: A Journal of Varieties of English* and *Annual Review of Applied Linguistics*.

CHERIS KRAMARAE is associate professor of speech communication at the University of Illinois, Urbana, where in her teaching and research she has focused on attitudes toward speaker of conflicting social groups. Organizer or co-organizer of four international meetings on language and gender or language and power, her publications include *The Voices and Words of Women and Men* (ed., 1980), *Women and Men Speaking* (1981), and *Language, Gender and Society* (co-ed. with Barrie Thorne and Nancy Henley, 1983).

NOËLLE BISSERET MOREAU is maître de recherche at the Centre National de la Recherche Scientifique in Paris, and author of *Education, Class Language and Ideology*. Her early research on sex and class relationships showed that the exercise of and submission to power are assigned meaning through a dominant ideology, which is the effect and the cause of the seizure, by dominant groups, of vital resources and of human beings. This dominant, naturalist ideology denies social violence and justifies power relationships by affirming that the dominated groups are biologically "destined" to serve. Her first study of class languages concluded that language practices, marked by this ideology, are constitutive of power relationships. With Claire Michard and Catherine Viollet, she is now studying gender in modern French, the linguistic forms of the socioconceptual category of sex.

PATRICIA C. NICHOLS teaches in the English Department of San Jose State University, where she has worked in teacher training programs, remedial composition, and English as a second language. Her research interests focus on minority languages and dialects in pluralistic societies. Articles about this research appear in *Language Arts, Language Problems and Language Planning, International Journal of the Sociology of Language,* and *American Speech.* Currently she is completing a sociolinguistic history of language and dialect in South Carolina. At Stanford, where she received a Ph.D. in linguistics, she was a founding co-editor of *Women and Language News.*

JEAN F. O'BARR teaches political science at Duke University, where she is director of women's studies. Her primary research interest is the political roles of women in the Third World, especially African women. She is currently studying protest literature as a means of analyzing social movements. Her publications include *Third World Women: Factors in their Changing Status* (1976), *Language and Politics* (co-ed. with William M. O'Barr, 1976), *Persepctives on Power: Women in Africa, Asia and Latin America* (1981), and *Passbook #47927: Women and the MauMau Emergency* (1984).

WILLIAM M. O'BARR, professor of anthropology at Duke University, has studied social and cultural change (1967-1968, Tanzania), language and politics in East Africa (1972), language in the courtroom (1974-1976, United States), language and advertising (1978-1980), and language and law in Kenya (since 1982). His books are *Survey Research in Africa* (ed. with D. Spain and M. Tessler, 1973), *Tradition and Identity in Changing Africa* (with D. Spain and M. Tessler, (1972), *The Student Africanist's Handbook* (with G. Hartwig, 1974), *Language and Politics* (co-ed. with Jean O'Barr, 1976), and *Linguistic Evidence: Language and Power in the Courtroom* (1982).

MARY CATHERINE O'CONNOR has an M.A. in linguistics from the University of California, Berkeley, and is continuing studies there, with work on language and power in institutional settings, including legal and educational contexts. She has worked with John Gumperz on courtroom studies of text comprehension strategies and juvenile waiver of Fifth Amendment rights. With Lily Fillmore and Susan Ervin-Tripp she has been studying the relation to school success of individual differences in second-langue acquisition of immigrant children.

PEDRO PEDRAZA, Jr., is director of the Language Policy Task Force of the Centro Puertorriquenos, Hunter College, City University of New York. Under his tenure the task force has completed several multidisciplinary research projects on language use and language policy in the Puerto Rican community of New York City. He is the author and co-author of reports and articles on these and related topics, such as bilingual education, language proficiency testing, literacy, bilingualism, and discourse analysis.

JARRETT ROSENBERG is a human factors psychologist at the Xerox Office Systems Division in Palo Alto, California, working on human-computer interaction. He received a Ph.D. in psychology at the University of California, Berkeley, working on the analysis of family interaction reported here.

JOAN RUBIN has been a pioneer in the development of language planning theory (societal control of language change) since 1968. From 1974-1977, she organized the Language Planning Program of the Culture Learning Institute at the East-West Center in Honolulu. She is founder and editor of the *Language Planning Newsletter*. In addition to her consulting work as bilingual specialist in Paraguay, Bolivia, Guatemala and Mexico, she has published a study on educational issues on the Indochinese children in the United States. Her publications include *Can Language Be Planned, Language Planning Processes* (both co-edited), *Directory of Language Planning Organizations,* and *References for Students of Language Planning*. She serves as consultant in language planning, bilingual education, and second-language learning, and as president of Joan Rubin Associates.

MURIEL SCHULZ, a linguist, is professor of English and coordinator of developmental writing at California State University, Fullerton. She has published many articles focusing on gender-related semantic differences in language, and has recently completed a book (with Ruth Wodak) on mother/daughter language. She is currently a consultant on a computer-aided instruction project at San Francisco State University.

GENEVA SMITHERMAN is professor of speech communication, senior research associate of Black Studies, and acting director of the linguistics program at Wayne State University. Involved in Black Liberation struggles and in the Black studies movement for nearly two decades, she utilizes her training, research, and scholarship in sociolinguistics and Black English in community, educational, and legal work throughout Black America. Author of more than 50 articles and papers, her publications also include three books: *Sounds of Soul* (1975), *Talkin & Testifyin: The Language of Black America* (1977) and *Black English and the Education of Black Children and Youth* (ed., 1981).

DALE SPENDER is a graduate of British and Australian universities and has undertaken research in a wide range of areas. She is the founding editor of *Women's Studies International Forum*, a member of the Fawcett Society, and the Honorary Librarian of the Fawcett Library. She is the author of *Man Made Language* (1980), *Invisible Woman: The Schooling Scandal* (1981), *Women of Ideas—And What Men Have Done to Them* (1983), and *There's Always Been a Women's Movement* (1983). She is editor of *Men's Studies Modified* (1981), *Learning to Lose* (1980), and *Feminist Theorists* (1983). In press are her books *Time and Tide Wait for No Man* and *For the Record*, and she is currently working on several books, including a novel.

PAULA A. TREICHLER is on the faculty of the University of Illinois, Urbana, with appointments in the College of Medicine, Speech Communication, Institute for Communications Research, and Unit for Criticism and Interpretive Theory. Interested in the linguistic changes that accompany the medical professionalization process, she teaches communication skills to medical students and directs an interdisciplinary course in medicine and society. She is also interested in language and gender, has published articles on that topic, and (with Cheris Kramarae) edits *Women and Language News*.

BRIAN WEINSTEIN, professor of political science, has taught at Howard University since 1966. He has conducted research on language planning in Africa and India. His books include *Gabon: Nation-Building on the Ogooué* (1967), *Eboué* (1972), *Introduction to African Politics: A Continental Approach* (2nd ed., 1977, with L. Rubin), *The Civic Tongue: Political Consequences of Language Choices* (1983), and *Haiti: Political Failures, Cultural Successes* (with A. Segal, 1984). He is currently preparing a book on language strategists.

RUTH WODAK-ENGEL is professor of applied linguistics, including socio-and psycholinguistics, at the Institute of Linguistics, University of Vienna. Her main fields of research (and topics of her 70 papers) are socio-, psycho-, and textlinguistics; sex, race, and class-specific speech behavior and socialization; therapeutic discourse;

schizophrenia; and mother-child interaction. Her publications (under the names Leodolter, Wodak-Leodolter, and Wodak) include four monographs and four co-edited books.

KATHLEEN ZOPPI is currently a research assistant at the University of Illinois, Urbana, in the College of Medicine and Speech Communication. She also does pregnancy and birth control counseling at McKinley Health Center. Working on a doctorate in communication at the University of Michigan, she is particularly interested in the ways patients and physicians define their relationships. Doctors and medical students use her videotapes of patient/doctor interactions to improve their understanding of problems in medical interviews.

LIBRARY OF D